Klaus Berold

Words You Can Use

Name: ______________________

Street: ______________________

Town/City: ______________________

Telephone no.: ______________________

School: ______________________

____

Cornelsen & Oxford University Press

Das Lernwörterbuch *Words You Can Use* wurde von Klaus Berold in Zusammenarbeit mit der Verlagsredaktion verfaßt.

Verlagsredaktion Michael Freyer

Illustrationen Hewett Street Studios, London; David Graham, London; Graham Humphreys, Shropshire; Liz Roberts, London; Sophie Grillet, London; Rod Tricker, Somerset.

1. Auflage

5.	4.	3.	2.	1.	Die letzten Ziffern bezeichnen Zahl und Jahr des Druckes.
1991	90	89	88	87	

Alle Drucke dieser Auflage können, weil untereinander unverändert, im Unterricht nebeneinander verwendet werden.
Bestellnummer 46761

Satz und Druck Saladruck, Berlin

Weiterverarbeitung Fritzsche-Ludwig, Berlin

ISBN 3-8109-4676-1

Vertrieb Cornelsen-Velhagen & Klasing, Verlagsgesellschaft, Bielefeld

Contents

1	**Space**	**Raum**	1
1.1	Universe and geography	Weltall und Erdkunde	1
1.2	Weather, light and colour	Wetter, Licht und Farbe	3
1.3	Travel	Reisen	5
1.4	Transport	Transport	8
1.5	Location and direction	Position und Richtung	12
1.6	Movement and motion	Bewegung und Bewegungsarten	16
2	**Time**	**Zeit**	22
2.1	Time in general	Allgemeine Zeitangaben	22
2.2	Divisions of time	Zeiteinteilungen	23
2.3	Beginning and end	Anfang und Ende	25
2.4	Old, young and new	Alt, jung und neu	26
2.5	Grammatical expressions of time	Grammatische Ausdrücke der Zeit	27
3	**Life on earth**	**Leben auf der Erde**	31
3.1	Life in general	Leben allgemein	31
3.2	Animals	Tierwelt	31
3.3	Plants	Pflanzenwelt	33
4	**Human being**	**Mensch**	35
4.1	Body	Körper	35
4.2	Health and medicine	Gesundheit und Medizin	37
4.3	Food and drink	Essen und Trinken	40
4.4	Clothing and personal care	Kleidung und Körperpflege	44
4.5	Housing and furniture	Wohnen und Möblierung	47
5	**Senses and feelings**	**Sinne und Gefühle**	52
5.1	Feelings in general	Gefühle allgemein	52
5.2	Qualities and emotions	Eigenschaften und Emotionen	54
5.3	Strong feelings and attitudes	Ausgeprägte Empfindungen und Haltungen	58
5.4	Senses and sensations	Sinne und Sinneswahrnehmungen	63
6	**Thinking, language and communication**	**Denken, Sprache und Kommunikation**	66
6.1	Thinking and learning	Denken und Lernen	66
6.2	Speaking and talking	Sprechen und Reden	70
6.3	Reading and writing	Lesen und Schreiben	75
6.4	Communication and the media	Kommunikation und Medien	79
6.5	Language and grammar	Sprache und Grammatik	82
6.6	Grammatical words and phrases	Strukturwörter und grammatische Ausdrücke	86
7	**Society**	**Gesellschaft**	91
7.1	Personal life	Persönliches Leben	91
7.2	Social life	Gesellschaftliches Leben	96
7.3	Education and religion	Erziehung und Religion	99
7.4	Government and politics	Regierung und Politik	104
7.5	Law and crime	Gesetz und Verbrechen	109
7.6	Entertainment and recreation	Unterhaltung und Freizeit	113
7.7	Sports and games	Sport und Spiele	117
8	**Working life**	**Arbeitswelt**	122
8.1	Arts, science and technology	Kunst, Wissenschaft und Technik	122
8.2	Work and production	Arbeit und Produktion	125
8.3	Money and trade	Geld und Handel	130
8.4	Numbers and measurements	Zahlen und Maße	135
8.5	Materials and objects	Materialien und Gegenstände	138
9	**General and abstract expressions**	**Allgemeine und abstrakte Ausdrücke**	145
9.1	General actions	Handlungen allgemeiner Art	145
9.2	Quantity and size	Menge und Größe	150
9.3	Quality	Beschaffenheit	155
9.4	Having and getting	Haben und Bekommen	158
9.5	Being, reality and possibility	Sein, Wirklichkeit und Möglichkeit	161
		Index Englisch	166
		Index Deutsch	188

1.

Words You Can Use . . .

1 ... gliedert den Wortschatz nach thematischen Sachgebieten.
Die Anordnung nach Themenbereichen fördert Gedankenverknüpfungen – die Wörter haften besser im Gedächtnis. Die Anwendung des Wortschatzes in verschiedenen Situationen wird erleichtert.

2 ... unterteilt den Wortschatz in 4 Stufen.
Man kann sich zuerst den häufig auftretenden Wörtern zuwenden und dann stufenweise seinen Wortschatz erweitern. Diese Aufteilung in einen Grund- und Erweiterungswortschatz ermöglicht ein systematisches Lernen:

1 2 1
- Stufe 1/2 = ***Grundwortschatz*** (grau unterlegte Kästchen) umfaßt den wichtigsten und am häufigsten gebrauchten Wortschatz. Dabei stellt die linke Seite der Kästchenspalte Stufe 1 dar, die rechte Seite Stufe 2.

4 4 3
- Stufe 3/4 = ***Erweiterungswortschatz*** (Kästchen ohne Unterlegung) umfaßt zusätzliche, aber wichtige Vokabeln, die zur Erlangung eines mittleren Bildungsabschlusses vorausgesetzt werden. Dabei stellt die linke Seite der Kästchenspalte Stufe 3 dar, die rechte Seite Stufe 4.

3 ... wendet sich an
Lernende, die einen Wortschatz aufbauen wollen, der einem mittleren Bildungsabschluß entspricht.

4 ... hilft
Anfängern zum Ersterwerb und gezielten Aufbau eines Wortschatzes und Fortgeschrittenen zur planmäßigen Wiederholung, Festigung und Erweiterung ihres Vokabulars.

5 ... dient
der zeitsparenden Prüfungsvorbereitung, z. B. durch gezielte Wiederholung des Grundwortschatzes (grau unterlegte Kästchen).

2.

Der Seitenaufbau von **Words You Can Use** im Überblick:

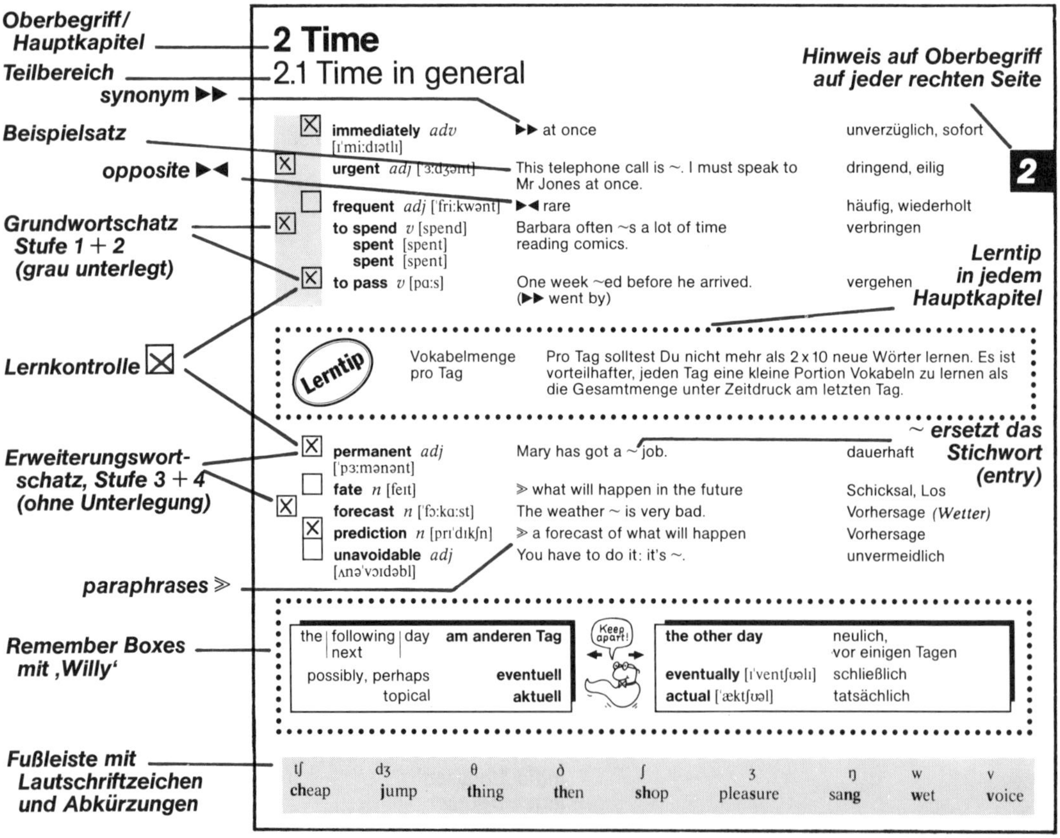

3. So arbeitet man mit **Words You Can Use**:

1 Man wählt sich ein Sachgebiet aus und prüft, ob man den Grundwortschatz durcharbeiten muß oder ob man bereits zum Erweiterungswortschatz übergehen kann.
Als Anfänger bearbeitet man z. B. zunächst Stufe 1, als Fortgeschrittener würde man Stufe 3 wählen.

2 Über das Inhaltsverzeichnis sucht man den gewünschten Oberbegriff bzw. Teilbereich aus. Dann liest man die Einzeleinträge der Sachgruppe durch und merkt sich z. B. Definitionen, *synonyms, opposites.*
Nun deckt man die rechte Spalte (deutsche Übersetzung) ab (Pappstreifen ca. 25 x 10 cm) und erschließt die deutsche Übersetzung mit Hilfe der beiden anderen Spalten.

3 Danach deckt man die linke Spalte (englisches Wort, [Lautschrift], *Wortart*) ab und wiederholt mit Hilfe der mittleren und rechten Spalte das englische Stichwort laut. Die Lautschrift hilft bei der Kontrolle der Aussprache (Lautschriftzeichen s. Fußleiste). Wörter, die man beherrscht, kennzeichnet man in den Kästchen am linken Rand (Kreuzchen, Textmarker o. ä.). Bei Fehlanzeige bekommen die Kästchen keine Markierung. So lassen sich nach einiger Zeit die Problemwörter deutlich erkennen.

4 In gewissen zeitlichen Abständen sollte man den gesamten Wortschatz wiederholen. Dazu kann man z. B. eine zweite Reihe Kreuzchen oder Markierungen neben den Kästchen anbringen.

5 Um ***langfristig*** den Wortschatz im Gedächtnis zu verankern, sollte man sich nicht zu große Lernabschnitte auf einmal vornehmen und von Zeit zu Zeit Wiederholungsphasen einlegen. Hat man nur noch wenig Zeit zum Lernen, z. B. vor einer Prüfung, wiederholt man zunächst Stufe 1/2, um so einen Mindestwortschatz ***sicher*** zur Verfügung zu haben.

4. **Words You Can Use**

bietet verschiedene Wege, eine gesuchte Vokabel bzw. ein Sachgebiet zu finden:

Contents

1	**Space**	**Raum**	1
1.1	Universe and geography	Weltall und Erdkunde	1
1.2	Weather, light and colour	Wetter, Licht und Farbe	3
1.3	Travel	Reisen	5
1.4	Transport	Transport	8
1.5	Location and direction	Position und Richtung	12
1.6	Movement and motion	Bewegung und Bewegungsarten	16
2	**Time**	**Zeit**	22
2.1	Time in general	Allgemeine Zeitangaben	22
2.2	Divisions of time	Zeiteinteilungen	23

Index Englisch

87 a *art*
151 a few
154 a good deal
154 a great deal
151 a little
151 a lot of
24 a quarter of an hour
163 a sort of
61 admire *vt*
19 admission
17 admit *vt+*
72 ~ *vt+*
~ *vt+*
75 adopt *vt+*
94 ~
91 adult *n,a*

Index Deutsch

123 Abbild
20 abbremsen
23 Abend
40 Abendessen
161 Abenteuer
76 Adresse
164 ähneln
162 ähnlich
164 Ähnlichkeit
27 älter

2 Time
2.1 Time in general

time *n* [taɪm]	T~ is measured in minutes, hours, weeks	Zeit
moment *n* ['məʊmənt]	≫ a very short time	Moment, Augenblick
occasion *n* [ə'keɪʒn]	a certain time when something happens	Gelegenheit, Anlaß
to hes		
past		
preser		
future		
long		
short		

2.2 Divisions of time — 23

on time [taɪm]	The bus arrived ~. (≫ at the right time)	pünktlich
punctual *adj* ['pʌŋktʃʊəl]		
age *n* [eɪdʒ]	e.g. the Middle A~s, the Stone A~	Zeitalter
historical *adj* [hɪ'stɒrɪkl]	e.g. a ~ play (≫ having to do with history)	historisch, geschichtlich

Im gesamten Wörterbuch befinden sich in dieser Fußleiste Hinweise zu Lautschriftzeichen und Erklärungen zu Abkürzungen und Symbolen.

Dem vorliegenden Wortschatz – etwa 4.980 Wörter in 4 Stufen – liegen verschiedene wissenschaftliche Quellen zugrunde (u.a. West, Hindmarsh). Auswahlkriterien für den Verfasser waren neben der Häufigkeit des Auftretens in gängigen Lehrwerken besonders der Gebrauchswert und die Verfügbarkeit in Alltagssituationen. Wortschatzlisten der curricularen Lehrpläne wurden ebenso berücksichtigt wie die Richtlinienwortschätze des Volkshochschulverbandes (Stufe 1 = VHS-GBS / Stufe 2 = VHS-Zertifikat) und des Europarats (Waystage/Threshold Level).

Die vielen Beispiele, Definitionen, *synonyms, opposites* und *paraphrases* helfen dem Lernenden, den Wortschatz im richtigen Zusammenhang zu lernen und zu verwenden. Die Begriffe *synonym* und *opposite* sind nicht streng sprachwissenschaftlich zu verstehen; sie stellen eine *„working terminology"* für den Lernenden dar.

Das assoziative Lernen wird durch die über- und unterordnenden Kategorien von ***Words you can use*** gestützt, der Lernende prägt sich also nicht nur sterile Vokabelgleichungen ein. Bei der produktiven Sprachanwendung (exercises, composition etc.) helfen die ausführlichen Hinweise zum Satzbau im alphabetischen Anhang Englisch (S. 166).

Der ***Index Englisch*** bringt nach der Wortart ***Angaben zum Satzbau***, z. B.:

72 ***agree***	*vi (**with**+indir o)(**on**+dir o)*	* I agree ***with*** you ***on*** this point.
~	*vi+to inf*	* He agreed ***to*** phone her.
~	*vi+**that***	* They agreed ***that*** they should leave at once.
55 ***enjoy***	*vt+o*	* We enjoyed our holiday.
~	*vt+v-**ing***	* We always enjoy go***ing*** to the cinema.
71 ***describe***	*vt+o **(to)***	* Bill described the way ***to*** the tourist.
~	*vt+wh*	* They described ***what*** had happened.

Die Abkürzungen zum Satzbau werden in der Fußleiste erläutert (ab S. 166).

1 Space
1.1 Universe and geography

space *n* [speɪs]	They went through ~ to the moon.	(Welt)Raum, Weltall
nature *n* [ˈneɪtʃə]	everything in the world which was not made by people	Natur
world *n* [wɜːld]	Mount Everest is the highest mountain in the ~.	Welt
sun *n* [sʌn]	The ~ gives us light and heat.	Sonne
sunny *adj* [ˈsʌnɪ]	It was a warm and ~ day.	sonnig
star *n* [stɑː]	At night we can often see ~s in the sky.	Stern
moon *n* [muːn]	The ~ moves around the earth.	Mond
earth *n* [ɜːθ]	the world in which we live	Erde
direction *n* [dɪˈrekʃn]	You are going in the wrong ~.	Richtung
north *n, adj* [nɔːθ]		Norden, Nord-
south *n, adj* [saʊθ]		Süden, Süd-
east *n, adj* [iːst]		Osten, Ost-
west *n, adj* [west]		Westen, West-

northern *adj* [ˈnɔːðən]	Sweden is in ~ Europe.	Nord-, nördlich
southern *adj* [ˈsʌðən]	Italy is in ~ Europe.	Süd-, südlich
eastern *adj* [ˈiːstən]	Poland is in ~ Europe.	Ost-, östlich
western *adj* [ˈwestən]	France is in ~ Europe.	West-, westlich
continent *n* [ˈkɒntɪnənt]	Australia is a ~.	Erdteil, Kontinent, Festland
land *n* [lænd]	the dry part of the earth	Land
ocean *n* [ˈəʊʃn]	e.g. the Pacific ~, the Atlantic ~	Ozean
map *n* [mæp]	Peter looked at the ~ to find the way.	Landkarte
scene *n* [siːn]	The sheep on the hill were a beautiful ~.	Anblick, Bild, Szene
sea *n* [siː]	Some boats are sailing **on the ~.**	Meer, die See
seaside *n* [ˈsiːsaɪd]	land by the sea	Küste(nbereich)
island *n* [ˈaɪlənd] ①		Insel
coast *n* [kəʊst] ②		Küste, Meeresufer
beach *n* [biːtʃ] ③		Strand (flach)
lake *n* [leɪk] ④		der See
river *n* [ˈrɪvə] ⑤		Fluß, Strom
stream *n* [striːm] ⑥		Bach, Wasserlauf

bank *n* [bæŋk] ⑦	We sat on the river ~.	Ufer
hill *n* [hɪl]	A ~ isn't as high as a mountain.	Hügel, Erhebung
mountain *n* [ˈmaʊntɪn]	Mount Everest is the highest ~ in the world.	Berg
steep *adj* [stiːp]	The hill was too ~ for me to climb.	steil
top *n* [tɒp]	the highest point of a mountain	Gipfel, Spitze
valley *n* [ˈvælɪ]	the land between hills or mountains	Tal
hole *n* [həʊl]	There is a ~ in the roof where the rain comes through.	Loch

bench	**Bank**
river	**Strom, Fluß**
briefcase	**Mappe**

bank [bæŋk]	Bankhaus; Ufer
stream [striːm]	Bach, Strömung
map [mæp]	Landkarte

iː	ɪ	e	æ	ɑː	ɒ	ɔː	ʊ	uː	ʌ	ɜː	ə
eat	bit	ten	bad	fast	got	saw	sure	too	cut	bird	about

wood *n* [wʊd]	an area of land with trees	Wald, Gehölz
forest *n* ['fɒrɪst]	A ~ is bigger than a wood.	Wald, Forst
universe *n* ['ju:nɪvɜ:s]	everything that exists	Universum, Kosmos
planet *n* ['plænɪt]	Mars is a ~.	Planet
satellite *n* ['sætəlaɪt]	The TV programme came from the United States by ~.	Satellit
worldwide *adj* [wɜ:ld'waɪd]	all over the world	weltweit
solar *adj* ['səʊlə]	S~ power comes from the sun.	Sonnen-, Solar-
pole *n* [pəʊl]	e.g. the North P~	Pol
orbit *n* ['ɔ:bɪt]	They put the spacecraft into ~.	Umlaufbahn
to orbit *v* ['ɔ:bɪt]	The spaceship ~ed the moon.	umkreisen
meridian *n* [mə'rɪdɪən]	a line from the North Pole to the South Pole	Längengrad
observatory *n* [əb'zɜ:vətrɪ]	Scientists watch the stars from an ~.	Observatorium
geography *n* [dʒɪ'ɒgrəfɪ]	the study of the earth, its mountains, rivers, towns etc	Geographie, Erdkunde
feature *n* ['fi:tʃə]	The flat wheat fields are a ~ of the area. (≫ a typical or interesting part)	Merkmal, Kennzeichen
scenery *n* ['si:nərɪ]	≫ natural surroundings	Landschaft, Gegend
landscape *n* ['lændskeɪp]	scenery such as hills or fields	Landschaft
continental *adj* [kɒntɪ'nentl]	e.g. a ~ climate, typical of Europe	kontinental, Festland-
territory *n* ['terɪtrɪ]	land belonging to a country	Gebiet, Territorium
gulf *n* [gʌlf]	e.g. the G~ of Mexico	Golf
loch *n* [lɒk]	►► a lake	See *(Schottland)*
tide *n* [taɪd]	the rise and fall of the sea	Ebbe und Flut
wave *n* [weɪv]		Welle, Woge
spring *n* [sprɪŋ]	a place where water comes up from the ground	Quelle
source *n* [sɔ:s]	where a river starts	Quelle
geyser *n* ['gi:zə]	a natural spring of hot water	Geysir
pond *n* [pɒnd]		Teich, Weiher
puddle *n* ['pʌdl]	After the rain there were ~s of water everywhere.	Pfütze
canal *n* [kə'næl]	a waterway made by people	Kanal
cliff *n* [klɪf]	e.g. the white ~s of Dover	Klippe, steiler Abhang
fiord *n* [fɪ'ɔ:d]	a narrow arm of sea between cliffs	Fjord
slope *n* [sləʊp]	There was a steep ~ up to the castle.	Abhang, Böschung
hilly *adj* ['hɪlɪ]	▶◀ flat	hügelig
plain *n* [pleɪn]	a flat area	Ebene
prairie *n* ['preərɪ]	a wide, grassy plain with no trees	Prairie, Grasland
desert *n* ['dezət]	e.g. the Sahara ~	Wüste
jungle *n* ['dʒʌŋgl]	Tigers live in the ~.	Dschungel
highlands *n* ['haɪləndz]	a mountain area	Hoch-, Bergland
highland *adj* ['haɪlənd]	e.g. a ~ tour of Scotland	
glacier *n* ['glæsɪə]	a mass of ice which moves down a mountain	Gletscher
cave n [keɪv]	People once lived in ~s.	Höhle
horizon *n* [hə'raɪzn]	The red sun sank below the ~.	Horizont
horizontal *adj* [hɒrɪ'zɒntl]	in a flat position, parallel to the horizon	horizontal, waagerecht

adj	*adv*	*art*	*conj*	*n*	*pl*	*prep*	*pron*	*sing*
adjective	adverb(ial)	article	conjunction	noun	plural	preposition	pronoun	singular

1

earthquake *n* [ˈɜːθkweɪk]	a strong shaking of the ground	Erdbeben
volcano *n* [vɒlˈkeɪnəʊ]		Vulkan

1.2 Weather, light and colour

weather *n* [ˈweðə]	What's the ~ like today? Oh, it's raining.	Wetter
degree *n* [dɪˈgriː]	Water boils at 100 ~s C.	Grad *(Temperatur)*
temperature *n* [ˈtemprətʃə]	The living-room had a ~ of 20 °C.	Temperatur
sky *n* [skaɪ]	The ~ is nice and blue. It's a fine day.	Himmel
air *n* [eə]	Let's go out into the fresh ~.	Luft
cloud *n* [klaʊd]	Dark ~s often bring rain.	Wolke
rain *n* [reɪn]	Look at the ~. You must take an umbrella.	Regen
to rain *v* [reɪn]	I hope it isn't going to ~ today.	regnen
shower *n* [ˈʃaʊə]	a short fall of rain	Schauer, Regenschauer
to pour *v* [pɔː]	You can't go out. It's ~ing. (≫ raining hard)	gießen, stark regnen
snow *n* [snəʊ]	There was a lot of ~ on the roads.	Schnee
to snow *v* [snəʊ]	It often ~s in winter.	schneien
ice *n* [aɪs]	Water becomes ~ at 0 °C.	Eis
fog *n* [fɒg]	I couldn't see the house opposite because of the ~.	Nebel
wind *n* [wɪnd]	air moving quickly across land or sea	Wind
storm *n* [stɔːm]	bad weather, with strong winds and rain	Unwetter, Sturm
flood *n* [flʌd]	After the heavy rain there was a big ~.	Flut, Überschwemmung
thunder *n* [ˈθʌndə]	a loud noise in the clouds when there is a storm	Donner
to blow *v* [bləʊ] **blew** [bluː] **blown** [bləʊn]	The wind is ~ing hard.	wehen, blasen
windy *adj* [ˈwɪndɪ]	≫ with a lot of wind	windig
cloudy *adj* [ˈklaʊdɪ]	▶◀ sunny	bewölkt
dry *adj* [draɪ]	≫ with no water; ▶◀ wet	trocken
to dry *v* [draɪ]	The shirts are ~ing in the sun. She is ~ing her hands on a towel.	trocknen abtrocknen
wet *adj* [wet]	▶◀ dry	naß, feucht

Temperatures of the day

freezing	cold	cool	mild	warm	hot	very hot	
0 °C	10 °C	15 °C	20 °C	25 °C	30 °C	35 °C	

hot *adj* [hɒt]	≫ at a high temperature; ▶◀ cold	heiß, warm
heat *n* [hiːt]	how hot something is	Hitze
warm *adj* [wɔːm]	▶▶ quite hot	warm
fine *adj* [faɪn]	It's a ~ day. (≫ clear and pleasant, not raining)	schön, klar

cold *adj* [kəʊld]	▶◀ hot	kalt
cool *adj* [ku:l]	≫ not warm but not too cold	kühl, erfrischend
freezing *adj* ['fri:zɪŋ]	▶▶ very cold	kalt, frierend
frozen *adj* ['frəʊzn]	You can keep ~ food for a long time.	gefroren
light *n* [laɪt]	The sun gives us ~. (▶◀ dark/darkness)	Licht, Helligkeit
dark(ness) *n* [dɑ:k(nɪs)]	≫ being without light	Dunkelheit
shadow *n* ['ʃædəʊ]	The ~s became longer in the evening.	Schatten(-bild)
shade *n* [ʃeɪd]	Let's sit in the ~ of the tree.	Schatten
sunshine *n* ['sʌnʃaɪn]	the light of the sun	Sonnenschein
to shine *v* [ʃaɪn] **shone** [ʃɒn] **shone** [ʃɒn]	The sun ~s in the day. (≫ gives out light)	scheinen
bright *adj* [braɪt]	≫ giving out a lot of light	strahlend, hell
clear *adj* [klɪə]	≫ easy to see or see through	hell, klar
dark *adj* [dɑ:k]	≫ with no or not much light	dunkel
dull *adj* [dʌl]	▶◀ bright or shiny	matt, stumpf
colour *n, adj* ['kʌlə] **color** *n, adj AE*	What ~ **is** his new car?	Farbe

Colours

white *adj, n* [waɪt]	○ weiß	**green** *adj, n* [gri:n]	○ grün
black *adj, n* [blæk]	○ schwarz	**brown** *adj, n* [braʊn]	○ braun
red *adj, n* [red]	○ rot	**grey** *adj, n* [greɪ]	○ grau
yellow *adj, n* ['jeləʊ]	○ gelb	**gray** *adj, n AE*	
orange *adj, n* ['ɒrɪndʒ]	○ orange	**pink** *adj, n* [pɪŋk]	○ rosa(rot)
blue *adj, n* [blu:]	○ blau	**purple** *adj, n* ['pɜ:pl]	○ purpurrot

climate *n* ['klaɪmɪt]	England has a colder ~ than Italy.	Klima
forecast *n* ['fɔ:kɑ:st]	The weather ~ says there will be snow.	Wettervorhersage, Wetterbericht
atmosphere *n* ['ætməsfɪə]	the air around the earth	Atmosphäre
mist *n* [mɪst]	a thin fog	Dunst, leichter Nebel
rainbow *n* ['reɪnbəʊ]		Regenbogen
frost *n* [frɒst]	≫ very cold, freezing weather	Frost
fair *adj* [feə]	We only take the boat out in ~ **weather.** (≫ fine)	heiter, wolkenlos
cloudless *adj* ['klaʊdlɪs]	a ~ sky (≫ clear, without clouds)	wolkenlos
foggy *adj* ['fɒgɪ]	≫ with fog	neblig
misty *adj* ['mɪstɪ]	≫ with mist	dunstig, leicht neblig
damp *adj* [dæmp]	≫ slightly wet	feucht
rainy *adj* ['reɪnɪ]	a ~ day (≫ wet, with a lot of rain)	regnerisch, Regen-
chilly *adj* ['tʃɪlɪ]	a ~ wind (≫ cold and uncomfortable)	frostig, kühl, kalt
frosty *adj* ['frɒstɪ]	It was a cold and ~ morning.	frostig
icy *adj* ['aɪsɪ]	≫ like ice, covered with ice	eisig

tʃ	dʒ	θ	ð	ʃ	ʒ	ŋ	w	v
cheap	**j**ump	**th**ing	**th**en	**sh**op	plea**s**ure	sa**ng**	**w**et	**v**oice

1

changeable *adj* ['tʃeɪndʒəbl]	The weather has been ~ this week. (≫ often changing)	veränderlich
gale *n* [geɪl]	a very strong wind	Sturmwind
hurricane *n* ['hʌrɪkən]	a storm with very strong fast winds	Orkan, Hurrikan, Wirbelsturm
thunderstorm *n* ['θʌndəstɔ:m]	a storm with heavy rain, thunder and lightning	Gewitter
lightning *n* ['laɪtnɪŋ]	a sudden flash of light in the sky often followed by thunder	Blitz
to rage *v* [reɪdʒ]	A storm was ~ing outside. (≫ blowing wildly)	toben, wüten
to dry up *v + adv* [draɪ]	This stream will ~ in summer. (≫ become dry)	austrocknen
	D~ the dishes, please.	abtrocknen
to drown *v* [draʊn]	The boy ~ed in the river. (≫ died under water)	ertrinken
	The old man ~ed the two cats. (≫ killed . . . by putting them in water)	ertränken
warmth *n* [wɔ:mθ]	He felt the ~ of the fire. (▶▶ heat)	Wärme
cold *n* [kəʊld]	▶◀ warmth, heat	Kälte
to freeze *v* [fri:z] **froze** [frəʊz] **frozen** ['frəʊzn]	Water ~s at 0 °C.	gefrieren
to melt *v* [melt]	The ice ~ed in the sun.	schmelzen
daylight *n* ['deɪlaɪt]	≫ the light of day	Tageslicht
flash *n* [flæʃ]	a sudden bright light	Blitz, Aufblitzen
to flash *v* [flæʃ]	The lights ~ed twice.	aufblitzen
to illuminate *v* [ɪ'lu:mɪneɪt]	The lights ~ed the place.	beleuchten
light *adj* [laɪt]	▶◀ dark	hell
shiny *adj* ['ʃaɪnɪ]	▶▶ bright; ▶◀ dull	strahlend, glänzend
pale *adj* [peɪl]	≫ with little colour	blaß, bleich

Lerntip

Zeitpunkt

Warte mit dem Wörterlernen nicht bis zum letzten Moment. Verteile den Lernstoff möglichst gleichmäßig auf die zur Verfügung stehende Zeit.

1.3 Travel

to visit *v* ['vɪzɪt]	I ~ my uncle once a year. (≫ go to see)	besuchen
	He wants to ~ the Tower.	besichtigen
visit *n* ['vɪzɪt]	a short stay	Besuch
to invite *v* [ɪn'vaɪt]	Mr Billows ~d me to tea. (≫ asked me to come)	einladen
	They ~d me to speak at the conference. (≫ asked me politely)	auffordern
invitation *n* [ɪnvɪ'teɪʃn]	He sent me an ~ to his party.	Einladung
to meet *v* [mi:t] **met** [met] **met** [met]	Let's ~ near the post office. (≫ come together)	sich treffen
	He wanted to ~ some interesting people.	treffen, kennenlernen
meeting *n* ['mi:tɪŋ]	the coming together of two or more people	Treffen, Versammlung
appointment *n* [ə'pɔɪntmənt]	a meeting at a fixed time	Verabredung, Termin

i:	ɪ	e	æ	ɑ:	ɒ	ɔ:	ʊ	u:	ʌ	ɜ:	ə
eat	bit	ten	bad	fast	got	saw	sure	too	cut	bird	about

interview *n* ['ɪntəvju:]	a meeting where a person is asked questions	Interview, (Vorstellungs)gespräch
abroad *adv* [ə'brɔ:d]	≫ in or to another country	im Ausland, ins Ausland
to travel *v* ['trævl]	≫ to make a journey	reisen
travel *n* ['trævl]	e.g. the ~s of Marco Polo	Reise(n)
journey *n* ['dʒɜ:nɪ]	They started early on their long ~.	Reise, Fahrt
trip *n* [trɪp]	a journey (usually for pleasure)	Reise, Ausflug, Fahrt
tour *n* [tʊə]	A group of Americans are doing a ~ of Germany.	Rundreise, Tour
sight *n* [saɪt]	The tourists had a tour of the main ~s of London.	Sehenswürdigkeit
sightseeing tour *n* ['saɪtsi:ɪŋtʊə]	a visit to a number of interesting places	(Stadt)Rundfahrt
tent *n* [tent]		Zelt
camping *n* ['kæmpɪŋ]	living in a tent (for a holiday)	Camping, Zelten
hotel *n* [həʊ'tel]	a building where you can get a room and buy meals	Hotel
reception *n* [rɪ'sepʃn]	the place in a hotel where people go when they arrive	Empfang, Rezeption
guesthouse *n* ['gesthaʊs]	a private house for visitors to stay and have meals	Gästehaus, Pension

restaurant	**Gasthaus**
boss	**Chef**
pot	**Kanne**
store	**Lager**
jam	**Marmelade**

guest-house ['gesthaʊs]	(Privat)Pension
chef [ʃef]	(Chef)Koch
can [kæn]	Dose
lager ['lɑ:gə]	Bier
marmalade ['mɑ:məleɪd]	Orangenmarmelade

bed and breakfast *n* [bed, 'brekfəst]	B~ cost him £9.	Übernachtung mit Frühstück
room *n* [ru:m]	I'd like a ~ for three nights, please.	Hotelzimmer, Zimmer
single room *n* ['sɪŋgl]	a room for one person	Einzelzimmer
double room *n* ['dʌbl]	a room for two people	Doppelzimmer
to book *v* [bʊk] **to reserve** *v* [rɪ'zɜ:v]	I managed to ~ a seat on the plane.	buchen, reservieren
to check in *v + prep* [tʃek]	You must ~ **at** the hotel before midnight. (≫ arrive and register)	einchecken, ankommen
visitor *n* ['vɪzɪtə]	He often has ~s from America. (≫ people who come to visit)	Besucher, Gast
guest *n* [gest]	They had eight ~s **to** dinner.	Gast
tourist *n* ['tʊərɪst]	a person who travels for pleasure	Tourist, Urlauber
passenger *n* ['pæsɪndʒə]	a person travelling by bus, train, ship, plane etc	Passagier, Fahrgast
guide *n* [gaɪd] **travel guide** *n* ['trævl gaɪd]	A ~ is a person or book giving information about a place.	Reiseführer
to call on *v + prep* [kɔ:l]	I'll ~ you on my way back. (≫ visit for a short time)	besuchen
to come and see [kʌm, si:]	≫ to come to visit	besuchen
to interview *v* ['ɪntəvju:]	≫ to meet someone and ask questions	interviewen
date *n* [deɪt]	►► an appointment, an agreement to meet	Verabredung

adj	*adv*	*art*	*conj*	*n*	*pl*	*prep*	*pron*	*sing*
adjective	adverb(ial)	article	conjunction	noun	plural	preposition	pronoun	singular

1

voyage *n* [ˈvɔɪɪdʒ]	≫ a sea journey	Seereise
tourism *n* [ˈtʊərɪzəm]	the business of providing transport, hotels etc for tourists	Tourismus
expedition *n* [ekspɪˈdɪʃn]	He took part in an ~ to the South Pole. (≫ a long journey with a special purpose)	Expedition
safari *n* [səˈfɑːrɪ]	an expedition to watch or hunt animals (in Africa)	Safari
package tour *n* [ˈpækɪdʒ tʊə]	a completely planned holiday tour at a fixed price	Package Tour, Pauschalreise
exchange visit *n* [ɪkˈstʃeɪndʒ ˈvɪzɪt]	one of a number of visits between young people in different countries	Schüleraustausch
overseas *adv* [əʊvəˈsiːz]	He has gone ~. (≫ to places across the sea)	in, nach Übersee
oversea *adj* [əʊvəˈsiː]	O~ trade has increased in the last three years.	überseeisch, Übersee-
immigration *n* [ɪmɪˈgreɪʃn]	≫ coming into a country	Einwanderung
immigrant *n* [ˈɪmɪgrənt]	a person who comes into a country to make his home there	Einwanderer
host *n* [həʊst]	▶◀ guest	Gastgeber
hostess *n* [ˈhəʊstɪs]	≫ a female host	Gastgeberin
travel agency *n* [ˈtrævl eɪdʒənsɪ]	A ~ organizes trips and helps people get tickets etc.	Reisebüro
booking office *n* [ˈbʊkɪŋ ɒfɪs]	You get your ticket at the ~.	Kasse, Kartenbüro, Vorverkaufsstelle
reservation *n* [rezəˈveɪʃn]	She made all the ~s for her holidays. (▶▶ bookings)	Reservierung, Buchung
information office *n* [ɪnfəˈmeɪʃn ɒfɪs]	Please ask at the tourist ~.	Auskunftsbüro
lost property office *n* [lɒstˈprɒpətɪ ɒfɪs]	You can go to the ~ if you've lost something.	Fundamt, Fundbüro
boarding-house *n* [ˈbɔːdɪŋ haʊs]	a house where people rent rooms and may have meals	Pension
youth hostel *n* [ˈjuːθ hɒstl]	a place where young people get cheap and simple accommodation	Jugendherberge
to camp *v* [kæmp]	to live in a tent	lagern, campen
camp *n* [kæmp]	a place where people live in tents	Lager, Camp
camping site *n* [ˈkæmpɪŋ saɪt] **camping ground** *n AE* [graʊnd]	a place where you can put up a tent	Zeltplatz, Campingplatz
caravan *n* [ˈkærəvæn]		Wohnwagen
camping van *n* [ˈkæmpɪŋ væn]		Wohnmobil
motel *n* [məʊˈtel]	a hotel for motorists	Motel
host family *n* [həʊst ˈfæməlɪ]	a family who receives guests	Gastfamilie
hospitality *n* [hɒspɪˈtælətɪ]	The guests thanked their hostess for her ~.	Gastfreundschaft
resort *n* [rɪˈzɔːt]	a place that lots of people visit for holidays	Ferienort, Zuflucht
seaside resort *n* [ˈsiːsaɪd]	≫ a resort by the sea	Seebad

v	*AE*	*BE*	☒	~	▶◀	▶▶	≫
verb	American English	British English	a word you have learnt	entry	opposite	synonym	paraphrase

1.4 Transport

traffic *n* ['træfɪk]	the movement of vehicles on the roads	Verkehr

car *n* [kɑː] ①	Auto
taxi *n* ['tæksɪ] ②	Taxi
lorry *n* ['lɒrɪ] ③ **truck** *n AE* [trʌk]	Lastwagen, LKW
bus *n* [bʌs] ④	Omnibus, Stadtbus
tram *n* [træm] ⑤	Tram, Straßenbahn
bicycle *n* ['baɪsɪkl] ⑥ **bike** *n, inf* [baɪk]	Fahrrad
motorbike *n* ['məʊtəbaɪk] ⑦	Motorrad
tyre *n* ['taɪə] ⑧ **tire** *n AE* ['taɪə]	Reifen

to give somebody a lift [lɪft]	≫ to take somebody along in a car	jemanden mitnehmen *(Auto)*
to park *v* [pɑːk]	You can't ~ here. (≫ leave your car)	parken
car park *n* ['kɑːpɑːk] **parking lot** *n AE* ['pɑːkɪŋ lɒt]	He left his car in a ~.	Parkplatz, Parkhaus
rush hour *n* ['rʌʃ aʊə]	the time when everyone is travelling to work or back home	Stoßzeit, Hauptverkehrszeit
accident *n* ['æksɪdənt]	Three people were killed in a **road** ~ last night.	Verkehrsunfall, Unfall
garage *n* ['gærɑːʒ]	A ~ is a place where petrol is sold and where cars are repaired.	Tankstelle, Kfz-Werkstatt
service *n* ['sɜːvɪs]	When did the car last have a ~?	Kundendienst
road *n* [rəʊd]	He bought a ~ map of France.	Straße, Weg
street *n* [striːt]	A car was coming along the ~.	Straße
main road *n* ['meɪn rəʊd]	A ~ is an important road from one town to another.	Hauptverkehrsstraße
motorway *n* ['məʊtəweɪ]	Traffic goes very fast on the ~.	Autobahn
way *n* [weɪ]	Can you tell me the ~ to the post office, please?	Weg
path *n* [pɑːθ]	A ~ is a narrow way for people or animals to walk on.	Pfad, Weg, Feldweg
bridge *n* [brɪdʒ]		Brücke
bend *n* [bend]	There are lots of ~s in the road.	Kurve, Biegung
turn *n* [tɜːn]	e.g. a ~ in the road	Biegung
detour *n* ['diːtʊə]	≫ a longer way round	Umweg
turning *n* ['tɜːnɪŋ]	He took the third ~ to the right.	Abzweigung, Seitenstraße
traffic lights *n* ['træfɪk laɪts]		Ampel
place *n* [pleɪs]	She lives at 6, Eaton P~.	Platz
square *n* [skweə]	an open place in a town	Platz
corner *n* ['kɔːnə]	the point where two streets meet	Ecke, Straßenecke
train *n* [treɪn]		Zug, Eisenbahn
rail *n* [reɪl]		Gleis

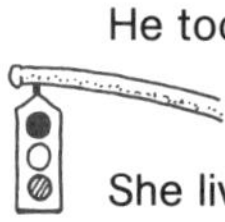

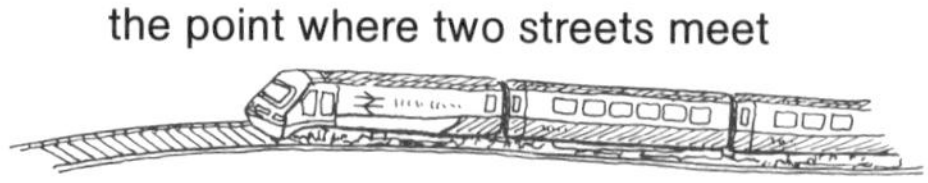

tʃ	dʒ	θ	ð	ʃ	ʒ	ŋ	w	v
cheap	**j**ump	**th**ing	**th**en	**sh**op	plea**s**ure	sa**ng**	**w**et	**v**oice

railway *n* [ˈreɪlweɪ] **railroad** *n AE* [ˈreɪlrəʊd]	the train service that carries people and goods	Eisenbahn
station *n* [ˈsteɪʃn] **railway station** *n* [ˈreɪlweɪ]	A ~ is a place where trains stop to take on or let off passengers.	Bahnhof
platform *n* [ˈplætfɔːm]	The train for Oxford leaves from ~ two.	Bahnsteig
porter *n* [ˈpɔːtə]	A ~ carries luggage at a railway station or hotel.	Gepäckträger, Portier
timetable *n* [ˈtaɪmteɪbl]	A ~ tells you when trains arrive and depart.	Fahrplan
ticket *n* [ˈtɪkɪt]		Fahrkarte
single ticket *n* [ˈsɪŋgl] **one-way ticket** *n AE* [ˈwʌnweɪ]	a ticket for one journey only	Einzelfahrkarte
return ticket *n* [rɪˈtɜːn] **round-trip ticket** *n AE* [ˈraʊndtrɪp]	a ticket for a journey to a place and back again	Rückfahrkarte
underground *n* [ˈʌndəgraʊnd] **tube** *n* [tjuːb] **subway** *n AE* [ˈsʌbweɪ]	the railway system under the ground	U-Bahn
boat *n* [bəʊt]	He crosses the lake in a small sailing ~.	Schiff, Boot
ship *n* [ʃɪp] ①	a large boat	Schiff
to sail *v* [seɪl]	The yacht ~ed yesterday. (≫ left the port) He ~ed the boat into the harbour.	segeln
to sink *v* [sɪŋk] **sank** [sæŋk] **sunk** [sʌŋk]	▶◀ to float	sinken, versenken
sailor *n* [ˈseɪlə]	A ~ is a person who works on a ship. (▶▶ seaman)	Seemann, Matrose
port *n* [pɔːt]	Hamburg and Bremen are German ~s.	Hafen(stadt)
aircraft *n* [ˈeəkrɑːft] *pl* **aircraft**	a machine that flies	Flugzeug
aeroplane *n* [ˈeərəpleɪn] **airplane** *n AE* [ˈeəpleɪn] **plane** *n* [pleɪn]		Flugzeug
airline *n* [ˈeəlaɪn]	*British Airways* and *Pan Am* are well-known ~s.	Fluggesellschaft
airport *n* [ˈeəpɔːt]	a place where you go to catch a plane	Flughafen
gate *n* [geɪt]	Go to ~ 6 for the flight to Rome.	Flugsteig
customs *n* [ˈkʌstəmz]	She was searched when she went through ~ at the airport.	Zollabfertigung
customs officer *n* [ˈɒfɪsə]	The ~ asked: "Have you anything to declare?"	Zollbeamter
to take off *v + adv* [teɪk]	to leave the ground	abheben, starten
to land *v* [lænd]	The plane ~ed at 7.15. (≫ came down onto the ground)	landen, aufsetzen
flight *n* [flaɪt]	a journey in a plane	Flug
crew *n* [kruː]	the group of people who work and look after a ship or plane	Mannschaft, Crew, Besatzung
captain *n* [ˈkæptɪn]	the person in command on a ship or plane	Kapitän
steward *n* [stjʊəd]	a man who looks after passengers on a plane or ship	Steward
air hostess *n BE* [ˈeə həʊstɪs] **stewardess** *n* [stjʊəˈdes]	a woman who looks after passengers on a plane	Stewardess
by *prep* [baɪ]	They went ~ bus. (≫ on a)	mit *(Verkehrsmittel)*

①

iː	ɪ	e	æ	ɑː	ɒ	ɔː	ʊ	uː	ʌ	ɜː	ə
eat	bit	ten	bad	fast	got	saw	sure	**too**	cut	bird	about

transport *n* ['trænspɔ:t]	carrying goods or people from one place to another	Transport, Beförderung
shipping company *n* ['ʃɪpɪŋ kɒmpənɪ]	a company that carries goods from one place to another (by sea)	Spedition, Transportfirma
mobile *adj* ['məʊbaɪl]	A ~ shop comes to the village three times a week.	fahrbar
means of transport *n* [mi:nz, 'trænspɔ:t]	A car is a ~.	Verkehrsmittel
vehicle *n* ['vi:ɪkl]	Cars, buses etc are ~s.	Fahrzeug
waggon *n* ['wægən] **wagon** *n AE*		Wagen, Waggon
automobile *n* ['ɔ:təməbi:l]	▶▶ car	Auto(mobil)
cab *n* [kæb]	▶▶ a taxi	Taxi
van *n* [væn]	≫ a small, covered lorry	Lieferwagen
coach *n* [kəʊtʃ] ①		Reisebus; Kutsche
minibus *n* ['mɪnɪbʌs] ②		Kleinbus
trailer *n* ['treɪlə] ③		Anhänger
bus stop *n* ['bʌsstɒp]	the place where buses stop for passengers	Bushaltestelle
fire engine *n* ['faɪə endʒɪn]		Feuerwehrauto
fireman *n* ['faɪəmən]		Feuerwehrmann
motorcycle *n* ['məʊtəsaɪkl]	▶▶ motorbike	Motorrad
gear *n* [gɪə]	The car is in first ~.	Gang
steering wheel *n* ['stɪərɪŋ wi:l]	You can steer the car with a ~.	Lenkrad
brake *n* [breɪk]	You can stop the car with the ~.	Bremse
driver *n* ['draɪvə]	a person who drives a vehicle	Fahrer
driving licence *n* ['draɪvɪŋ laɪsns]	You are only allowed to drive a car if you have a ~.	Führerschein

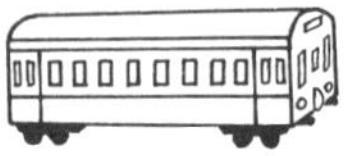

We go	**by**	car bus/taxi/lorry underground/tube/train ship/hovercraft/ferry	and	**by**	road rail/air/sea	but	**on foot**	and **on horseback**

cyclist *n* ['saɪklɪst]	a person who rides a bike	Radfahrer
conductor *n* [kən'dʌktə]	a person who sells tickets **on** a bus	Schaffner
motorist *n* ['məʊtərɪst]	a person who drives (and owns) a car	Kraftfahrer
pedestrian *n* [pɪ'destrɪən]	a person who is walking **in** the street	Fußgänger
pram *n* [præm]		Kinderwagen
locomotive *n* ['ləʊkəməʊtɪv] **engine** *n* ['endʒɪn]		Lokomotive
express *n* [ɪk'spres] **express train** *n* [ɪk'spres treɪn]	≫ a fast train	D-Zug
carriage *n* ['kærɪdʒ]	The engine was pulling nine ~s.	Wagen *(Eisenbahn)*
compartment *n* [kəm'pɑ:tmənt]	part of a railway carriage	Abteil
waiting room *n* ['weɪtɪŋ rʊm]	People wait for the trains in the ~.	Wartesaal

adj	*adv*	*art*	*conj*	*n*	*pl*	*prep*	*pron*	*sing*
adjective	adverb(ial)	article	conjunction	noun	plural	preposition	pronoun	singular

schedule *n AE* ['ʃedju:l, *AE:* 'skedʒʊl]	▶▶ timetable	Fahrplan, Arbeitsplan, Stundenplan
highway *n AE* ['haɪweɪ]	a main road on which cars can travel fast	Hauptverkehrsstraße, Überlandstraße
route *n* [ru:t]	the way from one place to another	Route, Strecke
lane *n* [leɪn]	He went down the ~. (≽ narrow road) The road has four ~s.	Gasse, Feldweg Fahrspur
avenue *n* ['ævənju:]	a wide street in a town	breite Straße, Allee
pavement *n* ['peɪvmənt] **sidewalk** *n AE* ['saɪdwɔ:k]	Pedestrians should always walk on the ~.	Gehsteig
by-pass *n* ['baɪpɑ:s]	a road round a busy town	Umgehungsstraße
subway *n BE* ['sʌbweɪ]	a path under a road or railway	Unterführung
crossroads *n* ['krɒsrəʊdz] **intersection** *n AE* [ɪntə'sekʃn]	He stopped his motorbike at the ~.	Straßenkreuzung
roundabout *n* ['raʊndəbaʊt] ① **traffic circle** *n AE* ['træfɪk sɜ:kl]		Kreisverkehr
crossing *n* ['krɒsɪŋ]	the place where you can cross a road	Straßenübergang
zebra crossing *n* [zi:brə 'krɒsɪŋ] ②		Zebrastreifen
speed limit *n* ['spi:d lɪmɪt]	the fastest speed allowed by law	Geschwindigkeits-begrenzung, Höchstgeschwindigkeit
to crash *v* [kræʃ]	The two cars ~ed on a bend. (≽ had an accident)	zusammenstoßen, (zusammen)krachen
crash *n* [kræʃ]	Four people were killed in a car ~. (▶▶ accident)	Zusammenstoß, Unfall
filling station *n* ['fɪlɪŋ steɪʃn] **petrol station** *n* ['petrəl steɪʃn] **gas station** *n AE* ['gæs steɪʃn]	You can buy petrol at a ~.	Tankstelle
tunnel *n* ['tʌnl]	an underground passage	Tunnel
suspension bridge *n* [sə'spenʃn brɪdʒ] ①		Hängebrücke
hovercraft *n* ['hɒvəkrɑ:ft] ②	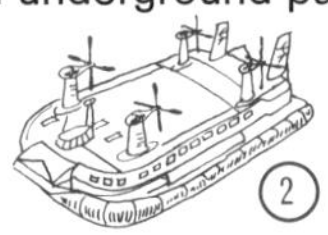	Hovercraft
ferry *n* ['ferɪ]	F~ies take people across water.	Fähre, Fährschiff
steamer *n* ['sti:mə]	a large boat driven by steam	Dampfer
deck *n* [dek] ③	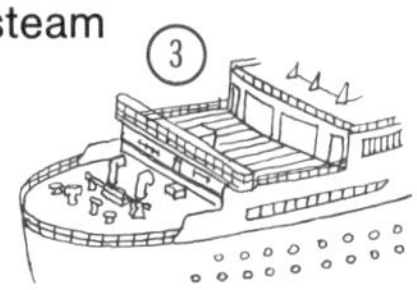	Deck
cabin *n* ['kæbɪn]	a room in a ship	Kabine, Kajüte
canoe *n* [kə'nu:] ④		Kanu
gangway *n* ['gæŋweɪ]	the bridge from a ship to the land	Landungsbrücke
aboard *adv* [ə'bɔ:d] **on board** *adv* [bɔ:d]	on a ship, plane etc	an Bord
harbour *n* ['hɑ:bə] **harbor** *n AE*	The ship came into ~.	Hafen
docks *n* [dɒks]	the place where ships are loaded and unloaded or repaired	Hafenanlagen

v	*AE*	*BE*	☒	~	▶◀	▶▶	≽
verb	American English	British English	a word you have learnt	entry	opposite	synonym	paraphrase

wreck *n* [rek]	They found the ~ of an old ship on the bottom of the sea.	Wrack
to go down *v + adv* [gəʊ]	▶▶ to sink	sinken
jet *n* [dʒet]	an aeroplane driven by engines that send out hot gas	Düsenflugzeug
supersonic *adj* [suːpəˈsɒnɪk]	A ~ aircraft can fly faster than the speed of sound.	Überschall-

helicopter *n* [ˈhelɪkɒptə] ①	Hubschrauber
parachute *n* [ˈpærəʃuːt] ②	Fallschirm
spaceship *n* [ˈspeɪsʃɪp] ③	Raumschiff
spacecraft *n* [ˈspeɪskrɑːft] *pl* **spacecraft**	Raumschiff
astronaut *n* [ˈæstrənɔːt] ④	Astronaut
capsule *n* [ˈkæpsjuːl] ⑤	Kapsel
rocket *n* [ˈrɒkɪt] ⑥	Rakete

landing *n* [ˈlændɪŋ]	The old aircraft made a smooth ~.	Landung
take-off *n* [ˈteɪkɒf]	The plane is ready for ~. (▶▶ the start)	Start *(Flugzeug)*
charter flight *n* [ˈtʃɑːtə flaɪt]	a journey in a hired aircraft	Charterflug
pilot *n* [ˈpaɪlət]	a person who flies a plane	Pilot, Flugkapitän
terminal *n* [ˈtɜːmɪnl]	We waited for them at the air ~.	Abfertigungsgebäude *(Flughafen)*
lounge *n* [laʊndʒ]	a sitting-room or waiting-room in a hotel or airport	Gesellschaftsraum, Wartehalle

1.5 Location and direction

place *n* [pleɪs]	Nobody can be in two ~s at the same time.	Ort, Stelle
situation *n* [sɪtʃʊˈeɪʃn]	The hotel was built in a beautiful ~. (▶▶ position)	Lage
room *n* [ruːm]	The big sofa takes **up** too much ~.	Platz, Raum
space *n* [speɪs]	▶▶ room, a gap	Raum, Platz, Abstand
border *n* [ˈbɔːdə]	a line between two countries	Grenze
to wait *v* [weɪt]	They ~ed **for** the bus.	warten
to stand *v* [stænd] **stood** [stʊd] **stood** [stʊd]	There were no seats, so we had to ~.	stehen
to sit *v* [sɪt] **sat** [sæt] **sat** [sæt]	The boss was ~ting **at** his desk.	sitzen, sich setzen
to sit down *v + adv* [sɪt]	▶▶ to take a seat	sich setzen
to lie *v* [laɪ] **lay** [leɪ] **lain** [leɪn]	The boy was ~ing on his back. (≫ resting flat)	liegen, sich hinlegen
to lie down *v + adv* [laɪ]	▶◀ to stand up	sich hinlegen
to hang *v* [hæŋ]	A nice picture was ~ing on the wall.	(auf)hängen
top *n* [tɒp]	She stood at the ~ of the mountain. (≫ highest part)	Spitze, Gipfel
on top of [tɒp]	They put the textbooks ~ the copybooks.	auf, obenauf

tʃ	dʒ	θ	ð	ʃ	ʒ	ŋ	w	v
cheap	**j**ump	**th**ing	**th**en	**sh**op	plea**s**ure	sa**ng**	**w**et	**v**oice

middle *n* ['mɪdl]	He was in the ~ of the hall. (▶▶ centre)	Mitte, Zentrum
centre *n* ['sentə] **center** *n AE*	▶▶ the middle	Mitte, Zentrum
bottom *n* ['bɒtəm]	▶◀ top	Boden, Grund, Fuß
surface *n* ['sɜːfɪs]	They could see nothing on the ~ of the water.	Oberfläche
front *n* [frʌnt]	The ~ of the building is painted green.	Vorderseite
back *n* [bæk]	▶◀ front	Rückseite
side *n, adj* [saɪd]	There was a door at the ~ of the house.	Seite(n)
side by side [saɪd]	They stood ~ in the hall. (⪢ next to each other)	nebeneinander
right *adj, adv, n* [raɪt]	Do you write with your ~ hand?	rechts, recht-
left *adj, adv, n* [left]	▶◀ right	links, link-
present *adj* ['preznt]	How many pupils are ~ today? (⪢ here)	anwesend
absent *adj* ['æbsənt]	▶◀ present	abwesend
missing *adj* ['mɪsɪŋ]	A ~ book is one that cannot be found.	fehlend
here *adv* [hɪə]	⪢ at, in or to this place	hier, hierher
there *adv* [ðeə]	that	dort, dorthin
everywhere *adv* ['evrɪweə]	▶◀ nowhere	überall
about *adv* [ə'baʊt]	The children were running ~ in the rain. (⪢ here and there)	umher, herum
around *adv* [ə'raʊnd]	There was nobody ~. (⪢ in the area)	in der Nähe
around *prep* [ə'raʊnd] **round** *adv BE* [raʊnd]	They were sitting ~ the table. (⪢ on all sides of)	herum, um ... herum
round *prep BE* [raʊnd]	The earth moves ~ the sun.	um, um herum
forward *adv* ['fɔːwəd]	The people moved ~. (⪢ to the front)	vorwärts
back *adv* [bæk]	She was out and then came ~.	zurück
after *prep* ['ɑːftə]	He came in ~ his friend.	hinter, nach

to *prep* **towards** *prep*	**at** *prep*	**from** *prep*	**away from** *prep* **away** *adv*

zu, in Richtung	an, in, zu	von, aus	weg von

on *prep* **onto** *prep*	**on** *prep, adv* **upon** *prep*	**off** *adv*	**off** *adv*

auf, hinauf	auf, an	herunter, weg von	entfernt von

iː	ɪ	e	æ	ɑː	ɒ	ɔː	ʊ	uː	ʌ	ɜː	ə
eat	bit	ten	bad	fast	got	saw	sure	too	cut	bird	about

into *prep* **in** *prep, adv* **inside** *adv, prep*	**in** *prep, adv* **inside** *prep, adv*	**out of** *prep* **out** *adv* **outside** *adv*	**out of** *prep* **outside** *prep, adv*
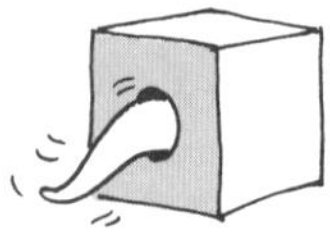			
in, hinein	in, innerhalb	aus, hinaus	außerhalb

in front of *prep* **in front** *adv*	**behind** *adv, prep*	**across** *prep, adv*	**through** *adv, prep*

vor	hinter, hinten	hinüber, quer über	durch, hindurch

inside *n* [ɪn'saɪd]	They were decorating the ~ of the house.	das Innere
outside *n* [aʊt'saɪd]	▶◀ inside	das Äußere
ahead *adv* [ə'hed]	▶▶ in front	voran
with *prep* [wɪð]	The man came ~ a dog. The pupil was fighting ~ his friend.	mit mit, gegen
without *prep* [wɪð'aʊt]	They left ~ him.	ohne
within *prep* [wɪð'ɪn]	The Queen passed ~ five metres of us.	innerhalb von

above *prep, adv*	**over** *prep, adv*	**below** *prep, adv*	**under** *prep, adv*

oberhalb, über	über	unterhalb, unter	unter

between *prep, adv*	**among** *prep*	**beyond** *prep, adv*	**away** *adv*
		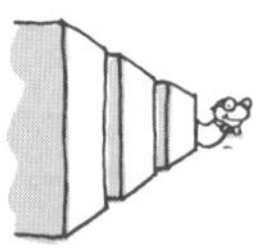	
(da)zwischen	unter, zwischen	jenseits	weg, entfernt

adj	*adv*	*art*	*conj*	*n*	*pl*	*prep*	*pron*	*sing*
adjective	adverb(ial)	article	conjunction	noun	plural	preposition	pronoun	singular

1

up *prep, adv*	**down** *prep, adv*	**along** *prep, adv*	**past** *prep, adv*

hinauf, auf	hinunter, unten	längs, entlang	(an) vorbei

up to *prep* [ʌp tə]	As I was waiting, a man came ~ me.	(bis) zu
as far as [əz 'fɑːrəz]	They walked ~ the house.	bis zu
together *adv* [tə'geðə]	The two girls always go to school ~. (≫ with each other)	zusammen
against *prep, adv* [ə'genst]	He put the ladder ~ the wall.	gegen
distance *n* ['dɪstəns]	What's the ~ from Paris to Rome? It's about 1,400 km.	Entfernung
near *prep* [nɪə]	His house is ~ the park. (≫ not far away from)	nahe, in der Nähe
near *adv* [nɪə] **close** *adv* [kləʊs]	She lives quite ~.	nahe, in der Nähe
beside *prep* [bɪ'saɪd]	Sit down ~ me.	neben
next to *prep* [nekst]	He sat down ~ me. (▶▶ beside)	neben
next *adj, adv* [nekst]	She lives in the ~ house. (≫ the one that comes after this one)	nächste(r,s)
far *adv* [fɑː]	She doesn't live ~ from here. (≫ a long way)	weit entfernt

I don't live **far** from here. *(negative sentences)*

How **far** is it? *(questions)*

He lives **a long way** from here. *(positive sentences)*

further *adv, adj* ['fɜːðə]	She was tired and couldn't go any ~.	weiter
furthest *adv, adj* ['fɜːðɪst]	She lives the ~ from London.	am weitesten
position *n* [pə'zɪʃn]	the place where something is	Position, Lage
to be located [ləʊ'keɪtɪd] **to be situated** ['sɪtʃʊeɪtɪd]	The factory is ~ outside the town. (≫ in a place)	gelegen sein, liegen
spot *n* [spɒt]	▶▶ place, point	Stelle, Platz
opening *n* ['əʊpənɪŋ]	There was an ~ in the wall. (≫ a way through)	Öffnung
gap *n* [gæp]	Leave a ~ before the next paragraph.	Lücke, Spalte
slot *n* [slɒt]	Put a coin in the ~.	Schlitz
range *n* [reɪndʒ]	the distance one can fire a gun	Reichweite
reach *n* [riːtʃ]	The boxer has a long ~.	Reichweite
within reach [wɪð'ɪn]	≫ near enough to reach	in Reichweite
out of reach [aʊtəv]	≫ too far away to reach	außer Reichweite
limit *n* ['lɪmɪt]	Fishing is not allowed inside the 12-mile ~.	Grenze, Einschränkung
frontier *n* ['frʌntɪə]	▶▶ border	Grenze, Grenzland
barrier *n* ['bærɪə]	A ~ stopped him from passing.	Schranke, Barriere
obstacle *n* ['ɒbstəkl]	something that stands in your way	Hindernis

edge *n* [edʒ]	▶◀ centre, middle	Rand, Kante
rim *n* [rɪm]	the edge of a round object	Rand, Kante
tip *n* [tɪp]	the pointed end of something	Spitze
all over *adv, prep* [ɔ:l'əʊvə]	▶▶ everywhere	überall
inner *adj* ['ɪnə]	▶◀ outer	inner, Innen-
inward(s) *adv* ['ɪnwəd(z)]	≫ on/towards the inside	(nach) innen
presence *n* ['prezns]	≫ being present	Anwesenheit
absence *n* ['æbsəns]	▶◀ presence	Abwesenheit
farther *adj, adv* ['fɑ:ðə]	▶▶ further	weiter *(räumlich)*
farthest *adj, adv* ['fɑ:ðɪst]	▶▶ furthest	am weitesten
far away *adv* [fɑ:rə'weɪ]	≫ a long way away	weit weg
distant *adj* ['dɪstənt]	▶▶ far away; ▶◀ close, near	entfernt
remote *adj* [rɪ'məʊt]	≫ far from other places, distant	abgelegen
apart *adv* [ə'pɑ:t]	The two houses are 40 metres ~. (≫ away from each other)	auseinander
aside *adv* [ə'saɪd]	She put her magazine ~ when he entered. (≫ away)	beiseite
backwards *adv* ['bækwədz]	▶◀ forwards	rückwärts
halfway down [hɑ:f'weɪ daʊn]	≫ half the distance down	halbwegs, auf halbem Wege, unten
beneath *prep, adv* [bɪ'ni:θ]	▶▶ under, below	unter
underneath *prep, adv* [ʌndə'ni:θ]		
via *prep* ['vaɪə]	They flew to Tokyo ~ Moscow. (≫ through)	über, via
by *prep, adv* [baɪ]	Mr Harris walked ~ without greeting me. (≫ past)	vorbei, an . . . vorbei

1.6 Movement and motion

to move *v* [mu:v]	Don't ~, I want to take your picture. (≫ change your position)	sich bewegen
	Our neighbours have ~d. (≫ changed their home)	umziehen
step *n* [step]	You take a ~ when you put one foot in front of the other.	Schritt
queue *n* [kju:]	a line of people who are waiting for something	Schlange, Warteschlange
to queue *v* [kju:]	to wait in a line	Schlange stehen
to come *v* [kʌm] **came** [keɪm] **come** [kʌm]	The little boy didn't ~ when I called him.	kommen
to come from *v + prep* [kʌm]	They ~ London.	kommen aus, stammen aus
to go *v* [gəʊ] **went** [went] **gone** [gɒn]	I must ~ now. We can ~ by train.	(weg)gehen gehen, fahren
to pass *v* [pɑ:s]	I ~ed him on my way to work.	vorübergehen
to appear *v* [ə'pɪə]	≫ to come into view	auftauchen, erscheinen
to disappear *v* [dɪsə'pɪə]	▶◀ to appear	verschwinden

tʃ	dʒ	θ	ð	ʃ	ʒ	ŋ	w	v
cheap	**j**ump	**th**ing	**th**en	**sh**op	plea**s**ure	sa**ng**	**w**et	**v**oice

1

to arrive *v* [ə'raɪv]	⩾ to come/get to a place	ankommen
to reach *v* [ri:tʃ]	She ~ed Paris the following day. (▶▶ arrived at/in)	erreichen
to get *v* [get] **got** [gɒt] **got** [gɒt]	He didn't ~ there in time. (▶▶ arrive)	sich begeben, gehen, kommen, gelangen
to get in *v + adv* [get]	▶▶ to arrive	ankommen
arrival *n* [ə'raɪvl]	His wife met him on his ~ at the airport.	Ankunft
to enter *v* ['entə]	They ~ed the house by the back door. (▶▶ came into)	betreten, eintreten
to get on *v + prep* [get] *v + adv*	We can't ~ the bus until it comes.	einsteigen, aufsteigen
to admit *v* [əd'mɪt]	▶▶ to let in	einlassen
to get off *v + adv* [get] *v + prep*	He wanted to ~. Nobody saw the man ~ the plane. (▶▶ leave)	aussteigen
stop *n* [stɒp] **halt** *n* [hɔ:lt]	The car came to a ~.	Halt, Aufenthalt
to leave *v* [li:v] **left** [left] **left** [left]	▶▶ to go out (of), go away from They ~ work at five o'clock.	weggehen verlassen, zurücklassen
to go away *v + adv* [gəʊ]	▶▶ to leave	weggehen, wegfahren
to return *v* [rɪ'tɜ:n]	Try to ~ before midnight.	zurückkehren
to get back *v + adv* [get]	▶▶ come back	
departure *n* [dɪ'pɑ:tʃə]	▶◀ arrival	Abfahrt, Abreise
to climb *v* [klaɪm]	The children ~ed the tree. (▶▶ went up)	klettern auf, besteigen
to fall *v* [fɔ:l] **fell** [fel] **fallen** ['fɔ:lən]	Don't ~ into the water!	fallen
to drop *v* [drɒp]	The coin ~ped onto the floor. (▶▶ fell) Tim's mother ~ped a plate. (▶▶ let fall) D~ me at the next crossroads.	fallen, sinken fallen lassen aussteigen lassen
to raise *v* [reɪz]	He ~d his arm. (⩾ moved . . . upward)	hochheben, anheben
to lift *v* [lɪft]	▶◀ to drop, to lower	hochheben
to get up *v + adv* [get]	When do you ~ in the morning? (⩾ leave your bed)	aufstehen *(Bett)*
to walk *v* [wɔ:k]	My brother likes ~ing. (⩾ going on foot)	zu Fuß gehen, laufen
to step *v* [step]	She ~ped aside to let her pass. (▶▶ walked)	treten, einen Schritt machen
walk *n* [wɔ:k]	a journey on foot	Spaziergang
to go for a walk	Let's ~. (⩾ walk somewhere for pleasure)	spazierengehen
to drive *v* [draɪv] **drove** [drəʊv] **driven** ['drɪvn]	His father ~s a bus.	(Auto)fahren, antreiben

GO FOR	**. . . a drive**	eine Fahrt machen	**. . . a run**	laufen gehen	**. . . a swim**	schwimmen gehen	**. . . a walk** spazieren-gehen

GO	**. . . climbing**	klettern gehen	**. . . hunting**	zur Jagd gehen	**. . . skiing**	Ski fahren gehen
	. . . dancing	tanzen gehen	**. . . sailing**	segeln gehen	**. . . swimming**	schwimmen gehen
	. . . fishing	fischen gehen	**. . . shopping**	einkaufen gehen	**. . . surfing**	surfen gehen

ride *n* [raɪd]	Let's go for a ~ in your new car.	Fahrt, Ritt
to fly *v* [flaɪ] **flew** [flu:] **flown** [fləʊn]	Birds can ~. (⩾ move through the air) He couldn't ~ the jet.	fliegen

to sail *v* [seɪl]	We're ~ing tomorrow. (⪢ starting a voyage)	abfahren *(Schiff)*
to cross *v* [krɒs]	⪢ to go from one side to the other	überqueren
to follow *v* [ˈfɒləʊ]	▶▶ to come after	folgen, verfolgen
to come along *v + adv* [kʌm]	Please go now. I'll ~ later. (▶▶ follow)	folgen, begleiten
to hurry *v* [ˈhʌrɪ]	Don't ~. You've got lots of time. (⪢ move quickly)	sich beeilen
to rush *v* [rʌʃ]	▶▶ to hurry	sich beeilen, rasen
hurry *n* [ˈhʌrɪ]	I'm **in a** ~ because I'm late.	Eile, Hast
to slip *v* [slɪp]	He ~ped on the ice and fell.	ausrutschen
speed *n* [spiːd]	The ~ of the car was 40 mph.	Geschwindigkeit, Tempo
progress *n* [ˈprəʊgres]	continual development or improvement	Fortschritt
quick *adj* [kwɪk]	Be ~ or we'll miss the start.	schnell
fast *adj* [fɑːst]	▶▶ quick	schnell
fast *adv* [fɑːst]	She can run ~. (▶▶ quickly)	schnell
slow *adj* [sləʊ]	▶◀ quick, fast. The ~ train takes ages.	langsam
to put *v* [pʊt] **put** [pʊt] **put** [pʊt]	P~ the parcel on the chair.	legen, stellen, setzen
to place *v* [pleɪs]	▶▶ to put	legen, stellen
to lay *v* [leɪ]	▶▶ to put, to place Would you please ~ **the table.** (⪢ put knives, forks, plates etc on)	legen Tisch decken
to carry *v* [ˈkærɪ]	Can you ~ this suitcase.	tragen, befördern
to fetch *v* [fetʃ]	F~ a doctor. (⪢ go and get)	holen, abholen
to bring *v* [brɪŋ] **brought** [brɔːt] **brought** [brɔːt]	Please ~ me my glasses. (⪢ carry the glasses to me) You can ~ a friend with you.	(her)bringen
to take *v* [teɪk] **took** [tʊk] **taken** [ˈteɪkən]	He always ~s his son to school in his car. Bill always ~s the bus on his way to work. (⪢ uses)	(weg)bringen nehmen, benutzen

Please **bring** me a cola.
(To the speaker)

Take the empty glasses to the kitchen.
(Away from the speaker)

to lead *v* [liːd] **led** [led] **led** [led]	L~ me to the exit, please. (⪢ show the way)	führen
to avoid *v* [əˈvɔɪd]	▶▶ to keep away from	vermeiden
to take away *v + adv* [teɪk]	T~ these old bottles.	wegnehmen
to remove *v* [rɪˈmuːv]	▶▶ to take away	wegnehmen
to pull *v* [pʊl]	Two horses ~ed the coach.	ziehen, zerren, reißen
pull *n* [pʊl]	e.g. to give it a ~ ⪢ to pull	Ziehen, Zerren
to draw *v* [drɔː] **drew** [druː] **drawn** [drɔːn]	▶▶ to pull	ziehen
to push *v* [pʊʃ]	▶◀ to pull	stoßen, schieben
push *n* [pʊʃ]	He gave me a ~ and I fell. (▶◀ pull)	Stoß, Schubs
to throw *v* [θrəʊ] **threw** [θruː] **thrown** [θrəʊn]	T~ me the ball. (⪢ send . . . through the air)	zuwerfen, werfen

adj	*adv*	*art*	*conj*	*n*	*pl*	*prep*	*pron*	*sing*
adjective	adverb(ial)	article	conjunction	noun	plural	preposition	pronoun	singular

to shake *v* [ʃeɪk] **shook** [ʃʊk] **shaken** ['ʃeɪkən]	S~ the bottle before you open it. (≫ move . . . quickly backwards and forwards)	schütteln
to turn *v* [tɜːn]	She ~ed the wheel. (≫ made . . . go round)	drehen, wenden
to pour *v* [pɔː]	She ~ed the beer into a large glass.	gießen, schütten
to spread *v* [spred] **spread** [spred] **spread** [spred]	The disease ~s quickly. S~ some butter on the breadroll.	sich ausbreiten (auf)streichen, verteilen
movement *n* ['muːvmənt]	There was no ~ in the air.	Bewegung
motion *v* [məʊʃn]	≫ a way of moving	Bewegung, Bewegungsart
standstill *n* ['stændstɪl]	a complete stop	Stillstand
stay *n* [steɪ]	a visit, a period of time that you are in a place	Aufenthalt
approach *n* [ə'prəʊtʃ]	the way that leads to a place ≫ getting near to a place	Zugang Näherkommen
crossing *n* ['krɒsɪŋ]	He had a rough ~ by hovercraft.	Überfahrt
passage *n* ['pæsɪdʒ]	She had no way of measuring the ~ of time.	Vorübergehen
destination *n* [destɪ'neɪʃn]	the place to which a person is travelling	Bestimmungsort, Reiseziel
admission *n* [əd'mɪʃn]	being allowed to enter a place	Eintritt, Zutritt
to approach *v* [ə'prəʊtʃ]	≫ to come near(er) to	sich nähern
to set off *v adv* [set]	≫ to begin a journey	aufbrechen
to depart *v* [dɪ'pɑːt]	▶▶ to leave, to go away, ▶◀ to arrive	abfahren
to part *v* [pɑːt]	≫ to go away from each other	(sich) trennen
to precede *v* [prɪ'siːd]	≫ to go in front (of), ▶◀ to follow	vorangehen
to turn up *v + adv* [tɜːn]	I think he'll ~ soon.	auftauchen
to pop up *v + adv* [pɒp]	≫ to appear (when not expected)	erscheinen (unerwartet)
to pop in *v + adv* [pɒp]	P~ whenever you're free. (≫ pay a short visit)	hereinschauen, vorbeischauen
to rise *v* [raɪz] **rose** [rəʊz] **risen** ['rɪzn]	After the rainfall the water in the rivers began to ~. (▶▶ go up)	steigen
to arise *v* [ə'raɪz] **arose** [ə'rəʊz] **arisen** [ə'rɪzn]	▶▶ to happen, to appear	sich erheben, entstehen
to hitchhike *v* ['hɪtʃhaɪk]	to travel by asking for lifts from motorists	trampen, per Anhalter fahren
to march *v* [mɑːtʃ]	The band ~ed down the street.	marschieren
march *n* [mɑːtʃ]	It was a day's ~ to the next settlement.	Marsch
to stroll *v* [strəʊl]	She ~ed along the street. (≫ walked slowly)	schlendern
stroll *n* [strəʊl]	a slow walk	Bummel
to lose one's way [luːz]	≫ to become lost	sich verirren, sich verlaufen
in single file ['sɪŋgl faɪl]	≫ one behind the other	im Gänsemarsch
to kneel *v* [niːl] **knelt** [nelt] **knelt** [nelt]	≫ to go down on one's knees	knien, niederknien
to crawl *v* [krɔːl]	The baby ~ed along the floor. (≫ moved slowly on the hands and knees)	krabbeln, kriechen
to slide *v* [slaɪd] **slid** [slɪd] **slid** [slɪd]	The children were ~ing along the ice.	rutschen, gleiten
to stumble *v* ['stʌmbl]	She ~d over the stone and fell.	stolpern
to float *v* [fləʊt]	▶◀ to sink	treiben, schwimmen

v	*AE*	*BE*	☒	~	▶◀	▶▶	≫
verb	American English	British English	a word you have learnt	entry	opposite	synonym	paraphrase

to flow *v* [fləʊ]	The river ~s into the sea. (≫ moves along)	fließen
to steer *v* [stɪə]	She ~ed the car into the parking place. (▶▶ guided)	steuern
to guide *v* [gaɪd]	≫ to show the way	führen
to cycle *v* ['saɪkl]	≫ to ride a bike	radfahren
to overtake *v* [əʊvə'teɪk] **overtook** [əʊvə'tʊk] **overtaken** [əʊvə'teɪkən]	≫ to go past (something moving more slowly)	überholen, einholen
to slow *v* [sləʊ] **to slow down** *v + adv*	He ~ed the car (down) to 40 mph.	langsamer fahren
to brake *v* [breɪk]	She ~d the car suddenly. (≫ caused . . . to slow down or stop)	abbremsen
to hasten *v* ['heɪsn]	▶▶ to hurry	eilen, sich beeilen

Read the words out loud: same sound but different spelling:

[ʌ]	[dʒ]	[u:]	[i:]	[k]	[ɑ:]
b **u** t	**j** ump	b **oo** t	f **ee** l	**k** ind	f **a** ther
s **o** me	e **dg** e	r **u** de	f **ie** ld	**c** ool	h **ear** t
d **oe** s	a **ge**	fl **ew**	t **ea** m	s **ch** ool	c **al** m
bl **oo** d	sol **di** er	sh **oe**	k **ey**	lo **ck**	l **au** gh
y **ou** ng	sandwi **ch**	thr **ough**	p **eo** ple	wal **k**	s **er** geant
			sc **e** ne	che **que**	

to escape *v* [ɪ'skeɪp]	He ~d from prison. (▶▶ got away)	entkommen, fliehen
to flee *v* [fli:] **fled** [fled] **fled** [fled]	People are ~ing from the war. (▶▶ running away)	fliehen
to hunt *v* [hʌnt]	The police are ~ing the gangsters. (▶▶ going after, searching for)	jagen, suchen, verfolgen
escape *n* [ɪ'skeɪp] **getaway** *n* ['getəweɪ]	The prisoner climbed over the wall and made his ~.	Flucht
narrow escape ['nærəʊ]	He only just avoided the car that was about to hit him. It was a ~.	mit knapper Not davonkommen
to abandon *v* [ə'bændən]	He ~ed the damaged car. (▶▶ left, gave up)	aufgeben, verlassen
busy *adj* ['bɪzɪ]	The supermarket was ~ on Friday. (≫ full of activity)	belebt
rapid *adj* ['ræpɪd]	▶▶ fast, quick	schnell
swift *adj* [swɪft]	▶▶ very fast	schnell, flink
advance *n* [əd'vɑ:ns]	forward movement	Vorrücken
to transport *v* [træn'spɔ:t]	They ~ed the coal in a ship. (▶▶ carried)	transportieren, befördern
delivery *n* [dɪ'lɪvərɪ]	There are two postal ~ies a day.	Lieferung, Zustellung
portable *adj* ['pɔ:təbl]	She bought a ~ TV-set. (≫ . . . that can be carried)	tragbar
to send for *v + prep* [send]	Let's ~ a doctor. (≫ ask . . . to come)	schicken nach
to show *v* [ʃəʊ] **showed** [ʃəʊd] **shown** [ʃəʊn]	She ~ed him to his seat. (▶▶ led)	führen, geleiten, bringen
to show (a)round *v + adv, v + prep* [ʃəʊ]	The manager ~ed the new employee ~ (the factory).	herumführen

to accompany *v* [əˈkʌmpənɪ]	He ~ied her on her trip to Paris. (▶▶ went with)	begleiten
to turn round *v + adv* [tɜːn]	I saw her ~ and look back.	sich umdrehen, umdrehen
to wind *v* [waɪnd] **wound** [waʊnd] **wound** [waʊnd]	Please ~ the handle. (⪢ turn . . . round and round)	drehen
to twist *v* [twɪst]	I ~ed the knob, but it wouldn't turn.	verdrehen, umdrehen
to bend *v* [bend] **bent** [bent] **bent** [bent]	Some people can ~ metal just by touching it.	biegen
	B~ down and pick up the coin.	sich bücken
to lean *v* [liːn] **leant** [lent] **leant** [lent]	Don't ~ out of the window.	(sich) lehnen
shake *n* [ʃeɪk]	She answered with a ~ of her head.	Schütteln
to wave *v* [weɪv]	She ~d her hand when she went away. (⪢ moved . . . backwards and forwards)	winken
to shrug *v* [ʃrʌg]	Fiona ~ged **her shoulders** because she didn't know the answer.	die Achseln zucken
to rub *v* [rʌb]	R~ your hands together to keep them warm.	reiben, einreiben
to rub out *v + adv* [rʌb]	The pupil ~bed ~ the word in his copybook. (⪢ removed . . . with a rubber)	ausradieren
to rub off *v + adv* [rʌb]	to remove or to come off by rubbing	sich abreiben lassen, abwischen
to scatter *v* [ˈskætə]	The crowd ~ed when the first shots were heard. (⪢ went in different directions)	sich zerstreuen, verstreuen
to sprinkle *v* [ˈsprɪŋkl]	He ~d some salt on the eggs.	streuen
to spray *v* [spreɪ]	The youngsters ~ed paint on the house walls.	sprühen, besprühen
spray *n* [spreɪ]	Helen bought some insect ~.	Spray, Spraydose

iː	ɪ	e	æ	ɑː	ɒ	ɔː	ʊ	uː	ʌ	ɜː	ə
eat	bit	ten	bad	fast	got	saw	sure	too	cut	bird	about

2 Time

2.1 Time in general

time *n* [taɪm]	T~ is measured in minutes, hours, weeks.	Zeit
moment *n* ['məʊmənt]	≫ a very short time	Moment, Augenblick
occasion *n* [ə'keɪʒn]	a certain time when something happens	Gelegenheit, Anlaß
to hesitate *v* ['hezɪteɪt]	Bill ~d before he took the money.	zögern
past *n* [pɑ:st]	≫ the time before now	Vergangenheit
present *n* ['preznt]	≫ the time now	Gegenwart
future *n* ['fju:tʃə]	≫ the time that is to come	Zukunft
long *adj, adv* [lɒŋ]	We've got a nice ~ holiday. I'm busy, so I can't stay ~.	lange
short *adj* [ʃɔ:t]	▶◀ long	kurz, kurze Zeit
early *adj* ['ɜ:lɪ] *adv*	She came back in the ~ morning. The train arrived 10 minutes ~. (▶◀ late)	früh zu früh
late *adj* [leɪt] *adv*	They returned in the ~ afternoon. The bus arrived 6 minutes ~. (▶◀ early)	spät zu spät
in time [taɪm]	≫ not too late for something	rechtzeitig
sudden *adj* ['sʌdn]	There was a ~ cry from upstairs.	plötzlich
suddenly *adv* ['sʌdnlɪ]	▶◀ gradually	plötzlich
immediate *adj* [ɪ'mi:dɪət]	I want an ~ answer.	unmittelbar, sofort
immediately *adv* [ɪ'mi:dɪətlɪ]	▶▶ at once	unverzüglich, sofort
urgent *adj* ['ɜ:dʒənt]	This telephone call is ~. I must speak to Mr Jones at once.	dringend, eilig
frequent *adj* ['fri:kwənt]	▶◀ rare	häufig, wiederholt
to spend *v* [spend] **spent** [spent] **spent** [spent]	Barbara often ~s a lot of time reading comics.	verbringen
to pass *v* [pɑ:s]	One week ~ed before he arrived. (▶▶ went by)	vergehen

Lerntip

Vokabelmenge pro Tag — Pro Tag solltest Du nicht mehr als 2 x 10 neue Wörter lernen. Es ist vorteilhafter, jeden Tag eine kleine Portion Vokabeln zu lernen als die Gesamtmenge unter Zeitdruck am letzten Tag.

to take *v* [teɪk] **took** [tʊk] **taken** ['teɪkən]	It ~s me two hours to get there. (≫ I need two hours) The flight ~s two hours.	erfordern *(Zeit)*, brauchen dauern
to last *v* [lɑ:st]	The film ~ed (for) two hours. (▶▶ went on)	(an)dauern
to continue *v* [kən'tɪnju:]	▶▶ to go on ▶▶ to start again	andauern fortsetzen, weitermachen
to go ahead *v + adv* [ə'hed]	You can ~ with this job now.	anfangen, weitermachen
period *n* ['pɪərɪəd]	a length of time	Zeitabschnitt
while *n* [waɪl]	I had to wait for a long ~. (▶▶ period)	Zeitraum, Weile
interval *n* ['ɪntəvl]	time between two things	Zwischenraum, Spanne, Pause
pause *n* [pɔ:z]	a short stop	Pause
to pause *v* [pɔ:z]	≫ to stop for a short time	pausieren
break *n* [breɪk]	▶▶ pause, short rest	(kurze) Pause
brief *adj* [bri:f]	▶▶ short	kurz

adj	*adv*	*art*	*conj*	*n*	*pl*	*prep*	*pron*	*sing*
adjective	adverb(ial)	article	conjunction	noun	plural	preposition	pronoun	singular

on time [taɪm] **punctual** *adj* [ˈpʌŋktʃʊəl]	The bus arrived ~. (≫ at the right time)	pünktlich
age *n* [eɪdʒ]	e.g. the Middle A~s, the Stone A~	Zeitalter
historical *adj* [hɪˈstɒrɪkl]	e.g. a ~ play (≫ having to do with history)	historisch, geschichtlich
historic *adj* [hɪˈstɒrɪk]	≫ important in history	geschichtlich (bedeutend)
gradually *adv* [ˈgrædʒʊlɪ]	step by step	schrittweise
urgency *n* [ˈɜːdʒənsɪ]	This is a matter of great ~.	Dringlichkeit
occasional *adj* [əˈkeɪʒənl]	I take an ~ trip to London.	gelegentlich
for once [fə ˈwʌns]	≫ on one occasion only, unusually	dieses eine Mal
to carry on *v + adv* [ˈkærɪ]	▶▶ to go on, to continue	weitermachen
to keep going [kiːp ˈgəʊɪŋ]	≫ to not stop, to go on	durchhalten, weitermachen
steady *adj* [ˈstedɪ]	This pupil is a ~ worker.	regelmäßig, beständig
continuous *adj* [kənˈtɪnjʊəs] **constant** *adj* [ˈkɒnstənt]	≫ without stopping	beständig, fortwährend
permanent *adj* [ˈpɜːmənənt]	Mary has got a ~ job.	dauerhaft
fate *n* [feɪt]	≫ what will happen in the future	Schicksal, Los
forecast *n* [ˈfɔːkɑːst]	The weather ~ is very bad.	Vorhersage *(Wetter)*
prediction *n* [prɪˈdɪkʃn]	≫ a forecast of what will happen	Vorhersage
unavoidable *adj* [ʌnəˈvɔɪdəbl]	You have to do it: it's ~.	unvermeidlich
inevitable *adj* [ɪnˈevɪtəbl]	≫ it is certain to happen	unentrinnbar, unvermeidlich

2.2 Divisions of time

day *n* [deɪ]	We can see by ~, but not by night.	Tag
sunrise *n* [ˈsʌnraɪz]	▶◀ sunset	Sonnenaufgang
morning *n* [ˈmɔːnɪŋ]	What time did you get up this ~?	Morgen
noon *n* [nuːn] **midday** *n* [mɪdˈdeɪ]	≫ 12 o'clock, in the middle of the day	Mittag
afternoon *n* [ɑːftəˈnuːn]	≫ the time between midday and evening	Nachmittag
evening *n* [ˈiːvnɪŋ]	≫ the later part of the day	Abend
sunset *n* [ˈsʌnset]	≫ the time when the sun goes down	Sonnenuntergang
night *n* [naɪt]	▶◀ day	Nacht
midnight *n* [ˈmɪdnaɪt]	≫ 12 o'clock at night, ▶◀ noon, midday	Mitternacht
today *n, adv* [təˈdeɪ]	T~ is her birthday. (≫ This day)	heute

the following / next day	**am anderen Tag**
possibly, perhaps	**eventuell**
topical	**aktuell**

the other day	neulich, vor einigen Tagen
eventually [ɪˈventʃʊəlɪ]	schließlich
actual [ˈæktʃʊəl]	tatsächlich

v	*AE*	*BE*	☒	~	▶◀	▶▶	≫
verb	American English	British English	a word you have learnt	entry	opposite	synonym	paraphrase

yesterday *n, adv* [ˈjestədɪ]	≫ (on) the day before this one	gestern
this morning [ˈmɔːnɪŋ]	≫ the morning of today	heute morgen
tomorrow *n, adv* [təˈmɒrəʊ]	≫ (on) the day after today	morgen
the day before yesterday [bɪˈfɔː ˈjestədɪ]	≫ two days ago	vorgestern
the day after tomorrow [ˈɑːftə təˈmɒrəʊ]	≫ two days after today	übermorgen
tonight *n, adv* [təˈnaɪt]	We're going to a party ~. (≫ this night)	heute nacht, heute abend
last night [lɑːst ˈnaɪt]	They arrived ~ and left this morning. (≫ the night of yesterday)	gestern abend, gestern nacht
this evening [ðɪs ˈiːvnɪŋ]	≫ the evening of today	heute abend
second *n* [ˈsekənd]	There are 60 ~s in a minute.	Sekunde
minute *n* [ˈmɪnɪt]	one of the sixty parts of an hour	Minute
hour *n* [aʊə]	sixty minutes	Stunde

a quarter of an hour

half an hour

three quarters of an hour

to *prep* [tuː, tʊ, tə] **before** *prep AE* [bɪˈfɔː]	It's five (minutes) ~ eight. (▶◀ past)	vor *(bei Zeitangaben)*
past *prep* [pɑːst] **after** *prep AE* [ˈɑːftə]	It's half ~ three now. (≫ 3.30)	nach *(bei Zeitangaben)*
day *n* [deɪ]	There are seven ~s in a week.	Tag

Days of the week

Monday [ˈmʌndɪ]	(Mon)	Montag	**Friday** [ˈfraɪdɪ]	(Fri)	Freitag
Tuesday [ˈtjuːzdɪ]	(Tues)	Dienstag	**Saturday** [ˈsætədɪ]	(Sat)	Samstag, Sonnabend
Wednesday [ˈwenzdɪ]	(Wed)	Mittwoch			
Thursday [ˈθɜːzdɪ]	(Thu)	Donnerstag	**Sunday** [ˈsʌndɪ]	(Sun)	Sonntag

week *n* [wiːk]	a period of seven days & nights	Woche
weekday *n* [ˈwiːkdeɪ]	≫ any day except Sunday (and Saturday)	Wochentag, Werktag
weekend *n* [wiːkˈend]	Saturday and Sunday	Wochenende
month *n* [mʌnθ]	January is the first ~ of the year.	Monat

Months of the year

January [ˈdʒænjʊərɪ]	(Jan)	Januar	**July** [dʒuːˈlaɪ]	(Jul)	Juli
February [ˈfebrʊərɪ]	(Feb)	Februar	**August** [ˈɔːgəst]	(Aug)	August
March [mɑːtʃ]	(Mar)	März	**September** [sepˈtembə]	(Sept)	September
April [ˈeɪprəl]	(Apr)	April	**October** [ɒkˈtəʊbə]	(Oct)	Oktober
May [meɪ]	(May)	Mai	**November** [nəʊˈvembə]	(Nov)	November
June [dʒuːn]	(Jun)	Juni	**December** [dɪˈsembə]	(Dec)	Dezember

year *n* [jɜː]	She was born in the ~ 1986.	Jahr
century *n* [ˈsentʃərɪ]	≫ one hundred years	Jahrhundert
clock *n* [klɒk] ①		Uhr
alarm clock *n* [əˈlɑːm klɒk] ②		Wecker

②

①

tʃ	dʒ	θ	ð	ʃ	ʒ	ŋ	w	v
cheap	**j**ump	**th**ing	**th**en	**sh**op	plea**s**ure	sa**ng**	**w**et	**v**oice

watch *n* [wɒtʃ]	a small clock that you wear or carry with you	(Armband-/Taschen-) Uhr
o'clock *adv* [ə'klɒk]	What time is it? – It's 8 ~.	Uhr *(bei Zeitangaben)*
a.m. *adv* [eɪ'em]	≫ before midday	vormittags
p.m. *adv* [pɪ'em]	▶◀ a.m.	nachmittags
date *n* [deɪt]	What's the ~ today?	Datum
season *n* ['si:zn]	A year has four ~s.	Jahreszeit

spring *n* [sprɪŋ]	**summer** *n* ['sʌmə]	**autumn** *n*/**fall** *n AE* ['ɔ:təm/fɔ:l]	**winter** *n* ['wɪntə]
Frühling	Sommer	Herbst	Winter

Easter *n* ['i:stə]	**Whit(sun)** *n* ['wɪt(sn)]	**Christmas** *n* ['krɪsməs]	**New Year's Day** *n* ['nju: jɜ:z deɪ]
Ostern	Pfingsten	Weihnachten	Neujahr

fortnight *n BE* ['fɔ:tnaɪt]	≫ two weeks, 14 days	vierzehn Tage
wristwatch *n* ['rɪstwɒtʃ]		Armbanduhr
calendar *n* ['kælɪndə]	≫ a list of the days, weeks and months of the year	Kalender
diary *n* ['daɪərɪ]	My little sister **keeps a** ~.	Tagebuch

hourly *adj, adv* ['aʊəlɪ]	≫ once every	hour	stündlich
daily *adj, adv* ['deɪlɪ]		day	täglich
weekly *adj, adv* ['wi:klɪ]		week	wöchentlich
monthly *adj, adv* ['mʌnθlɪ]		month	monatlich
yearly *adj, adv* ['jɜ:lɪ] / **annual** *adj* ['ænjʊəl]		year	jährlich

mid- *adj* [mɪd]	He starts his job in ~September.	Mitte, Mittel . . .

2.3 Beginning and end

to begin *v* [bɪ'gɪn] **began** [bɪ'gæn] **begun** [bɪ'gʌn]	You must ~ to work now.	anfangen, beginnen
to start *v* [stɑ:t]	I'll ~ my homework in a minute. (▶▶ begin)	beginnen, anfangen
to delay *v* [dɪ'leɪ]	The snowfalls ~ed all trains.	verschieben, verzögern
delay *n* [dɪ'leɪ]	You should do it **without** ~. (≫ at once)	Aufschub, Verzögerung
to stop *v* [stɒp]	Suddenly the rain ~ped.	aufhören, stoppen
to cancel *v* ['kænsl]	The manager ~led his flight to Tokyo. (▶▶ called off)	annullieren, rückgängig machen
to give up *v + adv* [gɪv]	▶▶ to stop	aufgeben
to finish *v* ['fɪnɪʃ]	Mary ~ed reading that thriller yesterday. The lesson ~ed with a song.	enden, beenden, aufhören mit

i:	ɪ	e	æ	ɑ:	ɒ	ɔ:	ʊ	u:	ʌ	ɜ:	ə
eat	bit	ten	bad	fast	got	saw	sure	too	cut	bird	about

to end *v* [end]	▶▶ to finish, to stop	enden, endigen
to be over *v + adv* [bɪ ˈəʊvə]	The storm will soon ~. (▶▶ stop)	zu Ende sein, aufhören
beginning *n* [bɪˈgɪnɪŋ]	There were several new pupils at the ~ of term.	Anfang, Beginn
start *n* [stɑːt]	▶▶ beginning	Anfang, Beginn
end *n* [end]	▶◀ beginning, start	Ende, Schluß
stop *n* [stɒp]	The runners made a ~ after 10 miles.	Halt
first *adj, adv, n* [fɜːst]	Armstrong was the ~ man to walk on the moon.	erste(r,s)
original *adj* [əˈrɪdʒənl]	The ~ inhabitants of America are the Red Indians. (▶▶ first)	ursprünglich, Ur-
last *adj, adv* [lɑːst]	Jane hurt her leg and came ~ in the race.	letzte(r,s)
later *adj, adv* [ˈleɪtə]	▶◀ earlier	später
latest *adj, adv* [ˈleɪtɪst]	What is the ~ news?	letzte, neueste
to launch *v* [lɔːntʃ]	to send (a boat, rocket etc) into the water or sky	starten, vom Stapel lassen
to halt *v* [hɔːlt]	to make something stop	(an)halten
to cease *v* [siːs]	▶▶ to stop, to end	aufhören, enden
to break down *v + adv* [breɪk]	My car often ~s ~. (≫ stops working)	versagen, eine Panne haben
breakdown *n* [ˈbreɪkdaʊn]	She had a ~ on the motorway.	Panne, Zusammenbruch
to postpone *v* [pəˈspəʊn]	≫ to move to a later date	verschieben, aufschieben
to put off *v + adv* [pʊt]	▶▶ to postpone	verschieben
delayed *adj* [dɪˈleɪd]	The arrival of the train was ~.	verzögert, aufgeschoben
origin *n* [ˈɒrɪdʒɪn]	the place or situation where something began	Ursprung, Quelle
source *n* [sɔːs]	the place where something starts or comes from	Quelle
halt *n* [hɔːlt]	The taxi **came to a** ~. (▶▶ stop)	Halt, Stillstand
first of all [fɜːst, ɔːl]	≫ before anything else	vor allen Dingen
originally *adv* [əˈrɪdʒənəlɪ]	▶▶ at first, in the beginning	ursprünglich, zuerst
former *adj* [ˈfɔːmə]	He is the ~ director of that firm. (≫ He used to be . . .)	frühere(r,s), ehemalig
previous *adj* [ˈpriːvɪəs]	Her ~ husband was very rich. (▶▶ earlier)	vorausgehend, vorhergehend
latter *adj* [ˈlætə]	▶▶ last	letzte(r,s)
final *adj* [ˈfaɪnl]	▶▶ last	letzte(r,s)
endless *adj* [ˈendlɪs]	His speech seemed ~. (≫ without end)	endlos

2.4 Old, young and new

old *adj* [əʊld]	My grandmother is very ~. (▶◀ young) He sold his ~ car and bought a new one.	alt
second-hand *adj* [sekəndˈhænd]	≫ already used by someone	aus zweiter Hand
new *adj* [njuː]	I'd like to buy a ~ motorbike. (▶◀ used; old)	neu
future *adj* [ˈfjuːtʃə]	This is his ~ wife. (≫ the woman he's going to marry)	zukünftig
modern *adj* [ˈmɒdn]	I don't like ~ music. (≫ . . . of the present time)	modern

adj	*adv*	*art*	*conj*	*n*	*pl*	*prep*	*pron*	*sing*
adjective	adverb(ial)	article	conjunction	noun	plural	preposition	pronoun	singular

fresh *adj* [freʃ]	The bread is still ~.	frisch, neu
youth *n* [juːθ]	In his ~ he was a famous star.	Jugend
age *n* [eɪdʒ]	What's your ~? – I'm 10 years old.	Alter
young *adj* [jʌŋ]	▶◀ old	jung
birthday *n* [ˈbɜːθdeɪ]	**Happy** ~ to you!	Geburtstag
to grow *v* [grəʊ] **grew** [gruː] **grown** [grəʊn]	Billy is ~ing fast. (⩾ becoming taller)	wachsen
to develop *v* [dɪˈveləp]	Henry has ~ed quickly.	(sich) entwickeln
development *n* [dɪˈveləpmənt]	⩾ growing, new happening	Entwicklung
out-of-date *adj* [aʊtəvˈdeɪt]	▶◀ modern	altmodisch
old-fashioned *adj* [əʊldˈfæʃnd]		
ancient *adj* [ˈeɪnʃənt]	▶▶ very old	einstig, alt
antique *adj* [ænˈtiːk]	My uncle collects ~ furniture. (⩾ old and valuable)	altertümlich, antik
antique *n* [ænˈtiːk]	an old and therefore valuable thing	Antiquität
up-to-date *adj* [ʌptəˈdeɪt]	▶▶ modern	modern
progressive *adj* [prəˈgresɪv]	e.g. ~ ideas	fortschrittlich
recent *adj* [ˈriːsnt]	⩾ a short time ago	jüngste(r,s), frisch
present *adj* [ˈpreznt]	Alan doesn't like his ~ job.	gegenwärtig
junior *adj* [ˈdʒuːnɪə]	Kim is three years ~ to me. (⩾ younger than I)	jünger
senior *adj* [ˈsiːnɪə]	▶◀ junior	älter, ranghöher
mature *adj* [məˈtjʊə]	⩾ fully developed	reif
ripe *adj* [raɪp]	That apple isn't quite ~. (⩾ ready to be eaten)	reif *(Obst, Getreide, Ernte)*
aged *adj* [eɪdʒd]	The man was ~ about thirty. (⩾ of the age of)	im Alter von
elderly *adj* [ˈeldəlɪ]	⩾ rather old	ältere(r,s)
childhood *n* [ˈtʃaɪldhʊd]	the time when one is a child	Kindheit
old age *n* [əʊld ˈeɪdʒ]	▶◀ youth	Greisenalter

2.5 Grammatical expressions of time

now *adv* [naʊ]	⩾ at the present time	jetzt
at once *adv* [ətˈwʌns]	You must do it ~! (▶▶ immediately)	sofort, augenblicklich
at the moment *adv* [ˈməʊmənt]	He's rather busy ~. (▶▶ now)	im Augenblick
recently *adv* [ˈrɪsntlɪ]	⩾ not long ago	kürzlich, neulich
during *prep* [ˈdjʊərɪŋ]	He had to go away ~ the meeting.	während
while *conj* [waɪl]	It was raining ~ we were walking.	während

during + NOUN (during the night)
while + VERB (while we sleep)

then *adv* [ðen]	⩾ at that time	damals
once *adv* [wʌns]	⩾ some time ago	einst, einmal

always *adv* ['ɔ:lweɪz]	▶◀ never	immer
all day [ɔ:l 'deɪ]	▶▶ the whole day	den ganzen Tag
forever *adv* [fə'revə] **for ever** *adv*	'I'll love you ~!' he said. (⪢ for all time)	für immer
sometimes *adv* ['sʌmtaɪmz]	I ~ go to the movies.	manchmal
often *adv* ['ɒfn]	▶▶ many times	oft
seldom *adv* ['seldəm]	⪢ almost never, ▶◀ often	selten
already *adv* [ɔ:l'redɪ]	▶◀ not . . . yet	schon, bereits
yet *adv* [jet]	I have**n't** finished my supper ~.	noch (nicht)
ever *adv* ['evə]	Have you ~ been to Japan? (⪢ at any time)	je, jemals
never *adv* ['nevə]	I've ~ seen Charlie Chaplin in my life.	nie, niemals
still *adv* [stɪl]	It's ten o'clock and Mary is ~ in bed.	(immer) noch
still not *adv*	It's very late but the children ~ are ~ back.	(immer) noch nicht
when *adv* [wen]	W~ do you get up in the morning? (⪢ at what time)	wann
when *conj, adv* [wen]	It was snowing ~ they arrived.	als
as soon as *conj* [əz 'su:n əz]	A~ she saw the burglar, Jill began to scream.	sobald
soon *adv* [su:n]	⪢ in a short time	bald
in a minute ['mɪnɪt]	I'll be back ~. (⪢ very soon)	gleich, sofort
again *adv* [ə'gen] **once again** *adv* [wʌns ə'gen] **once more** *adv* [wʌns 'mɔ:]	⪢ another time	wieder, noch einmal
at first *adv* [ət'fɜ:st]	▶▶ at the beginning	zuerst
till *prep, conj* [tɪl] **until** *prep, conj* [ən'tɪl]	She won't be back ~ 8 o'clock. She waited ~ they arrived.	bis
by *adv* [baɪ]	I'll be back ~ 9 o'clock. (⪢ not later than)	bis (spätestens)
before *prep, adv, conj* [bɪ:fɔ:]	My brother arrived ~ 7 o'clock. (⪢ earlier than)	vor
	Ring me up ~ you come.	bevor, ehe
after *prep, adv, conj* ['ɑ:ftə]	▶◀ before	nach
afterwards *adv* [ɑ:ftəwədz]	▶▶ later	später, nachher
finally *adv* ['faɪnəlɪ]	⪢ after a long time	schließlich
then *adv* [ðen]	Jane went home and ~ she met a friend. (▶▶ next, after that)	dann, darauf
towards *prep* [tə'wɔ:dz]	It was getting ~ midnight when they arrived home.	gegen
almost *adv* ['ɔ:lməʊst] **nearly** *adv* ['nɪəlɪ]	It's ~ midday. (⪢ a short time before)	beinahe, fast

in *prep* [ɪn]		**on** *prep* [ɒn]		**at** *prep* [æt, ət]	
~ 1984	*(Year)*	~ Friday	*(Day)*	~ 6 o'clock	*(Exact time)*
~ summer	*(Season)*			~ noon	
~ May	*(Month)*			~ night	
~ the morning	*(Part of the day)*			~ Christmas	*(Holidays)*
~ the afternoon				~ Easter	
				~ weekends	

tʃ	dʒ	θ	ð	ʃ	ʒ	ŋ	w	v
cheap	**j**ump	**th**ing	**th**en	**sh**op	plea**s**ure	sa**ng**	**w**et	**v**oice

for *prep* [fɔ:, fə]	She has been here ~ three months.	seit *(Zeitraum)*
since *prep, conj* [sɪns]	Mike has lived here ~ January. I haven't seen him ~ he left.	seit *(Zeitpunkt)* seit(dem)
ago *adv* [əˈgəʊ]	He left three days ~. (▶▶ before now)	vor

2

will/'ll *v* [wɪl/l]	I ~ be 17 next May.	werden
shall *v* [ʃæl, ʃl]	I ~ go there next week.	werden
nowadays *adv* [ˈnaʊədeɪz] **these days** [ði:z ˈdeɪz]	≫ at the present period	heutzutage
at present *adv* [ətˈpreznt]	▶▶ now, at the moment	jetzt, momentan
lately *adv* [ˈleɪtlɪ] **the other day** [ðɪ ʌðə ˈdeɪ]	▶▶ recently	kürzlich, vor kurzem, neulich
the next day [ðə nekst ˈdeɪ] **the day after** [ðə deɪ ˈɑ:ftə]	▶▶ the following day	am folgenden Tag

Don't mix them up:

then [ðen] dann, damals	**its** [ɪts] sein *pron*	**costume** [ˈkɒstju:m] Kostüm
than [ðən] als	**it's** [ɪts] es ist	**custom** [ˈkʌstəm] Sitte
		customs [ˈkʌstəmz] Zoll
at last [ətˈlɑ:st] schließlich	**whose** [hu:z] deren, dessen	**shirt** [ʃɜ:t] Hemd
at least [ətˈli:st] zumindest	**who's** [hu:z] wer ist	**skirt** [skɜ:t] Rock
quiet [ˈkwaɪət] ruhig	**sweat** [swet] Schweiß	**soup** [su:p] Suppe
quite [kwaɪt] ziemlich	**sweet** [swi:t] süß	**soap** [səʊp] Seife

some other time [səm ˈʌðə taɪm] **at a different time** [ˈdɪfrənt]	≫ not now	ein andermal
in the near future [ˈfju:tʃə]	≫ quite soon	ziemlich bald
shortly *adv* [ˈʃɔ:tlɪ] **before long** *adv* [bɪfɔ: ˈlɒŋ]	▶▶ soon	in kurzem

i:	ɪ	e	æ	ɑ:	ɒ	ɔ:	ʊ	u:	ʌ	ɜ:	ə
eat	bit	ten	bad	fast	got	saw	sure	too	cut	bird	about

in the end *adv* [ɪn ðɪ 'end]	►► finally	schließlich, endlich
at last *adv* [ət'lɑ:st]		
eventually *adv* [ɪ'ventʃʊəlɪ]		
in the meantime *adv* ['mi:ntaɪm]	≫ in the time between	inzwischen, mittlerweile
meanwhile *adv* ['mi:nwaɪl]		
throughout *prep, adv* [θru:'aʊt]	It rained ~ his holidays (≫ during the whole time of)	während, hindurch
for the time being [taɪm 'bi:ɪŋ]	≫ for a limited period	vorläufig, für jetzt
up to *adv* ['ʌp tʊ]	He always works ~ 7 o'clock. (►► till)	bis
up to now *adv* [ʌp tʊ 'naʊ]	≫ up to the present	bis jetzt
so far *adv* ['səʊ fɑ:]	≫ up to the present	bis jetzt
ever since *adv, conj* [evə 'sɪns]	Diana has liked animals ~ she was a child. (≫ from the time when)	seit der Zeit, seitdem
occasionally *adv* [ə'keɪʒnəlɪ]	►► sometimes	gelegentlich
now and then *adv* [naʊ ənd 'ðen]		von Zeit zu Zeit
rarely *adv* ['reəlɪ]	►► seldom	selten
invariably *adv* [ɪn'veərɪəblɪ]	►► always	(be)ständig
constantly *adv* ['kɒnstəntlɪ]		
whenever *conj* [wen'evə]	W~ I see him he is smoking a cigar.	immer wenn, wann immer
as *conj* [æz, əz]	A~ I went past, somebody hit me on the head. (►► when)	als, während
before now [bɪ'fɔ: naʊ]	≫ earlier than the present moment	vorher, zuvor
previously *adv* ['pri:vɪəslɪ]		
in advance [ɪn əd'vɑ:ns]	≫ before others	im voraus
later on *adv* [leɪtər' ɒn]	►► afterwards	später
through *prep* [θru:]	My brother had to work ~ the night. (≫ from the beginning to the end of)	hindurch, während
roughly *adv* ['rʌflɪ]	R~ when did you arrive?	ungefähr, etwa
approximately *adv* [ə'prɒksɪmətlɪ]	(≫ more or less), ►◄ exactly	
once upon a time [wʌns əpɒn ə 'taɪm]	≫ some time ago *(beginning of a story for children)*	(es war) einmal . . .
to be about to [bɪ ə'baʊt tʊ]	►► to be going to	im Begriff sein

adj	*adv*	*art*	*conj*	*n*	*pl*	*prep*	*pron*	*sing*
adjective	adverb(ial)	article	conjunction	noun	plural	preposition	pronoun	singular

3 Life on earth

3.1 Life in general

to be *v* [biː]	To ~ or not to ~, that is the question. *(Hamlet)*	sein, existieren
to live *v* [lɪv]	My uncle is very ill, but the doctor says he will ~.	leben, am Leben bleiben
to lead *v* [liːd]	He ~s a dangerous life.	führen
life *n* [laɪf] *pl* **lives** [laɪvz]	There is no ~ on the moon.	Leben
alive *adj* [əˈlaɪv]	▶◀ dead	lebend
born *adj* [bɔːn]	The baby was ~ at 11 o'clock.	geboren
birth *n* [bɜːθ]	The young woman gave ~ to a little girl.	Geburt
death *n* [deθ]	the end of life	Tod
dead *adj* [ded]	▶◀ alive	tot
to die *v* [daɪ]	The old man ~d after a long illness. (≫ stopped living)	sterben
to kill *v* [kɪl]	The terrorists ~ed three people.	töten
natural *adj* [ˈnætʃrəl]	She is a girl with great ~ charm.	natürlich
wild *adj* [waɪld]	A lion is a ~ animal.	wild
sex *n* [seks]	Here is a form. Please fill in your name, age and ~.	Geschlecht
	They shouldn't show ~ films on TV.	Sex, Erotik
male *adj, n* [meɪl]	Boys and men belong to the ~ sex.	männlich
female *adj, n* [ˈfiːmeɪl]	▶◀ male	weiblich

Lerntip Aussprache

Lies jeden Vokabeleintrag mehrmals laut, und präge Dir die Aussprache gut ein. Die Lautschrift hilft Dir, die richtige Aussprache zu finden. Wörter, die Du schwer behalten kannst, solltest Du besonders kennzeichnen, z. B. mit einem Textmarker.

to exist *v* [ɪgˈzɪst]	▶▶ to be, to live	existieren
to create *v* [kriːˈeɪt]	God ~ed the world.	(er)schaffen
to survive *v* [səˈvaɪv]	≫ to remain alive	überleben
living *adj* [ˈlɪvɪŋ]	▶▶ alive	lebend
live *adj* [laɪv]	The show is ~ from Aberdeen. (▶◀ recorded)	live, lebendig
existence *n* [ɪgˈzɪstəns]	This girl leads a sad ~.	Leben, Existenz
survival *n* [səˈvaɪvl]	The men who had that accident have a slight hope of ~.	Überleben, Fortbestand
organic *adj* [ɔːˈgænɪk]	≫ of living things	organisch
to lay *v* [leɪ] **laid** [leɪd] **laid** [leɪd]	Hens ~ eggs.	legen (Eier)
pregnant *adj* [ˈpregnənt]	She has been ~ for seven months.	schwanger
youthful *adj* [ˈjuːθfʊl]	▶▶ young-looking	jugendlich
natural history *n* [ˈnætʃrəl ˈhɪstrɪ]	the study of nature	Naturgeschichte

3.2 Animals

animal *n* [ˈænɪml]	a living thing that is not a plant (or a person)	Tier
bird *n* [bɜːd]	Most ~s can fly.	Vogel
fish *n pl* **fish** [fɪʃ]	Bill saw some ~ in the water.	Fisch, Fischarten

monkey *n* ['mʌŋkɪ] (1)		Affe
horse *n* [hɔ:s] (2)		Pferd
cow *n* [kaʊ] (3)		Kuh, Rind
cat *n* [kæt] (4)		Katze
dog *n* [dɒg] (5)		Hund
sheep *n, pl* **sheep** [ʃi:p] (6)		Schaf
lamb *n* [læm] (7)		Lamm
chicken *n* ['tʃɪkɪn]	a young hen	Hühnchen
fly *n* [flaɪ] (8)		Fliege
(living) creature *n* ['lɪvɪŋ 'kri:tʃə]	animal	Lebewesen
being *n* ['bi:ɪŋ]		
beast *n* [bi:st]	≫ a big animal with four feet	(vierfüßiges) Tier, Vieh
insect *n* ['ɪnsekt]	A fly is an ~.	Insekt
herd *n* [hɜ:d]	≫ a large group (e.g. of cattle)	Herde
nest *n* [nest]	Yesterday I saw a bird's ~ under the roof.	Nest
zoo *n* [zu:]	a place where you can see many different animals	Zoo, Zoologischer Garten, Tiergarten
stray *adj* [streɪ]	There are several ~ cats in our garden.	herrenlos, streunend
to bark *v* [bɑ:k]	Our dog ~ed when it saw the young man.	bellen
to growl *v* [graʊl]	The dog ~ed at the postman.	knurren
pony *n* ['pəʊnɪ]	≫ a small horse	Pony
donkey *n* ['dɒŋkɪ]		Esel

zebra *n* ['zi:brə]		Zebra
stripe *n* [straɪp]	Zebras and tigers have ~s.	Streifen
striped *adj* [straɪpt]	The zebra is a ~ animal.	gestreift
calf *n, pl* **calves** [kɑ:f, kɒ:vz]	a young cow	Kalb
ox *n, pl* **oxen** [ɒks, 'ɒksn]	There are five ~ on this farm.	Ochse
cattle *n* ['kætl]	Cows and bulls are ~.	Vieh
pig *n* [pɪg]		Schwein
goat *n* [gəʊt]		Ziege
lion *n* ['laɪən]		Löwe
lioness *n* ['laɪənes]	a female lion	Löwin

tiger *n* ['taɪgə] (1)		Tiger
elephant *n* ['elɪfənt] (2)		Elefant
camel *n* ['kæml] (3)		Kamel
hump *n* [hʌmp] (4)		Höcker
greyhound *n* ['greɪhaʊnd] (5)		Windhund
fox *n* [fɒks] (6)		Fuchs
wolf *n, pl* **wolves** [wʊlf, wʊlvz] (7)		Wolf
bear *n* [beə] (8)		Bär
deer *n, pl* **deer** [dɪə] (9)		Hirsch, Rotwild
polar bear *n* ['pəʊlə beə] (10)		Eisbär
seal *n* [si:l] (11)		Robbe, Seehund
fur *n* [fɜ:]	the hair of bears, cats etc	Pelz, Fell
rabbit *n* ['ræbɪt] (12)		Kaninchen
hare *n* [heə]	an animal like a rabbit, but larger	Hase

tʃ	dʒ	θ	ð	ʃ	ʒ	ŋ	w	v
cheap	**j**ump	**th**ing	**th**en	**sh**op	plea**s**ure	sa**ng**	**w**et	**v**oice

hedgehog *n* ['hedʒhɒg] ⑬		Igel
spine *n* [spaɪn] ⑭		Stachel
mouse *n, pl* **mice** [maʊs, maɪs] ⑮		Maus
squirrel *n* ['skwɪrəl] ⑯		Eichhörnchen
tail *n* [teɪl] ⑰		Schwanz
hen *n* [hen] ⑱		Henne
feather *n* ['feðə] ⑲		Feder
turkey *n* ['tɜ:kɪ] ⑳		Truthahn, Puter
duck *n* [dʌk] ㉑		Ente
goose *n, pl* **geese** [gu:s, gi:s] ㉒		Gans
swallow *n* ['swɒləʊ] ㉓		Schwalbe
wing *n* [wɪŋ] ㉔		Flügel
pigeon *n* ['pɪdʒɪn] ㉕		Taube

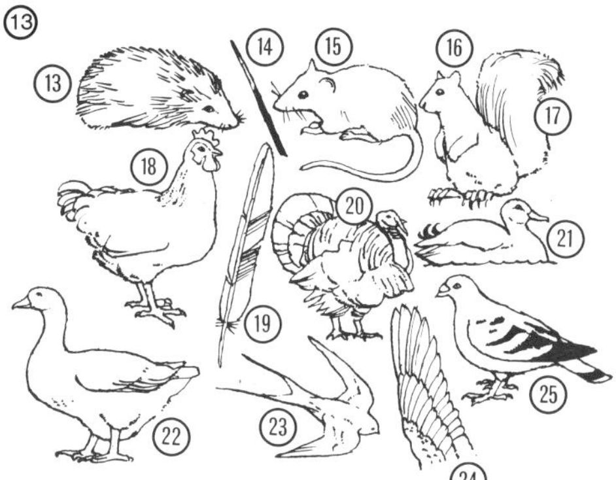

Irregular plurals

singular:	fish	sheep	deer	mouse	goose	calf	wolf	ox
plural:	fish	sheep	deer	mice	geese	calves	wolves	oxen

lark *n* [lɑ:k]	a small songbird	Lerche
parrot *n* ['pærət] ㉖		Papagei
kiwi *n* ['ki:wi:] ㉗		Kiwi
kea *n* ['keɪə] ㉘		Kea *(Papageienart)*
owl *n* [aʊl] ㉙		Eule
snake *n* [sneɪk] ㉚		Eule, Uhu
alligator *n* ['ælɪgeɪtə] ㉛		Alligator
frog *n* [frɒg] ㉜		Frosch
lobster *n* ['lɒbstə] ㉝		Hummer
shrimp *n* [ʃrɪmp] ㉞		Garnele, Krabbe
shell *n* [ʃel] ㉟		(Muschel)schale
worm *n* [wɜ:m] ㊱		Wurm
butterfly *n* ['bʌtəflaɪ] ㊲		Schmetterling
spider *n* ['spaɪdə] ㊳		Spinne
beetle *n* ['bi:tl] ㊴		Käfer
dinosaur *n* ['daɪnəsɔ:] ㊵		Dinosaurier

3.3 Plants

plant *n* [plɑ:nt]	Vegetables, flowers and trees are ~s.	Pflanze
flower *n* ['flaʊə]	Roses are ~s.	Blume, Blüte
rose *n* [rəʊz]		Rose
fruit *n* [fru:t]	Apples, pears and bananas are ~.	Frucht, Obst
leaf *n, pl* **leaves** [li:f, li:vz] ①		Blatt
tree *n* [tri:] ②		Baum
grass *n* [grɑ:s] ③		Gras
orange *n* ['ɒrɪndʒ] ④		Orange, Apfelsine
banana *n* [bə'nɑ:nə] ⑤		Banane
apple *n* ['æpl] ⑥		Apfel
pear *n* [peə] ⑦		Birne

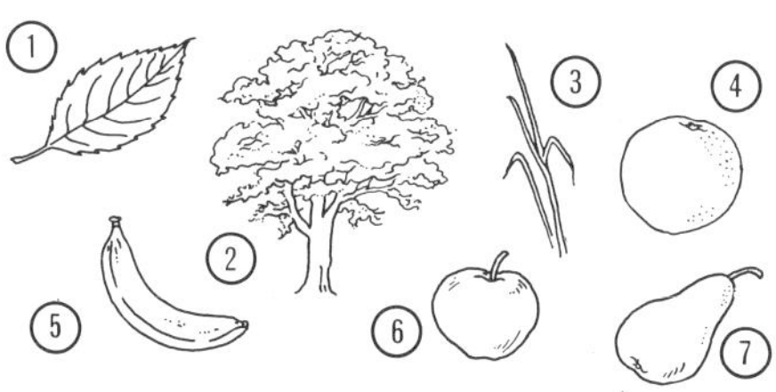

i:	ɪ	e	æ	ɑ:	ɒ	ɔ:	ʊ	u:	ʌ	ɜ:	ə
eat	bit	ten	bad	fast	got	saw	sure	too	cut	bird	about

nut *n* [nʌt] ⑧		Nuß
potato *n* [pəˈteɪtəʊ] ⑨ *pl* **potatoes**		Kartoffel
tomato *n* [təˈmɑːtəʊ] ⑩ *pl* **tomatoes**		Tomate
rice *n* [raɪs]	In China and Japan people eat a lot of ~.	Reis
root *n* [ruːt] ⑪		Wurzel
branch *n* [brɑːntʃ] ⑫		Ast, Zweig
stem *n* [stem] ⑬		Stengel, Stiel
stone *n* [stəʊn]	Cherries have ~s in them.	Stein, Kern
herb *n* [hɜːb]	a plant used in cooking or medicine	Kraut, Heilpflanze
mushroom *n* [ˈmʌʃrʊm] ⑭		(Speise)Pilz
watermelon *n* [ˈwɔːtəmelən] ⑮		Wassermelone
lemon *n* [ˈlemən] ⑯		Zitrone
grapefruit *n* [ˈgreɪpfruːt] ⑰		Grapefruit
peach *n* [piːtʃ] ⑱		Pfirsich
pinapple *n* [ˈpaɪnæpl] ⑲		Ananas
plum *n* [plʌm] ⑳		Pflaume
cherry *n* [ˈtʃerɪ] ㉑		Kirsche
strawberry *n* [ˈstrɔːbrɪ] ㉒		Erdbeere
gooseberry *n* [ˈgʊzbərɪ] ㉓		Stachelbeere
grape *n* [greɪp] ㉔		Traube
raisin *n* [ˈreɪzn]	She made the cake with ~s. (≥ dried grapes)	Rosine
cabbage *n* [ˈkæbɪdʒ] ㉕		Kohl, Kohlkopf
carrot *n* [ˈkærət] ㉖		Karotte, Möhre
lettuce *n* [ˈletɪs]	a green garden plant that you eat in salads	Kopfsalat
onion *n* [ˈʌnɪən] ㉗		Zwiebel
pea *n* [piː] ㉘		Erbse
beans *n* [biːnz] ㉙		Bohnen
spinach *n* [ˈspɪnɪdʒ]	a vegetable with green leaves	Spinat
parsley *n* [ˈpɑːslɪ]	a garden plant used in the kitchen	Petersilie
wheat *n* [wiːt] ㉚		Weizen
corn *n* [kɔːn] *AE*	plants such as oats and wheat ►► maize *BE*	Korn, Weizen Mais
chestnut *n* [ˈtʃesnʌt] ㉛		Kastanie
pine *n* [paɪn] ㉜		Kiefer, Föhre
cactus *n* [ˈkæktəs] ㉝		Kaktus
kauri *n* [ˈkaʊrɪ]	a tree from New Zealand	Kauribaum

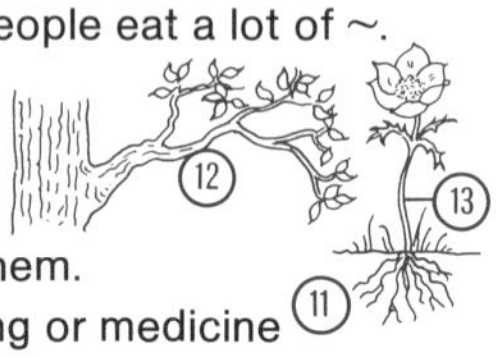

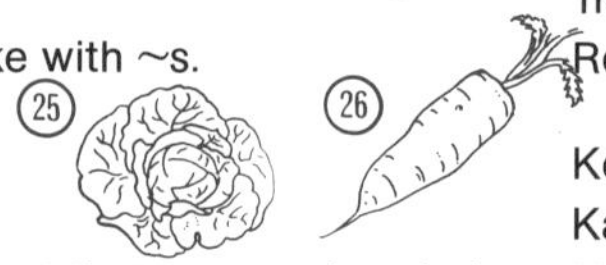

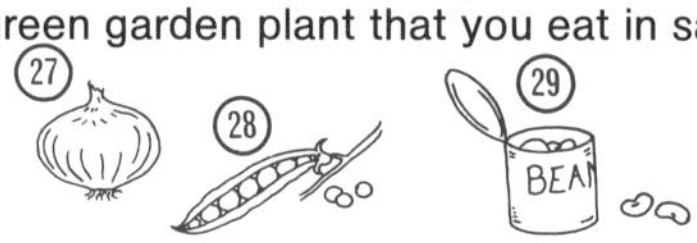

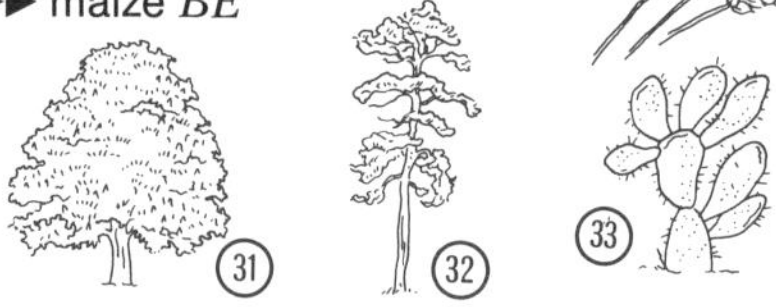

adj	*adv*	*art*	*conj*	*n*	*pl*	*prep*	*pron*	*sing*
adjective	adverb(ial)	article	conjunction	noun	plural	preposition	pronoun	singular

4 Human being
4.1 Body

body *n* ['bɒdɪ]	Arms, hands, legs, head etc are parts of our ~.	Körper
figure *n* ['fɪgə]	I could see the ~ of a man in the distance.	Figur, Gestalt
head *n* [hed] (1)		Kopf
neck *n* [nek] (2)		Hals
throat *n* [θrəʊt] (3)		Kehle, Hals
face *n* [feɪs]	Have you washed your ~?	Gesicht
hair *n* [heə] (4)		Haar, Haare
eye *n* [aɪ] (5)		Auge
ear *n* [ɪə] (6)		Ohr
nose *n* [nəʊz] (7)		Nase
mouth *n* [maʊθ] (8)		Mund
tooth *n, pl* **teeth** [tu:θ, ti:θ] (9)		Zahn
beard *n* [bɪəd] (10)		(Voll)bart
heart *n* [hɑ:t]	When you run, your ~ beats faster.	Herz
blood *n* [blʌd]	the red liquid in your body	Blut
bloody *adj* ['blʌdɪ]	≫ covered with blood	blutig
back *n* [bæk] (11)		Rücken
shoulder *n* ['ʃəʊldə] (12)		Schulter
arm *n* [ɑ:m] (13)		Arm
hand *n* [hænd] (14)		Hand
finger *n* ['fɪŋgə] (15)		Finger
stomach *n* ['stʌmək] (16)		Magen, Bauch
leg *n* [leg] (17)		Bein
knee *n* [ni:] (18)		Knie
foot *n, pl* **feet** [fʊt, fi:t] (19)		Fuß
skin *n* [skɪn]	When you sit in the sun for a long time, your ~ gets brown.	Haut
black *n* [blæk]	a person with dark skin	Farbige(r)
fair *adj* [feə]	What's the name of that ~-haired girl over there?	blond, hell
awake *adj* [ə'weɪk]	≫ not sleeping	wach
to sleep *v* [sli:p] **slept** [slept] **slept** [slept]	I normally ~ six hours every night.	schlafen
to fall asleep *v* [fɔ:l ə'sli:p]	≫ to start sleeping	einschlafen
asleep *adj* [ə'sli:p]	She was ~ when I arrived. (▶▶ sleeping), ▶◀ awake	eingeschlafen schlafend
to wake (up) *v* [weɪk] **woke** [wəʊk] **woken** ['wəʊkən]	I often ~ in the middle of the night. (≫ stop sleeping)	aufwachen
	Please don't ~ our baby.	aufwecken
sleep *n* [sli:p]	Did you have a good ~?	Schlaf
rest *n* [rest]	You should **take a** short ~.	Ruhepause
to rest *v* [rest]	≫ to take a rest	ausruhen
to dream *v* [dri:m] **dreamt** [dremt] **dreamt** [dremt]	He often ~s he is James Bond.	träumen
dream *n* [dri:m]	Last night my girlfriend had a strange ~.	Traum

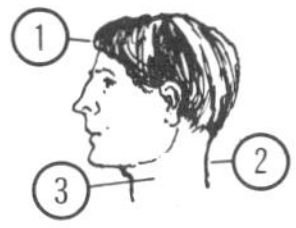

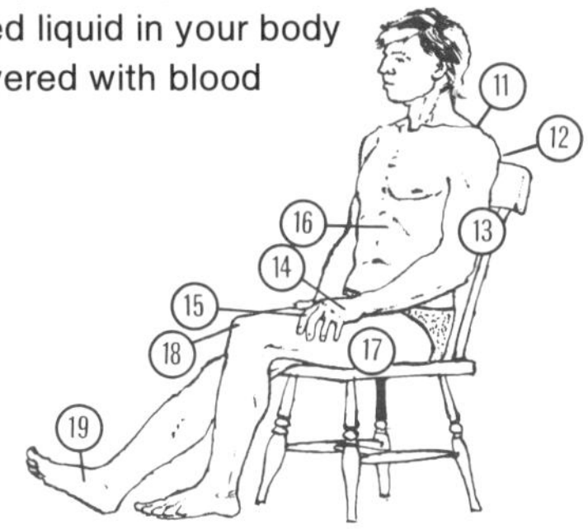

4

lazy *adj* ['leɪzɪ]	≫ unwilling to work	faul
active *adj* ['æktɪv]	My grandfather is 74 but still very ~. (▶▶ busy)	aktiv, tätig
to sweat *v* [swet]	The runner was ~ing after the race.	schwitzen
tired *adj* ['taɪəd]	I need a rest now: I'm very ~.	müde, erschöpft
fat *adj* [fæt]	Don't eat so much, you're getting too ~.	dick, fett
thin *adj* [θɪn]	▶◀ fat	dünn, dürr
slim *adj* [slɪm]	▶◀ fat	schlank
physical *adj* ['fɪzɪkl]	▶◀ mental	körperlich
bone *n* [bəʊn]	She broke a ~ in her hand.	Knochen
tissue *n* ['tɪʃuː]	The organs of the body are made of ~.	Gewebe
muscle *n* ['mʌsl]	He hurt a ~ in his right arm.	Muskel
nerve *n* [nɜːv]	N~s carry feelings through the body.	Nerv
limb *n* [lɪm]	a leg or an arm	Glied, Gliedmaßen
brain *n* [breɪn]	The ~ controls thought and feeling.	Gehirn, Verstand
brow *n* [braʊ] ①		Augenbraue
cheek *n* [tʃiːk] ②		Wange, Backe
lip *n* [lɪp] ③		Lippe
chin *n* [tʃɪn] ④		Kinn
moustache *n* [mə'stɑːʃ] ⑤ **mustache** *n AE* ['mʌstæʃ]		Schnurrbart

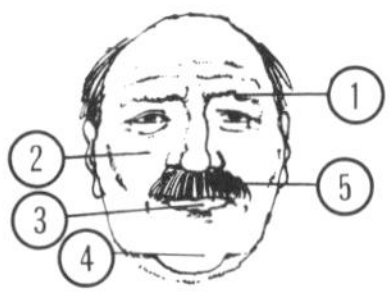

tongue *n* [tʌŋ]	When you talk, your ~ moves inside your mouth.	Zunge
chest *n* [tʃest] ⑥		Brust(korb)
waist *n* [weɪst] ⑦		Taille
to bleed *v* [bliːd] **bled** [bled] **bled** [bled]	Bill was ~ing from a cut. (≫ losing blood)	bluten

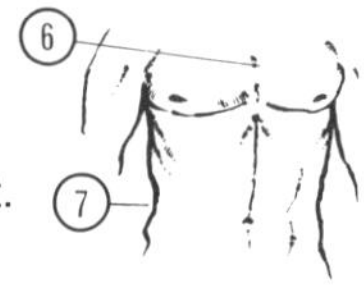

pulse *n* [pʌls]	The nurse felt the old lady's ~.	Puls(schlag)
lungs *n* [lʌŋz]	We breathe with our ~.	Lunge
to breathe *v* [briːð]	She was unconscious but still ~ing.	atmen
breath *n* [breθ]	He took a deep ~.	Atem(zug)
liver *n* ['lɪvə]	The ~ cleans the blood.	Leber
wrist *n* [rɪst] ⑧		Handgelenk
thumb *n* [θʌm] ⑨		Daumen
ankle *n* ['æŋkl] ⑩		(Fuß)knöchel
heel *n* [hiːl] ⑪		Ferse
toe *n* [təʊ] ⑫		Zehe

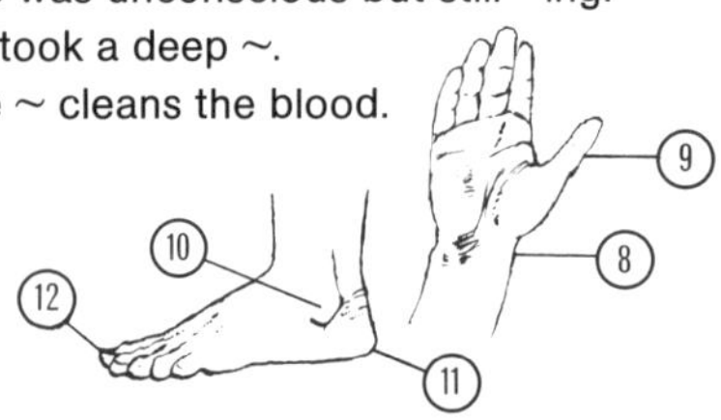

curly *adj* ['kɜːlɪ]	Is your hair ~? ▶◀ straight	lockig, gelockt
pale *adj* [peɪl]	Suddenly he **turned** ~. (≫ white in the face)	blaß, bleich
negro *n, pl* **negroes** ['niːgrəʊ, 'niːgraʊz]	A person with a black skin (living in America) was called a ~.	Neger, Schwarzer
tear *n* [tɪə]	a drop of water that comes from the eyes when you are unhappy	Träne
sweat *n* [swet]	drops of water that come out of the skin when it is hot	Schweiß
to spit *v* [spɪt] **spat** [spæt] **spat** [spæt]	The baby was ~ting out the banana.	(aus)spucken
conscious *adj* ['kɒnʃəs]	The girl was still ~ after the accident. (≫ awake)	bei Bewußtsein, bewußt
sleepy *adj* ['sliːpɪ]	▶▶ tired	schläfrig

tʃ	dʒ	θ	ð	ʃ	ʒ	ŋ	w	v
cheap	jump	thing	then	shop	pleasure	sang	wet	voice

to yawn *v* [jɔ:n]	I knew she was tired because she was ~ing.	gähnen
to oversleep *v* [əʊvə'sli:p] **overslept** [əʊvə'slept] **overslept** [əʊvə'slept]	≫ to sleep too long	verschlafen
to relax *v* [rɪ'læks]	≫ to rest from work	(sich) entspannen
to take it easy ['i:zɪ]	She told him to ~ and come home a little earlier. (≫ relax)	es leicht nehmen
nap *n* [næp]	a short sleep during the day	Nickerchen
kip *n informal* [kɪp]	≫ sleep	Schlaf
nightmare *n* ['naɪtmeə]	a very bad dream	Alptraum
lively *adj* ['laɪvlɪ]	≫ full of life, active	lebhaft
laziness *n* ['leɪzɪnɪs]	I've had enough of your ~. Do some work now!	Faulheit
exhausted *adj* [ɪg'zɔ:stɪd]	≫ extremely tired	erschöpft
breathless *adj* ['breθlɪs]	≫ out of breath	atemlos, außer Atem
slender *adj* ['slendə]	▶▶ slim	schlank
to slim *v* [slɪm]	I'm ~ming at the moment. (≫ trying to get thinner)	abnehmen, Schlankheitskur machen
out of shape [ʃeɪp]	She must be ~ because she gets tired easily.	nicht gut in Form

4

Lerntip

Problemwörter

Wörter, die Du Dir schwer merken kannst, solltest Du einer „Sonderbehandlung“ unterziehen. Schreibe sie groß auf ein Blatt und hänge es gut sichtbar in Deinem Zimmer auf, z. B. an der Tür oder am Spiegel, damit Du die schwierigen Wörter immer vor Augen hast.

4.2 Health and medicine

condition *n* [kən'dɪʃn]	a state of health	Gesundheitszustand
health *n* [helθ]	My father's ~ is excellent.	Gesundheit
illness *n* ['ɪlnɪs]	▶◀ health	Krankheit
well *adj* [wel]	He was ill but now he is ~ again. (≫ in good health)	gesund
fit *adj* [fɪt]	≫ strong and well	fit, gesund
better *adj* ['betə]	Are you feeling ~? (≫ less ill)	besser
all right [ɔ:l 'raɪt]	How are you? – A~, thank you. (≫ quite good)	ganz gut, ganz wohl
okay / OK *adj* [əʊkeɪ]	▶▶ all right	in Ordnung, OK
fine *adj* [faɪn]	How are you feeling? – F~, thank you. (≫ very well)	sehr gut, ausgezeichnet
ill *adj* [ɪl]	Jane can't come because she's ~. (≫ not well)	krank
sick *adj* [sɪk]	▶▶ ill	krank
to be sick *v*	She was ~ three times last night.	sich erbrechen
to feel sick *v* [fi:l]	I ~. Show me the bathroom.	Übelkeit verspüren
bad *adj* [bæd]	I feel ~! (≫ ill)	schlecht, übel
unconscious *adj* [ʌn'kɒnʃəs]	She was ~ for 4 days after the accident.	bewußtlos
sore *adj* [sɔ:]	I've had a ~ **throat** for two days. (▶▶ painful)	entzündet, wund, weh
pain *n* [peɪn]	I have a ~ **in** my leg.	Schmerz(en)

to hurt *v* [hɜːt] **hurt** [hɜːt] **hurt** [hɜːt]	My feet ~. Let's stop for a moment.	schmerzen, weh tun
painful *adj* ['peɪnfʊl]	⪢ giving pain	schmerzhaft
to suffer from *v+prep* ['sʌfə]	Her parents often ~ headaches. (⪢ have)	leiden an
to cut *v* [kʌt] **cut** [kʌt] **cut** [kʌt]	Don't ~ your finger with the knife.	schneiden, sich schneiden
cut *n* [kʌt]	She has a ~ on her finger.	Schnitt(wunde)
to bite *v* [baɪt] **bit** [bɪt] **bitten** ['bɪtn]	Don't tease the dog. He might ~ you.	beißen
to break *v* [breɪk] **broke** [brəʊk] **broken** ['brəʊkən]	Careful! Don't ~ your leg.	brechen, kaputtschlagen
blind *adj* [blaɪnd]	A ~ person cannot see.	blind
headache *n* ['hedeɪk]	a pain in the head	Kopfschmerzen
cold *n* [kəʊld]	Mary has a bad ~.	Erkältung
to catch (a) cold [kætʃ]	You can easily ~ in winter. (⪢ get a cold)	sich erkälten
to cough *v* [kɒf]	James was ~ing because of his cold.	husten
cough *n* [kɒf]	We heard a loud ~ in the kitchen.	Husten
flu *n* [fluː] **influenza** *n* [ɪnflʊ'enzə]	an illness with fever, headaches and a cold	Grippe
doctor *n* ['dɒktə]	I'm not feeling well. I'll have to see a ~.	Arzt
to examine *v* [ɪg'zæmɪn]	The doctor ~d the young woman and said she was healthy.	untersuchen
to test *v* [test]	▶▶ to examine	untersuchen, überprüfen
examination *n* [ɪgzæmɪ'neɪʃn] **test** *n* [test]	The doctor made an ~.	Untersuchung
to treat *v* [triːt]	The doctor ~ed Martha with a new drug.	behandeln
dentist *n* ['dentɪst]	A ~ repairs bad teeth.	Zahnarzt
toothache *n* ['tuːθeɪk]	a pain in a tooth	Zahnschmerzen
medicine *n* ['medsn]	We take ~ when we are ill.	Arznei, Medizin
medical *adj* ['medɪkl]	James is a ~ student. (⪢ . . . of medicine)	Medizin-
hospital *n* ['hɒspɪtl]	After the crash three people were taken to ~.	Krankenhaus
nurse *n* [nɜːs]	A ~ looks after sick people (in a hospital).	Krankenschwester
to look after *v+prep* [lʊk 'ɑːftə] **to take care of** [teɪk 'keər əv] **to care for** *v+prep* ['keə fə]	The nurse will ~ the patients.	sich kümmern um, sorgen für
chemist *n* ['kemɪst]	A ~ sells medicine, soap, make-up etc.	Apotheker, Drogist
drugstore *n AE* ['drʌgstɔː]		Apotheke, Drogerie

adj	*adv*	*art*	*conj*	*n*	*pl*	*prep*	*pron*	*sing*
adjective	adverb(ial)	article	conjunction	noun	plural	preposition	pronoun	singular

pill *n* [pɪl]	Have you taken your sleeping ~?	Pille, Dragee
toothpaste *n* ['tu:θpeɪst]	a special paste for cleaning your teeth	Zahnpasta
drug *n* [drʌg]	a medicine that makes sick people well	Arznei(mittel), Droge, Rauschgift
poison *n* ['pɔɪzn]	P~ will kill or harm you if you eat or drink it.	Gift
healthy *adj* ['helθɪ]	≫ in good health, ▶◀ ill, sick	gesund
handicapped *adj* ['hændɪkæpt]	He has a ~ child.	(körperlich/geistig) behindert
disabled *adj* [dɪs'eɪbld]	▶▶ handicapped	behindert, versehrt
wheelchair *n* ['wi:ltʃeə]	a special chair with wheels for disabled people	Rollstuhl
welfare *n* ['welfeə]	health and happiness	Wohlergehen, Wohlfahrt
disease *n* [dɪ'zi:z]	▶▶ illness	Krankheit, Erkrankung
sickness *n* ['sɪknɪs]		
to fall ill [fɔ:l 'ɪl]	≫ to become ill	erkranken
to sneeze *v* [sni:z]	Raquel had a bad cold and could not stop ~ing into her handkerchief.	niesen
to sigh *v* [saɪ]	She ~ed with relief when she heard the news.	seufzen
sigh *n* [saɪ]	She gave a ~.	Seufzer
to groan *v* [grəʊn]	to make a sound of suffering or despair	stöhnen
to ache *v* [eɪk]	▶▶ to hurt	schmerzen
ache *n* [eɪk]	a constant dull pain	dumpfer Schmerz
to sting *v* [stɪŋ] **stung** [stʌŋ] **stung** [stʌŋ]	If you're not careful the bee will ~ you.	stechen
severe *adj* [sɪ'vɪə]	Mike felt a ~ pain in his leg. (≫ strong)	stark, schwer
scar *n* [skɑ:]	the mark that is left by an old wound	Narbe
to wound *v* [wu:nd]	He ~ed Tarzan **in** the leg with his knife. (▶▶ hurt)	verletzen, verwunden
wound *n* [wu:nd]	He had a bad ~ **in** his leg.	Wunde, Verletzung
injury *n* ['ɪndʒərɪ]	The player suffered an ~ **to** his back.	Verletzung
to injure *v* ['ɪndʒə]	Seven people were ~d in a car accident. (▶▶ hurt)	verletzen
blow *n* [bləʊ]	Suddenly he got a ~ on his head.	Schlag
deaf *adj* [def]	A ~ person cannot hear.	taub
dumb *adj BE* [dʌm]	≫ unable to speak	stumm
blindness *n* ['blaɪndnɪs]	≫ being blind	Blindheit
deafness *n* ['defnɪs]	≫ being deaf	Taubheit
breakdown *n* ['breɪkdaʊn]	Her mother had a **nervous** ~.	(Nerven)Zusammenbruch
fever *n* ['fi:və]	an illness with a high temperature of the body	Fieber, Fieberzustand
backache *n* ['bækeɪk]	pain in the back	Rückenschmerzen
poisonous *adj* ['pɔɪzənəs]	The liquid is ~ and should be kept in a safe place.	giftig
physician *n formal* [fɪ'zɪʃn]	≫ doctor	Arzt
lady doctor *n* ['leɪdɪ dɒktə]	≫ a woman doctor	Ärztin
psychiatrist *n* [saɪ'kaɪətrɪst]	A ~ treats dieases of the mind.	Psychiater

4

patient *n* ['peɪʃnt]	There were too many ~s in the doctor's waiting room.	Patient
victim *n* ['vɪktɪm]	The ~s of the bomb attack were taken to hospital.	Opfer
to neglect *v* [nɪ'glekt]	≫ to give too little care to	vernachlässigen
to operate *v* ['ɒpəreɪt]	They ~ed (**on** the patient) last night.	operieren
to heal *v* [hi:l]	All his wounds are ~ing quickly. (≫ getting better)	heilen
to bandage *v* ['bændɪdʒ]	The nurse ~d his bleeding hand.	verbinden
bandage *n* ['bændɪdʒ]		Verband
to soothe *v* [su:ð]	to make calm, quiet or less painful	beruhigen, trösten, lindern
to recover *v* [rɪ'kʌvə]	to become well again	genesen, wieder gesund werden
treatment *n* ['tri:tmənt]	a way of curing an illness	Behandlung
operation *n* [ɒpə'reɪʃn]	She's gone into hospital for an ~.	Operation
recovery *n* [rɪ'kʌvərɪ]	He made a slow ~.	Genesung
first aid *n* [fɜ:st 'eɪd]	quick help before the doctor comes	Erste Hilfe
nursing *n* ['nɜ:sɪŋ]	the job of a nurse	Krankenpflege
ambulance *n* ['æmbjʊləns]	a car for taking people to hospital	Krankenwagen
prescription *n* [prɪ'skrɪpʃn]	The doctor wrote me a ~.	Rezept
remedy *n* ['remədɪ]	There is no ~ for this disease.	(Heil)mittel
tablet *n* ['tæblɪt]		Tablette
heroin *n* ['herəʊɪn]	H~ is a dangerous drug.	Heroin
addicted *adj* [ə'dɪktɪd]	He's ~ **to** drugs.	abhängig

4.3 Food and drink

hungry *adj* ['hʌŋgrɪ]	I'm ~. Give me something to eat, please.	hungrig
thirsty *adj* ['θɜ:stɪ]	I'm ~. Give me a glass of water, please.	durstig
food *n* [fu:d]	things we can eat	Nahrung, Essen
to eat *v* [i:t] **ate** [et] **eaten** ['i:tn]	Jane ~s an apple every evening.	essen, fressen
to feed *v* [fi:d] **fed** [fed] **fed** [fed]	She's ~ing her baby. (≫ giving food to)	füttern, ernähren
meal *n* [mi:l]	Breakfast, lunch and dinner are ~s.	Mahlzeit, Essen
picnic *n* ['pɪknɪk]	We went for a ~ with our friends.	Picknick
breakfast *n* ['brekfəst]	the first meal of the day	Frühstück
lunch *n* [lʌntʃ]	We had fish and chips for ~.	Mittagessen
dinner *n* ['dɪnə]	the main meal of the day	Hauptmahlzeit
supper *n* ['sʌpə]	the last meal of the day	Abendessen
dish *n* [dɪʃ]	I like Japanese ~es. (≫ food)	Gericht, Speise
soup *n* [su:p]	Henry is fond of chicken ~.	Suppe
vegetable *n* ['vedʒtəbl]	Potatoes, carrots and peas are ~s.	Gemüse
egg *n* [eg]	Hens lay ~s. He had a **boiled** ~ for breakfast. Two **fried** ~s, please.	Ei hartgekochtes Ei Spiegelei
meat *n* [mi:t]	The butcher sells different kinds of ~.	Fleisch
steak *n* [steɪk]	a thick piece of meat	Steak

sausage *n* ['sɒsɪdʒ]		Wurst, Würstchen
fish *n, pl* **fish** [fɪʃ]	They had ~ and chips for lunch.	Fisch
salt *n* [sɒlt]	There's not enough ~ in this soup.	Salz
oil *n* [ɔɪl]	The cook fried the meat in ~.	Öl
salad *n* ['sæləd]	vegetables or fruit mixed and eaten uncooked	Salat
bread *n* [bred]	Cut yourself a slice of ~.	Brot
loaf *n, pl* **loaves** [ləʊf, ləʊvz]	She bought a ~ **of bread** at the baker's. (⪢ big piece)	Laib *(Brot)*
roll *n* [rəʊl]	He bought 12 ~s at the baker's.	Brötchen
cake *n* [keɪk]	She had tea and a piece of ~.	Kuchen
biscuit *n* ['bɪskɪt]	⪢ a flat dry cake	Keks
sandwich *n* ['sænwɪdʒ]	two pieces of bread with e.g. cheese or meat between them	Sandwich
jam *n* [dʒæm]	Have some strawberry ~ on your bread.	Marmelade, Konfitüre
sugar *n* ['ʃʊgə]	I don't take ~ in my coffee.	Zucker
chocolate *n* ['tʃɒklət]	Most children like ~.	Schokolade
sweets *n* [swi:ts]	Toffees and chocolates are ~.	Süßigkeiten
butter *n* ['bʌtə]	yellow fat made from milk	Butter
cheese *n* [tʃi:z]	'Camembert' is a kind of ~.	Käse
milk *n* [mɪlk]	Many people drink cow's ~ every day.	Milch
cream *n* [kri:m]	C~ has more fat than milk.	Sahne, Creme
to drink *v* [drɪŋk] **drank** [dræŋk] **drunk** [drʌŋk]	He is fond of ~ing beer. I know that her husband ~s.	trinken *(gewohnheitsmäßig trinken)*
drink *n* [drɪŋk]	May I have a ~? (⪢ something to drink)	Getränk, Drink
to have *v* [hæv]	H~ another drink/piece of cake. (⪢ Take)	nehmen, zu sich nehmen
coffee *n* ['kɒfɪ]	I'd like a cup of ~, please!	Kaffee
tea *n* [ti:]	James likes his ~ with milk and sugar in it.	Tee, schwarzer Tee
beer *n* [bɪə]	Bavarians drink of lot of ~.	Bier
wine *n* [waɪn]	W~ is made from grapes.	Wein
alcohol *n* ['ælkəhɒl]	A~ makes a person drunk.	Alkohol
drunk *adj* [drʌŋk]	Bill had too much whiskey and became ~.	betrunken
juice *n* [dʒu:s]	Have some more orange ~.	Saft
ice-cream *n* [aɪs'kri:m]		Speiseeis
to mix *v* [mɪks]	She ~ed sugar and eggs together. Oil and water don't ~.	mischen, vermischen sich vermischen
to bake *v* [beɪk]	I'll ~ you a cake.	backen
to cook *v* [kʊk]	Jill ~ed a chicken for dinner.	kochen, zubereiten
to boil *v* [bɔɪl]	▶◀ to freeze	kochen, sieden
to prepare *v* [prɪ'peə]	Her husband ~ed a meal for us.	zubereiten
to serve *v* [sɜ:v]	James will ~ the soup. The waitress ~d the customers.	servieren bedienen
to wash up *v + adv* [wɒʃ]	to wash the dishes	Geschirr spülen
pot *n* [pɒt] (1)		Topf
plate *n* [pleɪt] (2)		Teller
fork *n* [fɔ:k] (3)		Gabel
spoon *n* [spu:n] (4)		Löffel
knife *n, pl* **knives** [naɪf, naɪvz] (5)		Messer
to cut *v* [kʌt] **cut** [kʌt] **cut** [kʌt]	He ~s the bread with a knife. The lady ~ a piece of cake for her guest.	schneiden abschneiden

i:	ɪ	e	æ	ɑ:	ɒ	ɔ:	ʊ	u:	ʌ	ɜ:	ə
eat	bit	ten	bad	fast	got	saw	sure	too	cut	bird	about

4

cup *n* [kʌp] ⑥		Tasse
glass *n* [glɑːs] ⑦		Glas, Trinkglas
jar *n* [dʒɑː] ⑧		gläsernes Gefäß
bottle *n* ['bɒtl] ⑨		Flasche

restaurant *n* ['restrɒnt]	a place where you can buy a meal and eat it	Restaurant, Speiselokal
menu *n* ['menjuː]	a list of dishes in a restaurant	Speisenkarte, Speisenfolge
snack *n* [snæk]	a small quick meal	Imbiß
snack bar *n* ['snækbɑː]	You can have light meals at a ~.	Imbißstube, Snackbar
café *n* ['kæfeɪ]	a small restaurant	kleine Gaststätte
pub *n* [pʌb]	People drink beer and talk to friends in a ~.	Pub, Kneipe
bar *n* [bɑː]	They went to a ~ to have a drink.	Bar
waiter *n* ['weɪtə]	A ~ serves food in a restaurant.	Kellner, Ober
waitress *n* ['weɪtrɪs]	a female waiter	Kellnerin
tip *n* [tɪp]	a small amount of money given for a service	Trinkgeld
cook *n* [kʊk]	A ~ prepares meals.	Koch, Köchin
tobacco *n* [tə'bækəʊ]	T~ is made into cigarettes or smoked in pipes.	Tabak
cigarette *n* [sɪgə'ret] ①		Zigarette
cigar *n* [sɪ'gɑː] ②		Zigarre
pipe *n* [paɪp] ③		Pfeife
ashtray *n* ['æʃtreɪ] ④		Aschenbecher

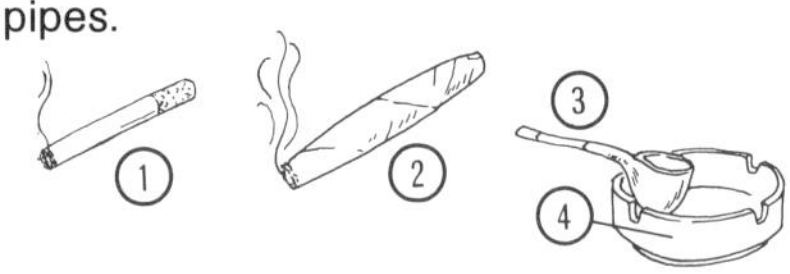

to smoke *v* [sməʊk]	It's bad for your health to ~ cigarettes.	rauchen

„Guten Appetit" does **not** exist in English! Don't say anything!

"Talkmaster" does **not** exist in English! Use **'host'** instead.

hunger *n* ['hʌŋgə]	the wish for food	Hunger
starvation *n* [stɑː'veɪʃn]	Lots of people died of ~ in the Sahel area.	Verhungern, Hungern
to starve *v* [stɑːv]	Quite a few animals ~d to death last winter.	(ver)hungern
thirst *n* [θɜːst]	the wish for something to drink	Durst
appetite *n* ['æpɪtaɪt]	I can't eat. I've got no ~. (⋟ wish to eat)	Appetit
to nourish *v* ['nʌrɪʃ]	The baby should be given food that will ~ her.	ernähren, nähren
to chew *v* [tʃuː]	He couldn't ~ the hard meat.	kauen
to swallow *v* ['swɒləʊ]	I can't ~ these pills. They're too big.	schlucken
raw *adj* [rɔː]	not cooked	roh
refreshments *n* [rɪ'freʃmənts]	There's a dining-room where ~ are served.	Erfrischungen
hamburger *n* ['hæmbɜːgə]		Hamburger
course *n* [kɔːs]	The first ~ was soup. (⋟ part of the meal)	Gang, Speisenfolge
portion *n* ['pɔːʃn]	He ordered two ~s of salad.	Portion
helping *n* ['helpɪŋ]	I'd like a second ~, please. (▶▶ portion)	Portion
to help oneself to [help]	H~ yourself ~ another piece of cake. (⋟ serve yourself with)	sich bedienen, sich etwas nehmen
starter *n* ['stɑːtə]	a course at the start of a meal	Vorspeise
main course *n* [meɪn 'kɔːs]	the main dish, the most important part of a meal	Hauptgericht
dessert *n* [dɪ'zɜːt]	We had ice cream for ~.	Nachtisch
pudding *n* ['pʊdɪŋ]	I'm very fond of rice ~.	Pudding

adj	*adv*	*art*	*conj*	*n*	*pl*	*prep*	*pron*	*sing*
adjective	adverb(ial)	article	conjunction	noun	plural	preposition	pronoun	singular

chips *n* [tʃɪps]	He likes to eat fish and ~.	Pommes frites
French fries *n AE* [frentʃ 'fraɪz]	I'd like steak and ~.	
hot dog *n* [hɒt 'dɒg]		Hotdog, Bockwurst
roast meat *n* [rəʊst 'mi:t]	meat that has been cooked over a fire or in an oven	Braten
mince *n BE* [mɪns]	meat cut into very small pieces	Hackfleisch

What you buy at the butcher's

beef *n* [bi:f] ①		Rindfleisch
pork *n* [pɔ:k] ②		Schweinefleisch
veal *n* [vi:l] ③		Kalbfleisch
mutton *n* ['mʌtn] ④		Hammelfleisch

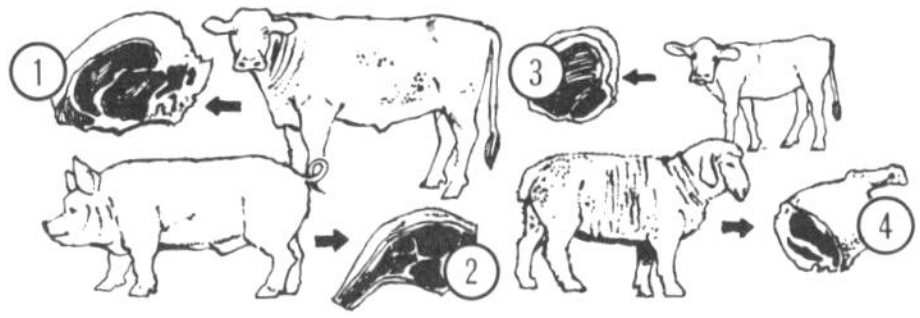

ham *n* [hæm]	meat from a pig's leg	Schinken
bacon *n* ['beɪkən]	I often eat ~ **and eggs**.	Speck
sauce *n* [sɔ:s]	Do you like pork with apple ~?	Sauce, Soße
gravy *n* ['greɪvɪ]	a thin meat sauce	Bratensaft
fat *n* [fæt]	the white part of the meat	Fett
omelette *n* ['ɒmlɪt]	eggs beaten together and fried	Omelette
kipper *n* ['kɪpə]	a salted herring, dried or smoked	Kipper, geräucherter Hering
pepper *n* ['pepə]		Pfeffer
mustard *n* ['mʌstəd]	In Germany people usually eat their sausages with ~.	Senf
spice *n* [spaɪs]	We use ~s to give food more taste.	Gewürz
mint *n* [mɪnt]	My sister doesn't like ~ **sauce**.	Pfefferminze, (-Soße)
vinegar *n* ['vɪnɪgə]	We put oil and ~ on our salad.	Essig
toast *n* [təʊst]	Bill had tea and a piece of ~.	Toast
to toast *v* [təʊst]	We ~ed some bread.	toasten, rösten
flour *n* ['flaʊə]	We use ~ to make bread.	Mehl
tart *n* [tɑ:t]	I'd like an apple ~, please.	(Frucht)torte
pie *n* [paɪ]		Pastete, Pie
plum pudding *n* [plʌm'pʊdɪŋ]	≫ Christmas pudding	Plumpudding
gingerbread *n* ['dʒɪndʒəbred]	a kind of cake with ginger	Pfefferkuchen
cornflakes *n* ['kɔ:nfleɪks]		Cornflakes
porridge *n* ['pɒrɪdʒ]	P~ is made from oats and milk.	Porridge, Haferbrei
margarine *n* [mɑ:dʒə'ri:n]	He doesn't eat butter, he only eats ~.	Margarine
marmalade *n* ['mɑ:məleɪd]	jam made from oranges	Orangenmarmelade
jelly *n* ['dʒelɪ]	J~ is made from fruit juice and sugar.	Gelee
honey *n* ['hʌnɪ]	a sweet food made by bees	Honig
yogurt *n* ['jəʊgət]	a food which is made from milk	Joghurt
dairy *n* ['deərɪ]	Butter and milk are ~ **products**.	Molkerei
fruit juice *n* ['fru:tdʒu:s]	Have a glass of ~.	Fruchtsaft
soft drink *n* [sɒft 'drɪŋk]	a non-alcoholic drink	alkoholfreies Getränk

cola *n* [ˈkəʊlə]	a kind of soft drink	Cola
to sip *v* [sɪp]	Diana ~ped the hot tea.	nippen an
spirits *n* [ˈspɪrɪts]	Whisky, brandy and gin are ~.	Spirituosen
ale *n* [eɪl]	beer with a pale colour	Ale *(Bier)*
bitter *n* [ˈbɪtə]	A pint of ~, please.	Bitter *(Bier)*
lager *n* [ˈlɑːgə]	a light kind of beer	Lager *(Bier)*
whisky *n* [ˈwɪskɪ] **whiskey** *n AE* [ˈwɪskɪ]	A lot of ~ is produced in Scotland.	Whisky
sober *adj* [ˈsəʊbə]	▶◀ drunk	nüchtern
recipe *n* [ˈresəpɪ]	A ~ tells you how to prepare food.	Kochrezept
mixture *n* [ˈmɪkstʃə]	The drink is a ~ of rum and cola.	Mischung
ingredient *n* [ɪnˈgriːdɪənt]	one of a mixture of things	Zutat(en)
additive *n* [ˈædɪtɪv]	a substance added to something else to improve e.g. taste or colour	Zusatzstoff
to stir *v* [stɜː]	S~ the porridge, please.	umrühren
to fry *v* [fraɪ]	≫ to cook in hot fat	braten
frying-pan *n* [ˈfraɪɪŋpæn]	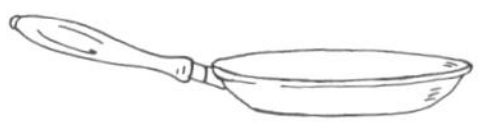	Bratpfanne
saucepan *n* [ˈsɔːspən]		Stieltopf, Kasserolle
to roast *v* [rəʊst]	He was ~ing the meat over the fire.	braten, rösten, schmoren
barbecue *n* [ˈbɑːbɪkjuː]	a party where meat is cooked over a fire	Grillparty
grill *n* [grɪl]	a part of a cooker	Grill
to carve *v* [kɑːv]	≫ to cut e.g. meat	tranchieren
to peel *v* [piːl]	P~ the apple with that knife.	schälen
to cut up *v + adv* [kʌt]	≫ to cut into little pieces	zerschneiden
baking tin *n* [ˈbeɪkɪŋ tɪn]		Backform
batter *n* [ˈbætə]	You make ~ with flour, eggs and milk.	Eierteig
pastry *n* [ˈpeɪstrɪ]	There is ~ in pies and tarts.	Blätterteig
fudge *n* [fʌdʒ]	a kind of sweet	Karamel
tablespoon *n* [ˈteɪblspuːn]	a large spoon	Eßlöffel
napkin *n* [ˈnæpkɪn]	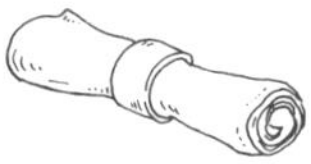	Serviette
kettle *n* [ˈketl]	a metal pot for boiling water	(Tee)kessel
saucer *n* [ˈsɔːsə] ①	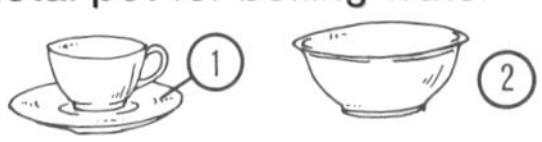	Untertasse
bowl *n* [bəʊl] ②		Napf, Schüssel, Schale
cafeteria *n* [kæfɪˈtɪərɪə]	We have to serve ourselves at a ~.	Cafeteria
coffee bar *n* [ˈkɒfɪ bɑː]	a small café serving drinks and snacks	Imbißstube
canteen *n* [kænˈtiːn]	a place in a factory or school where people buy food and drink	Kantine
to tip *v* [tɪp]	He ~ped the waiter £1.	Trinkgeld geben

4.4 Clothing and personal care

clothes *n* [kləʊðz]	the things we wear	Kleidung, Kleider
dress *n* [dres]	Mary put on her new ~.	Kleid, Kleidung
to dress *v* [dres]	≫ to put on clothes	(sich) anziehen
to wear *v* [weə] **wore** [wɔː] **worn** [wɔːn]	My sister is ~ing a new dress.	tragen, anhaben

to put on *v + adv* [pʊt]	▶◀ to take off	anziehen
to try on *v + adv* [traɪ]	T~ the sweater, but I think it's too small.	anprobieren
to suit *v* [su:t]	That dress doesn't ~ you.	passen
suit *n* [su:t]	e.g. a man's jacket and trousers	Anzug, Kostüm
skirt *n* [skɜ:t] ①	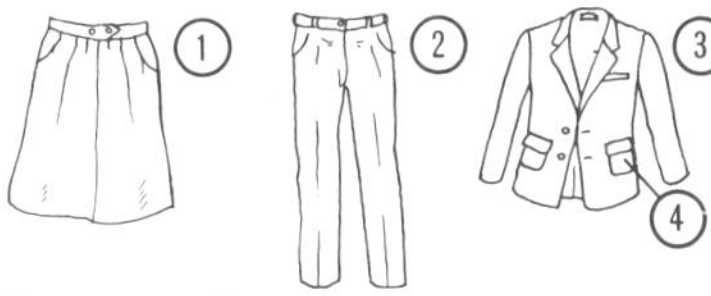	Rock
trousers *n* ['traʊzəz]		Hose(n)
pants *n AE* [pænts] ②		
jacket *n* ['dʒækɪt] ③		Jacke
pocket *n* ['pɒkɪt] ④		Tasche *(Kleidung)*
tights *n* [taɪts]	Dancers often wear ~.	Strumpfhose
shorts *n* [ʃɔ:ts] ⑤		kurze Hose(n)
coat *n* [kəʊt] ⑥		Mantel
umbrella *n* [ʌm'brelə] ⑦		(Regen)schirm
pullover *n* ['pʊləʊvə] ⑧		Pullover
sweater *n* ['swetə]	▶▶ pullover	Pullover
shirt *n* [ʃɜ:t] ⑨		Hemd
tie *n* [taɪ] ⑩		Krawatte, Binder
button *n* ['bʌtn] ⑪		Knopf
blouse *n* [blaʊz] ⑫		Bluse
hat *n* [hæt] ⑬		Hut
purse *n* [pɜ:s] ⑭		Geldbörse
wallet *n* ['wɒlɪt]	a small leather case to carry money, personal papers etc	Brieftasche
handkerchief *n* ['hæŋkətʃɪf] **hankie** *n informal* ['hæŋkɪ]	You dry your nose with a ~.	Taschentuch
shoe *n* [ʃu:] ⑮	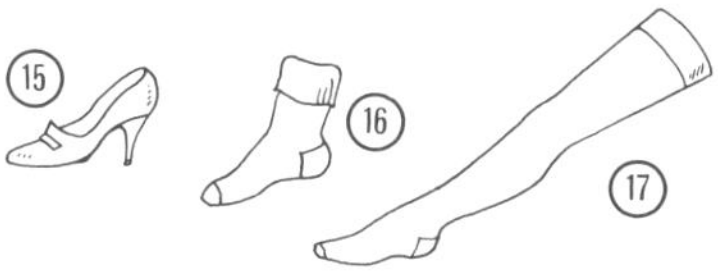	Schuh
sock *n* [sɒk] ⑯		Socke
stocking *n* ['stɒkɪŋ] ⑰		(Damen-)Strumpf
pair *n* [peə]	e.g. a ~ of socks	Paar
to wash *v* [wɒʃ]	My hands are dirty. I'll just ~ them.	(sich) waschen
to shave *v* [ʃeɪv]	≫ to cut off hair (from the skin)	(sich) rasieren
shaver *n* ['ʃeɪvə]	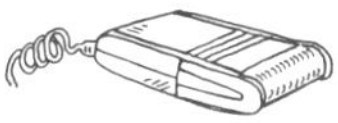 	(elektrischer) Rasierapparat
toothbrush *n* ['tu:θbrʌʃ]		Zahnbürste
to clean *v* [kli:n]	Always ~ your teeth after meals.	putzen, saubermachen
to tidy *v* ['taɪdɪ]	T~ your room before you go away.	aufräumen, in Ordnung bringen
to bath *v* [bɑ:θ]	Don't have the water too hot when you ~ the baby.	baden, ein Bad nehmen
shower *n* ['ʃaʊə]	She's going to **have/take a** ~.	Dusche, Duschbad
to have *v* [hæv]	I'm ~ing **a bath/shower.**	(ein Bad)nehmen/duschen
comb *n* [kəʊm]		Kamm
to comb *v* [kəʊm]	Jill ~ed her hair.	kämmen
brush *n* [brʌʃ]		Bürste, Pinsel
clean *adj* [kli:n]	≫ free from dirt, ▶◀ dirty	sauber, rein
tidy *adj* ['taɪdɪ]	≫ arranged in good order	ordentlich, sauber
pure *adj* [pjʊə]	The air is very ~ in this area. (▶▶ clean)	rein, sauber
dirty *adj* ['dɜ:tɪ]	▶◀ clean	schmutzig
dirt *n* [dɜ:t]	There was a lot of ~ on his shoes.	Schmutz, Dreck
dust *n* [dʌst]	Jim wiped the ~ off his desk.	Staub
spot *n* [spɒt]	There were ~s of dirt on his trousers.	Fleck

i:	ɪ	e	æ	ɑ:	ɒ	ɔ:	ʊ	u:	ʌ	ɜ:	ə
eat	bit	ten	bad	fast	got	saw	sure	too	cut	bird	about

4

hairdresser *n* ['heədresə]	A ~ cuts and shapes hair.	Friseur, Friseuse
haircut *n* ['heəkʌt]	Your hair is very long. You need a ~.	Haarschnitt
clothing *n* ['kləʊðɪŋ]	►► clothes	Kleidung
uniform *n* ['ju:nɪfɔ:m]	Policemen wear ~s.	Uniform
costume *n* ['kɒstju:m]	The actors were wearing historical ~s.	Kostüm
fancy dress *n* ['fænsɪ dres]	a funny costume e.g. for a party	(Masken)Kostüm
to dress up *v + adv* [dres]	to wear special clothes for fun	(sich) kostümieren
outfit *n* ['aʊtfɪt]	all the clothes for a special purpose	Ausrüstung, Ausstattung
appearance *n* [ə'pɪərəns]	what a person or thing looks like	Erscheinungsbild
outward appearance ['aʊtwəd]	His ~ is very smart.	äußere Erscheinung
to undress *v* [ʌn'dres]	to take off your clothes	(sich) ausziehen
to change *v* [tʃeɪndʒ]	to put on different clothes	(sich) umziehen
naked *adj* ['neɪkɪd]	≫ without any clothes	nackt
bare *adj* [beə]	▶◀ covered	nackt, bloß
barefoot *adv* ['beəfʊt]	≫ without shoes	barfuß
bareheaded *adv* [beə'hedɪd]	≫ without a hat	ohne Kopfbedeckung
shabby *adj* ['ʃæbɪ]	≫ old and worn-out	schäbig
fashion *n* ['fæʃn]	a style of dressing	Mode
craze *n* [kreɪz]	a very popular fashion for a short time	Mode(torheit), Manie
fashionable *adj* ['fæʃnəbl]	▶◀ old-fashioned	modisch
elegant *adj* ['elɪgənt]	≫ very well dressed	elegant
model *n* ['mɒdl]	She is a very famous fashion ~.	Modell, Fotomodell
to be in *v + adv* [bɪ 'ɪn]	≫ to be in fashion	in (Mode) sein
gown *n* [gaʊn]	a woman's long dress	langes Kleid
slacks *n* [slæks]	trousers worn by women	lange Damenhose
AE	long, loose trousers	lange Hose
kilt *n* [kɪlt] ①		Kilt, Schottenrock
overcoat *n* ['əʊvəkəʊt]	a long coat worn in cold weather	Überzieher, Mantel
raincoat *n* ['reɪnkəʊt] **waterproof** *n* ['wɔ:təpru:f] ②		Regenmantel
scarf *n, pl* **scarves** [skɑ:f, skɑ:vz] ③		Schal
zip *n* [zɪp] ④		Reißverschluß
belt *n* [belt] ⑤		Gürtel
jersey *n* ['dʒɜ:zɪ]	I always wear a ~ in cold weather.	Pullover
long-sleeved *adj* [lɒŋ'sli:vd]	≫ with long sleeves	langärmlig
cap *n* [kæp]		Mütze
helmet *n* ['helmɪt]		Helm, Schutzhelm
underclothes *n* ['ʌndəkləʊðz] **underwear** *n* ['ʌndəweə]	the clothes we wear under a shirt, trousers or dress	Unterwäsche
petticoat *n* ['petɪkəʊt]	►► an underskirt	Unterrock
pyjamas *n* [pə'dʒɑ:məz]	clothes worn when sleeping	Schlafanzug
handbag *n* ['hændbæg]	a woman's bag for small things	Handtasche

① 

② 

③ 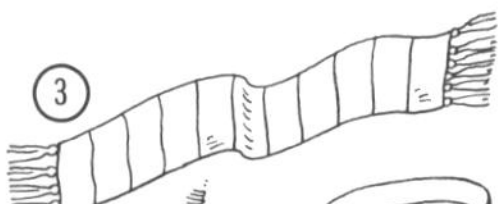

④ 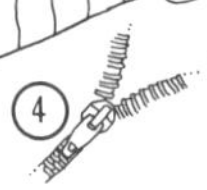

⑤ 

adj	*adv*	*art*	*conj*	*n*	*pl*	*prep*	*pron*	*sing*
adjective	adverb(ial)	article	conjunction	noun	plural	preposition	pronoun	singular

glove *n* [glʌv] ①	 	Handschuh
boot *n* [bu:t] ②		Stiefel
heel *n* [hi:l] ③		Absatz *(Schuh)*
jewellery *n BE* ['dʒu:əlrɪ] **jewelry** *n AE*	rings, precious stones etc	Schmuck, Juwelen, Edelsteine
plated *adj* ['pleɪtɪd]	This gold-~ spoon belonged to my grandmother. 	plattiert, vergoldet, versilbert
necklace *n* ['neklɪs] ④		Halskette
collar *n* ['kɒlə] ⑤		Kragen
sleeve *n* [sli:v] ⑥		Ärmel
tailor *n* ['teɪlə]	A ~ makes clothes for men.	Schneider
dressmaker *n* ['dresmeɪkə]	A ~ makes clothes for women.	Damenschneider(in)
to wipe *v* [waɪp]	He ~d his hands on a towel. (⋙ dried or cleaned)	(ab)wischen
sponge *n* [spʌndʒ]	We use a ~ for washing and cleaning.	Schwamm
to brush *v* [brʌʃ]	Jane ~ed her hair.	bürsten
to trim *v* [trɪm]	The hairdresser ~med my hair. (⋙ cut a little off)	stutzen, zurückschneiden
to dust *v* [dʌst]	They ~ed all the tables in the room.	abstauben
to scrub *v* [skrʌb]	He ~bed the floor clean. (⋙ rubbed . . . with a brush)	schrubben, scheuern
neat *adj* [ni:t]	▶▶ tidy, in good order	ordentlich, gepflegt
smart *adj* [smɑ:t]	She's looking very ~ in her new dress. (⋙ elegant)	elegant, schick, gepflegt
trim *adj* [trɪm]	⋙ neat and tidy	nett, geputzt
dusty *adj* ['dʌstɪ]	⋙ covered with dust	staubig
filthy *adj* ['fɪlθɪ]	▶▶ very dirty	dreckig, schmutzig
to pollute *v* [pə'lu:t]	Industrial waste ~s our rivers and streams. (⋙ makes . . . dirty)	verunreinigen, verschmutzen
pollution *n* [pə'lu:ʃn]	The ~ of rivers has killed a lot of fish.	(Umwelt)Verschmutzung
mess *n* [mes]	What a ~ your room is in! (⋙ dirty, untidy state)	Unordnung, Schmutz
to get ready *v + adv* [get 'redɪ]	Mother must ~ the boys ~ for school. (⋙ make . . . ready)	(sich) fertig machen
make-up *n* ['meɪkʌp]	Janet is wearing too much eye ~.	Make-up
to sunbathe *v* ['sʌnbeɪð]	to lie in the sun	ein Sonnenbad nehmen
iron *n* ['aɪən]		Bügeleisen
to iron *v* ['aɪən]	Jim has ~ed seven shirts.	bügeln
to fold *v* [fəʊld]	He ~ed the shirts and put them in his suitcase.	falten, zusammenlegen
laundry *n* ['lɔ:ndrɪ]	a place where clothes are washed; clothes that need washing	Wäscherei (schmutzige) Wäsche

4.5 Housing and furniture

to live *v* [lɪv]	She still ~s in London. (⋙ has her home)	wohnen, leben
to stay *v* [steɪ]	She's ~ing **with** her uncle. (⋙ living for a short time)	wohnen
	Can't you ~ for tea?	bleiben
to remain *v* [rɪ'meɪn]	▶▶ to stay	bleiben
to occupy *v* ['ɒkjʊpaɪ]	⋙ to live in (e.g. a house)	bewohnen

to put up *v + adv* [pʊt 'ʌp]	Can you ~ me ~ for one night? (⩾ give me a bed)	unterbringen
	They wanted to ~ at a hotel. (⩾ stay)	unterkommen
home *n* [həʊm]	the place where you live	Heim, Zuhause
at home [ət 'həʊm]	He stayed ~. (⩾ in the house or family)	zu Hause
landlord *n* ['lændlɔ:d]	A ~ is a person from whom one rents a flat or house.	Hauswirt
	Mr Smith is the ~ of the 'Red Lion'.	Gastwirt
landlady *n* ['lændleɪdɪ]	His ~ has just put up the rent.	Hauswirtin
to build *v* [bɪld] **built** [bɪlt] **built** [bɪlt]	My father wants to ~ a house. (▶▶ make)	(er)bauen, errichten
building *n* ['bɪldɪŋ]	Houses, shops, towers etc are ~s.	Gebäude, Bau(werk)
castle *n* ['kɑ:sl]		Burg, Schloß

tower *n* ['taʊə]	a tall, narrow building	Turm

house *n* [haʊs] ①		Haus
roof *n, pl* **roofs** [ru:f, ru:fs] ②		Dach
basement *n* ['beɪsmənt] ③		Untergeschoß
garage *n* ['gærɑ:ʒ] ④		Garage
garden *n* ['gɑ:dn] ⑤		Garten

park *n* [pɑ:k]	a piece of land with trees and grass	Park, Grünanlage
yard *n* [jɑ:d]	A ~ is a space beside a house with buildings around it.	Hof
flat *n* [flæt]	a set of rooms in a building	Wohnung
apartment *n AE* [ə'pɑ:tmənt]	where you can live	
block (of flats) *n* [blɒk]	Mary lives in a ~ in Hull.	Wohnblock
wall *n* [wɔ:l]	a side of a building or room	Wand; Mauer
ceiling *n* ['si:lɪŋ]	There was a light hanging from the ~. (▶◀ floor)	(Zimmer)Decke
window *n* ['wɪndəʊ] ①		Fenster
balcony *n* ['bælkənɪ] ②		Balkon
door *n* [dɔ:] ③		Tür
gate *n* [geɪt] ④		Tor, Pforte

entrance *n* ['entrəns]	the way into a place	Eingang
exit *n* ['eksɪt]	the way out of a place	Ausgang
ground *n* [graʊnd]	The red apple fell to the ~. (▶▶ earth)	(Erd)Boden, Erde
floor *n* [flɔ:]	We walk on the ~ of a room.	Fußboden
	My office is on the 6th ~.	Stockwerk
lift *n* [lɪft]		Aufzug, Lift
elevator *n AE* ['elɪveɪtə] ①		
stairs *n* [steəz] ②		Treppe
downstairs *adv* [daʊn'steəz] ③		(nach) unten
upstairs *adv* [ʌp'steəz] ④		(nach) oben

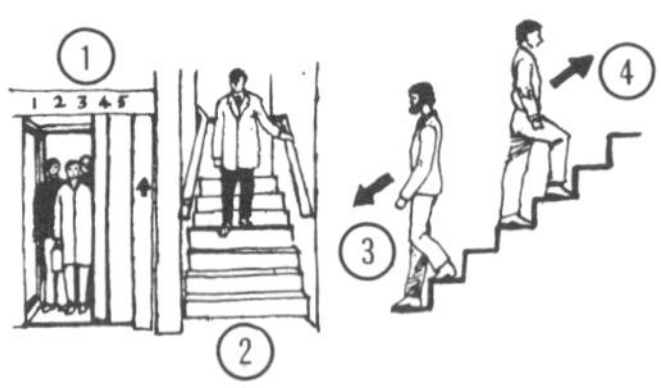

tʃ	dʒ	θ	ð	ʃ	ʒ	ŋ	w	v
cheap	**j**ump	**th**ing	**th**en	**sh**op	plea**s**ure	sa**ng**	**w**et	**v**oice

room *n* [ru:m]	Our house has six ~s.	Zimmer, Raum
living room *n* ['lɪvɪŋrʊm] ⑤		Wohnzimmer
dining room *n* ['daɪnɪŋrʊm] ⑥		Eß-, Speisezimmer
bedroom *n* ['bedrʊm] ⑦		Schlafzimmer
kitchen *n* ['kɪtʃɪn] ⑧		Küche
hall *n* [hɔ:l] ⑨		Eingangshalle
bathroom *n* ['bɑ:θrʊm] ⑩		Bad, Badezimmer
bath *n* [bɑ:θ] ⑪		Badewanne

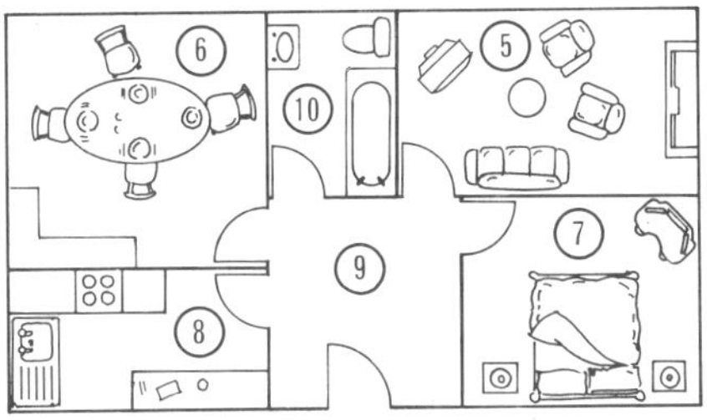

towel *n* ['taʊəl]	She dried her hands with a ~.	Handtuch
toilet *n* ['tɔɪlɪt]	I must go to the ~. (▶▶ WC)	Toilette, WC
heating *n* ['hi:tɪŋ]	It's cold. Switch the ~ on.	(Zentral)heizung
central heating *n* ['sentrəl]		

furniture *n* ['fɜ:nɪtʃə]	tables, sofas, beds etc	Mobiliar, Möbel
furnished *adj* ['fɜ:nɪʃt]	He rented a ~ flat.	möbliert
table *n* ['teɪbl] ⑫		Tisch
desk *n* [desk] ⑬		Pult, Schreibtisch
chair *n* [tʃeə] ⑭		Stuhl, Sessel
seat *n* [si:t]	a place where you sit	Sitz(platz)

bed *n* [bed] ⑮		Bett
sheet *n* [ʃi:t] ⑯		Bettlaken
blanket *n* ['blæŋkɪt] ⑰		Bettdecke, Decke
curtain *n* ['kɜ:tn] ⑱		Vorhang, Gardine
cupboard *n* ['kʌbəd] ⑲		(Speise/Geschirr) Schrank

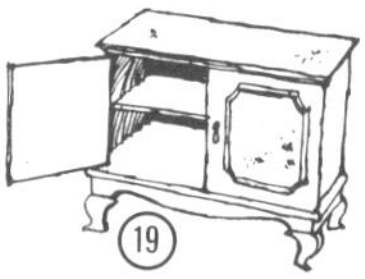

carpet *n* ['kɑ:pɪt]	a thick covering for floors	Teppich
mirror *n* ['mɪrə]	You can see yourself in a ~.	Spiegel
residence *n* ['rezɪdəns]	He has a ~ in London.	Wohnsitz, Residenz
lodgings *n* ['lɒdʒɪŋz]	Most university students stay in ~. (⪢ a furnished room or flat)	Unterkunft
accommodation *n* [əkɒmə'deɪʃn]	a place to live	Unterkunft
inhabitant *n* [ɪn'hæbɪtənt]	The little village has only 766 ~s. (⪢ people who live there)	Einwohner, Bewohner
resident *n* ['rezɪdənt]	a person who lives in a place	Bewohner
caretaker *n* ['keəteɪkə]	a person who looks after a building	Hausmeister
to settle *v* ['setl]	He left England and ~d in Canada. (⪢ made his home)	sich niederlassen ansiedeln, besiedeln
to settle down *v + adv*	He married and wanted to ~.	zur Ruhe kommen
settler *n* ['setlə]	He read a book about the first ~s of America.	Siedler
pioneer *n* [paɪə'nɪə]	A ~ is one of the first settlers in a new country.	Pionier
to construct *v* [kən'strʌkt]	▶▶ to build	errichten, bauen
to put up *v + adv* [pʊt 'ʌp]	▶▶ to build	bauen, errichten
construction *n* [kən'strʌkʃn]	This road is **under** ~. (⪢ being built)	Bau, Konstruktion
shed *n* [ʃed]	a small wooden building	Schuppen
hut *n* [hʌt]	a small building, made of wood or stone	Hütte
cottage *n* ['kɒtɪdʒ]	a small house in the country	Hütte

i:	ɪ	e	æ	ɑ:	ɒ	ɔ:	ʊ	u:	ʌ	ɜ:	ə
eat	bit	ten	bad	fast	got	saw	sure	too	cut	bird	about

cabin *n* ['kæbɪn]	a small wooden house	(Block)hütte
lodge *n* [lɒdʒ]	a small house (e.g. one used during the hunting season)	Jagdhütte
bungalow *n* ['bʌŋgələʊ]	a house with only one floor	Bungalow
semi-detached house *n* [semɪdɪ'tætʃt haʊs]	a house which is built together with another house	Doppelhaushälfte
Council house *n* ['kaʊnsl]	A ~ is rented from a local Council.	stadteigenes Wohnhaus
estate *n* [ɪ'steɪt]	They live on a big **housing** ~.	Wohnanlage
skyscraper *n* ['skaɪskreɪpə]	a very tall building	Wolkenkratzer
skyline *n* ['skaɪlaɪn]	the picture of tall buildings against the sky	Skyline, Kontur(en)
mansion (house) *n* ['mænʃn]	a very big house	Villa, Herrenhaus
palace *n* ['pælɪs]	We visited the ~ where the Queen lives. (⋟ big, beautiful house)	Palast
fortress *n* ['fɔ:trɪs]	a strong castle or town that can be defended	Festung
fort *n* [fɔ:t]	a building that can be easily defended	Fort
doorway *n* ['dɔ:weɪ] **way in** *n* [weɪ'ɪn]	A man was standing in the ~. (▶▶ entrance)	Eingang
way out *n* [weɪ'aʊt]	▶▶ exit	Ausgang
wing *n* [wɪŋ]	one side of a large building	Flügel, Seitenflügel
level *n* ['levl]	We are about 200 metres above sea ~.	Niveau, Ebene, Höhe

GB	USA	
first floor *n* [fɜ:st 'flɔ:]	**second floor** *n*	erster Stock
ground floor *n* [graʊnd]	**first floor** *n*	Erdgeschoß
cellar *n* ['selə]	**cellar** *n*	Keller

passage *n* ['pæsɪdʒ] **corridor** *n* ['kɒrɪdɔ:]	a narrow way through a building	Passage, Verbindungsgang
cloakroom *n* ['kləʊkrʊm]	a room for hats, coats, bags etc	Garderobe

staircase *n* ['steəkeɪs] ①	Treppe, Treppenhaus
ladder *n* ['lædə] ②	Leiter
escalator *n* ['eskəleɪtə] ③	Rolltreppe
ramp *n* [ræmp] ④	Rampe

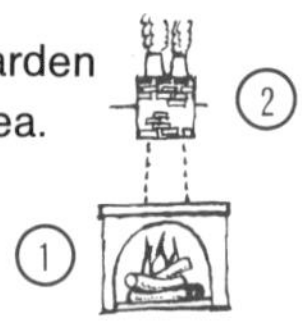

fence *n* [fens]	There was a high ~ round the field.	Zaun
court *n* [kɔ:t] **courtyard** *n* ['kɔ:tjɑ:d]	an open area inside a large building	Hof
lawn *n* [lɔ:n]	an area of short grass in a garden	Rasen
terrace *n* ['terəs]	They sat on the ~, drinking tea.	Terrasse
hall *n* [hɔ:l]	a large room for meetings	Halle, Saal
fireplace *n* ['faɪəpleɪs] ①		offener Kamin
chimney *n* ['tʃɪmnɪ] ②		Schornstein, Kamin
shutter(s) *n* ['ʃʌtə(z)]	a wooden or metal cover for a window	Fensterladen, Jalousie
study *n* ['stʌdɪ]	The professor was working in his ~.	Studier-, Arbeitszimmer
bedsitter *n* [bed'sɪtə]	a single room for living and sleeping in	Wohnschlafzimmer

adj	*adv*	*art*	*conj*	*n*	*pl*	*prep*	*pron*	*sing*
adjective	adverb(ial)	article	conjunction	noun	plural	preposition	pronoun	singular

☐ **wash basin** *n* ['wɒʃ beɪsn] ③		Waschbecken
☐ **hanger** *n* ['hæŋə] ④		Haken, Halterung
☐ **lavatory** *n* ['lævətrɪ] ⑤		Toilette, Klosett
☐ **WC** *n* [dʌbljʊ'siː]		WC
☐ **tap** *n* [tæp] ⑥		(Wasser)hahn

☐ **to furnish** *v* ['fɜːnɪʃ]	We are ~ing our flat at the moment. (≫ putting furniture in)	möblieren, einrichten, ausstatten
☐ **to decorate** *v* ['dekəreɪt]	They ~d the Christmas tree with coloured lights.	dekorieren, ausschmücken
	You must have this room ~d. (≫ painted)	anstreichen
☐ **decoration** *n* [dekə'reɪʃn]	The ~ of her house was very expensive.	Anstrich, Dekorierung
☐ **decorative** *adj* ['dekərətɪv]	These flowers are very ~. (▶▶ beautiful)	dekorativ
☐ **air-conditioned** *adj* ['eəkəndɪʃənd]	All the rooms are ~.	klimatisiert, mit Klimaanlage
☐ **bench** *n* [bentʃ] ①		(Sitz)bank
☐ **armchair** *n* ['ɑːmtʃeə] ②		Sessel
☐ **couch** *n* [kaʊtʃ] ③		Couch
☐ **sofa** *n* ['səʊfə] ④		Sofa

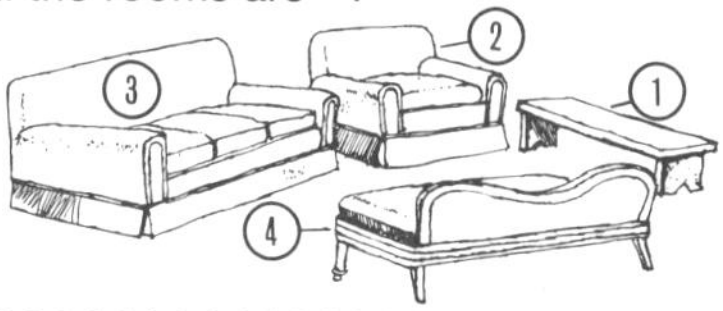

☐ **mattress** *n* ['mætrɪs] ⑤		Matratze
☐ **wardrobe** *n* ['wɔːdrəʊb] ⑥		Kleiderschrank
☐ **rug** *n* [rʌg] ⑦		(kleiner) Teppich, Läufer

☐ **mat** *n* [mæt]	a small piece of covering for the floor	Matte
☐ **cushion** *n* ['kʊʃn]	a bag filled with soft material to sit on	Kissen, Polster

v	*AE*	*BE*	☒	~	▶◀	▶▶	≫
verb	American English	British English	a word you have learnt	entry	opposite	synonym	paraphrase

5 Senses and feelings
5.1 Feelings in general

feeling *n* [ˈfiːlɪŋ]	I have a ~ that he doesn't like me.	Gefühl
mood *n* [muːd]	He's in a bad ~ at the moment. (≫ state of mind)	Laune, Stimmung
sense of humour *n* [sens, ˈhjuːmə]	He has a very good ~.	Sinn für Humor
to feel *v* [fiːl] **felt** [felt] **felt** [felt]	Mary was ~ing rather annoyed. I ~ very tired. I ~ (that) you don't understand my question. (≫ think, believe)	fühlen, spüren sich fühlen das Gefühl haben, glauben
to want *v* [wɒnt]	She ~s the comic. I ~ you to go there now.	wollen wünschen, daß
to be willing to [ˈwɪlɪŋ]	≫ to be ready to, to want to	gewillt sein
would like *v* [wʊd ˈlaɪk]	She ~ to go to the cinema.	mögen, wollen
to care for *v + prep* [keə]	Would you ~ a drink? (▶▶ like)	lieben, mögen
to be keen on [kiːn]	Is he really so ~ Susan?	sehr mögen, lieben
to wish *v* [wɪʃ]	I ~ (that) I had a car. I ~ you a merry Christmas.	wollen, wünschen
wish *n* [wɪʃ]	It's her ~ to go there.	Wunsch, Verlangen
to prefer *v* [prɪˈfɜː]	I like Jane's dress, but I ~ Fiona's. (▶▶ like . . . better)	vorziehen
favour *n* [ˈfeɪvə] **favor** *n AE*	Please **do me a** ~.	Gefallen, Wohlwollen
I would rather [wʊd ˈrɑːðə] **I had rather** [həd ˈrɑːðə]	≫ I would prefer to do	ich möchte lieber
to miss *v* [mɪs]	I ~ed you while you were away.	vermissen
to hope *v* [həʊp]	Will he come? – I ~ so/not. I ~ (that) you understand my decision.	(er)hoffen
hope *n* [həʊp]	She has no ~ of succeeding.	Hoffnung
to need *v* [niːd]	I ~ a new bike. My old one is too small for me.	brauchen, benötigen
to like *v* [laɪk]	Do you ~ dancing?	lieben, gern haben
to love *v* [lʌv]	≫ to like very much	gern haben, lieben
to be fond of *v + adv + prep* [fɒnd]	She's very ~ her dog.	gern haben, gern tun
love *n* [lʌv]	I'm not **in** ~ **with** her. He has a great ~ **for/of** Chinese food. (≫ liking for)	Liebe (zu)
to hate *v* [heɪt]	▶◀ to love	hassen
interest *n* [ˈɪntrəst]	Have you any hobbies or ~s?	Interesse
to interest *v* [ˈɪntrəst]	I don't watch quiz shows. They don't ~ me at all.	interessieren
to care *v* [keə]	I don't ~ any more. (≫ am not interested)	interessiert sein
interested *adj* [ˈɪntrəstɪd]	He's not ~ **in** politics.	interessiert (an)

Lerntip — Wiederholen

Ohne Wiederholung vergißt Du nach ein paar Tagen die Hälfte der neu gelernten Vokabeln. Baue deshalb in gewissen zeitlichen Abständen, z. B. alle 14 Tage, Wiederholungsphasen ein und arbeite die gelernten Vokabeln nochmals durch oder lasse Dich von Freunden, Geschwistern oder Eltern abfragen.

tʃ	dʒ	θ	ð	ʃ	ʒ	ŋ	w	v
cheap	jump	thing	then	shop	pleasure	sang	wet	voice

interesting *adj* [ˈɪntrəstɪŋ]	That's a very ~ idea.	interessant
popular *adj* [ˈpɒpjʊlə]	≫ liked by many people Her brother is ~ with girls. (≫ well liked by)	populär beliebt bei
sensation *n* [senˈseɪʃn]	I have no ~ in my right hand. (▶▶ feeling)	Empfindung, Gefühl
emotion *n* [ɪˈməʊʃn]	a strong feeling	Gefühlsregung
frame of mind [freɪm, maɪnd]	▶▶ mood	Gemütszustand, Stimmung
attitude *n* [ˈætɪtjuːd]	I don't like her unfriendly ~. (≫ way of thinking or behaving)	Haltung, Verhalten Einstellung
passion *n* [ˈpæʃn]	a very strong feeling (e.g. love, hate, anger)	Leidenschaft
emotional *adj* [ɪˈməʊʃənl] **sentimental** *adj* [sentɪˈmentl]	full of feeling	gefühlsbetont, empfindsam
to lack *v* [læk]	They all ~ed food and medicine. (≫ were without)	nicht haben, dringend benötigen
to require *v* [rɪˈkwaɪə]	▶▶ to need	brauchen, benötigen
requirement *n* [rɪˈkwaɪəmənt]	What are your ~s, sir?	Bedarf, Bedürfnis, Bedingung
lack *n* [læk] **want** *n* [wɒnt]	All the flowers died **from/for** ~ **of** water.	Mangel, Fehlen
need *n* [niːd]	She's in great ~ of help. There's **no** ~ **for** panic.	Verlangen, Bedürfnis, Notwendigkeit
hopeful *adj* [ˈhəʊpfʊl]	I'm ~ that I can win the game.	voller Hoffnung, erwartungsvoll
hopefully *adv* [ˈhəʊpfəlɪ]	≫ I hope so	hoffentlich
hopeless *adj* [ˈhəʊplɪs]	≫ without hope	hoffnungslos
despair *n* [dɪˈspeə]	▶◀ hope	Verzweiflung
desperate *adj* [ˈdespərət]	≫ completely hopeless	verzweifelt
to bear *v* [beə] **bore** [bɔː] **borne** [bɔːn]	I can't ~ sleeping in a hot room.	ertragen
to stand *v* [stænd] **stood** [stʊd] **stood** [stʊd]	I can't ~ that fool. (▶▶ bear)	ertragen
to tolerate *v* [ˈtɒləreɪt]	We won't ~ that noise.	dulden, ertragen, zulassen
to put up with *v + adv + prep* [pʊt ˈʌp wɪð]	We won't ~ his bad manners. (▶▶ tolerate)	sich gefallen lassen, dulden

Never pronounce the b, d, l, t, k, h **or** w **in these words:**

[b]	[d]	[l]	[t]	[k]	[h]	[h]	[w]
subtle	**handkerchief**	**calm**	**castle**	**knee**	**exhausted**	**what**	**sword**
doubt	**handsome**	**could**	**chestnut**	**to kneel**	**exhibition**	**when**	**who**
debt	**landlady**	**folk**	**Christmas**	**knife**	**heir**	**where**	**whole**
bomb	**landlord**	**half**	**to fasten**	**knight**	**honest**		**whom**
to climb				**to knit**			**whose**
							to wrap

to behave *v* [bɪˈheɪv]	He ~d very badly. Please, ~ yourself!	sich benehmen
Be good! [bɪ ˈgʊd]	≫ Behave yourself!	Benimm dich, sei brav.
manners *n* [ˈmænəz]	It's good ~ to say 'please' and 'thank you'.	Manieren, Benehmen

iː	ɪ	e	æ	ɑː	ɒ	ɔː	ʊ	uː	ʌ	ɜː	ə
eat	bit	ten	bad	fast	got	saw	sure	too	cut	bird	about

behaviour *n* [bɪˈheɪvɪə] **behavior** *n AE*	Her ~ towards me is very surprising. (≫ way of behaving)	Verhalten, Benehmen
conduct *n* [ˈkɒndʌkt]	▶▶ behaviour	Benehmen
action *n* [ˈækʃn]	His ~s were rather strange.	Tat, Vorgang
will *n* [wɪl]	He did it against his ~.	Willen
self-control *n* [selfkənˈtrəʊl]	the ability to control one's feelings	Selbstbeherrschung
discipline *n* [ˈdɪsɪplɪn]	correct behaviour, self-control	Disziplin
prejudice *n* [ˈpredʒʊdɪs]	a feeling or opinion formed without knowledge or experience	Vorurteil
disinterested *adj* [dɪsˈɪntrəstɪd]	not influenced by private feelings	unparteiisch, uneigennützig
to fancy *v* [ˈfænsɪ]	≫ to like and want	mögen
favourite *adj* [ˈfeɪvərɪt]	Golf is my ~ sport.	Lieblings-
preferable *adj* [ˈprefrəbl]	≫ better than	vorzuziehen, besser als
preference *n* [ˈprefrəns]	≫ liking one thing more than another	Vorliebe
rather than *adv* [ˈrɑːðə ðən]	▶▶ instead of	lieber als
to dislike *v* [dɪsˈlaɪk]	Helen ~s being touched by people. (≫ doesn't like)	nicht mögen
dislike *n* [dɪsˈlaɪk]	She has a ~ of snakes.	Abneigung
hate *n* [heɪt] **hatred** *n* [ˈheɪtrɪd]	▶◀ love	Haß
revenge *n* [rɪˈvendʒ]	doing harm to someone to pay him back for doing harm to you	Rache
popularity *n* [pɒpjʊˈlærətɪ]	Football has great ~.	Beliebtheit
unpopular *adj* [ʌnˈpɒpjʊlə]	≫ not liked by people	unbeliebt

5.2 Qualities and emotions

good *adj* [gʊd] **better** [ˈbetə] **best** [best]	That's a ~ idea.	gut besser am besten
well *adv* [wel]	You did the job very ~. (≫ in a very good way)	gut
fine *adj* [faɪn]	▶▶ good; beautiful	gut; schön
nice *adj* [naɪs]	It's ~ to see you again.	nett; hübsch
pleasant *adj* [ˈpleznt]	They had a ~ day at the seaside. (▶▶ nice)	angenehm, froh
wonderful *adj* [ˈwʌndəfʊl]	They gave him a ~ present. (▶▶ very nice)	wunderbar
great *adj* [greɪt]	It's ~ to see you again. (▶▶ wonderful) They are ~ friends. (≫ very good)	großartig, toll groß
super *adj* [ˈsuːpə]	It was great. We had a ~ time.	toll, prima
beautiful *adj* [ˈbjuːtɪfʊl]	Jane is a very ~ woman.	schön, hübsch
attractive *adj* [əˈtræktɪv]	She's an ~ girl. (▶▶ beautiful)	reizvoll, attraktiv
good-looking *adj* [gʊdˈlʊkɪŋ]	▶▶ attractive	gutaussehend
pretty *adj* [ˈprɪtɪ]	≫ nice to look at	hübsch, nett
lovely *adj* [ˈlʌvlɪ]		reizend
charming *adj* [ˈtʃɑːmɪŋ]		bezaubernd

adj	*adv*	*art*	*conj*	*n*	*pl*	*prep*	*pron*	*sing*
adjective	adverb(ial)	article	conjunction	noun	plural	preposition	pronoun	singular

average *adj* ['ævərɪdʒ]	His work at school is just ~.	durchschnittlich
bad *adj* [bæd] **worse** [wɜːs] **worst** [wɜːst]	▶◀ good	schlecht schlechter am schlechtesten
poor *adj* [pʊə]	≫ bad	schlecht, dürftig
terrible *adj* ['terəbl]	Stop that ~ noise.	schrecklich, furchtbar
awful *adj* ['ɔːfl]	▶▶ terrible, very bad	furchtbar
nasty *adj* ['nɑːstɪ]	▶◀ nice	garstig, häßlich
ugly *adj* ['ʌglɪ]	▶◀ beautiful	häßlich
right *adj* [raɪt]	It's not ~ to tell lies.	recht, richtig
to be right [raɪt]	I was ~, but he wasn't. (≫ correct)	recht haben
wrong *adj* [rɒŋ]	It's ~ to tell lies. (≫ bad)	falsch, unrichtig
to be wrong [rɒŋ]	▶◀ to be right	unrecht haben
right *n* [raɪt]	She has no ~ to say that.	Recht
duty *n* ['djuːtɪ]	It's my ~ to help her.	Pflicht
honest *adj* ['ɒnɪst]	An ~ man doesn't tell lies.	aufrichtig, ehrlich
to trust *v* [trʌst]	Don't ~ him, he's not honest.	vertrauen
to cheat *v* [tʃiːt]	She ~ed him (out of £50). He always ~s at cards.	betrügen um schwindeln, mogeln
trick *n* [trɪk]	She fooled me with a ~.	Trick
secret *adj* ['siːkrɪt]	The plans must remain ~. Nobody should know about them.	geheim
secret *n* ['siːkrɪt]	This is a ~. Don't tell anyone.	Geheimnis
happy *adj* ['hæpɪ]	She was ~ to be home again.	glücklich, froh
glad *adj* [glæd]	She was ~ to see him again. (▶▶ happy)	froh, sich freuen über
pleased *adj* [pliːzd]	I was very ~ to pass the exam.	erfreut (über)
satisfied *adj* ['sætɪsfaɪd]	We are not ~ with the results. (▶▶ pleased)	zufrieden
to satisfy *v* ['sætɪsfaɪ]	≫ to be good enough for	zufriedenstellen, befriedigen
pleasure *n* ['pleʒə]	She takes great ~ in doing her job.	Vergnügen, Gefallen
to enjoy *v* [ɪn'dʒɔɪ]	They all ~ed listening to rock music. (≫ liked)	Freude haben an, Gefallen finden an
sad *adj* [sæd]	▶◀ happy	traurig
poor *adj* [pʊə]	P~ Jim, he has lost all his money.	arm, bemitleidenswert
to disappoint *v* [dɪsə'pɔɪnt]	▶◀ to please	enttäuschen
pity *n* ['pɪtɪ]	He felt no ~ for the killer. **It's a/What a** ~ you can't come to my party. (≫ It's sad . . .)	Mitleid wie schade
to pity *v* ['pɪtɪ]	Everybody will ~ him. (≫ feel sorry for)	bemitleiden
to regret *v* [rɪ'gret]	Bill ~ted his stupid behaviour. (≫ was sorry for)	bedauern
kind *adj* [kaɪnd]	It was ~ of you to help us.	freundlich, nett

These words have different meanings:

kind [kaɪnd]: nett, freundlich / Art	**race** [reɪs]: Rennen / Rasse	**mine** [maɪn]: meines / Mine, Bergwerk
yard [jɑːd]: Hof / Längenmaß	**like** [laɪk]: lieben / wie, gleich	**ball** [bɔːl]: Ball, Kugel / Ball, Tanzabend

v	*AE*	*BE*	☒	~	▶◀	▶▶	≫
verb	American English	British English	a word you have learnt	entry	opposite	synonym	paraphrase

5

helpful *adj* ['helpfʊl]	He's a very ~ boy. He always does what is wanted.	hilfsbereit, hilfreich
polite *adj* [pə'laɪt]	Chris is a very ~ child. He has good manners.	höflich
generous *adj* ['dʒenərəs]	He's too ~ with his money.	großzügig
to consider *v* [kən'sɪdə]	We must ~ her feelings. (▶▶ think of)	berücksichtigen
grateful *adj* ['greɪtfʊl]	I'm ~ to you for your help.	dankbar
to thank *v* [θæŋk]	Did you ~ Mr Watson for the lift?	danken
please *interj* [pli:z]	Can I borrow your pen, ~	bitte
excellent *adj* ['eksələnt]	This is an ~ book. You'll enjoy it. (▶▶ very good)	ausgezeichnet
splendid *adj* ['splendɪd]	▶▶ very fine	prächtig
marvellous *adj* ['mɑ:vələs]	▶▶ wonderful	wunderbar
magnificent *adj* [mæg'nɪfɪsnt]	He lives in a ~ palace. (▶▶ splendid)	prächtig, großartig
sensational *adj* [sen'seɪʃənl]	e.g. a ~ piece of news	aufsehenerregend
gorgeous *adj* ['gɔ:dʒəs]	They had a ~ tea. (▶▶ wonderful)	großartig, toll, phantastisch
to attract *v* [ə'trækt]	The match ~ed a large crowd.	anziehen
attraction *n* [ə'trækʃn]	She had no ~ for him.	Anziehungskraft
handsome *adj* ['hænsəm]	Jim is a ~ young man. (▶▶ good-looking)	gutaussehend
satisfactory *adj* [sætɪs'fæktərɪ]	≫ good enough, quite good	zufriedenstellend
unpleasant *adj* [ʌn'pleznt]	The cheese had an ~ smell.	unangenehm

active	**engagiert**
lazy	**faul**
full of life	**vital**
criticism	**Kritik**

engaged [ɪn'geɪdʒd]	verlobt; besetzt
foul [faʊl]	stinkend; faul
vital ['vaɪtl]	notwendig, unerläßlich
critic ['krɪtɪk]	Kritiker

naughty *adj* ['nɔ:tɪ]	Peter is a ~ child. (▶◀ good)	ungezogen, frech
bully *n* ['bʊlɪ]	a person who enjoys hurting weaker people	Raufbold, Tyrann
dreadful *adj* ['dredfʊl]	▶▶ terrible, very unpleasant	fürchterlich
horrible *adj* ['hɒrəbl]	▶▶ awful, very unpleasant or ugly	schrecklich
conscience *n* ['kɒnʃəns]	She has a **clear/guilty** ~.	Gewissen
sincere *adj* [sɪn'sɪə]	▶▶ honest, really meaning what you say	aufrichtig
frank *adj* [fræŋk]	Give me a ~ reply. (▶▶ honest)	offen, aufrichtig
frankly *adv* ['fræŋklɪ]	F~ speaking, I don't like her.	offen (gesagt)
open *adj* ['əʊpən]	He's a frank, ~ young man. (▶▶ honest)	offen, ehrlich
reliable *adj* [rɪ'laɪəbl]	She's a ~ girl. If she says she will do her homework, she'll do it.	zuverlässig
decent *adj* ['di:snt]	Our neighbours are ~ people. (≫ kind and respectable)	anständig
loyal *adj* ['lɔɪəl]	She has always been ~ to her friends.	treu
faithful *adj* ['feɪθfʊl]	Bill is a ~ friend. (▶▶ loyal)	treu
confidence *n* ['kɒnfɪdəns]	trust and belief	Vertrauen
honesty *n* ['ɒnəstɪ]	His ~ is well known everywhere.	Aufrichtigkeit

trust *n* [trʌst]	We have ~ in him.	Vertrauen
loyalty *n* [ˈlɔɪəltɪ]	You can be sure of his ~.	Treue
reliability *n* [rɪlaɪəˈbɪlətɪ]	ability to be relied on	Zuverlässigkeit
to depend on *v + prep* [dɪˈpend]	Babies ~ their parents. We ~ you to do it.	abhängen von sich verlassen auf
to rely on *v + prep* [rɪˈlaɪ]	Don't ~ her. (▶▶ depend on)	sich verlassen auf
dependent *adj* [dɪˈpendənt]	She's ~ **on** her parents.	abhängig von
independent *adj* [ɪndɪˈpendənt]	She took up a part-time job to be ~ **of** her husband.	unabhängig von
to lie *v* [laɪ]	▶◀ to tell the truth	lügen, belügen
to trick *v* [trɪk]	▶▶ to cheat	überlisten, täuschen
to fool *v* [fu:l]	▶▶ to cheat	täuschen, zum Narren halten
to mislead *v* [mɪsˈli:d] **misled** [mɪsˈled] **misled** [mɪsˈled]	Her friendly behaviour can ~ people who don't really know her.	irreführen
to pretend *v* [prɪˈtend]	She ~s to love me, but she doesn't.	vorgeben, vortäuschen, so tun als ob
unreliable *adj* [ʌnrɪˈlaɪəbl]	▶◀ reliable	unzuverlässig
dishonest *adj* [dɪsˈɒnɪst]	Don't trust him. He's a very ~ man. (▶◀ honest)	unehrlich
false *adj* [fɒls]	The newspaper gave a ~ picture of what really happened.	unaufrichtig
lie *n* [laɪ]	Don't believe her. It's all ~s.	Lüge
to disguise *v* [dɪsˈgaɪz]	He ~d himself as a clown.	sich verkleiden
mask *n* [mɑ:sk]	The burglar wore a ~ over his face.	Maske
to mask *v* [mɑ:sk]	She couldn't ~ her feelings. (▶▶ hide) The gangsters were ~ed.	verbergen maskieren
to conceal *v* [kənˈsi:l]	▶▶ to hide	verbergen
secrecy *n* [ˈsi:krəsɪ]	⩾ keeping secrets	Verschwiegenheit
to reveal *v* [rɪˈvi:l]	They finally ~ed the secret.	enthüllen, aufdecken
cheerful *adj* [ˈtʃɪəfʊl]	Mike came in with a ~ smile. (▶▶ happy)	fröhlich, heiter
joyful *adj* [ˈdʒɔɪfʊl]	▶▶ very happy	freudig, froh
enjoyable *adj* [ɪnˈdʒɔɪəbl]	It was an ~ party.	erfreulich, unterhaltsam, schön
delighted *adj* [dɪˈlaɪtɪd]	He was ~ at the news. (▶▶ very pleased with)	erfreut, entzückt
gay *adj* [geɪ]	⩾ happy and cheerful	heiter, lustig
happiness *n* [ˈhæpɪnɪs]	Your ~ is very important to me.	Glück, Glücksgefühl
joy *n* [dʒɔɪ]	great happiness	Freude
satisfaction *n* [sætɪsˈfækʃn]	His success gives me great ~.	Befriedigung, Zufriedenheit
to please *v* [pli:z]	The team's win ~d their fans. (⩾ made . . . happy)	erfreuen, eine Freude machen
unhappy *adj* [ʌnˈhæpɪ]	▶▶ sad	unglücklich
miserable *adj* [ˈmɪzrəbl]	▶▶ very sad	elend, kläglich
bored *adj* [bɔ:d]	▶◀ interested	gelangweilt
fed up *adj* [fed ˈʌp]	I'm ~ **with** my present job. (▶▶ bored)	überdrüssig, satt haben
disappointment *n* [dɪsəˈpɔɪntmənt]	The film was a ~ because the actors were bad.	Enttäuschung
misery *n* [ˈmɪzərɪ]	great unhappiness	Not, Elend

5

Read the words out loud: same sound but different spelling:

[ɒ]	[f]	[e]	[s]	[ʒ]	[z]
J**o**hn	**f**ast	b**e**d	**s**un	plea**s**ure	**z**oo
c**ou**gh	enou**gh**	h**ea**d	ri**ce**	vi**si**on	wa**s**
w**a**tch	**ph**ysics	fr**ie**nd	**sc**ene	u**su**al	sci**ss**ors
	ca**lf**	**a**ny	**ps**ychology		
	o**ft**en	s**ai**d	**sw**ord		
			citizen		

sorrow *n* ['sɒrəʊ]	Her death caused him great ~. (▶▶ sadness)	Kummer, Sorge
regret *n* [rɪ'gret]	She feels no ~ about what she did. (⩾ being sorry)	Bedauern
tender *adj* ['tendə]	⩾ gentle and loving	zärtlich, zart
gentle *adj* ['dʒentl]	⩾ kind and friendly, ▶◀ rough	sanft, freundlich
delicate *adj* ['delɪkət]	⩾ soft and tender	feinfühlig, taktvoll
severe *adj* [sɪ'vɪə]	The judge had a ~ look on his face.	streng
strict *adj* [strɪkt]	The teacher is very ~ with his pupils. (▶▶ severe)	streng
formal *adj* ['fɔ:ml]	The first meeting between the two leaders was a very ~ affair.	förmlich, formell
informal *adj* [ɪn'fɔ:ml]	▶◀ formal	ungezwungen
casual *adj* ['kæʒʊəl]	He's fond of wearing ~ clothes.	zwanglos, salopp
impolite *adj* [ɪmpə'laɪt]	⩾ without good manners	unhöflich
rude *adj* [ru:d]	It was very ~ of you not to thank your host. (▶▶ impolite)	frech, unhöflich
vulgar *adj* ['vʌlgə]	Please don't use such ~ language. (⩾ very rude and low)	ordinär, unanständig, vulgär
tolerant *adj* ['tɒlərənt]	⩾ friendly and understanding	tolerant
politeness *n* [pə'laɪtnɪs]	⩾ polite manners	Höflichkeit
kindness *n* ['kaɪndnɪs]	Thank you for all your ~ to me.	Freundlichkeit, Liebenswürdigkeit
sympathy *n* ['sɪmpəθɪ]	I have no ~ for people who beat their children.	Verständnis *(Mitgefühl)*
tolerance *n* ['tɒlərəns]	⩾ being tolerant	Toleranz, Duldsamkeit
mercy *n* ['mɜ:sɪ]	The soldiers showed no ~ to/towards their enemies. (▶▶ pity)	Gnade, Mitleid
charity *n* ['tʃærətɪ]	sympathy and kindness	Nächstenliebe, Mildtätigkeit
generosity *n* [dʒenə'rɒsətɪ]	She's a woman of great ~.	Großzügigkeit
greedy *adj* ['gri:dɪ]	It would be ~ to have a third helping.	gierig
mean *adj* [mi:n]	▶◀ generous It's ~ to tease him. (▶▶ unkind)	geizig gemein
thankful *adj* ['θæŋkfʊl]	▶▶ grateful	dankbar
gratitude *n* ['grætɪtju:d]	Peter was full of ~. (⩾ very grateful)	Dankbarkeit

5.3 Strong feelings and attitudes

smile *n* [smaɪl]	Sabine has a lovely ~.	Lächeln
to smile *v* [smaɪl]	She ~d because she was happy. (⩾ had a happy look on her face)	lächeln
to laugh *v* [lɑ:f]	Stop ~ing (at me)!	lachen (über)

adj	*adv*	*art*	*conj*	*n*	*pl*	*prep*	*pron*	*sing*
adjective	adverb(ial)	article	conjunction	noun	plural	preposition	pronoun	singular

to cry *v* [kraɪ]	She was ~ing because her dog had died.	weinen
angry *adj* ['æŋgrɪ]	Barbara was ~ because she could not see the film.	böse, ärgerlich
to quarrel *v* ['kwɒrəl]	I don't want to ~ with you. (≫ talk angrily)	streiten
quarrel *n* ['kwɒrəl]	The two boys had a ~ over the girl. (≫ angry argument)	Streit, Auseinandersetzung
to argue *v* ['ɑ:gju:]	Please don't ~ with me. (▶▶ quarrel, disagree)	streiten
argument *n* ['ɑ:gjʊmənt]	▶▶ a quarrel, disagreement	Streit
cruel *adj* ['krʊəl]	It is ~ to beat a child.	grausam, roh, unbarmherzig
to disturb *v* [dɪ'stɜ:b]	Don't ~ her while she is asleep.	stören, beunruhigen
to bother *v* ['bɒðə]	Don't ~ me. I'm busy. (▶▶ disturb, interrupt) Shall I fetch it? – No, don't ~ (≫ take the trouble)	jem. belästigen sich bemühen
to worry *v* ['wʌrɪ]	His driving ~ies his mother. Don't ~. It's O.K.	beunruhigen sich sorgen
to be afraid *v + adj* [ə'freɪd]	Don't be ~ **of** our dog. He was ~ to climb the ladder.	Angst haben (vor)
fear *n* [fɪə]	Her hands were shaking with ~.	Furcht, Angst
shock *n* [ʃɒk]	an unpleasant surprise	Schock, Schlag
to shock *v* [ʃɒk]	The murder ~ed everybody.	schockieren
upset *adj* [ʌp'set]	≫ anxious and unhappy	bestürzt
nervous *adj* ['nɜ:vəs]	≫ rather afraid and worried	reizbar, nervös
tense *adj* [tens]		angespannt
problem *n* ['prɒbləm]	I did it easily. It was no ~.	Problem
trouble *n* ['trʌbl]	▶▶ difficulty	Mühe, Schwierigkeit
brave *adj* [breɪv]	▶▶ fearless	tapfer, mutig

5

fearful, timid, shy	**ängstlich**
to be surprised at	**sich wundern**
good, well-behaved	**brav**

anxious ['æŋkʃəs]	besorgt um, bedacht auf
to wonder ['wʌndə]	sich fragen, wissen wollen
brave [breɪv]	tapfer

hero *n, pl* **heroes** ['hɪarau, 'hɪarauz]	The man who saved the boy from drowning was a ~. (≫ very brave person)	Held
to risk *v* [rɪsk]	She ~ed all her money. (≫ put . . . in danger)	riskieren, aufs Spiel setzen
firm *adj* [fɜ:m]	≫ strong and sure	unnachgiebig, standhaft
proud *adj* [praʊd]	Jack is very ~ **of** his new car.	stolz
ashamed of *adj* [ə'ʃeɪmd]	▶◀ proud of	beschämt, voll Scham
to embarrass *v* [ɪm'bærəs]	I was ~ed by having to answer a lot of personal questions.	in Verlegenheit bringen
comfortable *adj* ['kʌmftəbl]	Are you ~ in that armchair?	bequem
quiet *adj* ['kwaɪət]	Nothing much happens here. It's very ~.	ruhig, ausgeglichen
calm *adj* [kɑ:m]	▶▶ quiet	ruhig
exciting *adj* [ɪk'saɪtɪŋ]	▶◀ boring	aufregend, anregend, spannend
keen *adj* [ki:n]	She is very ~ **on** pop music. Paul is ~ **to** pass the exam. (≫ wants very much)	interessiert an begierig, eifrig

boring *adj* ['bɔ:rɪŋ]	▶◀ interesting	langweilig
surprise *n* [sə'praɪz]	His answer caused some ~.	Überraschung
wonder *n* ['wʌndə]	He was full of ~ at what he saw.	Erstaunen, Verwunderung, Wunder
to surprise *v* [sə'praɪz]	She ~d me with a visit.	überraschen
to wonder *v* ['wʌndə]	I ~ where she is. (≫ ask myself) I ~ **at** her behaviour. (≫ am surprised)	gerne wissen mögen erstaunt sein
laugh *n* [lɑ:f]	You friend has a loud ~.	Lachen
laughter *n* ['lɑ:ftə]	We could hear ~ from the classroom next door. (≫ laughing)	Gelächter, Lachen
to grin *v* [grɪn]	They were all ~ning when they heard the good news. (≫ showing a broad smile)	grinsen
grin *n* [grɪn]	a broad smile	Grinsen
to whistle *v* ['wɪsl]	Fitzgerald ~d a tune as he came down the stairs.	pfeifen
whistle *n* ['wɪsl]	When Jim saw his friend he gave a loud ~.	Pfiff, Pfeifen
to weep *v* [wi:p] **wept** [wept] **wept** [wept]	The little boy began to ~. (▶▶ cry)	weinen
to annoy *v* [ə'nɔɪ]	≫ to make angry	ärgern
to tease *v* [ti:z]	Stop ~ing the cat. (≫ annoying/making fun of)	necken, ärgern
to mess about *v + adv* [mes ə'baʊt]	≫ to behave in a silly way for fun	Unfug treiben
anger *n* ['æŋgə]	He was filled with ~ when he heard about it.	Ärger, Zorn
rage *n* [reɪdʒ]	▶▶ great anger	Wut
temper *n* ['tempə]	He's in a **bad** ~ today. So keep away from him. (▶▶ mood)	Laune, Stimmung
to lose one's temper [lu:z, 'tempə]	≫ to get angry	wütend werden
good-tempered *adj* [gʊd'tempəd]	≫ in a good temper, not angry	gutgelaunt
bad-tempered *adj* [bæd'tempəd]	▶◀ good-tempered	schlechtgelaunt
annoyed *adj* [ə'nɔɪd]	≫ a little angry	etwas verärgert
furious *adj* ['fjʊərɪəs] **mad** *adj informal* [mæd]	▶▶ very angry	wütend
annoying *adj* [ə'nɔɪɪŋ]	It's ~ to miss the bus.	ärgerlich, lästig
to disagree *v* [dɪsə'gri:]	I ~ **with** you **on/about** that matter. (▶◀ agree)	verschiedener Meinung sein
to take sides with [teɪk 'saɪdz]	Jane didn't ~ her father in the argument. (≫ wasn't on the side of)	Partei ergreifen für
fuss *n* [fʌs]	Don't make such a ~ about it.	Getue
nuisance *n* ['nju:sns]	What a ~. I've lost my keys.	Ärgernis
disagreement *n* [dɪsə'gri:mənt]	They had a violent ~. (▶▶ quarrel)	Streit
cruelty *n* ['krʊəltɪ]	It's a film about the ~ of war.	Grausamkeit
violence *n* ['vaɪələns]	Many people think that too much ~ is shown on TV.	Gewalt, Gewalttätigkeit
violent *adj* ['vaɪələnt]	John is always ~ when he's drunk.	gewalttätig, heftig
fierce *adj* [fɪəs]	The building is guarded by a ~ dog.	wild, heftig
to upset *v* [ʌp'set] **upset** [ʌp'set] **upset** [ʌp'set]	to make someone feel anxious or disturbed	beunruhigen

tʃ	dʒ	θ	ð	ʃ	ʒ	ŋ	w	v
cheap	jump	thing	then	shop	pleasure	sang	wet	voice

to trouble *v* ['trʌbl]	What's ~ing you? (≫ making you sad, bothering you)	beunruhigen, stören
anxious *adj* ['æŋkʃəs]	▶▶ worried	besorgt
worried *adj* ['wʌrɪd]	▶▶ fearful, anxious	besorgt
terror *n* ['terə]	great fear	Schrecken, Terror
to be frightened ['fraɪtnd]	▶▶ to be afraid	Angst haben (vor)
to be scared [skeəd]		
to fear *v* [fɪə]	The king ~ed he would lose the battle.	fürchten
to frighten *v* ['fraɪtn]	The strange men ~ed her. (≫ made . . . afraid)	erschrecken, verjagen
to terrify *v* ['terɪfaɪ]	≫ to fill with fear	in Angst versetzen

IN

. . . in danger in Gefahr	**. . . in common** gemeinsam	**. . . in general** allgemein	**. . . in fact** tatsächlich	**. . . in love** verliebt	**. . . in particular** besonders
. . . in pieces kaputt	**. . . in sight** in Sicht	**. . . in private** privat	**. . . in public** öffentlich	**. . . in time** rechtzeitig	

shy *adj* [ʃaɪ]	Billy is a ~ child. He is unwilling to meet strangers.	schüchtern
timid *adj* ['tɪmɪd]	▶▶ shy, easily frightened	schüchtern, ängstlich
self-conscious *adj* [self'kɒnʃəs]	nervous and shy in the presence of others	gehemmt, unsicher, befangen
to blush *v* [blʌʃ]	She ~ed with shame. (≫ became red in the face)	erröten
courageous *adj* [kə'reɪdʒəs]	▶▶ brave	tapfer
self-confident *adj* [self'kɒnfɪdənt]	sure of your power to succeed	selbstbewußt
coward *n* ['kaʊəd]	▶◀ hero	Feigling
courage *n* ['kʌrɪdʒ]	The girl showed great ~ at the scene of the accident.	Mut, Beherztheit
to dare *v* [deə]	to be brave enough	wagen
to pull oneself together *v + adv* [pʊl wʌn'self tə'geðə]	P~ yourself ~! (≫ Control your feelings)	sich zusammenreißen
to show off *v + adv* ['ʃəʊ ɒf]	He's just ~ing ~. (≫ trying to impress others)	angeben, prahlen
determined *adj* [dɪ'tɜːmɪnd]	The team are ~ to win.	entschlossen
stubborn *adj* ['stʌbən]	He's a ~ young man. He won't change his mind.	stur, starrköpfig
to admire *v* [əd'maɪə]	We all ~d her courage.	bewundern
to respect *v* [rɪ'spekt]	I ~ him for what he did. (≫ think well of)	achten, respektieren
to honour *v* ['ɒnə] **to honor** *v AE*	▶▶ to respect	ehren, verehren
honour *n* ['ɒnə] **honor** *n AE*	▶◀ shame	Ehre
respect *n* [rɪ'spekt]	Criminals have no ~ for the law.	Achtung, Respekt
admiration *n* [ædmə'reɪʃn]	a feeling of pleasure and respect	Bewunderung
glory *n* ['glɔːrɪ]	≫ great honour	Ruhm
majesty *n* ['mædʒəstɪ]	≫ greatness	Majestät
impressive *adj* [ɪm'presɪv]	His work is really ~. (≫ very good and important)	eindrucksvoll, beeindruckend

5

humble *adj* ['hʌmbl] **modest** *adj* ['mɒdɪst]	▶◀ proud	bescheiden
pride *n* [praɪd]	≫ a proud feeling	Stolz
jealous *adj* ['dʒeləs]	Harry is always ~ when his wife talks to other men.	eifersüchtig
jealousy *n* ['dʒeləsɪ]	≫ a jealous feeling	Eifersucht
to envy *v* ['envɪ]	I don't ~ you (your money).	neidisch sein auf
envy *n* ['envɪ]	Her luck filled him with ~.	Neid
to offend *v* [ə'fend]	I didn't want to ~ you. (≫ hurt your feelings)	beleidigen
offence *n* [ə'fens] **offense** *n AE*	I hope she didn't cause any ~.	Beleidigung
shame *n* [ʃeɪm]	He felt no ~ for what he had done. **What a** ~ to work on a day like this. (≫ What a pity . . .)	Scham, Schande wie schade
embarrassing *adj* [ɪm'bærəsɪŋ]	She asked me an ~ question.	peinlich
at a loss [lɒs]	≫ uncertain, not knowing what to do	in Verlegenheit
convenient *adj* [kən'vi:nɪənt]	free from trouble and difficulty	bequem, passend
peaceful *adj* ['pi:sfʊl]	They spent a ~ evening. (▶▶ quiet)	ruhig, friedlich
patient *adj* ['peɪʃnt]	≫ ready to wait	geduldig
quiet(ness) *n* ['kwaɪət(nɪs)] **peace** *n* [pi:s] **calmness** *n* ['kɑ:mnɪs]	I love the ~ of the country.	Ruhe, Frieden
comfort *n* ['kʌmfət]	He has enough money to **live in** ~. Sabine ran to her mother for ~.	Behaglichkeit, Zufriedenheit, Trost
to comfort *v* ['kʌmfət]	They tried to ~ the crying boy. (≫ make . . . feel better)	trösten

AT	**. . . at first** zuerst	**. . . at last** schließlich	**. . . at least** zumindest	**. . . at once** sofort	**. . . at work** bei der Arbeit
	. . . at present jetzt		**. . . at breakfast** beim Frühstück		**. . . at home** zu Hause

to get excited [ɪk'saɪtɪd]	▶◀ to keep cool	sich aufregen
to stimulate *v* ['stɪmjʊleɪt]	The speaker's words failed to ~ much interest.	stimulieren, anregen
excited *adj* [ɪk'saɪtɪd]	▶◀ calm	begeistert (von)
impatient *adj* [ɪm'peɪʃnt]	≫ not ready to wait	ungeduldig
eager *adj* ['i:gə]	She's ~ **for** success. He's ~ **to** win. (▶▶ keen)	begierig, eifrig
anxious *adj* ['æŋkʃəs]	She's ~ to meet him. (▶▶ eager)	bestrebt
thrilling *adj* ['θrɪlɪŋ]	▶▶ very exciting	spannend
dramatic *adj* [drə'mætɪk]	▶▶ exciting	dramatisch
unexpected *adj* [ʌnɪk'spektɪd]	≫ not expected	unerwartet
curious *adj* ['kjʊərɪəs]	I'm ~ to find out where he is.	neugierig
indifferent *adj* [ɪn'dɪfrənt]	She's ~ **to** other people's problems. (≫ not interested in)	gleichgültig gegenüber
excitement *n* [ɪk'saɪtmənt]	After his heart attack he should avoid all ~.	Aufregung

adj	*adv*	*art*	*conj*	*n*	*pl*	*prep*	*pron*	*sing*
adjective	adverb(ial)	article	conjunction	noun	plural	preposition	pronoun	singular

sensation *n* [senˈseɪʃn]	The first landing on the moon was a great ~.	Sensation
impatience *n* [ɪmˈpeɪʃns]	inability to wait calmly	Ungeduld
to bore *v* [bɔː]	to make tired and uninterested	langweilen
sensitive *adj* [ˈsensətɪv]	I'm very ~ **to** cold.	empfindlich, sensibel
tension *n* [ˈtenʃn]	▶▶ mental strain	Spannung, Streß
astonishment *n* [əˈstɒnɪʃmənt]	▶▶ great surprise	Erstaunen
amazement *n* [əˈmeɪzmənt]		
to astonish *v* [əˈstɒnɪʃ] **to amaze** *v* [əˈmeɪz]	≫ to greatly surprise	erstaunen
to startle *v* [ˈstɑːtl]	A sudden noise ~d us. (≫ surprised and shocked)	aufschrecken, alarmieren
amazing *adj* [əˈmeɪzɪŋ]	▶▶ very surprising, astonishing	überraschend
puzzle *n* [ˈpʌzl]	something that is difficult to understand	Rätsel, Puzzle
mystery *n* [ˈmɪstərɪ]	I like reading ~ stories.	Geheimnis, Rätsel
mysterious *adj* [mɪˈstɪərɪəs]	difficult to explain or understand	geheimnisvoll
miracle *n* [ˈmɪrəkl]	a wonderful happening	Wunder

5.4 Senses and sensations

to see *v* [siː] **saw** [sɔː] **seen** [siːn]	We couldn't ~ them in the pub.	sehen
to look *v* [lʊk]	She ~ed **at** the young man. He ~s ill.	ansehen aussehen
to watch *v* [wɒtʃ]	Peter often ~es TV. He ~ed his friend cross the street.	schauen beobachten
to glance *v* [glɑːns]	The manager ~d **at** his watch. (≫ had a quick look)	blicken auf
to have/take a look [lʊk]	Let me ~ **at** the photo.	einen Blick werfen auf
to face *v* [feɪs]	He ~d his opponent without fear.	ins Auge blicken, gegenüberstehen
look *n* [lʊk]	He had a good ~ **at** the man.	Blick
glance *n* [glɑːns]	a quick look	flüchtiger Blick
sight *n* [saɪt]	His ~ isn't very good. He must wear glasses.	Sehkraft, Sicht
at first sight	It was love ~. (≫ at the first time of meeting)	auf den ersten Blick
in sight	▶▶ in view	in Sicht
out of sight	The car was ~.	außer Sicht(weite)

OUT OF
- ... **out of danger** – außer Gefahr
- ... **out of date** – veraltet
- ... **out of order** – kaputt
- ... **out of sight** – außer Sichtweite
- ... **out of work** – arbeitslos
- ... **out of stock** – nicht vorrätig

to know ... by sight	I don't know his name, I only ~ him ~.	vom Sehen kennen
view *n* [vjuː]	From my room I have a good ~ of the mountains.	Blick, Aussicht
clear *adj* [klɪə]	His handwriting is ~ and easy to read.	deutlich, klar

v	*AE*	*BE*	☒	~	▶◀	▶▶	≫
verb	American English	British English	a word you have learnt	entry	opposite	synonym	paraphrase

CATCH	**... a cold**	sich erkälten	**COME TO**	**... an agreement**	zu einer Einigung kommen
	... a bus/train	den Bus/Zug erreichen		**... a conclusion**	zu einer Folgerung gelangen
				... a decision	eine Entscheidung erreichen
DO	**... one's best**	sein Bestes geben		**... somebody a favour**	jemandem einen Gefallen tun
	... one's duty	seine Pflicht tun		**... one's homework**	seine Hausaufgabe(n) machen
				... somebody a service	jemandem einen Dienst erweisen

to hear *v* [hɪə] **heard** [hɜ:d] **heard** [hɜ:d]	I couldn't ~ a sound.	hören
to listen *v* [lɪsn]	Are you ~ing (**to** the music)?	zuhören
noise *n* [nɔɪz]	There was so much ~ in the pub that I couldn't hear him.	Lärm
noisy *adj* ['nɔɪzɪ]	≫ full of noise; ▶◀ quiet	lärmend, geräuschvoll
sound *n* [saʊnd]	Light travels faster than ~.	Ton, Klang, Schall
quiet *adj* ['kwaɪət]	≫ with little noise	ruhig, leise
silent *adj* ['saɪlənt]	▶▶ quiet, calm; ▶◀ loud, noisy	still, leise
loud *adj* [laʊd]	▶◀ quiet	laut
aloud *adv* [ə'laʊd]	Shall I read ~ or silently?	laut
to ring *v* [rɪŋ] **rang** [ræŋ] **rung** [rʌŋ]	The telephone was ~ing.	läuten
to notice *v* ['nəʊtɪs]	≫ to see, hear, recognize	bemerken
notice *n* ['nəʊtɪs]	Don't take any ~ of what he says. (≫ pay any attention to) The ~ on the wall says "NO PARKING"	Notiz, Beachtung Hinweis(schild)
smell *n* [smel]	Roses have a sweet ~.	Geruch
to smell *v* [smel]	I could ~ that the meat wasn't fresh. That man ~s **of** tobacco.	riechen (nach)
to taste *v* [teɪst]	The cook ~d the soup. This soup doesn't ~ **of** anything.	kosten, versuchen schmecken (nach)
taste *n* [teɪst]	Sugar has a sweet ~.	Geschmack

guesthouse	**Pension**	**pension** ['penʃn]	Rente
corridor	**Flur**	**floor** [flɔ:]	Stockwerk; Fußboden
trade	**Handel**	**handle** ['hændl]	Griff
button, key	**Taste**	**taste** [teɪst]	Geschmack

sweet *adj* [swi:t]	Sugar tastes ~.	süß
bitter *adj* ['bɪtə]	For some people black coffee without sugar has a ~ taste.	bitter
sour *adj* ['saʊə]	Lemons have a ~ taste.	sauer
to touch *v* [tʌtʃ]	He ~ed her shoulder. (≫ put his finger or hand on)	berühren
to handle *v* ['hændl]	'Don't ~ the oranges,' he said. (▶▶ touch)	berühren
touch *n* [tʌtʃ]	I felt a ~ on my arm. I haven't been **in** ~ **with** him for 5 years.	Berührung in Verbindung mit
senses *n* ['sensɪz]	The five ~ are sight, hearing, touch, tasting and smelling.	Sinne
vision *n* ['vɪʒn]	the ability to see	Sehvermögen, Vision
to observe *v* [əb'zɜ:v]	▶▶ to watch	beobachten

tʃ	dʒ	θ	ð	ʃ	ʒ	ŋ	w	v
cheap	**j**ump	**th**ing	**th**en	**sh**op	plea**s**ure	sa**ng**	**w**et	**v**oice

to stare *v* [steə]	The pupils ~d at the teacher in surprise.	starren, anstarren
survey *n* ['sɜːveɪ]	a general view	Überblick, Übersicht, Umfrage
glimpse *n* [glɪmps]	I **caught/got a** ~ of Paul when the bus went past our house.	flüchtiger Blick, Einblick
spectacle *n* ['spektəkl]	a great public show	Schauspiel, Anblick
visible *adj* ['vɪzəbl]	The sun isn't ~ at night. (≫ can't be seen)	sichtbar
obvious *adj* ['ɒbvɪəs] **evident** *adj* ['evɪdənt]	▶▶ quite clear	offensichtlich, offenbar
obviously *adv* ['ɒbvɪəslɪ]	▶▶ clearly	offensichtlich
prominent *adj* ['prɒmɪnənt]	≫ easily seen He's a ~ actor. (▶▶ famous)	auffallend prominent, berühmt
transparent *adj* [træns'pærənt]	Glass is ~. You can see through it.	durchsichtig
dense *adj* [dens]	The fog was ~. (▶▶ thick)	dicht, undurchsichtig
to sound *v* [saʊnd]	That ~s interesting. A bell ~ed.	klingen ertönen (lassen)
silence *n* ['saɪləns]	▶◀ noise	Stille, Ruhe
to knock *v* [nɒk]	Someone ~ed on the front door.	klopfen, schlagen
to crash *v* [kræʃ]	The tree ~ed to the ground. (≫ hit the ground with a loud noise)	krachen, krachend stürzen
crash *n* [kræʃ]	a sudden loud noise	Krach(en)
perfume *n* ['pɜːfjuːm]	My girlfriend loves French ~s.	Parfüm
scent *n* [sent]	a (sweet and pleasing) smell	Duft
flavour *n* ['fleɪvə] **flavor** *n AE*	What ~ is your ice-cream? (▶▶ taste)	Wohlgeschmack, Aroma
tasteful *adj* ['teɪstfʊl]	≫ showing good taste	geschmackvoll
tasteless *adj* ['teɪstlɪs]	This meat is ~. (≫ has no taste)	fade, unschmackhaft
tasty *adj* ['teɪstɪ] **delicious** *adj* [dɪ'lɪʃəs]	very good to eat	schmackhaft köstlich
hot *adj* [hɒt]	The curry is very ~. It leaves a burning taste in the mouth.	scharf (gewürzt)
to feel *v* [fiːl] **felt** [felt] **felt** [felt]	I had to ~ my way through the darkness.	berühren, betasten
to pinch *v* [pɪntʃ]	She ~ed her fingers in the door. My shoes ~. (≫ hurt because they're too tight)	(ein)zwicken, einklemmen drücken
contact *n* ['kɒntækt]	She has no ~ with other people.	Kontakt, Verbindung

5

iː	ɪ	e	æ	ɑː	ɒ	ɔː	ʊ	uː	ʌ	ɜː	ə
eat	bit	ten	bad	fast	got	saw	sure	too	cut	bird	about

6 Thinking, language and communication
6.1 Thinking and learning

mind *n* [maɪnd]	What are you thinking? What's going on in your ~?	Verstand, Geist
reason *n* [ˈriːzn]	▶▶ clear thinking	Vernunft, Verstand
idea *n* [aɪˈdɪə]	It was a good ~ to go there. (▶▶ plan) I don't have any ~ how to do it. (▶▶ understanding)	Idee, Plan Ahnung, Vorstellung
to think *v* [θɪŋk] **thought** [θɔːt] **thought** [θɔːt]	I often ~ **about** that girl. He was ~ing what to do next.	denken, nachdenken über, sich überlegen
to consider *v* [kənˈsɪdə]	I have to ~ this idea. (⩾ think carefully about)	bedenken, erwägen
to think over *v + adv* [θɪŋk ˈəʊvə]	This idea is very interesting but I have to ~ it ~. (▶▶ consider)	nachdenken über
to solve *v* [sɒlv]	to find an answer (to a problem)	lösen
to plan *v* [plæn]	The show was ~ned months ago. (▶▶ prepared)	planen
plan *n* [plæn]	He has worked out a ~ for making a lot of money.	Plan, Entwurf
purpose *n* [ˈpɜːpəs]	What was the ~ of his call?	Zweck, Absicht
on purpose	He did it ~, not by accident. (⩾ by intention)	absichtlich
by chance [baɪ ˈtʃɑːns]	▶▶ by accident; ▶◀ on purpose	zufällig
aim *n* [eɪm]	Her only ~ in life is to marry a rich man. (▶▶ purpose)	Ziel
to decide *v* [dɪˈsaɪd]	I couldn't ~ what to do. He ~d to leave.	entscheiden sich entschließen
decision *n* [dɪˈsɪʒn]	The boss makes all the important ~s.	Entscheidung
in favour of [ˈfeɪvə]	I'm ~ the idea.	für etwas (sein)
to make up one's mind [maɪnd]	▶▶ to decide	sich entschließen
to change one's mind [tʃeɪndʒ]	She wanted to go to the cinema, but then she ~d her ~.	sich anders besinnen
to remember *v* [rɪˈmembə]	I can't ~ his name. Please ~ to phone him. (⩾ don't forget)	sich erinnern (an) daran denken
to remind *v* [rɪˈmaɪnd]	Please ~ me to phone her. (⩾ make me remember)	erinnern an

Lerntip

Rechtschreibung Um Deine Rechtschreibkenntnisse zu testen deckst Du am besten die englische Spalte mit einem Blatt Papier zu und schreibst die deutschen Entsprechungen ab. Dann ergänzt Du diese Liste mit den englischen Vokabeln. Vergleiche dann die Wörter im Lernwörterbuch. Die fehlerhaften solltest Du markieren oder noch einmal richtig ausschreiben.

to remind of *v + prep* [rɪˈmaɪnd]	She ~ed me of your sister. (⩾ made me think of)	jem. erinnern an
to forget *v* [fəˈget] **forgot** [fəˈgɒt] **forgotten** [fəˈgɒtn]	▶◀ to remember	vergessen
to know *v* [nəʊ] **knew** [njuː] **known** [nəʊn]	Do you ~ the answer? He's in France at the moment. – Yes, I ~.	wissen, kennen
knowledge *n* [ˈnɒlɪdʒ]	He has little ~ of mathematics. K~ is power. (▶▶ knowing, understanding)	Kenntnisse Wissen
experience *n* [ɪkˈspɪərɪəns]	knowledge from practice (rather than from books)	Erfahrung

famous *adj* ['feɪməs]	The town is ~ **for** its cathedral.	berühmt
well-known *adj* [wel'nəʊn]		
to believe *v* [bɪ'li:v]	I ~ (that) he's wrong. (▶▶ think)	glauben, annehmen
to suppose *v* [sə'pəʊz]	▶▶ to think, to believe	annehmen, vermuten
to guess *v* [ges]	Can you ~ her age?	erraten, ahnen
AE	I ~ I'll have to meet him. (▶▶ think, suppose)	glauben, meinen
to imagine *v* [ɪ'mædʒɪn]	I~ her face when she hears it.	sich vorstellen
	I ~ that she'll be late. (▶▶ suppose)	glauben, denken
opinion *n* [ə'pɪnɪən]	**In my** ~ he is wrong. (▶▶ I think)	Meinung
view *n* [vju:]	**In my** ~, he's stupid. (▶▶ opinion)	Meinung
to expect *v* [ɪk'spekt]	She's ~ing a baby.	erwarten
	He ~s to be back by 10 o'clock.	annehmen, glauben
	They ~ me to work 6 days a week.	
to look forward to *v + adv + prep* [lʊk 'fɔ:wəd]	I'm ~ing ~ my birthday. (≫ waiting with pleasure for) I'm ~ing ~ seeing you soon.	sich freuen auf
to recognize *v* ['rekəgnaɪz]	You won't ~ her. She has changed so much! (≫ know her again)	(wieder)erkennen
to be aware of [ə'weə]	Is she ~ the dangers? (≫ Does she know ...)	sich bewußt sein
to realize *v* ['rɪəlaɪz] **-ise**	She ~d her mistake. (▶▶ understood, was aware of)	einsehen, (be)merken
to appreciate *v* [ə'pri:ʃɪeɪt]	He doesn't ~ our problems.	ermessen
	I ~ good wine. (≫ understand and enjoy)	(zu) schätzen (wissen)
to understand *v* [ʌndə'stænd] **understood** [ʌndə'stʊd] **understood** [ʌndə'stʊd]	I think I ~ what you feel.	verstehen, begreifen
to see *v* [si:] **saw** [sɔ:] **seen** [si:n]	Do you ~ what I mean? (▶▶ understand) Yes, I ~.	verstehen
to learn *v* [lɜ:n] **learnt (learned)** [lɜ:nt (lɜ:nd)] **learnt (learned)** [lɜ:nt (lɜ:nd)]	His daughter is ~ing quickly.	lernen
	They'll soon ~ of his success.	erfahren (von)
to study *v* ['stʌdɪ]	Cynthia is ~ing Japanese. (▶▶ learning)	lernen
clever *adj* ['klevə]	Laura is a ~ girl.	klug, schlau
intelligent *adj* [ɪn'telɪdʒənt]	▶▶ clever	intelligent
bright *adj* [braɪt]		gescheit, aufgeweckt
wise *adj* [waɪz]	No, that wouldn't be a very ~ thing to do. (▶▶ sensible)	klug, weise
good *adj* [gʊd]	She's very ~ at English.	gut in
skilful *adj* ['skɪlfʊl] **skillful** *adj AE*	Her brother is a very good and ~ player.	geschickt
able *adj* ['eɪbl]	He's an ~ pupil. (▶▶ clever)	begabt, tüchtig
ability *n* [ə'bɪlətɪ]	He has the ~ to do this job.	Fähigkeit, Befähigung
skill *n* [skɪl]	the ability to do something well	Geschicklichkeit
normal *adj* ['nɔ:məl]	She's a ~ teenager in every way.	normal
mad *adj* [mæd]	He went ~ after the death of his wife.	verrückt
stupid *adj* ['stju:pɪd]	≫ slow at understanding	dumm
silly *adj* ['sɪlɪ]	▶◀ sensible	albern
fool *n* [fu:l]	a silly person	Narr, Dummkopf

6

thought *n* [θɔ:t]	▶▶ idea	(Nach)Denken, Gedanke
presence of mind *n* ['prezns, maɪnd]	the ability to decide quickly and calmly in a dangerous situation	Geistesgegenwart
attention *n* [ə'tenʃn]	The teacher had the pupils' full ~.	Aufmerksamkeit
to pay attention [peɪ ə'tenʃn]	P~, please.	aufpassen

PAY ... **attention** to somebody/something — aufpassen auf jemanden/etwas
... **a call** on somebody — jemanden besuchen
... **a visit** — jemanden besuchen

TAKE ... **care of** — sich kümmern um
... **interest in** — sich interessieren für
... **a notice of** — etwas beachten
... **a photograph** — fotografieren
... **a trip** — eine Reise machen

solution *n* [sə'lu:ʃn]	an answer to a problem	Lösung
consideration *n* [kənsɪdə'reɪʃn]	careful thought	Erwägung, Überlegung; Rücksicht
to consider *v* [kən'sɪdə]	They ~ed him (to be) a fool.	halten für
to regard *v* [rɪ'gɑ:d]	His neighbours ~ him **as** a fool.	halten für
to fancy *v informal* ['fænsɪ]	▶▶ to imagine, to think	sich vorstellen, glauben, annehmen
guess *n* [ges]	I don't know how old he is; I can only make a ~.	Vermutung, Schätzung
public opinion *n* [pʌblɪk ə'pɪnɪən]	what people in general think about something	öffentliche Meinung
imagination *n* [ɪmædʒɪ'neɪʃn]	the ability to think new thoughts and form pictures in your mind	Phantasie, Vorstellungskraft
impression *n* [ɪm'preʃn]	He made a good ~ **on** her father.	Eindruck
theory *n* ['θɪərɪ]	an explanation or idea which has not yet been fully proved	Theorie
to conclude *v* [kən'klu:d]	≫ to come to believe, to finally decide	folgern, schließen
to gather *v* ['gæðə]		
conclusion *n* [kən'klu:ʒn]	They **came to the** ~ that he had stolen the money.	Folgerung
belief *n* [bɪ'li:f]	the feeling that something is true	Glaube
incredible *adj* [ɪn'kredəbl]	≫ hard to believe	unglaublich
to judge *v* [dʒʌdʒ]	to form an opinion, to make a decision	beurteilen
to criticize *v* ['krɪtɪsaɪz] **-ise**	▶▶ to judge, to blame, ▶◀ to praise	kritisieren, beurteilen
to review *v* [rɪ'vju:]	They ~ed his film in the paper. (≫ considered and judged)	beurteilen, besprechen
judg(e)ment *n* ['dʒʌdʒmənt]	▶▶ opinion	Urteil, Meinung
review *n* [rɪ'vju:]	a written report on a book, play or film	Kritik, Besprechung

re- = "again"

re-arrange
re-enter
re-open

rebuild
redecorate
redo

tʃ	dʒ	θ	ð	ʃ	ʒ	ŋ	w	v
cheap	**j**ump	**th**ing	**th**en	**sh**op	plea**s**ure	sa**ng**	**w**et	**v**oice

criticism *n* ['krɪtɪsɪzəm]	She hates ~. (⩾ being criticized)	Kritik
critical *adj* ['krɪtɪkl]	He was ~ **of** my plan.	kritisch
critic *n* ['krɪtɪk]	a person who judges and writes about books, plays, films, etc	Kritiker
common sense *n* ['kɒmən sens]	If he has any ~ he'll leave as soon as possible.	gesunder Menschenverstand
philosophy *n* [fɪ'lɒsəfɪ]	the study of knowledge and truth	Philosophie
philosopher *n* [fɪ'lɒsəfə]	a person who studies philosophy	Philosoph
logic *n* ['lɒdʒɪk]	reasonable thinking	Logik
abstract *adj* ['æbstrækt]	▶◀ concrete	abstrakt
mental *adj* ['mentl]	▶◀ physical	geistig, Geistes-
to intend *v* [ɪn'tend]	Our aim is victory. We ~ to win.	beabsichtigen
intention *n* [ɪn'tenʃn]	She had no ~ of doing that.	Absicht
ambition *n* [æm'bɪʃn]	His sister is full of ~. (⩾ a strong desire for success)	Ehrgeiz
	It's his ~ to be a filmstar. (▶▶ aim)	Ziel, Wunsch
ambitious *adj* [æm'bɪʃəs]	She's ~ to succeed in her work. (⩾ she has a strong desire)	ehrgeizig
project *n* ['prɒdʒekt] **scheme** *n* [ski:m]	▶▶ plan	Projekt, Plan
resolution *n* [rezə'lu:ʃn]	He made a ~ to work more. (▶▶ decision)	Entschluß
expectation *n* [ɪkspek'teɪʃn]	Did the film **come up to your** ~s?	Erwartung
to think of *v + prep* [θɪŋk] **to recall** *v* [rɪ'kɔ:l]	I **can't** ~ his name. (▶▶ remember)	sich erinnern
to omit *v* [ə'mɪt] **to leave out** *v + adv* [li:v]	▶◀ to include	auslassen, unterlassen
to skip *v* [skɪp]	They ~ped lunch and had a drink instead. (▶◀ left out)	überspringen, ausfallen lassen
memory *n* ['memərɪ]	When you have a good ~ you can remember things well.	Gedächtnis, Erinnerung
forgetful *adj* [fə'getfʊl]	He's very ~ of things.	vergeßlich
fame *n* [feɪm]	His films brought him ~.	Ruhm
distinguished *adj* [dɪ'stɪŋgwɪʃt]	Einstein was a ~ scientist. (▶▶ famous)	ausgezeichnet, berühmt
outstanding *adj* [aʊt'stændɪŋ]	▶▶ excellent; very important and famous	herausragend
to get *v informal* [get]	I'm afraid I don't ~ it. (▶▶ understand)	kapieren, verstehen
to misunderstand *v* [mɪsʌndə'stænd] **misunderstood** [mɪsʌndə'stʊd] **misunderstood** [mɪsʌndə'stʊd]	to understand in the wrong way	mißverstehen
comprehension *n* [kɒmprɪ'henʃn]	▶▶ understanding	Verständnis(test)
recognition *n* [rekəg'nɪʃn]	When I met her after five years, she showed no sign of ~.	Erkennen
	He got the money **in** ~ **of** his work.	Anerkennung
to train *v* [treɪn]	She's ~ed her children well.	erziehen; trainieren
	Kim is ~ing to be a teacher. (⩾ studying)	(sich) ausbilden (lassen)
learning *n* ['lɜ:nɪŋ]	Universities are centres of ~.	Gelehrsamkeit, Gelehrtheit
by heart [baɪ 'hɑ:t]	He **knows/learns it** ~ so that he is able to repeat it from memory.	auswendig
smart *adj* [smɑ:t]	⩾ clever and quick	gewitzt, pfiffig

6

i:	ɪ	e	æ	ɑ:	ɒ	ɔ:	ʊ	u:	ʌ	ɜ:	ə
eat	bit	ten	bad	fast	got	saw	sure	too	cut	bird	about

subtle *adj* ['sʌtl]	That's a ~ plan. (▶▶ very clever)	ausgeklügelt
intelligence *n* [ɪn'telɪdʒəns]	the ability to learn and understand	Intelligenz
cleverness *n* ['klevənɪs]	≫ being clever	Schlauheit, Klugheit
wisdom *n* ['wɪzdəm]	W~ often comes with age.	Weisheit
genius *n* ['dʒi:nɪəs]	Einstein was a ~. (≫ very clever person)	Genie; Begabung
gift *n* [gɪft]	a natural ability to do something	Begabung
talent *n* ['tælənt]	Bob has a ~ for painting.	Talent
competence *n* ['kɒmpɪtəns]	▶▶ skill	Geschicktheit
capacity *n* [kə'pæsətɪ]	Your ~ for remembering numbers is very great. (▶▶ ability)	Fähigkeit
tact *n* [tækt]	the ability to say or do the right thing at the right time	Takt(gefühl)
tactful *adj* ['tæktfʊl]	Be ~ with him. Don't show that you are angry.	taktvoll
skilled *adj* [skɪld]	Lionel is ~ in repairing watches.	geschickt in
capable *adj* ['keɪpəbl]	He is ~ of doing better. (≫ able to do)	fähig zu
competent *adj* ['kɒmpɪtənt]	▶▶ capable, able	fähig, kompetent
talented *adj* ['tæləntɪd] **gifted** *adj* ['gɪftɪd]	Joan is very ~.	talentiert
slow *adj* [sləʊ]	Mildred is a little ~ at school.	schwerfällig, langsam von Begriff
uneducated *adj* [ʌn'edʒʊkeɪtɪd]	≫ without (good) education	ungebildet
incapable *adj* [ɪn'keɪpəbl]	She's ~ **of** stealing. (≫ not able to steal)	unfähig zu
tactless *adj* ['tæktlɪs]	It was ~ of you to mention the trip to Dave. He can't afford to go.	taktlos
ignorance *n* ['ɪgnərəns]	▶◀ knowledge	Unkenntnis
to ignore *v* [ɪg'nɔ:]	▶◀ to pay attention to	nicht beachten
sane *adj* [seɪn]	≫ healthy in mind; ▶◀ mad	geistig gesund
dumb *adj AE* [dʌm]	▶▶ stupid	dumm
crazy *adj* ['kreɪzɪ] **insane** *adj* [ɪn'seɪn]	▶▶ mad	verrückt
ridiculous *adj* [rɪ'dɪkjʊləs]	≫ very foolish or silly	lächerlich
madness *n* ['mædnɪs]	It's ~ to do a thing like that!	Wahnsinn, Verrücktheit

6.2 Speaking and talking

to speak *v* [spi:k] **spoke** [spəʊk] **spoken** ['spəʊkən]	My father doesn't ~ Spanish.	sprechen
to say *v* [seɪ] **said** [sed] **said** [sed]	I can't ~ when he'll be back.	sagen
to tell *v* [tel] **told** [təʊld] **told** [təʊld]	T~ me the whole story. You should always ~ the truth.	erzählen sagen
to call *v* [kɔ:l]	They ~ed him Lionel.	nennen
to name *v* [neɪm]	▶▶ to call	(be)nennen

adj	*adv*	*art*	*conj*	*n*	*pl*	*prep*	*pron*	*sing*
adjective	adverb(ial)	article	conjunction	noun	plural	preposition	pronoun	singular

to talk *v* [tɔːk]	Animals can't ~. (▶▶ speak)	sprechen
to speak to *v + prep* [spiːk]	▶▶ to talk to	reden, Rede halten
conversation *n* [kɒnvəˈseɪʃn]	He interrupted our ~.	Unterhaltung
speech *n* [spiːtʃ]	The Prime Minister **gave/made a** ~ on TV last week. (▶▶ long talk)	Rede
talk *n* [tɔːk]	He gave a ~ on physics. She had a ~ with him. (▶▶ conversation)	Rede (über) Gespräch
to interrupt *v* [ɪntəˈrʌpt]	He ~ed Jill while she was speaking.	unterbrechen.
to shout *v* [ʃaʊt]	He ~ed for help.	(an)schreien (heraus)schreien
to cry *v* [kraɪ]	▶▶ to shout	schreien (um)
to call *v* [kɔːl]		
to scream *v* [skriːm]	People ~ed **with** terror when the fire broke out.	schreien, kreischen
shout *n* [ʃaʊt]	She gave a loud ~ to warn him.	Schrei
scream *n* [skriːm]	a loud high cry	Schrei
to repeat *v* [rɪˈpiːt]	≫ to say or do again	wiederholen
to explain *v* [ɪkˈspleɪn]	E~ the problem **to** me. (≫ Make . . . clear)	erklären
to describe *v* [dɪˈskraɪb]	Try to ~ the gangster. (≫ say what . . . is like)	beschreiben
to express *v* [ɪkˈspres]	He ~ed his thanks for her help.	äußern, ausdrücken
to talk about *v + prep* [tɔːk]	▶▶ to speak about	sprechen über
explanation *n* [ekspləˈneɪʃn]	There are several ~s for the accident.	Erklärung
to discuss *v* [dɪˈskʌs]	They ~ed the matter with their boss. (▶▶ talked about)	diskutieren, sprechen über
to argue *v* [ˈɑːgjuː]	to give reasons to support an opinion	argumentieren
discussion *n* [dɪˈskʌʃn]	They had a ~ **on** the matter.	Diskussion, Debatte
argument *n* [ˈɑːgjʊmənt]	reasons given to support an opinion	Argument, Grund

HAVE	**. . . an argument**	streiten	**. . . a bath**	baden	**. . . a drink**	etwas trinken
	. . . a game	spielen	**. . . a look**	ansehen	**. . . a rest**	sich ausruhen
	. . . a sleep	schlafen	**. . . a swim**	schwimmen	**. . . a talk**	sich unterhalten

6

debate *n* [dɪˈbeɪt]	Parliament **held a** ~ **on** nuclear energy.	Debatte
to mention *v* [ˈmenʃn]	▶▶ to speak of	erwähnen
to ask *v* [ɑːsk]	He ~ed her a question. They ~ed him to leave.	fragen auffordern
question *n* [ˈkwestʃən]	Mary didn't answer my ~.	Frage
inquiry *n* [ɪnˈkwaɪərɪ] **enquiry** *n* [ɪnˈkwaɪərɪ]	She **made** ~**ies** about her stolen handbag. (≫ asked for information)	Nachforschung, Erkundigung
doubt *n* [daʊt]	▶▶ uncertainty	Zweifel
to doubt *v* [daʊt]	≫ to be uncertain about	(be)zweifeln
to make sure [meɪkˈʃʊə]	≫ to find out for certain	sich vergewissern
to answer *v* [ˈɑːnsə]	▶◀ to ask	(be)antworten
to reply *v* [rɪˈplaɪ]	▶▶ to answer	antworten auf
answer *n* [ˈɑːnsə] **reply** *n* [rɪˈplaɪ]	I said 'hello' but he gave no ~.	Antwort
to ask for *v + prep* [ɑːsk]	Let's ~ a drink. (≫ say that we want)	bitten um
to excuse *v* [ɪkˈskjuːz]	Please ~ me for being late.	entschuldigen

to admit *v* [ədˈmɪt]	He ~ed his mistake.	eingestehen
excuse *n* [ɪkˈskjuːs]	She has no ~ for being late.	Entschuldigung
pardon *n* [ˈpɑːdn]	I beg your ~? Can you say that again?	Verzeihung
pardon *interj* [ˈpɑːdn]	P~? (≽ What did you say?)	Wie bitte?
to forgive *v* [fəˈgɪv] **forgave** [fəˈgeɪv] **forgiven** [fəˈgɪvn]	I'll ~ you, but don't do it again.	vergeben, nachsehen
to promise *v* [ˈprɒmɪs]	She ~d to phone me.	versprechen
promise *n* [ˈprɒmɪs]	If you **make a** ~, you must keep it.	Versprechen
to suggest *v* [səˈdʒest]	John ~ed going for a walk.	vorschlagen
suggestion *n* [səˈdʒestʃən]	His ~ was that we should go to the meeting.	Vorschlag
to recommend *v* [rekəˈmend]	Can you ~ me a good restaurant?	empfehlen
advice *n* [ədˈvaɪs]	We asked the expert for his ~. (≽ opinion about what to do)	Rat, Ratschläge

GIVE	**... somebody some advice**	jemandem einen Rat geben	**... an answer**	eine Antwort geben
	... an explanation	eine Erklärung geben	**... some help**	Hilfe leisten
	... a reply	eine Antwort geben	**... somebody a kiss**	jemanden küssen
	... somebody trouble	jemandem Schwierigkeiten bereiten		

to order *v* [ˈɔːdə]	They ~ed me to leave the room. (►► told)	befehlen, anordnen
instruction *n* [ɪnˈstrʌkʃn]	Read the ~s before you use that machine.	Anweisung
direction *n* [dɪˈrekʃn]		
to support *v* [səˈpɔːt]	Nobody ~ed my plans. (≽ was in favour of)	unterstützen
support *n* [səˈpɔːt]	help and encouragement	Unterstützung
to warn *v* [wɔːn]	They ~ed him not to go near the edge of the cliff.	warnen
warning *n* [ˈwɔːnɪŋ]	When there is fog on the motorway, the ~ signs light up.	Warnung
to threaten *v* [ˈθretn]	The gangster ~ed him with a gun.	(be)drohen
to complain *v* [kəmˈpleɪn]	People are always ~ing about the high cost of living.	klagen über
to swear *v* [sweə] **swore** [swɔː] **sworn** [swɔːn]	Please don't ~ at me! (≽ use bad language)	fluchen
to accept *v* [əkˈsept]	I can't ~ your offer. (≽ say yes to)	akzeptieren, annehmen
to agree *v* [əˈgriː]	They ~d **to** our plan. She ~d **with** me. They ~d **on** a date for the next meeting.	einverstanden sein zustimmen übereinkommen
agreement *n* [əˈgriːmənt]	They are all in ~. (≽ all have the same opinion)	Übereinstimmung, Zustimmung
to refuse *v* [rɪˈfjuːz]	►◄ to accept	ablehnen, sich weigern, verweigern
to turn down *v + adv* [tɜːn]	►► refuse	abweisen
to mind *v* [maɪnd]	**Would you** ~ wait**ing** for a moment?	etwas dagegen haben

to mind is normally used in **Would you mind ...?**
Do you mind ...?
I don't mind ...

tʃ	dʒ	θ	ð	ʃ	ʒ	ŋ	w	v
cheap	**j**ump	**th**ing	**th**en	**sh**op	plea**s**ure	sa**ng**	**w**et	**v**oice

named *adj* [neɪmd]	A girl ~ Jill phoned a moment ago. (▶▶ called)	mit Namen, genannt
to chat *v* [tʃæt]	≫ to talk in a friendly way	plaudern
to inform *v* [ɪn'fɔ:m]	Please ~ me **of** your plans. (≫ tell me about)	informieren (über)
to contact *v* ['kɒntækt]	Have you ~ed her? (▶▶ written, phoned, talked to)	Verbindung aufnehmen mit
to communicate *v* [kə'mju:nɪkeɪt]	to talk, write, pass information to	mitteilen, sich verständigen
speaker *n* ['spi:kə]	someone who speaks e.g. to an audience	Sprecher, Redner
chat *n* [tʃæt]	a friendly conversation	Plauderei, Gespräch
conference *n* ['kɒnfərəns]	a meeting for discussions	Konferenz
dialogue *n* ['daɪəlɒg] **dialog** *n AE*	a written conversation in a story or play	Dialog
lecture *n* ['lektʃə]	The professor gave a ~ to his students on modern history.	Vorlesung, Vortrag
cry *n* [kraɪ] **call** *n* [kɔ:l]	There was a ~ **for** help.	Rufen, Schrei
to whisper *v* ['wɪspə]	≫ to speak very softly	flüstern
to murmur *v* ['mɜ:mə]	The little boy ~ed in his sleep (≫ made a soft sound)	murmeln
to raise one's voice [reɪz, vɔɪs]	≫ to speak more loudly than normal	lauter reden
to remark *v* [rɪ'mɑ:k]	▶▶ to say, to comment	bemerken, anmerken
to comment *v* ['kɒment]	≫ to give an opinion	kommentieren
to congratulate *v* [kən'grætʃʊleɪt]	We ~d him **on** the birth of his son.	gratulieren, beglückwünschen
to compliment *v* ['kɒmplɪment]	The guests all ~ed Tom **on** his cooking.	loben, Komplimente machen
to praise *v* [preɪz]	The teacher ~d Jill for her good work. (▶◀ criticized)	loben
praise *n* [preɪz]	▶◀ criticism	Lob
to flatter *v* ['flætə]	to praise someone in order to please him/her	schmeicheln
remark *n* [rɪ'mɑ:k]	▶▶ a statement, a comment	Bemerkung
comment *n* ['kɒment]	an opinion given in speech or writing	Kommentar
compliment *n* ['kɒmplɪmənt]	You look very smart! – Thanks for the ~.	Kompliment
to declare *v* [dɪ'kleə]	I ~ the bazaar open. He ~d that he was innocent. (≫ said clearly)	erklären versichern, verkünden, behaupten
to announce *v* [ə'naʊns]	They ~d the date of the wedding.	ankündigen
announcement *n* [ə'naʊnsmənt]	The President wants to make an important ~.	Ankündigung, Bekanntmachung
declaration *n* [deklə'reɪʃn]	▶▶ announcement	Erklärung
statement *n* ['steɪtmənt]	The company has made a ~ to the press.	Aussage, Erklärung
to insist *v* [ɪn'sɪst]	I must ~ **on** it.	bestehen (auf)
to stress *v* [stres]	The Minister ~ed the need for more schools.	betonen, hervorheben
to emphasize *v* **-ise** ['emfəsaɪz]	▶▶ to stress	betonen

to underline *v* [ʌndəˈlaɪn]	Please ~ the following words in your text: ... (⩾ put a line under)	unterstreichen, hervorheben
emphasis *n* [ˈemfəsɪs]	stress put on certain words	Betonung
stress *n* [stres]	The ~ is on the first part of the word 'effort'.	Betonung
to exaggerate *v* [ɪgˈzædʒəreɪt]	You shouldn't ~ the seriousness of the affair.	übertreiben
to define *v* [dɪˈfaɪn]	⩾ to explain the meaning of	definieren
definition *n* [defɪˈnɪʃn]	You can find the ~ of the word in a dictionary.	Definition
description *n* [dɪˈskrɪpʃn]	She gave me a ~ **of** the place.	Beschreibung
to debate *v* [dɪˈbeɪt]	▶▶ to talk about, to discuss	debattieren, erörtern
to justify *v* [ˈdʒʌstɪfaɪ]	How can you ~ your behaviour? (⩾ give a good reason for)	rechtfertigen
to refer to *v + prep* [rɪˈfɜː]	▶▶ to speak about, to mention	sich beziehen auf
to quote *v* [kwəʊt]	He ~d Shakespeare. (⩾ repeated the exact words of)	zitieren
to raise *v* [reɪz]	She wants to ~ **the question/matter** at the next meeting. (▶▶ mention)	zur Sprache bringen, (eine Frage) aufwerfen
according to *prep* [əˈkɔːdɪŋ]	A~ Bill she is a silly girl. (⩾ Bill says that . . .)	laut, gemäß, nach
to look up *v + adv* [lʊk]	L~ the word in a dictionary.	nachschlagen
reference *n* [ˈrefrəns]	His book is full of ~s to contemporary history.	Hinweis, Verweis, Erwähnung
quotation *n* [kwəʊˈteɪʃn]	His book contained ~s from several authors.	Zitat
to propose *v* [prəˈpəʊz]	▶▶ to suggest	vorschlagen
to hint *v* [hɪnt]	⩾ to say indirectly	andeuten
to persuade *v* [pəˈsweɪd]	They ~d him of his mistake. I ~d her to go.	überzeugen überreden
to convince *v* [kənˈvɪns]	▶▶ to persuade	überzeugen
to assure *v* [əˈʃʊə]	They ~d us of his honesty.	zusichern
proposal *n* [prəˈpəʊzl]	▶▶ suggestion	Vorschlag
conviction *n* [kənˈvɪkʃn]	She was **speaking from** ~.	Überzeugung
hint *n* [hɪnt]	a small suggestion	Hinweis, Anspielung
to inquire *v* [ɪnˈkwaɪə] **to enquire** *v* [ɪnˈkwaɪə]	I don't know the date. I must ~. (⩾ ask for information)	erfragen, sich erkundigen
to question *v* [ˈkwestʃən]	The police ~ed the burglar.	verhören
to suspect *v* [səˈspekt]	Everybody ~ed him **of** murder.	verdächtigen
no doubt [daʊt] **without doubt**	⩾ it is certain	zweifellos
doubtful *adj* [ˈdaʊtfʊl]	▶◀ sure	zweifelhaft
doubtless *adj* [ˈdaʊtlɪs]	▶▶ certainly, very probably	zweifellos, sicher
suspicion *n* [səˈspɪʃn]	Mr Evans is **under** ~ **of** murder.	Verdacht; Mißtrauen
response *n* [rɪˈspɒns]	▶▶ answer, reaction	Antwort, Reaktion
to respond *v* [rɪˈspɒnd]	The pupils didn't ~ to the teacher's question. (▶▶ answer, react to)	antworten, reagieren
to demand *v* [dɪˈmɑːnd]	⩾ to ask for (as a right)	verlangen, fordern
to request *v* [rɪˈkwest]	The visitor ~ed a glass of water. (⩾ asked politely for)	bitten um, höflich ersuchen
to claim *v* [kleɪm]	to say that you have the right to	beanspruchen
to beg *v* [beg]	to ask for (e.g. money) as a gift	betteln; bitten

☐ **request** *n* [rɪ'kwest]	They will only come **on** ~. (≫ when asked for)	Bitte, Ersuchen
☐ **demand** *n* [dɪ'mɑ:nd]	There's a big ~ for these shoes. We're selling a lot of them.	Nachfrage, Bedarf
☐ **to blame** *v* [bleɪm]	She ~d the other man **for** the accident.	Schuld geben für; tadeln
☐ **complaint** *n* [kəm'pleɪnt]	Does he have any ~s against us?	Klage
☐ **to grumble** *v* ['grʌmbl]	to complain in a bad-tempered way	herumnörgeln
☐ **blame** *n* [bleɪm]	They **put the** ~ **on** her. (▶▶ responsibility, guilt)	Schuld
☐ **acceptable** *adj* [ək'septəbl]	Your standard of work is not ~. (≫ good enough)	annehmbar, akzeptabel
☐ **to confirm** *v* [kən'fɜ:m]	I'd like to ~ the details of my flight. (≫ make sure about)	bestätigen (lassen)
☐ **to approve of** *v + prep* [ə'pru:v]	I don't ~ his foolish behaviour.	zustimmen, billigen
☐ **compromise** *n* ['kɒmprəmaɪz]	an agreement in which each side gives up something	Kompromiß
☐ **to adopt** *v* [ə'dɒpt]	They ~ed our proposal. (▶▶ accepted)	annehmen
☐ **to apologize** *v* [ə'pɒlədʒaɪz]	≫ to say you are sorry	sich entschuldigen
☐ **apology** *n* [ə'pɒlədʒɪ]	I must **make an** ~ to my neighbour.	Entschuldigung
☐ **to guarantee** *v* [gærən'ti:]	▶▶ to promise	garantieren
☐ **guarantee** *n* [gærən'ti:]	She got a 1-year ~ with her new typewriter.	Garantie
☐ **to swear** *v* [sweə] **swore** [swɔ:] **sworn** [swɔ:n]	≫ to promise formally	schwören, geloben
☐ **recommendation** *n* [rekəmen'deɪʃn]	They gave him the job on my ~.	Empfehlung
☐ **to advise** *v* [əd'vaɪz]	▶▶ to recommend	(be)raten
☐ **you had better** [həd 'betə]	▶▶ you should/ought to	du solltest lieber
☐ **order** *n* ['ɔ:də]	An ~ tells you what to do. (▶▶ instruction, command)	Befehl, Anordnung
☐ **to obey** *v* [ə'beɪ]	Pupils should ~ their teachers. (≫ do what . . . tell them to do)	gehorchen, hören auf
☐ **threat** *n* [θret]	There have been several ~s against the Prime Minister's life.	Drohung
☐ **to deny** *v* [dɪ'naɪ]	He couldn't ~ the truth of the story. (▶◀ admit)	leugnen, abstreiten
☐ **to object** *v* [əb'dʒekt]	Does she ~ to smoking? (≫ Is she against smoking?)	etwas dagegen haben
☐ **refusal** *n* [rɪ'fju:zl]	She had to do it. R~ was impossible. (≫ saying no)	Weigerung, Ablehnung
☐ **objection** *n* [əb'dʒekʃn]	Do you have any ~s to/against our plan? (≫ reason to object, protest against)	Einwand, Einspruch Bedenken
☐ **denial** *n* [dɪ'naɪəl]	▶◀ admission	Ablehnung, Abweisung, Verneinung

6

6.3 Reading and writing

☐ **to write** *v* [raɪt] **wrote** [rəʊt] **written** ['rɪtn]	His girlfriend ~s him a letter every day.	schreiben
☐ **to write down** *v + adv* [raɪt]	W~ this address.	aufschreiben
☐ **to put down** *v + adv* [pʊt]		

to note down *v + adv* [nəʊt]	▶▶ to write down	niederschreiben
to type (out) *v + adv* [taɪp]	Please ~ the letter for me. (≫ write . . . with a typewriter)	mit der Maschine schreiben, tippen
to copy *v* ['kɒpɪ]	Please ~ this letter into your exercise book.	abschreiben
to sign *v* [saɪn]	≫ to write your name on	unterschreiben, unterzeichnen
signature *n* ['sɪgnətʃə]	the special way of writing one's name	Unterschrift
stamp *n* [stæmp]		Stempel
to stamp *v* [stæmp]	He ~ed the 5 receipts. (≫ put a stamp on)	stempeln
to read *v* [ri:d] **read** [red] **read** [red]	Granny ~s the boy a story every evening.	(vor)lesen
reader *n* ['ri:də]	a person who reads	Leser(in)
to spell *v* [spel] **spelt** [spelt] **spelt** [spelt]	Do you ~ 'doubt' with a 'b'?	buchstabieren
letter *n* ['letə]	A, B, C, . . . are ~s.	Buchstabe
capital (letter) *n* ['kæpɪtl]	A, B, C, . . . are ~s, a, b, c, . . . are not.	Großbuchstabe
print *n* [prɪnt]	I can't read the small ~ on this page.	Gedrucktes, Druck

Punctuation/Zeichensetzung

.	**full stop** *n BE*/**period** *AE* [fʊl'stɒp, 'pɪərɪəd]	'	**apostrophe** *n* [ə'pɒstrəfɪ]
.	**point** *n* [pɔɪnt]	' '	**quotation marks** *n* [kwəʊ'teɪʃn mɑ:ks]
,	**comma** *n* ['kɒmə]	:	**colon** *n* ['kəʊlən]
;	**semicolon** *n* [semɪ'kəʊlən]	-	**hyphen** *n* ['haɪfn]
?	**question mark** *n* ['kwestʃn mɑ:k]	–	**dash** *n* [dæʃ]
!	**exclamation mark** *n* [eksklə'meɪʃn mɑ:k]	( )	**brackets** *n* ['brækɪts]

pen *n* [pen]		Federhalter, Füller
ball pen *n* ['bɔ:l pen]		Kugelschreiber
pencil *n* ['pensl]		(Blei)stift
paper *n* ['peɪpə]		Papier
typewriter *n* ['taɪpraɪtə]		Schreibmaschine
sheet *n* [ʃi:t]	a piece of paper	Blatt
form *n* [fɔ:m]	Please fill in this ~.	Formular
list *n* [lɪst]	She made a ~ of the things she wanted to buy.	Liste
arrangement *n* [ə'reɪndʒmənt]	They made ~s to sell the car.	Abmachung
card *n* [kɑ:d]	Send me a Christmas ~.	Karte
page *n* [peɪdʒ]	The exercise is on ~ 56.	Seite
letter *n* ['letə]	Yesterday the postman brought me a ~.	Brief
note *n* [nəʊt]	a short letter	Notiz
notebook *n* ['nəʊtbʊk] ①		Notizheft, Notizblock
postcard *n* ['pəʊstkɑ:d] ②		Postkarte
address *n* [ə'dres] ③		Adresse
envelope *n* ['envələʊp] ④		Briefumschlag, Kuvert

tʃ	dʒ	θ	ð	ʃ	ʒ	ŋ	w	v
cheap	jump	thing	then	shop	pleasure	sang	wet	voice

book *n* [bʊk]		Buch
story *n* ['stɔ:rɪ]	She wrote a good ~.	Geschichte
poem *n* ['pəʊɪm]	a piece of writing in verse	Gedicht
brochure *n* ['brəʊʃə]	He brought along some holiday ~s.	Broschüre, Prospekt
report *n* [rɪ'pɔ:t]	I read a ~ about the accident.	Bericht
record *n* ['rekɔ:d]	exact notes about past actions or events	Niederschrift, Aufzeichnung
article *n* ['ɑ:tɪkl]	a piece of writing (in a newspaper or magazine)	Zeitungsartikel
heading *n* ['hedɪŋ]		Überschrift
title *n* ['taɪtl]	the name of a book, film etc	Titel
chapter *n* ['tʃæptə]	I've just read ~ 6 of this book. (≫ part)	Kapitel
copy *n* ['kɒpɪ]	Please buy three ~ies of today's newspaper.	Exemplar
writer *n* ['raɪtə]	a person who writes books, stories etc	Schriftsteller
library *n* ['laɪbrərɪ]	a building where books can be borrowed	Bibliothek
reading *n* ['ri:dɪŋ]	His hobby is ~.	Lesen, Lektüre
writing *n* ['raɪtɪŋ]	The Japanese use a different system of ~.	Schreiben, Schrift
draft *n* [drɑ:ft]	the first rough form of a letter, etc	Entwurf, Skizze
in writing ['raɪtɪŋ]	▶▶ written	schriftlich
handwriting *n* ['hændraɪtɪŋ]	I can't read the doctor's ~.	Handschrift
shorthand *n* ['ʃɔ:thænd]	S~ is a way of writing quickly, with special signs	Kurzschrift, Steno
italics *n* [ɪ'tælɪks]	The word ***history*** is in ~.	Kursivdruck
alphabet *n* ['ælfəbet]	the letters from A to Z	Alphabet
spelling *n* ['spelɪŋ]	the way of writing a word correctly	Rechtschreibung, Buchstabieren

Beginning a letter

Neutral	**Informal**	**Formal**
Dear Mr Williams, Mrs White, Miss Guthrie, John,	Dear Pat, My dear Pete,	Dear Sir, Dear Madam,

Ending a letter

Neutral	**Informal**	**Formal**
(with best wishes) Yours sincerely, *BE* Sincerely yours, *AE* James Cook	(Best wishes) Yours, Love, Lots of love, Mike	Yours faithfully, J K Smith (Personnel Manager)

i:	ɪ	e	æ	ɑ:	ɒ	ɔ:	ʊ	u:	ʌ	ɜ:	ə
eat	bit	ten	bad	fast	got	saw	sure	too	cut	bird	about

code *n* [kəʊd]	a system of secret writing	Kode
dot *n* [dɒt]	The 'i' has a ~ over it.	Punkt
to dot *v* [dɒt]	D~ the i, please. (⩾ put a dot on)	punktieren, pünkteln
rubber *n* ['rʌbə] **eraser** *n AE* [ɪ'reɪzə]		Radiergummi
to erase *v* [ɪ'reɪz]	to remove with a rubber	ausradieren
stationery *n* ['steɪʃənrɪ]	writing materials (2)	Schreibwaren
label *n* ['leɪbl] (1)		Etikette, Aufkleber
pad *n* [pæd] (2)		(Schreib)Block
ruler *n* ['ru:lə] (3)		Lineal

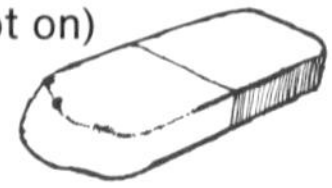

(1)

(2)

(3)

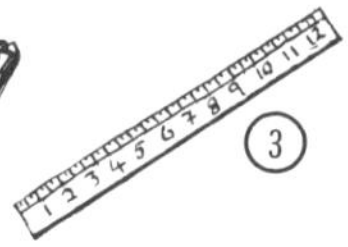

seal *n* [si:l]	a piece of wax on the back of a letter	Siegel
to seal *v* [si:l]	The letter was signed and ~ed. (⩾ closed tightly)	versiegeln
file *n* [faɪl]	Please put all the letters on my table in a ~.	(Brief/Akten)Ordner
register *n* ['redʒɪstə]	an official list (of e.g. names)	Verzeichnis, Liste, Register
to register *v* ['redʒɪstə]	to put (e.g. a name) on a list	registrieren, eintragen
document *n* ['dɒkjʊmənt]	a paper giving important information	Dokument
papers *n* ['peɪpəz]	Can I see your ~, please?	(Ausweis)Papiere
headline *n* ['hedlaɪn]	'40 KILLED IN BOMB ATTACK' was the ~ in the Evening News.	Schlagzeile
summary *n* ['sʌmərɪ]	I've written a short ~ of what was said at the meeting.	Zusammenfassung
to sum up *v + adv* [sʌm]	to give the main points (of what has been said)	zusammenfassen
introduction *n* [ɪntrə'dʌkʃn]	The ~ at the beginning of the book tells you what it is about.	Einleitung
contents *n* ['kɒntents]	(the list of) things written in a book	Inhalt(sverzeichnis)
ending *n* ['endɪŋ]	She likes stories with happy ~s.	Ende *(Geschichte, Film)*
paragraph *n* ['pærəgrɑ:f]	A ~ starts on a new line.	Absatz *(Text)*
appendix *n* [ə'pendɪks]	a part with extra information at the end of a book	Anhang
cover *n* ['kʌvə]	the outside of a book	Einband(deckel)
volume *n* ['vɒlju:m]	one of a series of books	Band
leaflet *n* ['li:flɪt]	a small printed piece of paper containing information	Flugblatt, Prospekt Broschüre
textbook *n* ['tekstbʊk]	Where is your English ~?	(Lehr)Buch
catalogue *n* ['kætəlɒg] **catalog** *n AE*	a list of e.g. names, places or goods	Katalog
classical *adj* ['klæsɪkl]	I'm fond of ~ literature.	klassisch
literature *n* ['lɪtrətʃə]	e.g. novels, plays, poetry	Literatur
poetry *n* ['pəʊɪtrɪ]	He gave her a book of ~. (▶▶ poems)	Dichtung
verse *n* [vɜ:s]	He wrote the poem in 7 ~s.	Vers, Strophe
limerick *n* ['lɪmərɪk]	a special type of amusing poem of five lines	Limerick
rhyme *n* [raɪm]	Not all poets use ~.	Reim
to rhyme *v* [raɪm]	'But' ~s with 'hut'.	sich reimen
fiction *n* ['fɪkʃn]	stories or novels which tell about imaginary events	frei erfundene Erzählung, Dichtung
novel *n* ['nɒvl]	*'Oliver Twist'* is a ~.	Roman
science fiction *n* [saɪəns 'fɪkʃn]	stories about future times on Earth or in space	Science Fiction
author *n* ['ɔ:θə]	▶▶ a writer	Autor, Verfasser

adj	*adv*	*art*	*conj*	*n*	*pl*	*prep*	*pron*	*sing*
adjective	adverb(ial)	article	conjunction	noun	plural	preposition	pronoun	singular

poet *n* ['pəʊɪt]	a person who writes poems	Poet, Dichter
editor *n* ['edɪtə]	a person who prepares books or newspapers for printing	Herausgeber, Redakteur
publisher *n* ['pʌblɪʃə]	a person who brings out books or newspapers	Verleger, Verlag
to print *v* [prɪnt]	The newspaper is ~ed daily.	drucken
to publish *v* ['pʌblɪʃ]	to bring out a book, newspaper or magazine	veröffentlichen
to issue *v* ['ɪʃu:]	▶▶ to bring out, to publish	publizieren, veröffentlichen
issue *n* ['ɪʃu:]	Have you read the latest ~ of *TIME* magazine?	Ausgabe
edition *n* [ɪ'dɪʃn]	There is no paperback ~ of this book.	Ausgabe, Auflage
publication *n* [pʌblɪ'keɪʃn]	a book or magazine that has been brought out	Veröffentlichung
bookshop *n* ['bʊkʃɒp]	a shop that sells books	Buchhandlung
librarian *n* [laɪ'breərɪən]	A ~ works in a library.	Bibliothekar(in)

6.4 Communication and the media

sign *n* [saɪn]		Zeichen; Schild
signal *n* ['sɪgnəl]		Signal
to mean *v* [mi:n] **meant** [ment] **meant** [ment]	'Zeit' in German ~s 'time' in English. He ~s to leave tomorrow. (▶▶ intends)	bedeuten beabsichtigen
meaning *n* ['mi:nɪŋ]	Some words have two different ~s.	Bedeutung

opinion, view	**Meinung**	**meaning** ['mi:nɪŋ]	Bedeutung, Sinn
to think	**meinen**	**to mean** [mi:n]	bedeuten
severe	**streng**	**strong** [strɒŋ]	stark, kräftig
recipe, prescription	**Rezept**	**receipt** [rɪ'si:t]	Quittung, Empfang

sense *n* [sens]	▶▶ meaning	Sinn, Bedeutung
nonsense *n* ['nɒnsns]	▶▶ rubbish	Unsinn
information *n* [ɪnfə'meɪʃn]	That's an interesting **piece of** ~. (▶▶ knowledge)	Information
news *n* [nju:z]	He heard the bad ~ on the radio. This is an important **piece/item of** ~.	Nachricht(en)
message *n* ['mesɪdʒ]	a piece of information sent to someone	Botschaft, Mitteilung
post *n BE* [pəʊst]	They sent the parcel **by** ~.	Post
to post *v* [pəʊst]	Please ~ this postcard for me.	zur Post geben, abschicken
post office *n* ['pəʊst ɒfɪs]	a building where you can send letters, parcels and buy stamps	Postamt
postman *n* ['pəʊstmən] **postwoman** *n* ['pəʊstwʊmən]	a man/woman who takes letters etc to people's houses	Postbote, Briefträger(in)
to send *v* [send] **sent** [sent] **sent** [sent]	I'll ~ you the money by post.	(ab)schicken, senden
to deliver *v* [dɪ'lɪvə]	▶◀ to collect	austragen, liefern
parcel *n* ['pɑ:sl]	I got a ~ in the post yesterday.	Paket
postage *n* ['pəʊstɪdʒ]	the money you must pay when you send a letter	Briefporto, Postgebühr
stamp *n* [stæmp]		Briefmarke

6

telegram *n* ['telɪgræm]	a fast message sent by electric signals	Telegramm
airmail *n* ['eəmeɪl]		Luftpost
telephone *n* ['telɪfəʊn] **phone** *n* [fəʊn]		Telefon
call *n* [kɔ:l] **ring** *n* [rɪŋ]	≫ a telephone call Give me a ~ when you're back.	Anruf
to telephone *v* ['telɪfəʊn] **to phone** *v* [fəʊn] **to ring (up)** *v* [rɪŋ]	I'll ~ you this afternoon. (≫ speak to you by telephone)	anrufen, telephonieren
to ring back *v* [rɪŋ]	≫ to telephone in reply	zurückrufen
press *n* [pres]	▶▶ newspapers	Presse
newspaper *n* ['nju:speɪpə] ① **paper** *n* ['peɪpə]		Zeitung
magazine *n* [mægə'zi:n] ②		Zeitschrift
daily *n* ['deɪlɪ]	He always buys three ~ies.	Tageszeitungen
weekly *n* ['wiklɪ]	a paper or magazine coming out once a week	Wochenzeitung
to report *v* [rɪ'pɔ:t]	The newspapers ~ important events. (▶▶ write about)	berichten über, melden
radio *n* ['reɪdɪəʊ]	They heard the news **on the** ~.	Radio
television *n* ['telɪvɪʒn] **TV** *n* [ti:'vi:]	I'd like to watch ~ tonight.	Fernsehen
television (set) *n* ['telɪvɪʒn set]		Fernsehgerät
to turn on *v + adv* [tɜ:n]	Please ~ the radio ~. (≫ put . . . on)	einschalten
to turn off *v + adv* [tɜ:n]	▶◀ to turn on	aus/abschalten
programme *n* ['prəʊgræm] **program** *n AE*	I saw a good ~ on TV last night.	Sendung
advertisement *n* [əd'vɜ:tɪsmənt] **ad** *n* [æd]	He put an ~ in the daily newspaper.	Anzeige, Reklame, Werbung
cinema *n* ['sɪnəmə]	Let's go to the ~ tomorrow.	Kino
film *n* [fɪlm]	Let's see the new James Bond ~.	Film
communication *n* [kəmju:nɪ'keɪʃn]	the exchange of information, news or opinions	Kommunikation, Gedankenaustausch
to signal *v* ['sɪgnəl] **to sign** *v* [saɪn]	She ~led to the waiter to bring the menu. (≫ gave a sign)	signalisieren, zu verstehen geben
to signify *v* ['sɪgnɪfaɪ]	▶▶ to mean	bedeuten, bezeichnen
symbol *n* ['sɪmbl]	Red is a ~ of danger.	Symbol, Sinnbild
symbolic *adj* [sɪm'bɒlɪk]	There was a ~ handshake between the two politicians.	symbolisch
gesture *n* ['dʒestʃə]	He made an unfriendly ~.	Geste, Gebärde
by word of mouth [wɜ:d, maʊθ]	≫ by speaking and not by writing	mündlich
rumour *n* ['ru:mə] **rumor** *n AE*	I've heard a ~ that the President is very ill.	Gerücht
gossip *n* ['gɒsɪp]	unkind talk about other people's private lives	Klatsch, Tratsch
messenger *n* ['mesɪndʒə]	a person who carries information from one place to another	Bote

tʃ	dʒ	θ	ð	ʃ	ʒ	ŋ	w	v
cheap	**j**ump	**th**ing	**th**en	**sh**op	plea**s**ure	sa**ng**	**w**et	**v**oice

correspondence *n* [kɒrɪ'spɒndəns]	I've been in ~ with him for 15 years.	Briefwechsel
to correspond *v* [kɒrɪ'spɒnd]	≫ to exchange letters	korrespondieren, (sich) entsprechen
mail *n AE* [meɪl]	letters, parcels etc sent by post	Post
postcode *n* ['pəʊstkəʊd] **zip code** *n AE* ['zɪp kəʊd]		Postleitzahl
postal *adj* ['pəʊstl]	≫ of the post	Post-
poste restante *n, adj* [pəʊst 'restɑ:nt]	She went to the ~ counter in the post.	postlagernd
letterbox *n* ['letəbɒks] ①		Briefkasten
pillar-box *n* ['pɪləbɒks] ②		Postkasten
to call up *v + adv* [kɔ:l]	▶▶ to phone	anrufen
telephone box *n* ['telɪfəʊn bɒks] ③ **telephone booth** *n T* ['telɪfəʊn bu:ð] **phone booth** *n* ['fəʊn bu:ð]		Telefonzelle, Fernsprechzelle
receiver *n* [rɪ'si:və] ④		Telefonhörer
telephone number *n* ['telɪfəʊn nʌmbə]	I can't remember his ~! – It's Hammersmith 2644.	Telefonnummer
operator *n* ['ɒpəreɪtə]		Vermittlung
to dial *v* ['daɪəl]	D~ 999 to get the police.	wählen *(Telefon)*
to hang on *v + adv* [hæŋ]	Please ~. The line is busy. (▶▶ wait)	warten, ausharren
to hang up *v + adv* [hæŋ]	to put the receiver down	auflegen, einhängen
media *n* ['mi:dɪə]	Newspapers, radio and television are (news) ~.	Medien
mass media *n* [mæs 'mi:dɪə]	media such as newspapers and TV which reach a great number of people	Massenmedien
periodical *n* [pɪərɪ'ɒdɪkl]	a magazine that is issued regularly	Zeitschrift
journalist *n* ['dʒɜ:nəlɪst]	a person who writes articles for newspapers or magazines	Journalist(in)
reporter *n* [rɪ'pɔ:tə]	Several ~s drove to the scene of the crime.	Reporter(in)
newsagent *n* ['nju:zeɪdʒənt]	a person who sells newspapers and magazines	Zeitungshändler
station *n* ['steɪʃn]	Sabine works for a **radio** ~.	Rundfunkstation
channel *n* ['tʃænl]	Which ~ is the concert on?	Frequenz, Kanal
wireless (set) *n* ['waɪəlɪs set]	▶▶ radio	Radiogerät
video *n, adj* ['vɪdɪəʊ]	Hundreds of films are available on ~ cassettes.	Video
video recorder *n* ['vɪdɪəʊ rɪkɔ:də]		Videorecorder
broadcast *n* ['brɔ:dkɑ:st]	This is a BBC English language ~. (▶▶ programme)	Sendung
to broadcast *v* ['brɔ:dkɑ:st] **broadcast** ['brɔ:dkɑ:st] **broadcast** ['brɔ:dkɑ:st]	The BBC ~s every day. (≫ sends out radio or TV programmes)	senden
to receive *v* [rɪ'si:v]	The ship ~d a radio message.	empfangen
receiver *n* [rɪ'si:və]	equipment that can receive messages	Empfänger

6

i:	ɪ	e	æ	ɑ:	ɒ	ɔ:	ʊ	u:	ʌ	ɜ:	ə
eat	bit	ten	bad	fast	got	saw	sure	too	cut	bird	about

announcer *n* [ə'naʊnsə]	The ~ told viewers about the next programme.	Sprecher *(Radio/TV)*
to switch on *v + adv* [swɪtʃ]	▶▶ to turn on	einschalten
to switch off *v + adv* [swɪtʃ]	▶▶ to turn off	ausschalten
viewer *n* ['vju:ə]	a person watching TV etc	(Fernseh)Zuschauer
soap opera *n* ['səʊp ɒprə]	'Dallas' is an American ~.	Familienserie
documentary *n* [dɒkjʊ'mentərɪ]	a film that gives information on a particular subject	Dokumentarfilm
feature *n* ['fi:tʃə]	a full-length film, the main film	Spielfilm
movie *n AE* ['mu:vɪ]	a cinema film	Film *(Kino)*
pictures *n* ['pɪktʃəz] **movies** *n AE* ['mu:vɪz]	Let's go to the ~ tonight! (▶▶ cinema)	Kino
to advertise *v* ['ædvətaɪz]	They ~d in all the papers.	werben, inserieren
commercial *n* [kə'mɜ:ʃl]	a TV or radio advertisement	Werbung *(Radio/TV)*
slogan *n* ['sləʊgən]	e.g. 'Allan's beer is super'	Werbespruch

6.5 Language and grammar

language *n* ['læŋgwɪdʒ]	Chinese is a difficult ~ to learn.	Sprache
slang *n* [slæŋ]	A ~ word for policeman is 'copper'.	Slang
voice *n* [vɔɪs]	The sound that you make when you speak or sing is called your ~.	Stimme
to pronounce *v* [prə'naʊns]	Don't ~ the 'l' in 'half'.	aussprechen
text *n* [tekst]	There is too much ~ in the book and there aren't enough pictures.	Text
sentence *n* ['sentəns]	A ~ contains a subject and a verb.	Satz
expression *n* [ɪk'spreʃn]	'To kick the bucket' is a slang ~ for 'to die'. (⋙ group of words)	Ausdruck
word *n* [wɜ:d]	There are thousands of ~s in the dictionary.	Wort
name *n* [neɪm]	Does your dog have a ~? Yes, it's called 'Rex'.	Name

Parts of speech – Wortarten/Satzteile

The	**man** in the	**green** shirt	**quickly**	**opened** the door
article	**noun**	**adjective**	**adverb**	**verb**
['ɑ:tɪkl]	[naʊn]	['ædʒɪktɪv]	['ædvɜ:b]	[vɜ:b]
Artikel	Hauptwort	Eigenschaftswort	Umstandswort	Tätigkeitswort

of	**his** car	**and** said	**"phew",**	**because it was so hot.**
preposition	**pronoun**	**conjunction/linking word**	**interjection**	**clause**
[prepə'zɪʃn]	['prəʊnaʊn]	[kən'dʒʌŋktʃn/'lɪŋkɪŋ wɜ:d]	[ɪntə'dʒekʃn]	[klɔ:z]
Verhältniswort	Fürwort	Bindewort	Ausruf	Nebensatz

subject *n* ['sʌbdʒɪkt]	Let's change the ~. I don't want to talk about mathematics.	Thema
to translate *v* [træns'leɪt]	Can you ~ this Spanish letter for me? (⋙ put . . . into English)	übersetzen
dictionary *n* ['dɪkʃənrɪ]	He bought a German-English ~.	Wörterbuch

adj	*adv*	*art*	*conj*	*n*	*pl*	*prep*	*pron*	*sing*
adjective	adverb(ial)	article	conjunction	noun	plural	preposition	pronoun	singular

☐	**foreign language** *n* ['fɒrɪn 'læŋgwɪdʒ]	He's learning two ~s.	Fremdsprache
☐	**mother tongue** *n* ['mʌðə tʌŋ]	My ~ is German. I was born in Germany.	Muttersprache
☐	**native language** *n* ['neɪtɪv 'læŋgwɪdʒ]		
☐	**accent** *n* ['æksənt]	He speaks English with a German ~.	Akzent
☐	**dialect** *n* ['daɪəlekt]	They're speaking in Scottish ~.	Dialekt
☐	**intonation** *n* [ɪntə'neɪʃn]	the rise and fall of a voice	Intonation
☐	**pronunciation** *n* [prənʌnsɪ'eɪʃn]	a way of saying a word	Aussprache
☐	**drawling** *adj* ['drɔ:lɪŋ]	≫ speaking slowly, making speech sounds longer than normal	schleppend
☐	**vocabulary** *n* [və'kæbjʊlərɪ]	all the words of a language	Wortschatz

grown-up	▶▶	adult	synonym ['sɪnənɪm]	Wort mit gleicher Bedeutung
long	▶◀	short	opposite ['ɒpəzɪt]	Gegenteil
incredible	≫	hard to believe	paraphrase ['pærəfreɪz]	Umschreibung
reader		a person who reads	definition [defɪ'nɪʃn]	Definition

☐	**phrase** *n* [freɪz]	a small group of words, e.g. "They arrived **after dinner.**"	Phrase
☐	**clause** *n* [klɔ:z]	a group of words containing a subject and a verb, forming part of a sentence	(Teil)Satz, Satzteil
☐	**question tag** *n* ['kwestʃn tæg]	". . ., isn't it?" is a ~.	Frageanhängsel
☐	**exclamation** *n* [eksklə'meɪʃn]	"Oh dear!" is an ~.	Ausruf
☐	**idiom** *n* ['ɪdɪəm]	e.g. 'It's raining cats and dogs.'	Redewendung
☐	**saying** *n* ['seɪɪŋ]	a well-known remark e.g. All's well that ends well!	Redensart, Sprichwort
☐	**proverb** *n* ['prɒvɜ:b]	'The early bird catches the worm' is an English ~.	Sprichwort
☐	**grammar** *n* ['græmə]	She's an expert **on** French ~.	Grammatik
☐	**colloquial** *adj* [kə'ləʊkwɪəl]	≫ used in everyday, spoken language	umgangssprachlich
☐	**oral** *adj* ['ɔ:rəl]	▶◀ written	mündlich, verbal
☐	**verbal** *adj* ['vɜ:bl]		
☐	**orally** *adv* ['ɔ:rəlɪ]	Let's do the exercise ~.	mündlich
☐	**fluent** *adj* ['flu:ənt]	His French is ~.	flüssig
☐	**passage** *n* ['pæsɪdʒ]	a part of a text	Passage, Stelle
☐	**context** *n* ['kɒntekst]	You can tell the meaning of this word from its ~.	Kontext, Textzusammenhang
☐	**topic** *n* ['tɒpɪk]	a subject for conversation	Thema, Gesprächsthema
☐	**theme** *n* [θi:m]		
☐	**matter** *n* ['mætə]	Let's discuss this ~ now. (▶▶ subject)	Angelegenheit, Thema
☐	**translation** *n* [træns'leɪʃn]	T~ into English is quite difficult.	Übersetzung
☐	**version** *n* ['vɜ:ʃn]	I've heard two different ~s of the story.	Version; Übersetzung

6

Tenses – Zeitformen

He **comes** here every day. — simple present [sɪmpl ˈpreznt]	Jim **is reading** a magazine. — present progressive/continuous [preznt prəˈgresɪv, kənˈtɪnjʊəs]
They **came** here last week. — simple past [sɪmpl ˈpɑ:st]	He **was reading** when she came. — past progressive/continuous [pɑ:st prəˈgresɪv, kənˈtɪnjʊəs]
She **will come** here next week. — future [ˈfju:tʃə]	They **will be working** here soon. — future progressive/continuous [fju:tʃə prəˈgresɪv, kənˈtɪnjʊəs]
She **has lived** here for years. — present perfect [preznt ˈpɜ:fɪkt]	He **has been reading** for two hours. — present perfect progressive/continuous [preznt ˈpɜ:fɪkt prəˈgresɪv, kənˈtɪnjʊəs]
He **had worked** for two hours . . . — past perfect [pɑ:st ˈpɜ:fɪkt]	She **had been working** there for two hours . . . — past perfect progressive/continuous [pɑ:st ˈpɜ:fɪkt prəˈgresɪv, kənˈtɪnjʊəs]
He **will have finished** by 8 o'clock. — future perfect [fju:tʃə ˈpɜ:fɪkt]	At 5 o'clock he **will have been working** for 12 hours. — future perfect progressive/continuous [fju:tʃə ˈpɜ:fɪkt prəˈgresɪv, kənˈtɪnjʊəs]

to interpret *v* [ɪnˈtɜ:prɪt]	He will ~ for me because I can't understand Chinese.	dolmetschen
interpreter *n* [ɪnˈtɜ:prɪtə]	a person who gives an oral translation	Dolmetscher
number *n* [ˈnʌmbə]	The word 'dogs' is plural in ~.	Numerus
singular *n, adj* [ˈsɪŋgʊlə]	'Cat' is ~ and 'cats' is plural.	Singular, Einzahl
plural *n, adj* [ˈplʊərəl]	'Cats' is a ~ noun.	Plural, Mehrzahl
countable *adj* [ˈkaʊntəbl]	'Knife' and 'fork' are ~ nouns.	zählbar
uncountable *adj* [ʌnˈkaʊntəbl]	'Sugar' and 'milk' are ~ nouns.	nicht zählbar
person *n* [ˈpɜ:sn]	'We' is the first ~ plural in English.	Person

Comparison – Steigerung

positive [ˈpɒzətɪv]	**comparative** [kəmˈpærətɪv]	**superlative** [su:ˈpɜ:lətɪv]
big	bigger	biggest
Positiv	Komparativ	Superlativ

tʃ	dʒ	θ	ð	ʃ	ʒ	ŋ	w	v
cheap	**jump**	**thing**	**then**	**shop**	**pleasure**	**sang**	**wet**	**voice**

Types of Sentences – Satztypen

positive	negative	interrogative	imperative	conditional
['pɒzətɪv]	['negətɪv]	[ɪntə'rɒgətɪv]	[ɪm'perətɪv]	[kən'dɪʃənl]
I like bananas.	I don't like hamburgers.	Do you like spinach?	Eat your porridge!	If you eat too many hamburgers, you'll get fat.
positiv, im Positiv	negativ, in der Verneinung	interrogativ, in der Frageform	imperativ, in der Befehlsform	konditional, in der Bedingungsform

voice *n* [vɔɪs]	Is the verb in the active or passive ~?	Aktiv oder Passiv (Genus des Verbs)
active *adj, n* ['æktɪv]	'The gangster killed the policeman' is in the ~ voice.	Aktiv, aktiv
passive *adj, n* ['pæsɪv]	'The policeman was killed by the gangster' is in the ~ voice.	Passiv, passiv
syllable *n* ['sɪləbl]	The word 'fat' has one ~. The word 'disagree' has three ~s.	Silbe
vowel *n* ['vaʊəl]	The letters a, e, i, o, u are ~s.	Vokal
consonant *n* ['kɒnsənənt]	e.g. b, c, d, f, g	Konsonant
voiced *adj* [vɔɪst]	e.g. [d] and [g] are ~ consonants	stimmhaft
voiceless *adj* ['vɔɪslɪs]	e.g. [f], [k] and [t] are ~ consonants	stimmlos

Parts of the sentence – Satzteile

The little girl	**gave**	**her mother**	**some flowers.**
subject	verb	indirect object	direct object
['sʌbdʒɪkt]	[vɜ:b]	[ɪndɪrekt 'ɒbdʒɪkt]	[dɪrekt 'ɒbdʒɪkt]
Satzgegenstand	Verb	indirektes Objekt	direktes Objekt

He **is a doctor.**	He tried **to kill** him.	He was **fighting** and	got **killed.**
predicate	infinitive	present participle	past participle
['predɪkət]	[ɪn'fɪnətɪv]	[preznt 'pɑ:tɪsɪpl]	[pɑ:st 'pɑ:tɪsɪpl]
Satzaussage	Infinitiv	Partizip Präsens	Partizip Perfekt

She **heard** **the burglar** because he **was coughing.**

heard the burglar	**was coughing**
transitive verb (vt)	intransitive verb (vi)
['trænsətɪv vɜ:b]	[ɪn'trænsətɪvɜ:b]
Verb mit direktem Objekt	Verb ohne direktes Objekt

He **walked** and **ran** 10 miles. Now he **is** tired and **must** relax.

walked	**ran**	**is** / **must**
regular verb	irregular verb	auxiliary verb/modal verb
['regjʊlə]	[ɪ'regjʊlə]	[ɔ:g'zɪlɪərɪ/'mɒdl vɜ:b]
Regelmäßiges Verb	Unregelmäßiges Verb	Hilfsverb/Modalverb

He said: "I am hungry".	He said (that) he was hungry.
direct speech [dɪrekt 'spi:tʃ]	indirect speech/reported speech [ɪndɪrekt/rɪpɔ:tɪd 'spi:tʃ]
direkte Rede	indirekte Rede

prefix *n* [ˈpriːfɪks]	e.g. un-, in, non-	Vorsilbe
suffix *n* [ˈsʌfɪks]	e.g. -able, -ible, -ment	Nachsilbe
prepositional *adj* [prepəˈzɪʃənl]	e.g. **in the morning, on the road, after breakfast** etc are ~ phrases	präpositional
phrasal verb *n* [ˈfreɪzl vɜːb]	"to give up" is a ~.	Verb-Adverb-Verbindung

6.6 Grammatical words and phrases

We use these words to talk about people (and things) . . .

Personal pronoun – Personalpronomen

. . . as subject	I [aɪ]	you [juː]	he [hiː]	she [ʃiː]	it [ɪt]	we [wiː]	you [juː]	they [ðeɪ]
. . . as object	me [miː]	you [juː]	him [hɪm]	her [hɜː]	it [ɪt]	us [ʌs]	you [juː]	them [ðem]

These words show that something belongs to somebody.

Possessive pronoun – Possessivpronomen

. . . with a noun	my [maɪ]	your [jɔː]	his [hɪz]	her [hɜː]	its [ɪts]	our [aʊə]	your [jɔː]	their [ðeə]
. . . without a noun	mine [maɪn]	yours [jɔːz]	his [hɪz]	hers [hɜːz]	–	ours [aʊəz]	yours [jɔːz]	theirs [ðeəz]

We use these words to talk about the same person/thing as in the subject of the sentence.

Reflexive pronoun – Reflexivpronomen

myself [maɪˈself	yourself jɔːˈself	himself hɪmˈself	herself hɜːˈself	itself ɪtˈself	ourselves aʊəˈselvz	yourselves jɔːˈselvz	themselves ðəmˈselvz]

Jane looked at herself (= at Jane)

each other *pron* [iːtʃ ˈʌðə] **one another** *pron* [wʌn əˈnʌðə]	Tom and Mary kissed ~. (≫ Tom kissed Mary and Mary kissed Tom).	einander, sich
some *adj* [sʌm, səm]	He went to the baker's and bought ~ cakes and ~ bread. (≫ a number of/≫ an amount of)	einige, etwas
some *pron* [sʌm]	S~ of the pupils came to the concert. (≫ a number/an amount)	einige, etwas
any *adj* [ˈenɪ]	Have you got ~ money? No, I don't have ~ money.	etwas, einige
any *pron* [ˈenɪ]	Do you want ~ of these? – Yes, I'd like some.	irgend etwas, irgendwelche
no *adj* [nəʊ]	They have ~ food. (≫ not any)	kein, keine
every *adj* [ˈevrɪ]	E~ family has a TV set. (≫ All the families have a TV set.)	jede(r, s)

adj	*adv*	*art*	*conj*	*n*	*pl*	*prep*	*pron*	*sing*
adjective	adverb(ial)	article	conjunction	noun	plural	preposition	pronoun	singular

Words with every some any no

	every	some	any	no
... for people:	**everyone** ['evrɪwʌn] **everybody** ['evrɪbɒdɪ] jeder	**someone** ['sʌmwʌn] **somebody** ['sʌmbɒdɪ] jemand	**anyone** ['enɪwʌn] **anybody** ['enɪbɒdɪ] irgendeiner	**no one** ['nəʊwʌn] **nobody** ['nəʊbɒdɪ] niemand
... for things:	**everything** ['evrɪθɪŋ] alles	**something** ['sʌmθɪŋ] etwas	**anything** ['enɪθɪŋ] etwas	**nothing** ['nʌθɪŋ] nichts
... for places:	**everywhere** ['evrɪweə] überall	**somewhere** ['sʌmweə] irgendwo	**anywhere** ['enɪweə] irgendwo	**nowhere** ['nəʊweə] nirgends

somehow *adv* ['sʌmhaʊ]	S~ he managed to get the piano through the door. (≫ in some way)	irgendwie
anyway *adv* ['enɪweɪ]	≫ in any case	sowieso, auf jeden Fall
the *art* [ðə, ðɪ]	I got a letter yesterday. Where is ~ letter?	der, die, das
a *art* [ə] **an** *art* [ən]	There's ~ man at the door.	ein(e)

Relative Pronouns

... for people

Subject (der, die, das)

The actor **who/(that)** played the part of James Bond was Sean Connery.

The gangster **who(m)/(that)** he looked for.

(den, die, das) Object

... for things

Subject (der, die, das)

The camera **which/that** filmed Sean Connery broke down.

The car **which/that** he used was a Jaguar.

(den, die, das) Object

Possessive dessen, deren

The girl **whose** father disappeared was Bond's girlfriend.

These words ask for

... things	**what** *pron, adj* [wɒt] (was)	... reason	**why** *adv* [waɪ] (warum)
... people	**who** *pron* [hu:] (wer)	... means	**how** *adv* [haʊ] (wie)
... places	**where** *adv* [weə] (wo)	... possession	**whose** *pron* [hu:z] (wessen)
... time	**when** *adv* [wen] (wann)		

Words to show that something is

. . . here [hɪə]	**. . . there** [ðeə]
 diese, dieser, dieses	 jene, jener, jenes
 diese	 jene

and *conj* [ənd]	She opened the door ~ went inside.	und
than *conj* [ðən]	Jack is bigger ~ his brother.	als
so *conj* [səʊ]	≫ that is why	so, deshalb
therefore *adv* [ˈðeəfɔː]	We have no money. T~ we can't go to the concert.	daher, deshalb
although *conj* [ɔːlˈðəʊ] **though** *conj* [ðəʊ] **even though** *conj* [ˈiːvn ðəʊ]	I'm going to the party ~ I don't really want to.	obwohl
in spite of *prep* [ɪn ˈspaɪt əv]	She left the flat ~ the heavy rain. (≫ although it was raining heavily)	trotz
but *conj* [bʌt]	He was rich ~ she was poor.	aber
however *conj* [haʊˈevə]	Later, ~, he came back. (≫ But later he . . .)	jedoch
if *conj* [ɪf]	I~ he goes now, he'll catch the train. Do you know ~ Bill is at home?	wenn, falls ob
whether *conj* [ˈweðə]	I don't know ~ I can meet you tonight (or not). (▶▶ if)	ob
on condition (that) [kənˈdɪʃn]	He agreed to sign the contract ~ he was paid £500.	unter der Bedingung, daß
as if [əz ˈɪf] **as though** [əz ˈðəʊ]	He talks ~ he knows everything. (≫ in a way that makes you think)	als ob
at all [ət ˈɔːl]	I'm not ~ happy about it. (≫ in any way)	überhaupt
unless *conj* [ʌnˈles]	Don't go ~ he phones. (≫ if he does not telephone)	wenn nicht, es sei denn, außer wenn
because *conj* [bɪˈkɒz]	He can't come ~ he is ill. (≫ for the reason that)	weil
because of *prep* [bɪˈkɒz əv]	They didn't go out ~ the rain.	wegen, aufgrund
since *conj* [sɪns]	S~ you want to know, I will tell you. (▶▶ Because)	da, weil
so that [ˈsəʊ ðət]	Speak up ~ I can hear you! (≫ in order that)	so daß
hello *interj* [həˈləʊ] **hallo** *interj* [həˈləʊ] **hullo** *interj* [həˈləʊ]	H~, everybody!	Hallo

hi *interj informal* [haɪ] **hi there** *interj informal* ['haɪ ðə]	H~, everybody! (▶▶ hello)	Hallo, Hi
yes *interj, adv* [jes]	Are you leaving? – Y~, I am. He said ~.	Ja
no *interj, adv* [nəʊ]	Are you going, too? – N~, I'm not. He said ~.	Nein
such as ['sʌtʃ əz] **for example** [fər ɪg'zɑ:mpl]	▶▶ like, e.g.	zum Beispiel, wie
well *interj* [wel]	W~, you know, I can't believe it.	nun

Exclamations-Ausrufe

Good heavens! [gʊd 'hevnz]

Ah! [ɑ:]

Ouch! [aʊtʃ]

Ugh! [ɜ:]

Phew! [fju:]

Hey! [heɪ]

What a . . .! ['wɒt ə]

one *pron* [wʌn]	O~ can fly to New York in 8 hours. (⩾ any person)	man
somewhat *adv* ['sʌmwɒt]	She is ~ sad. (▶▶ a little, rather)	etwas
anyhow *adv* ['enɪhaʊ]	▶▶ anyway	sowieso
nothing but ['nʌθɪŋ bʌt]	They talked about ~ football all evening.	nichts als, nur
whatever *adj, pron* [wɒt'evə]	Show me ~ you have. (⩾ no matter what)	was (auch immer), alles was
whichever *adj, pron* [wɪtʃ'evə]	Here are two records – take ~ you like. (⩾ any one)	welch(er, -e, -es) auch immer
whoever *pron* [hu:'evə]	⩾ any person who	wer auch immer
wherever *adv, conj* [weər'evə]	Take a seat ~ you like.	wo immer
whenever [wen'evə]	⩾ at whatever time	wann immer
so as to ['səʊ əz tʊ]	▶▶ in order to	so daß, um zu
despite *prep* [dɪ'spaɪt]	▶▶ in spite of	trotz
nevertheless *conj, adv* [nevəðə'les]	▶▶ however, in spite of that	jedoch, dennoch
after all *conj, adv* [ɑ:ftər 'ɔ:l]	He was right ~. (⩾ in spite of everything)	nach alledem, trotz alledem
even so *adv* ['i:vn səʊ]	It rained but ~ it was a nice day. (⩾ in spite of that)	trotzdem
whereas *conj* [weər'æz]	He's young ~ I'm old. (▶▶ but)	wohingegen, während
thus *adv* [ðʌs]	▶▶ in this way; ▶▶ for this reason	so; daher
provided (that) *conj* [prə'vaɪdɪd]	⩾ on condition (that)	vorausgesetzt, daß
as *conj* [əz]	A~ she wasn't there, we left. (▶▶ Because, Since)	da, weil
on account of *prep* [ɒn ə'kaʊnt əv] **due to** *prep* ['dju: tʊ] **owing to** *prep* ['əʊɪŋ tʊ]	We're late ~ the traffic. (▶▶ because of)	wegen, infolge

6

for the sake of [seɪk] **for . . .'s sake** [seɪk]	They went abroad ~ his wife's health. (⪢ for the good of) He did it ~ his wife~. (⪢ to please)	um . . . willen, zuliebe
in view of [vju:]	I~ the facts, he decided to resign.	angesichts
seeing that *conj* ['si:ɪŋ ðət]	S~ she's old enough, I don't want to tell her what to do. (▶▶ since)	in Anbetracht dessen, daß
indeed *adv* [ɪn'di:d]	Alan ran very well. He did ~. He came first. (▶▶ certainly, really) I like it **very much** ~.	wirklich, tatsächlich
for instance [fər 'ɪnstəns] **e.g.** [i:dʒi:]	▶▶ for example	zum Beispiel z.B.
etc [ɪt 'setərə] **and so on** [ənd səʊ 'ɒn]	. . .	usw.
ie [ɪd'est] **i.e.** [əɪi:]	⪢ id est ⪢ that is/means	das heißt, d.h.

Abbreviations-Abkürzungen

etc	[ɪt 'setərə]	and so on	usw.	**GB**	Great Britain
a.m.	[eɪ'em]	before noon	vormittags	**UK**	United Kingdom
p.m.	[pɪ'em]	after noon	nachmittags	**US**	United States
e.g.	[i:'dʒi:]	for example	z. B.	**MP**	Member of Parliament
i.e.	[aɪ'i:]	that is	d. h.	**BBC**	British Broadcasting Corporation

namely *adv* ['neɪmlɪ] **that is to say** [ðət iz tə 'seɪ] **in other words** [ɪn ʌðə 'wɜ:dz]	▶▶ that is	nämlich das heißt
so-called *adj* ['səʊkɔ:ld]	His ~ friends didn't care. (⪢ . . . (falsely) named so)	sogenannt
including *prep* [ɪn'klu:dɪŋ]	All of us left, ~ me.	einschließlich, inklusive

adj	*adv*	*art*	*conj*	*n*	*pl*	*prep*	*pron*	*sing*
adjective	adverb(ial)	article	conjunction	noun	plural	preposition	pronoun	singular

7 Society
7.1 Personal life

person *n* ['pɜːsn]	a man, woman or child	Person
people *n* ['piːpl]	There were lots of ~ in the streets.	Leute
personal *adj* ['pɜːsənl]	This letter is ~. Nobody else should read it.	persönlich
private *adj* ['praɪvɪt]	▶◀ public	privat
human *adj* ['hjuːmən]	≫ of people (rather than animals)	menschlich
man *n* [mæn] *pl* **men** [men]	≫ male adult	Mann, Männer
woman *n* ['wʊmən] *pl* **women** ['wɪmɪn]	≫ female adult	Frau, Frauen

Lerntip — Wo und wie

Am besten lernst Du zu Hause immer am gleichen Arbeitsplatz. Gestalte ihn so, daß Du Dich wohl fühlst. Gute Lichtverhältnisse sind genauso wichtig wie eine angenehme Raumtemperatur.

boy *n* [bɔɪ]	≫ a male child	Junge, Bub
girl *n* [gɜːl]	≫ a female child	Mädchen
parents *n* ['peərənts]	≫ father(s) and mother(s)	Eltern
child *n* [tʃaɪld] *pl* **children** ['tʃɪldrən]	≫ a boy or girl	Kind, Kinder
baby *n* ['beɪbɪ]	≫ a very young child	Baby, Säugling
adult *n, adj* ['ædʌlt] **grown-up** *n, adj* ['grəʊnʌp]	An ~ is a person over 18 (or 21).	Erwachsener, erwachsen
Mr *n* ['mɪstə]	His name was ~ Williams.	Herr (+ *Name*)
sir *n* [sɜː] **Sir** *n* [sɜː]	Excuse me, ~!	mein Herr
gentleman *n* ['dʒentlmən] *pl* **gentlemen** ['dʒentlmən]	a man who is polite and honest	Gentleman, Herr
Mrs *n* ['mɪsɪz]	Where is ~ Lee?	Frau (+ *Name*)
Miss *n* [mɪs] **miss** *n* [mɪs]	M~ Whitby phoned this morning. Where is the exit, ~?	Fräulein
lady *n* ['leɪdɪ]	She's a sweet old ~. (≫ woman)	Dame
madam *n* ['mædəm] **Madam** *n* ['mædəm]	I really can't thank you enough, ~.	gnädige Frau, gnädiges Fräulein
family *n* ['fæməlɪ]	mother, father and their child/children	Familie
father *n* ['fɑːðə]	His ~ is a doctor. (≫ male parent)	Vater
mother *n* ['mʌðə]	Her ~ works as a lawyer. (▶◀ father)	Mutter
son *n* [sʌn]	The Eastwoods have two ~s. (≫ male children)	Sohn
daughter *n* ['dɔːtə]	▶◀ son	Tochter
sister *n* ['sɪstə]	a girl or a woman who has the same parents as another person	Schwester
brother *n* ['brʌðə]	▶◀ sister	Bruder
grandfather *n* ['grændfɑːðə]	the father of your father or mother	Großvater
grandmother *n* ['grændmʌðə]	the mother of your father or mother	Großmutter
grandchild *n* ['grændtʃaɪld]	the child of your child	Enkelkind

grandson *n* ['grændsʌn]	the son of your child	Enkelsohn
granddaughter *n* ['grænddɔ:tə]	the daughter of your child	Enkeltochter
grandparents *n* ['grændpeərənts]	The mother(s) and father(s) of your parents are your ~.	Großeltern
relation *n* [rɪ'leɪʃn] **relative** *n* ['relətɪv]	a member of one's family	Verwandte(r)
aunt *n* [ɑ:nt]	the sister of your father or mother	Tante
uncle *n* ['ʌŋkl]	▶◀ aunt	Onkel
first name *n* ['fɜ:st neɪm]	Miller's ~ is James.	Vorname
family name *n* ['fæməlɪ neɪm]	His ~ is Smith.	Name

Irregular plurals

singular:	man	woman	gentleman	child	person
plural:	men	women	gentlemen	children	people

to bring up *v + adv* [brɪŋ]	They had to ~ three children.	erziehen, aufziehen
welcome *n* ['welkəm]	He gave me a **warm** ~.	Begrüßung
to introduce *v* [ɪntrə'dju:s]	I ~d him to my sister.	vorstellen, einführen
to kiss *v* [kɪs]	She ~ed her husband on the lips.	küssen
kiss *n* [kɪs]	He gave her a ~.	Kuß
to marry *v* ['mærɪ]	to take somebody as a husband/wife	heiraten
to get married [get 'mærɪd]	≫ to marry, to become husband and wife	heiraten
single *adj* ['sɪŋgl]	≫ not married	ledig
engaged *adj* [ɪn'geɪdʒd]	Alison is ~ **to** a nice young man.	verlobt mit
married *adj* ['mærɪd]	My sister is ~ **to** Jim's brother.	verheiratet mit
divorced *adj* [dɪ'vɔ:st]	≫ no longer married	geschieden
husband *n* ['hʌzbənd]	Mr Halliday is Mrs Halliday's ~.	Ehemann, Mann, Gatte
wife *n pl* **wives** [waɪf, waɪvz]	the woman to whom a man is married	Ehefrau, Frau, Gattin

Words for people

wife	mother	girl	sister	aunt	niece	queen	nun	Mrs, Miss, Ms
husband	father	boy	brother	uncle	nephew	king	monk	Mr

housewife *n pl* **housewives** ['haʊswaɪf, 'haʊswaɪvz]	A woman who works at home for her family is a ~.	Hausfrau
partner *n* ['pɑ:tnə]	I need a ~ to dance with.	Partner
colleague *n* ['kɒli:g]	a person who works with you	Kollege
friend *n* [frend]	I like Jane. She's my best ~.	Freund(in)
enemy *n* ['enəmɪ]	▶◀ friend	Feind
to make friends (with) [frendz]	He is able ~ with people very easily. (≫ start a friendship)	sich anfreunden (mit)
friendly *adj* ['frendlɪ]	He is very ~ **with** his neighbours. She is not very ~ **to** strangers. (▶▶ helpful, kind)	freundschaftlich freundlich gesinnt
member *n* ['membə]	A person who belongs to a group, club or society is a ~.	Mitglied
lonely *adj* ['ləʊnlɪ]	≫ sad because alone	einsam, allein

tʃ	dʒ	θ	ð	ʃ	ʒ	ŋ	w	v
cheap	**j**ump	**th**ing	**th**en	**sh**op	plea**s**ure	sa**ng**	**w**et	**v**oice

lonely – alone

lonely	means	unhappy because no one is near	We often say: He is quite / all alone.
alone	means	without any other person or thing near	

human being *n* [hjuːmən ˈbiːɪŋ]	a person, but not an animal	Mensch
human *n* [ˈhjuːmən]		
folk *n* [fəʊk] **folks** *n AE* [fəʊks]	The ~ in this village are very friendly. (▶▶ people)	Leute, Volk
kid *n infomal* [kɪd]	▶▶ child	Kind
childish *adj* [ˈtʃaɪldɪʃ]	Don't be ~! (⩾ silly, like a child)	kindisch
childlike *adj* [ˈtʃaɪldlaɪk]	She had a ~ faith in her husband. (⩾ innocent, like a child)	kindlich
twin *n* [twɪn]	⩾ one of two children born of the same mother at the same time	Zwilling
guy *n AE* [gaɪ]	I know him, he's a nice ~.	Bursche, Kerl
youth *n* [juːθ]	⩾ a young person	Jugendlicher
youngster *n* [ˈjʌŋstə]	⩾ a child or young person	Junge, Jugendlicher
teenager *n* [ˈtiːneɪdʒə]	a person between 13 and 19 years old	Teenager
teenage *adj* [ˈtiːneɪdʒ]	They've got a ~ daughter.	Teenager
elder *adj, n* [ˈeldə]	He has three ~ brothers. (▶▶ older)	älter *(Familienmitglieder)*
eldest *adj, n* [ˈeldɪst]	Her ~ brother is 27 years old. (▶▶ oldest)	ältest(er, -e, -es) *(Familienmitglied)*
individual *n* [ɪndɪˈvɪdʒʊəl]	An ~ is a single person.	Einzelperson, Individuum
personality *n* [pɜːsəˈnælətɪ]	⩾ a well-known person	Persönlichkeit

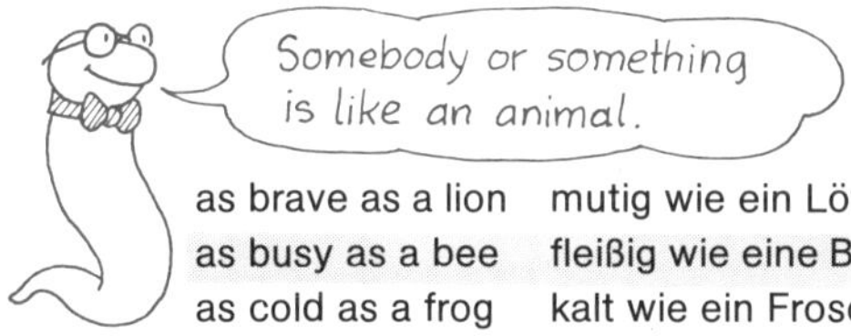

as brave as a lion	mutig wie ein Löwe
as busy as a bee	fleißig wie eine Biene
as cold as a frog	kalt wie ein Frosch
as fat as a pig	fett wie ein Schwein
as free as a bird	frei wie ein Vogel
as strong as a horse	stark wie ein Pferd
as poor as a church mouse	arm wie eine Kirchenmaus

household *n* [ˈhaʊshəʊld]	all the people living together in a house	Haushalt
tribe *n* [traɪb]	Many Indian ~s are forced to live in reservations nowadays.	Stamm, Sippe
clan *n* [klæn]	a large family group in Scotland	Clan
dad *n* [dæd]	His ~ is not at home. (▶▶ father)	Papi, Vati
mum *n* [mʌm] **mom** *n AE* [mɒm]	Where is your ~, Arthur? (▶▶ mother)	Mutti, Mami
nephew *n* [ˈnevjuː]	the son of your brother or sister	Neffe
niece *n* [niːs]	▶◀ nephew	Nichte
cousin *n* [ˈkʌzn]	the child of an uncle or aunt	Cousin, Cousine, Vetter, Base
related *adj* [rɪˈleɪtɪd]	We're both called Price, but we're not ~.	verwandt

iː	ɪ	e	æ	ɑː	ɒ	ɔː	ʊ	uː	ʌ	ɜː	ə
eat	bit	ten	bad	fast	got	saw	sure	too	cut	bird	about

ancestor *n* ['ænsestə]	His ~s came from France in 1750.	Vorfahr(en)
generation *n* [dʒenə'reɪʃn]	all the people born at about the same time	Generation
father-in-law *n* ['fɑːðər ɪn lɔː]	Mr Nickols is my ~. (⩾ wife's father/husband's father)	Schwiegervater
mother-in-law *n* ['mʌðər ɪn lɔː]	▶◀ father-in-law	Schwiegermutter
brother-in-law *n* ['brʌðər ɪn lɔː]	the brother of one's husband or wife or the husband of one's sister	Schwager
sister-in-law *n* ['sɪstər ɪn lɔː]	▶◀ brother-in-law	Schwägerin
Christian name *n* ['krɪstʃən neɪm]	▶▶ first name	Vorname
surname *n* ['sɜːneɪm]	▶▶ family name	Name, Nachname
nickname *n* ['nɪkneɪm]	Neil's ~ was Fatty, because he was so fat.	Spitzname
baby-sitting *n* ['beɪbɪsɪtɪŋ]	looking after a young child whose parents are out	Babysitten
to raise *v* [reɪz]	She has ~d a large family. (▶▶ brought up)	erziehen, aufziehen
to adopt *v* [ə'dɒpt]	Since they had no children of their own they ~ed a little boy. (⩾ took... as their own)	adoptieren, an Kindesstatt annehmen
to greet *v* [griːt]	⩾ to say hello to	grüßen, begrüßen
to welcome *v* ['welkəm]	He ~d us at the front door.	willkommen heißen, begrüßen
introduction *n* [ɪntrə'dʌkʃn]	The host made the ~s and everybody shook hands.	Vorstellen, Einführung
handshake *n* ['hændʃeɪk]	She gave me a friendly ~. 	Händedruck

adj	*adv*	*art*	*conj*	*n*	*pl*	*prep*	*pron*	*sing*
adjective	adverb(ial)	article	conjunction	noun	plural	preposition	pronoun	singular

to receive *v formal* [rɪˈsiːv]	▶▶ to welcome	empfangen
to date *v* [deɪt]	She has been ~ing Tom for two months. (≫ going out with)	gehen mit, sich zum Ausgehen verabreden
girl-friend *n* [ˈgɜːlfrend]	a girl or young woman who is the special friend of a boy or man	(feste) Freundin
boy-friend *n* [ˈbɔɪfrend]	a boy or young man who is the special friend of a girl or woman	(fester) Freund
couple *n* [ˈkʌpl]	≫ boyfriend and girlfriend	Pärchen
darling *n, adj* [ˈdɑːlɪŋ] **sweetheart** *n* [ˈswiːthɑːt]	D~, I love you.	Liebling, Schatz
to pat *v* [pæt]	He ~ted the dog. (≫ touched . . . gently)	tätscheln, einen Klaps geben
pat *n* [pæt]	Kim gave the boy a ~ on the shoulder.	Klaps
to fall in love [fɔːl, lʌv]	≫ to begin to love (each other)	sich verlieben
to be in love [bɪ, lʌv]	The young couple **were** ~. He **was** deeply ~ with her.	verliebt sein in
to propose to *v + prep* [prəˈpəʊz]	He wants to ~ her. (≫ make an offer of marriage to)	einen Heiratsantrag machen
to get engaged [ɪnˈgeɪdʒd]	Mary and Edward will ~ soon. (≫ agree to marry)	sich verloben
to get divorced [dɪˈvɔːst]	Their marriage had broken down, so they decided to ~.	sich scheiden lassen
engagement *n* [ɪnˈgeɪdʒmənt]	an agreement to marry	Verlobung
marriage *n* [ˈmærɪdʒ]	Their ~ lasted for two years only. (▶▶ married life)	Ehe, Hochzeit
wedding *n* [ˈwedɪŋ]	≫ marriage ceremony	Hochzeit
honeymoon *n* [ˈhʌnɪmuːn]	the holiday taken by a man and a woman who have just married	Flitterwochen, Hochzeitsreise
wedding anniversary *n* [ˈwedɪŋ ænɪˈvɜːsərɪ]	Their ~ is on August 7th.	Hochzeitstag
divorce *n* [dɪˈvɔːs]	the end of a marriage by law	Scheidung
bachelor *n* [ˈbætʃələ]	A man who is not married is a ~.	Junggeselle
fiancé *n* [fɪˈɒnseɪ]	Her ~ lives in Tunbridge Wells. (≫ the man to whom she is engaged)	Verlobter
fiancée *n* [fɪˈɒnseɪ]	His ~ comes from Thailand. (≫ the girl to whom he is engaged)	Verlobte
(married) couple *n* [(mærɪd) ˈkʌpl]	≫ husband and wife	Ehepaar
widow *n* [ˈwɪdəʊ]	a woman whose husband has died	Witwe
widower *n* [ˈwɪdəʊə]	a man whose wife has died	Witwer
bride *n* [braɪd]	a woman on her wedding-day	Braut
bridegroom *n* [ˈbraɪdgrʊm]	a man on his wedding-day	Bräutigam
acquaintance *n* [əˈkweɪntəns]	An ~ is a person one knows only a little.	Bekannte(r)
pen-friend *n* [ˈpenfrend] **pen-pal** *n* [ˈpenpæl]	My son has a ~ in Japan.	Brieffreund
opponent *n* [əˈpəʊnənt]	The boxer knocked out his ~.	Gegner, Widersacher
friendship *n* [ˈfrendʃɪp]	There was great ~ between the girls.	Freundschaft
company *n* [ˈkʌmpənɪ]	the presence of a friend	Gesellschaft, Begleitung
to get to know [get, nəʊ]	≫ to become familiar with	kennenlernen
to be acquainted with [əˈkweɪntɪd]	≫ to be familiar with	bekannt sein mit

to get on with *v + adv + prep* [get 'ɒn]	Does he ~ his teacher? (≫ have a friendly relationship with)	(gut) auskommen mit
warm *adj* [wɔ:m]	≫ friendly and kind	warm, herzlich
unfriendly *adj* [ʌn'frendlɪ]	He was very ~ **towards** her.	unfreundlich
cool *adj* [ku:l]	Relations between the two countries have become rather ~.	reserviert, kühl
cold *adj* [kəʊld]	His smile was ~. (≫ very unfriendly)	kalt, unfreundlich, teilnahmslos
loneliness *n* ['ləʊnlɪnɪs]	sadness caused by being alone	Einsamkeit

7.2 Social life

social *adj* ['səʊʃl]	≫ living in groups	sozial
neighbour *n* ['neɪbə] **neighbor** *n AE*	a person who lives near another	Nachbar(in)
group *n* [gru:p] **party** *n* ['pɑ:tɪ]	a number of persons together	Gruppe
crowd *n* [kraʊd]	a large number of people together	Menge, Gedränge
club *n* [klʌb]	e.g. a tennis ~, a social ~	Klub
society *n* [sə'saɪətɪ]	Terrorists are a danger to ~.	Gesellschaft

town *n* [taʊn]	a place with houses, shops, schools etc where people live	Stadt
city *n* ['sɪtɪ]	a large, important town	Großstadt, Stadt
centre *n* ['sentə] **center** *n AE*	There's a new department store in the ~ of town.	Zentrum
capital (city) *n* ['kæpɪtl (sɪtɪ)]	Tokyo is the ~ of Japan. (≫ the city of government)	Hauptstadt
suburb *n* ['sʌbɜ:b]	the outside areas of a city	Vorstadt
in the country ['kʌntrɪ]	▶◀ in a town	auf dem Land
village *n* ['vɪlɪdʒ]	A ~ is smaller than a town.	Dorf
district *n* ['dɪstrɪkt]	They live in the English Lake D~.	Bezirk, Distrikt
area *n* ['eərɪə]	a particular space or place	Gebiet, Raum
country *n* ['kʌntrɪ]	France is a European ~.	Land
state *n* [steɪt]	a (part of a) country	Staat, Bundesland
nation *n* ['neɪʃn]	Spain is a European ~.	Nation
people *n* ['pi:pl]	The Japanese are a hard-working ~. (▶▶ nation)	Volk
pl **peoples** ['pi:plz]	He wrote a book on the ~s of Africa.	Völker
race *n* [reɪs]	a group of people with the same physical features, e.g. colour of skin	Rasse

tʃ	dʒ	θ	ð	ʃ	ʒ	ŋ	w	v
cheap	**jump**	**thing**	**then**	**shop**	pleasure	sa**ng**	**w**et	**v**oice

local *adj* [ˈləʊkl]	He buys everything in the ~ shops. (⪢ in the place where he lives)	örtlich, am Ort
national *adj* [ˈnæʃnəl]	⪢ of a nation/country	Staats-, national
international *adj* [ɪntəˈnæʃnəl]	They went to a conference on ~ trade. (⪢ . . . between nations)	international
foreign *adj* [ˈfɒrən]	I've never been to a ~ country. (⪢ another)	fremd, ausländisch
national *n* [ˈnæʃnəl]	His passport shows that he is a German ~.	Staatsbürger
citizen *n* [ˈsɪtɪzn]	a person who lives in a certain country or town	Bürger
foreigner *n* [ˈfɒrənə]	a person from another country	Ausländer
stranger *n* [ˈstreɪndʒə]	He met a ~ in the building. (⪢ person he didn't know)	Fremde(r)
public *adj* [ˈpʌblɪk]	There will be a ~ meeting at 11. (▶◀ private)	öffentlich
class *n* [klɑːs]	All the people of one social rank are a ~.	Schicht, Gesellschaftsklasse
leader *n* [ˈliːdə]	a person who leads a group	Anführer
master *n* [ˈmɑːstə]	a person who has others working for him	Herr
free *adj* [friː]	The men were ~. They could go where they wanted.	frei
freedom *n* [ˈfriːdəm]	President Lincoln gave ~ to all American slaves in 1863.	Freiheit

the upper class *n* [ˈʌpə klɑːs]	Oberschicht
the middle class *n* [ˈmɪdl klɑːs]	Mittelklasse, mittlere Gesellschaftsschicht
the working class *n* [ˈwɜːkɪŋ klɑːs]	Arbeiterklasse
the lower class *n* [ˈləʊə klɑːs]	Unterschicht

band *n* [bænd] **gang** *n* [gæŋ]	They caught the leader of a ~ of thieves. (▶▶ group)	Bande, Gruppe, Gang
society *n* [səˈsaɪətɪ] **association** *n* [əsəʊsɪˈeɪʃn]	She joined a drama ~. (▶▶ club)	Gesellschaft, Verein
institution *n* [ɪnstɪˈtjuːʃn]	Parliament and the courts are ~s.	öffentliche Einrichtung
union *n* [ˈjuːnɪən]	e.g. the Mothers' U~	Vereinigung
alliance *n* [əˈlaɪəns]	a group or association with the same interests	Bündnis
membership *n* [ˈmembəʃɪp]	All the members of a club are its ~.	Mitgliederzahl, Mitgliederschaft
public *n* [ˈpʌblɪk]	The museum is open to **the** ~ every day. (⪢ people in general)	Öffentlichkeit
community *n* [kəˈmjuːnətɪ]	A ~ is a group of people who live in the same place.	Gemeinschaft, Gemeinde
civilization *n* [sɪvəlaɪˈzeɪʃn] **-sation** *n*	a society and its way of life	Zivilisation
way of life [weɪ, laɪf]	Many Europeans try to imitate the American ~. (⪢ life style, way of living)	Lebensart, Lebensweise
culture *n* [ˈkʌltʃə]	She has studied the ~ of East Asia. (⪢ customs, art and way of thinking)	Kultur
cultural *adj* [ˈkʌltʃərəl]	There are many ~ differences in the Americans. (⪢ . . . in culture)	kulturell
population *n* [pɒpjʊˈleɪʃn]	the number of people living in a place	Bevölkerung(szahl)

7

mankind *n* [mæn'kaɪnd] **humanity** *n* [hjuː'mænətɪ]	all the people in the world	Menschheit
borough *n* ['bʌrə]	a town or part of a big city	Bezirk
uptown *adv AE* [ʌp'taʊn]	≫ away from the city center	außerhalb des Zentrums
downtown *adv, n AE* [daʊn'taʊn]	≫ in/to the city center	(in der) Innenstadt
quarter *n* ['kwɔːtə]	She lives in the Chinese ~ of London. (▶▶ part)	Stadtviertel
slum *n* [slʌm]	an area of dirty, unhealthy houses where poor people live	Elendsviertel, Slum
countryside *n* ['kʌntrɪsaɪd]	The ~ is very beautiful in autumn. (≫ open country)	Landschaft
region *n* ['riːdʒən]	a large part of a country	Gegend, Gebiet, Region
zone *n* [zəʊn]	Do not enter the danger ~.	Zone
province *n* ['prɒvɪns]	Britain was once a Roman ~. (▶▶ state)	Provinz
county *n* ['kaʊntɪ]	Kent and Sussex are ~ies.	Grafschaft
settlement *n* ['setlmənt]	The Pilgrim Fathers made a ~ in North America.	Siedlung
neighbourhood *n* ['neɪbəhʊd] **neighborhood** *n AE*	the area and the people around a place	Nachbarschaft
environment *n* [ɪn'vaɪərənmənt]	We should protect the ~ from destruction.	Umwelt
surroundings *n* [sə'raʊndɪŋz]	The ~ of the town are very nice.	Umgebung
outskirts *n* ['aʊtskɜːts]	the outer areas of a town	Vororte, Außenbezirke
setting *n* ['setɪŋ]	≫ surroundings, environment	Umgebung, Schauplatz

Words for people: -ess [ɪs] **= a female . . .**

manager**ess**	act**ress** ['æktrɪs]	host**ess**	wait**ress** ['weɪtrɪs]	steward**ess**
manager	actor	host	waiter	steward
prince**ss**	count**ess**	baron**ess**	emp**ress** ['emprɪs]	duch**ess** ['dʌtʃɪs]
prince	count	baron	emperor	duke

nationality *n* [næʃə'nælətɪ]	She has British ~.	Nationalität, Staatsbürgerschaft
native *n* ['neɪtɪv]	Chris is a ~ of San Francisco. (≫ person who was born in S.F.) Columbus thought the ~s he met were Indians. (≫ original inhabitants)	Einheimischer, ein geborener . . . Eingeborene(r)
native *adj* ['neɪtɪv]	Jennifer is a ~ speaker of English.	gebürtig
racial *adj* ['reɪʃl]	The population is a mixture of ~ groups.	Rassen-
in public ['pʌblɪk]	≫ in front of other people	in der Öffentlichkeit
civil *adj* ['sɪvl]	C~ **war** is a war inside a state.	Bürger-, bürgerlich
regional *adj* ['riːdʒənl]	He read an article about ~ problems. (▶◀ national)	regional, örtlich
multi-national *adj* [mʌltɪ'næʃnəl]	≫ of many nations	multinational
position *n* [pə'zɪʃn]	A man in his ~ in society must be careful what he says.	Position, gesellschaftliche Stellung
rank *n* [ræŋk]	position in the armed forces, police	Rang
establishment *n* [ɪ'stæblɪʃmənt] **Establishment** *n*	**The** ~ are/is against these new plans. (≫ people who control public life)	Establishment

adj	*adv*	*art*	*conj*	*n*	*pl*	*prep*	*pron*	*sing*
adjective	adverb(ial)	article	conjunction	noun	plural	preposition	pronoun	singular

reputation *n* [repjʊ'teɪʃn]	He has **a** ~ **for** being funny. She has **the** ~ **of** being lazy. (≫ People think that she is lazy.)	Ruf
noble *n, adj* ['nəʊbl]	Prince Frederic was a man of ~ birth.	adelig, edel
common *adj* ['kɒmən]	▶◀ noble	gewöhnlich, ohne Rang *(bürgerlich)*
nobleman *n* ['nəʊblmən] **noblewoman** *n* ['nəʊblwʊmən]	a man/woman of noble birth	Adelige(r)
duke *n* [dju:k]	He became a ~ when his father died.	Herzog
duchess *n* ['dʌtʃɪs]	≫ the wife of a duke	Herzogin
earl *n* [3:l]	An ~ is a British nobleman of high rank.	(engl.) Graf
baron *n* ['bærən]	a nobleman with the lowest rank in the House of Lords	Baron
baroness *n* ['bærənɪs]	the wife of a baron	Baronin
knight *n* [naɪt]	A ~ was a noble soldier on horseback in former times. Nowadays a ~ is a man who has the title 'Sir'.	Ritter
lady *n* ['leɪdɪ]	title used for a noblewoman	Lady
Sir *n* [s3:]	the title of a knight, e.g. ~ Winston and Lady Churchill	Sir *(Anrede)*
head *n* [hed]	The ~s of government had a conference. (▶▶ leaders)	Chef, Führer, Leiter
chief *n* [tʃi:f]	Sitting Bull was a famous Sioux ~. (▶▶ leader)	Häuptling
maid *n* [meɪd]	a woman servant	Hausmädchen, Dienst-mädchen

Words for people

nurse	(lady) doctor	(female) student	(woman) driver	(woman) engineer
(male) nurse	doctor	student	driver	engineer

slave *n* [sleɪv]	a servant owned by a master/mistress	Sklave
slavery *n* ['sleɪvərɪ]	S~ has been abolished in most countries.	Sklaverei
privilege *n* ['prɪvəlɪdʒ]	≫ a special right	Vorrecht
liberty *n* ['lɪbərtɪ]	▶▶ freedom (e.g. from slavery)	Freiheit
liberation *n* [lɪbə'reɪʃn] **lib** *n* [lɪb]	Women's ~ is a movement that wants equal rights for women.	Befreiung
to free *v* [fri:]	On the West Indian plantations the slaves were ~d in 1860. (≫ made free)	befreien
tramp *n* [træmp]	a (poor) person with no home and no job	Landstreicher, Tramp
gipsy *n* ['dʒɪpsɪ] **gypsy** *n*	G~ies live in caravans and travel from one place to another.	Zigeuner, Landfahrer

7

7.3 Education and religion

school *n* [sku:l]	S~ is a place where (young) people learn things.	Schule
university *n* [ju:nɪ'v3:sətɪ]	He has studied **at** ~.	Universität
college *n* ['kɒlɪdʒ]	A ~ is a part of a university: King's C~ is in Cambridge.	Hochschule, Teil der Universität
AE	He went to ~ last fall. (≫ a school of higher learning)	Kolleg

education *n* [edʒʊ'keɪʃn]	learning, training of mind and character	Bildung, Erziehung
teacher *n* ['ti:tʃə]		Lehrer
blackboard *n* ['blækbɔ:d]		Tafel, Wandtafel
board *n* [bɔ:d]		
chalk *n* [tʃɔ:k]		Kreide
classroom *n* ['klɑ:srʊm]	Children have lessons in a ~.	Klassenzimmer
lady teacher *n* ['leɪdɪ ti:tʃə]	a female teacher	Lehrerin
to teach *v* [ti:tʃ] **taught** [tɔ:t] **taught** [tɔ:t]	My friend ~es French at a girls' school.	lehren, unterrichten
pupil *n* ['pju:pl]	There are 30 ~s in the class.	Schüler
schoolboy *n* ['sku:lbɔɪ]	a boy who goes to school	Schüler
schoolgirl *n* ['sku:lgɜ:l]	a girl who goes to school	Schülerin
student *n* ['stju:dnt]	a person who is studying at a university or college	Student
AE	a pupil at school	Schüler
class *n* [klɑ:s] **form** *n* [fɔ:m]	A group of pupils who are taught together is a ~.	Klasse
lesson *n* ['lesn]	They have an English ~ every day.	Unterrichtsstunde; Lektion
course *n* [kɔ:s]	Carl is taking an Italian ~ this summer.	Lehrgang, Kurs
timetable *n* ['taɪmteɪbl]	French was the first lesson on his ~.	Stundenplan
exercise *n* ['eksəsaɪz]	Copy ~ 4 into your ~-book.	Übung
homework *n* ['həʊmwɜ:k]	Jim didn't **do** his ~ yesterday.	Hausaufgaben, Schularbeiten
test *n* [test]	There will be a maths ~ tomorrow.	Prüfung, Test
to correct *v* [kə'rekt]	Mr Swift ~ed the essays.	korrigieren
examination *n* [ɪgzæmɪ'neɪʃn] **exam** *n* [ɪg'zæm]	a test of ability or knowledge	Prüfung
certificate *n* [sə'tɪfɪkət]	When you've passed the exam you get a ~.	Zeugnis

Certificates in Great Britain

C.S.E.	Certificate of Secondary Education	etwa: Hauptschulabschluß
G.C.E. – O level	General Certificate of Education – Ordinary level	mittlerer Bildungsabschluß

The G.C.S.E. (General Certificate of Secondary Education) is about to replace these.

G.C.E. – A level	General Certificate of Education – Advanced level	höherer Bildungsabschluß

degree *n* [dɪ'gri:]	A ~ is a title you get after an exam at a university.	akademischer Grad
holidays *n* ['hɒlədeɪz] **school holidays** *n* [sku:l]	Where are you going for your ~?	Ferien
religion *n* [rɪ'lɪdʒən]	e.g. Islam, Christianity . . .	Religion
god *n* [gɒd]	Neptune was the Roman ~ of the sea.	Gott, Gottheit
God *n* [gɒd]	The Bible says: G~ created the world.	Gott
in God's name [gɒdz 'neɪm]	Why ~ did you do that?	um Gottes willen
hell *n* [hel]	The journey was ~.	Hölle

tʃ	dʒ	θ	ð	ʃ	ʒ	ŋ	w	v
cheap	**j**ump	**th**ing	**th**en	**sh**op	plea**s**ure	sa**ng**	**w**et	**v**oice

church *n* [tʃɜːtʃ]	Alistair goes to ~ every Sunday.	Kirche
primary school *n* ['praɪmərɪ skuːl]	a school for pupils from the age of 5 to 11	Grundschule
elementary school *n* *AE* [elɪ'mentərɪ]		
secondary school *n* ['sekəndrɪ skuːl]	a school for pupils of 11 or 12 to 18	weiterführende Schule (GB)
high school *n AE* ['haɪ skuːl]	a secondary school for pupils over 14	weiterführende Schule (USA)
grammar school *n BE* ['græmə skuːl]	a school where pupils study languages and scientific subjects	Gymnasium (GB)
comprehensive school *n* [kɒmprɪ'hensɪv skuːl]	a secondary school for children of all abilities	Gesamtschule
public school *n BE* ['pʌblɪk skuːl]	A ~ is a private school for pupils between 13 and 18.	Privatschule (mit Internat) (GB)
polytechnic *n* [pɒlɪ'teknɪk]	a kind of university for technical subjects	technische Fachhochschule
staff room *n* ['stɑːf rʊm]	a room in a school where teachers can sit, talk or work	Lehrerzimmer
professor *n* [prə'fesə]	a teacher at a university	Professor
headmaster *n* [hed'mɑːstə]	A ~ is in charge of a school.	Direktor
headmistress *n* [hed'mɪstrɪs]		Direktorin
principal *n* ['prɪnsəpl]	the head of a school/university	Direktor
to attend *v* [ə'tend]	She ~s school regularly. (▶▶ goes to)	besuchen *(Schule)*
to educate *v* ['edʒʊkeɪt]	▶▶ to teach	erziehen, ausbilden

School timetable [skuːl 'taɪmteɪbl]

Mon	Tues	Wed	Thurs	Fri
English *n* ['ɪŋglɪʃ] Englisch	**French** *n* [frentʃ] Französisch	**German** *n* ['dʒɜːmən] Deutsch	**Latin** *n* ['lætɪn] Latein	**history** *n* ['hɪstrɪ] Geschichte
geography *n* [dʒɪ'ɒgrəfɪ] Erdkunde	**mathematics** *n* **maths** *BE*/**math** *AE* [mæθə'mætɪks, mæθs] Mathematik	**physics** *n* ['fɪzɪks] Physik	**chemistry** *n* ['kemɪstrɪ] Chemie	**music** *n* ['mjuːzɪk] Musik
Break [breɪk]				
art *n* [ɑːt] Kunsterziehung	**technical drawing** *n* ['teknɪkl 'drɔːɪŋ] Technisches Zeichnen	**biology** *n* [baɪ'ɒlədʒɪ] Biologie	**religious education** [rɪ'lɪdʒəs edʒʊ'keɪʃn] Religionslehre	**needlework** ['niːdlwɜːk] Handarbeit
autoshop *n AE* ['ɔːtəʊʃɒp] Kurs für Autoreparatur	**woodwork** *n* ['wʊdwɜːk] Werken	**domestic science** *n* **home economics** [də'mestɪk 'saɪəns] [həʊm iːkə'nɒmɪks] Hauswirtschaft	**physical education** ['fɪzɪkl edʒʊ'keɪʃn] Sport	**choir** *n* ['kwaɪə] Chor

iː	ɪ	e	æ	ɑː	ɒ	ɔː	ʊ	uː	ʌ	ɜː	ə
eat	bit	ten	bad	fast	got	saw	sure	too	cut	bird	about

7

to instruct *v* [ɪnˈstrʌkt]	He ~ed me in French. (▶▶ taught)	unterrichten
instruction *n* [ɪnˈstrʌkʃn]	≫ teaching	Unterweisung
scholar *n* [ˈskɒlə]	a person who has learned a lot about something	Gelehrter
scholarship *n* [ˈskɒləʃɪp]	money which is paid to a student to help him with his studies	Stipendium
subject *n* [ˈsʌbdʒɪkt]	French is my favourite ~ at school.	Fach, Gegenstand

secondary school grammar school	**Gymnasium**
university, college	**Hochschule**
reading	**Lektüre**
stamp	**Marke**

gymnasium [dʒɪmˈneɪzɪəm]	Turnhalle
high school [haɪ skuːl]	Gymnasium
lecture [ˈlektʃə]	Vorlesung
mark [mɑːk]	Note, Zeichen

assembly *n* [əˈsemblɪ]	A~ is at nine o'clock every morning.	Schulversammlung, Morgenandacht
term *n* [tɜːm]	There are 3 ~s in the British school year.	Trimester
semester *n AE* [sɪˈmestə]	half a school year	Semester, Halbjahr
break *n* [breɪk]	After the second lesson there's a ~.	Pause
vacation *n AE* [vəˈkeɪʃn]	▶▶ holidays	Ferien
overhead projector *n* [ˈəʊvəhed prəˈdʒektə]	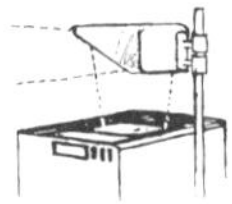	Overheadprojektor
transparency *n* [trænsˈpærənsɪ]	The teacher showed a ~ on the overhead projector.	Folie, Diapositiv
preparation *n* [prepəˈreɪʃn] **prep** *n* [prep]	≫ homework (in private schools)	Hausaufgabe, Unterrichtsvorbereitung
composition *n* [kɒmpəˈzɪʃn]	We have to write a ~ for next Monday. (≫ piece of writing)	Aufsatz
essay *n* [ˈeseɪ]	▶▶ composition	Aufsatz
dictation *n* [dɪkˈteɪʃn]	We got a French ~ today.	Diktat
to dictate *v* [dɪkˈteɪt]	He ~d a long text to the pupils.	diktieren
mark *n* [mɑːk] **grade** *n AE* [greɪd]	She got **good** ~s in the final examination.	Note
to mark *v* [mɑːk]	The teacher has 30 exam papers to ~.	zensieren, bewerten
correction *n* [kəˈrekʃn]	Most teachers make ~s in red ink.	Korrektur
final examination *n* [faɪnl ɪgzæmɪˈneɪʃn]	the last and most important test in a course	Abschlußprüfung
report *n* [rɪˈpɔːt]	James had a very good **school** ~ last year.	Schulzeugnis

Never pronounce the b, d, l, t, k, h **or** w **in these words:**

[b]	[d]	[l]	[t]	[k]	[h]	[h]	[w]
comb	**landscape**	**should**	**to listen**	**to knock**	**honour**	**whether**	**wreck**
lamb	**sandwich**	**talk**	**often**	**knot**	**hour**	**which**	**wretched**
limb	**Wednesday**	**walk**	**to whistle**	**to know**	**vehicle**	**why**	**wrist**
thumb	**windmill**	**would**		**knowledge**			**to write**
							wrong

adj	*adv*	*art*	*conj*	*n*	*pl*	*prep*	*pron*	*sing*
adjective	adverb(ial)	article	conjunction	noun	plural	preposition	pronoun	singular

qualification *n* [kwɒlɪfɪˈkeɪʃn]	I haven't got the necessary ~s for the job.	Qualifikation, Befähigung
to qualify *v* [ˈkwɒlɪfaɪ]	He wants to ~ as a doctor.	sich qualifizieren
prize *n* [praɪz]	One of the students got a ~ for his good work.	Preis, Auszeichnung
belief *n* [bɪˈliːf] **faith** *n* [feɪθ]	He talked about his ~ in God.	Glaube, religiöse Überzeugung
paradise *n* [ˈpærədaɪs]	Adam and Eve were in ~.	Paradies
angel *n* [ˈeɪndʒəl]	≫ a messenger of God	Engel
soul *n* [səʊl]	Christians believe that the ~ doesn't die with the body.	Seele
spirit *n* [ˈspɪrɪt]	▶▶ soul	Geist, Seele
ghost *n* [gəʊst]	the spirit of a dead person	Geist, Gespenst
poltergeist *n* [ˈpɒltəgaɪst]	a ghost that moves furniture etc	Poltergeist
pilgrim *n* [ˈpɪlgrɪm]	Lots of Islamic ~s go to Mecca.	Pilger
to believe in *v + prep* [bɪˈliːv]	Do you really ~ ghosts?	glauben an
to worship *v* [ˈwɜːʃɪp]	The ancient Romans ~ped lots of different gods.	verehren, anbeten
to pray *v* [preɪ]	They ~ed for God's help.	beten
prayer *n* [preə]	He said his ~s before going to bed.	Gebet
ceremony *n* [ˈserɪmənɪ]	The wedding ~ was very short.	Zeremonie; Feier
worship *n* [ˈwɜːʃɪp]	A church is a place of ~.	religiöse Verehrung
service *n* [ˈsɜːvɪs]	The **church** ~ is at 10 a.m. every Sunday.	Gottesdienst
sacrifice *n* [ˈsækrɪfaɪs]	a gift offered to the Gods	Opfer(gabe)
to sacrifice *v* [ˈsækrɪfaɪs]	He ~d his life to save the boy.	opfern
magic *n, adj* [ˈmædʒɪk]	pretending to use strange powers to cause unusual things or events	Magie, Zauberei magisch
superstition *n* [suːpəˈstɪʃn]	belief in magic	Aberglaube
legend *n* [ˈledʒənd]	an old story the truth of which is uncertain	Legende
fable *n* [ˈfeɪbl]	a ~ about animals, e.g. Aesop's ~s	Fabel, Sage
holy *adj* [ˈhəʊlɪ]	The bible is a ~ book.	heilig
religious *adj* [rɪˈlɪdʒəs]	Mary is a very ~ person.	religiös
spiritual *adj* [ˈspɪrɪtʃʊəl]	▶▶ religious	geistlich, religiös
saint *n* [seɪnt]	e.g. S~ Peter	Sankt
saint *n* [seɪnt]	≫ a good, holy person	Heilige(r)
priest *n* [priːst]	A ~ looks after a church and its people.	Priester *(Röm.Kath.)*
missionary *n* [ˈmɪʃənrɪ]	A ~ is a person who teaches religion in a foreign country.	Missionar

monk *n* [mʌŋk]		Mönch
nun *n* [nʌn]		Nonne
archbishop *n* [ɑːtʃˈbɪʃəp]	An ~ is a Christian priest of high rank.	Erzbischof
Pope *n* [pəʊp]	The ~ is the head of the Roman Catholic Church.	Papst
cathedral *n* [kəˈθiːdrəl]	a large and important church	Kathedrale
abbey *n* [ˈæbɪ]	a kind of church	Abteikirche
chapel *n* [ˈtʃæpl]	a room or small church for Christian service	Kapelle
churchyard *n* [ˈtʃɜːtʃjɑːd] **graveyard** *n* [ˈgreɪvjɑːd]	a place around a church where dead people are buried	Kirchhof, Friedhof

v	*AE*	*BE*	☒	~	▶◀	▶▶	≫
verb	American English	British English	a word you have learnt	entry	opposite	synonym	paraphrase

to bury *v* ['berɪ]	Many English queens and kings are ~ied in Westminster Abbey.	begraben, beerdigen
monument *n* ['mɒnjʊmənt]	A ~ is built in memory of a person or event.	Denkmal
monastery *n* ['mɒnəstrɪ]	Monks live together in a ~.	Kloster
temple *n* ['templ]		Tempel
mosque *n* [mɒsk]		Moschee

Religious beliefs	Christian	Catholic	Protestant	Puritan
	['krɪstʃən]	['kæθəlɪk]	['prɒtɪstənt]	['pjʊərɪtən]
	Christ	Katholik	Protestant	Puritaner

Quaker	Mormon	Jew	Muslim	Hindu	Buddhist
['kweɪkə]	['mɔːmən]	['dʒuː]	['mʊzlɪm]	[hɪn'duː]	['bʊdɪst]
Quäker	Mormone	Jude	Moslem	Hindu	Buddhist

7.4 Government and politics

ruler *n* ['ruːlə]	A king is a ~.	Herrscher
king *n* [kɪŋ]	George III was ~ of England and Scotland.	König
queen *n* [kwiːn]	a female ruler or the wife of a king	Königin
to rule *v* [ruːl]	The king ~d the country for 50 years. (≽ was in control of)	beherrschen, herrschen über
government *n* ['gʌvernmənt]	a group of people who rule a country	Regierung
president *n* ['prezɪdənt]	≽ the head of a state or government	Präsident, Staatspräsident
prime minister *n* [praɪm 'mɪnɪstə]	Margaret Thatcher became ~ in 1979.	Premier(minister)
minister *n* ['mɪnɪstə]	a member of a government	Minister
politics *n* ['pɒlətɪks]	matters of government	Politik
politician *n* [pɒlɪ'tɪʃn]	a person who works in politics	Politiker(in)
party *n* ['pɑːtɪ] **political party** *n* [pə'lɪtɪkl 'pɑːtɪ]	a group of people with the same political views: The **Conservative** ~, the **Labour** ~, the **Liberal** ~	Partei
democratic *adj* [demə'krætɪk]	West Germany is a ~ country. (≽ . . . governed by the people)	demokratisch
election *n* [ɪ'lekʃn]	E~s to Parliament will be held next spring.	Wahl
to elect *v* [ɪ'lekt]	They ~ed Reagan president.	wählen (zu)
to vote *v* [vəʊt]	I ~ed **for/against** him in the last election.	wählen, Stimme abgeben für
political *adj* [pə'lɪtɪkl]	He did it for ~ reasons.	politisch
to protest *v* [prə'test]	▶▶ to complain about	protestieren
war *n* [wɔː]	fighting between two or more countries	Krieg
peace *n* [piːs]	▶◀ war	Frieden
fight *n* [faɪt]	The leader has had a long ~ to control his party.	Kampf, Streit
to fight *v* [faɪt] **fought** [fɔːt] **fought** [fɔːt]	In 1940 the Chinese started to ~ with/against the Japanese.	kämpfen mit/gegen, bekämpfen

tʃ	dʒ	θ	ð	ʃ	ʒ	ŋ	w	v
cheap	**j**ump	**th**ing	**th**en	**sh**op	plea**s**ure	sa**ng**	**w**et	**v**oice

struggle *n* ['strʌgl]	▶▶ fight	Kampf, Streit
to attack *v* [ə'tæk]	≫ to start a fight against	angreifen
to occupy *v* ['ɒkjʊpaɪ]	The foreign army ~ied the town.	besetzen
to defend *v* [dɪ'fend]	The soldiers ~ed the town against the enemy. (▶▶ protected/guarded)	verteidigen
to lose *v* [lu:z] **lost** [lɒst] **lost** [lɒst]	▶◀ to win	verlieren
to give in *v + adv* [gɪv] **to give up** *v + adv* [gɪv]	Our soldiers were forced to ~ because the enemy was too strong. (≫ stop fighting)	aufgeben, sich ergeben
to defeat *v* [dɪ'fi:t]	In the end they ~ed the enemy. (≫ won a victory over)	völlig besiegen, eine Niederlage zufügen
soldier *n* ['səʊldʒə]	a person who works in the army	Soldat
army *n* ['ɑ:mɪ]	the soldiers of a country	Armee, Heer
officer *n* ['ɒfɪsə]	a person in a position of command in the armed forces	Offizier
weapon *n* ['wepən]	Guns and knives are ~s.	Waffe
gun *n* [gʌn]	A revolver is a sort of ~.	Feuerwaffe, Kanone
to fire *v* ['faɪə]	They ~d their guns **at** us.	feuern, schießen
to shoot *v* [ʃu:t]	They wanted to ~ a tiger. (≫ kill . . . with a bullet) He started to ~ at it. (▶▶ fire)	erschießen schießen auf
bomb *n* [bɒm]	In 1945 they dropped an **atomic** ~ on Hiroshima.	Bombe
monarchy *n* ['mɒnəkɪ] **kingdom** *n* ['kɪŋdəm]	a state which has a king/queen	Monarchie, Königreich
republic *n* [rɪ'pʌblɪk]	a state that is governed by a president and parliament	Republik
union *n* ['ju:niən]	The USA is a ~ of 51 states.	Union, Vereinigung
federal *adj* ['fedərəl]	e. g. the F~ Republic of Germany	Bundes-
empire *n* ['empaɪə]	The British once had a huge ~.	Weltreich, Kaiserreich, Imperium
commonwealth *n* ['kɒmənwelθ]	a group of countries that work together because they have the same interests (≫ former parts of the British Empire)	Staatenbund
colony *n* ['kɒlənɪ]	an area controlled by another country	Kolonie
dominion *n* [də'mɪnɪən]	land(s) held in complete control by a king or government	Herrschaftsgebiet
to colonize *v* ['kɒlənaɪz] **-ise**	The English ~d New England in 1620.	kolonisieren
colonization *n* [kɒlənaɪ'zeɪʃn] **-isation**	The ~ of Africa began in the 16th century.	Kolonisierung
democracy *n* [dɪ'mɒkrəsɪ]	(a country with) a government of the people	Demokratie
independence *n* [ɪndɪ'pendəns]	200 years ago the Americans fought for their ~ from Britain. (▶▶ freedom)	Unabhängigkeit
republican *adj* [rɪ'pʌblɪkən]	France has a ~ system of government.	republikanisch
prince *n* [prɪns]	the son of a king or queen	Prinz, Fürst
princess *n* [prɪn'ses]	the daughter of a king or queen	Prinzessin
emperor *n* ['empərə] **empress** *n* ['emprɪs]	the ruler of a group of countries	Kaiser Kaiserin
monarch *n* ['mɒnɑ:k]	a king, queen, emperor or empress	Monarch

7

i:	ɪ	e	æ	ɑ:	ɒ	ɔ:	ʊ	u:	ʌ	ɜ:	ə
eat	bit	ten	bad	fast	got	saw	sure	too	cut	bird	about

Your Majesty	Eure Majestät
His Majesty **Her Majesty**	Seine/Ihre Königliche Hoheit

royal *adj* ['rɔɪəl]	≫ of the king/queen	königlich
crown *n* [kraʊn]		Krone
to crown *v* [kraʊn]	They ~ed him King of England.	krönen (zu)
throne *n* [θrəʊn]	a special chair for a ruler	Thron
rule *n* [ru:l]	India was once under British ~. (▶▶ control)	Herrschaft
reign *n* [reɪn]	The time when a king or queen rules is called his/her ~.	Regierungszeit
administration *n* [ədmɪnɪ'streɪʃn]	the control of a country or business	Verwaltung
authority *n* [ɔ:'θɒrətɪ]	The teacher tried to show his ~. (≫ ability to control)	Autorität
	The ~ies didn't allow the open-air festival.	Behörde
civil service *n* [sɪvl 'sɜ:vɪs]	the people who do government work	öffentlicher Dienst
civil servant *n* [sɪvl 'sɜ:vənt]	a person who works for the government	Beamter (im öff. Dienst)
official *n* [ə'fɪʃl]	a person who works for the government	Beamter, Beamtin
social worker *n* ['səʊʃl wɜ:kə]	A ~ helps people and families in need.	Sozialarbeiter(in)
counsellor *n* ['kaʊnsələ]	a person who gives advice	Berater(in)
to govern *v* ['gʌvn]	≫ to control, to rule	regieren
to reign *v* [reɪn]	≫ to rule as a queen/king	herrschen, regieren
parliament *n* ['pɑ:ləmənt]	The laws are made by the ~.	Parlament

GB

Houses of Parliament
[haʊzɪz əv 'pɑ:ləmənt]
Parlament

USA

Congress
['kɒŋgres]
Kongreß

House of Commons	**House of Lords**	**House of Representatives**	**Senate**
[haʊs əv 'kɒmənz]	[haʊs əv 'lɔ:dz]	[reprɪ'zentətɪvz]	['senɪt]
Unterhaus	Oberhaus	Repräsentantenhaus	Senat

assembly *n* [ə'semblɪ]	≫ a meeting, a parliament	Versammlung
council *n* ['kaʊnsl]	The **District/County** C~ meets every Friday.	Rat(sversammlung)
committee *n* [kə'mɪtɪ]	a small group that makes decisions	Komitee, Ausschuß
chancellor *n* ['tʃɑ:nsələ]	the chief minister of state	Kanzler
vice-president *n* [vaɪs'prezɪdənt]	the person next in rank below a president	Vizepräsident
ex-president *n* [eks'prezɪdənt]	a former president	Expräsident
senator *n* ['senətə]	a member of a senate	Senator
mayor *n* [meə]	the head of a town or city	Bürgermeister

adj	*adv*	*art*	*conj*	*n*	*pl*	*prep*	*pron*	*sing*
adjective	adverb(ial)	article	conjunction	noun	plural	preposition	pronoun	singular

☐ **Lord Mayor** *n* [lɔ:d 'meə]	The ~ of London received the foreign guests.	Oberbürgermeister *(nur in den Städten London, Dublin, Liverpool, Manchester)*

Don't mix them up:

to **accept** [ək'sept] annehmen	**great** [greɪt] großartig	to **afford** [ə'fɒ:d] sich leisten
except [ɪk'sept] außer	to **greet** [gri:t] grüßen	**effort** ['efət] Anstrengung
to **expect** [ɪk'spekt] erwarten		
to **lose** [lu:z] verlieren	**coast** [kəʊst] Küste	**mayor** [meə] Bürgermeister
loose [lu:s] lose, locker	to **cost** [kɒst] kosten	**major** ['meɪdʒə] größer

☐ **town hall** *n* ['taʊn hɔ:l]	The mayor of a town has his office in the ~.	Rathaus
☐ **predecessor** *n* ['pri:dɪsesə]	the person who had the same job before another one	(Amts)Vorgänger
☐ **successor** *n* [sək'sesə]	▶◀ predecessor	Nachfolger
☐ **ambassador** *n* [æm'bæsədə]	a person who represents his country in a foreign state	Botschafter
☐ **embassy** *n* ['embəsɪ]	An ambassador works in an ~.	Botschaft(sgebäude)
☐ **policy** *n* ['pɒləsɪ]	the plan of action of a political party or government	politische Linie, Taktik, Politik
☐ **opinion poll** *n* [ə'pɪnɪən pəʊl]	O~s measure public opinion.	Meinungsumfrage
☐ **to nominate** *v* ['nɒmɪneɪt]	They ~d four people for president of the club.	nominieren, aufstellen
☐ **to campaign** *v* [kæm'peɪn]	The farmers have been ~ing for better facilities.	Feldzug, Kampagne veranstalten
☐ **by-election** *n* ['baɪ ɪlekʃn]	a special election held when a seat in Parliament becomes vacant	Nachwahl
☐ **vote** *n* [vəʊt]	the right to vote	Stimmrecht
☐ **majority** *n* [mə'dʒɒrətɪ]	≫ the greater number/part	Mehrheit
☐ **minority** *n* [maɪ'nɒrətɪ]	≫ the smaller number/part	Minderheit
☐ **nomination** *n* [nɒmɪ'neɪʃn]	He hopes to get the ~ for president.	Ernennung
☐ **constituency** *n* [kən'stɪtjʊənsɪ]	an area represented in Parliament by an MP.	Wahlkreis
☐ **candidate** *n* ['kændɪdət]	a person who wants to be elected	Kandidat
☐ **Member of Parliament MP** *n* [membə əv 'pɑ:ləmənt]	a representative of the people	Abgeordnete(r) des Unterhauses
☐ **representative** *n* [reprɪ'zentətɪv]	a person who acts in the name of other people	Abgeordnete(r), Vertreter(in)
☐ **democrat** *n* ['deməkræt]	a person who believes in democracy	Demokrat(in)
☐ **liberal** *n, adj* ['lɪbərəl]	(a person) in favour of freedom in political and other matters	Liberaler liberal
☐ **conservative** *n, adj* [kən'sɜ:vətɪv]	(a person) who does not like change or believes in conservatism	Konservativer konservativ
☐ **Tory** *n* ['tɔ:rɪ]	a member of the Conservative Party in Britain	Tory
☐ **socialist** *n, adj* ['səʊʃəlɪst]	(a person) in favour of socialism	Sozialist sozialistisch

7

v	*AE*	*BE*	☒	~	▶◀	▶▶	≫
verb	American English	British English	a word you have learnt	entry	opposite	synonym	paraphrase

to reform *v* [rɪ'fɔ:m]	They ~ed the unjust laws. (▶▶ improved)	reformieren, eine Reform durchführen
reform *n* [rɪ'fɔ:m]	an improvement in the social or political system	Reform
to impeach *v* [ɪm'pi:tʃ]	to say that someone is guilty of a serious crime against the state	eines Amtsvergehens anklagen
veto *n* ['vi:təʊ]	the right (of e.g. a president) to stop something by declaring himself/herself against it	Veto
to veto *v* ['vi:təʊ]	The plan was ~ed by the president. (▶▶ prevented)	Veto einlegen gegen
to resist *v* [rɪ'zɪst]	The soldiers ~ed the enemy attack. (▶▶ fought against)	sich widersetzen, widerstehen
resistance *n* [rɪ'zɪstəns]	The army offered no ~ when the enemy attacked.	Widerstand
to oppose *v* [ə'pəʊz]	▶▶ to resist, to be against	sich widersetzen
opposition *n* [ɒpə'zɪʃn]	The Conservatives have been in ~ to our policies for years.	Opposition
Opposition *n* [ɒpə'zɪʃn]	▶◀ government	Oppositionspartei
protest *n* ['prəʊtest]	▶▶ opposition	Protest, Einspruch
to demonstrate *v* ['demənstreɪt]	Thousands of students ~d against nuclear power plants.	demonstrieren
demonstration *n* [demən'streɪʃn]	There were several ~s against unemployment.	Demonstration
rebel *n* ['rebl]	a person who fights against authority	Rebell, Aufrührer
rebellion *n* [rɪ'belɪən]	There have been several ~s in South American countries lately.	Rebellion
revolution *n* [revə'lu:ʃn]	a total change in the governing of a country by force	Revolution, Umsturz
revolutionary *adj* [revə'lu:ʃənərɪ]	completely new and different	revolutionär
terrorist *n* ['terərɪst]	The ~s kidnapped the ambassador.	Terrorist(in)
terrorism *n* ['terərɪzəm]	the actions and methods of terrorists	Terrorismus
hostage *n* ['hɒstɪdʒ]	The terrorists **took** two passengers as ~s.	Geisel
to spy *v* [spaɪ]	≫ to watch secretly, to get secret information	(aus)spionieren
spy *n* [spaɪ]	a person who tries to get secret information about another country	Spion
(secret) agent *n* [('si:krɪt) 'eɪdʒənt]	James Bond is a ~. (▶▶ spy)	Geheimagent
plot *n* [plɒt]	A ~ is a secret plan.	Komplott, Verschwörung
battle *n* ['bætl]	The troops fought the first ~ of the war.	Schlacht
conflict *n* ['kɒnflɪkt]	▶▶ fight, quarrel	Kampf, Konflikt
attack *n* [ə'tæk]	a military action against a person or country	Angriff
invasion *n* [ɪn'veɪʒn]	the entering of a country with an army	Invasion
occupation *n* [ɒkjʊ'peɪʃn]	the taking and keeping of a country or town in war	Besetzung
raid *n* [reɪd]	a sudden attack	Überfall
to invade *v* [ɪn'veɪd]	In 1066 the Normans ~d England.	eindringen in
to struggle *v* ['strʌgl]	▶▶ to fight	kämpfen, streiten
to raid *v* [reɪd]	to make a sudden attack on	überfallen, stürmen auf
defence *n* [dɪ'fens] **defense** *n AE*	▶◀ attack	Verteidigung
to conquer *v* ['kɒŋkə]	The Romans ~ed part of England in 55 B.C. (≫ defeated and took control of)	erobern

conqueror *n* [ˈkɒŋkərə]	a person who defeats a country completely: e.g. **William the C~**	Eroberer
to surrender *v* [səˈrendə]	The general refused to ~. (▶▶ stop fighting, give in)	sich ergeben
	They ~ed the weapons to their enemies. (▶▶ handed . . . over)	übergeben
victory *n* [ˈvɪktərɪ]	the winning of a fight or game	Sieg
defeat *n* [dɪˈfiːt]	▶◀ victory	Niederlage
military *n* [ˈmɪlɪtrɪ]	▶▶ the army, soldiers	Militär
troops *n* [truːps]	▶▶ soldiers	Truppe(n)
navy *n* [ˈneɪvɪ]	a country's war-ships and its officers and men	(Kriegs)Marine
volunteer *n* [vɒlənˈtɪə]	a person who joins e.g. the armed forces without being forced to	Freiwilliger
sergeant *n* [ˈsɑːdʒənt]	a rank in the army	Feldwebel
general *n* [ˈdʒenrəl]	His father was a ~ in the US army.	General
on duty [ˈdjuːtɪ]	Most of the soldiers are ~ tonight. (▶▶ at work)	im Dienst
off duty [ˈdjuːtɪ]	You can rest when you go ~.	dienstfrei
cannon *n* [ˈkænən]		Kanone
gunpowder *n* [ˈgʌnpaʊdə]	G~ is used to fire a cannon.	Schießpulver

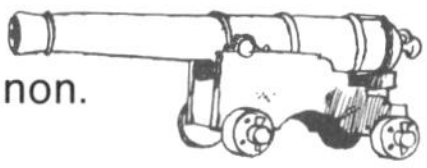

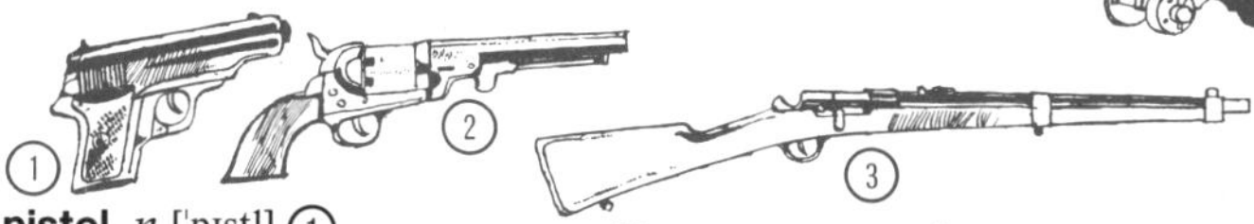

pistol *n* [ˈpɪstl] (1)		Pistole
revolver *n* [rɪˈvɒlvə] (2)		Revolver
rifle *n* [ˈraɪfl] (3)		Gewehr, Flinte
bullet *n* [ˈbʊlɪt] (4)		(Gewehr)Kugel
tank *n* [tæŋk] (5)		Panzer
shot *n* [ʃɒt]	the noise made by the firing of a gun ▶▶ a bullet	Schuß
submarine *n* [sʌbməˈriːn] **sub** *n* [sʌb]		U-Boot
periscope *n* [ˈperɪskəʊp]		Sehrohr
missile *n* [ˈmɪsaɪl]	▶▶ rocket	Rakete, Geschoß

7.5 Law and crime

rule *n* [ruːl]	You must follow the ~s.	Regel
exception *n* [ɪkˈsepʃn]	All pupils came **with the ~ of** Chris. (⩾ Chris was the only pupil who didn't come.)	Ausnahme
law *n* [lɔː]	It's **against the ~** to drive without a licence.	Gesetz
custom *n* [ˈkʌstəm]	It's her ~ to go to Spain every year. (⩾ She usually goes . . .)	Sitte, Gewohnheit
habit *n* [ˈhæbɪt]	Smoking is a very **bad ~**.	Gewohnheit
to let *v* [let]	Don't ~ her go. I need her at home.	lassen
to allow *v* [əˈlaʊ]	Will they ~ us to leave early?	erlauben, zulassen
official *adj* [əˈfɪʃl]	We got the ~ report.	offiziell
licence *n* [ˈlaɪsns] **license** *n AE*	Could I see your **driving ~**?	Lizenz, Erlaubnis
passport *n* [ˈpɑːspɔːt]	You need a ~ when you want to travel abroad.	(Reise)Paß

7

iː	ɪ	e	æ	ɑː	ɒ	ɔː	ʊ	uː	ʌ	ɜː	ə
eat	bit	ten	bad	fast	got	saw	sure	too	cut	bird	about

police *n* [pə'li:s]	The ~ have to catch criminals.	Polizei
policeman *n* [pə'li:smən] **policewoman** *n* [pə'li:swʊmən]		Polizist(in)
police station *n* [pə'li:s steɪʃn]	Where is the nearest ~?	Polizeiwache
officer *n* ['ɒfisə]	Two police ~s were injured.	Polizeibeamter
detective *n* [dɪ'tektɪv]	Sherlock Holmes was a famous ~.	Detektiv
guard *n* [gɑ:d]	A ~ protects people or places.	Wache, Wärter
to arrest *v* [ə'rest]	Two members of the gang were caught and ~ed.	verhaften
crime *n* [kraɪm]	Murder is a ~. (⋙ an act against the law)	Verbrechen, Vergehen
criminal *n* ['krɪmɪnl]	a person who has broken the law	Verbrecher, Krimineller
to steal *v* [sti:l] **stole** [stəʊl] **stolen** ['stəʊlən]	to take something without any right	stehlen
murder *n* ['mɜ:də]	killing a person on purpose	Mord

poison	**Gift**
to die	**sterben**
murderer	**Mörder**
detective	**Kriminaler**

gift [gɪft]	Geschenk
to starve [stɑ:v]	(ver)hungern
murder ['mɜ:də]	Mord
criminal ['krɪmɪnl]	Verbrecher; kriminell

court (of law) *n* [kɔ:t (əv lɔ:)] **law court** *n* ['lɔ: kɔ:t]	A ~ is a place where judges and lawyers listen to criminal cases.	Gericht(shof)
judge *n* [dʒʌdʒ]	a person in a law court who decides how a criminal is punished	Richter
lawyer *n* ['lɔ:jə]	A ~ helps people with the law and speaks for them in court.	(Rechts)Anwalt
guilty *adj* ['gɪltɪ]	The man was found ~ of the crime.	schuldig
to punish *v* ['pʌnɪʃ]	They ~ed him for stealing.	bestrafen
to sentence *v* ['sentəns]	The murderer was ~d to ten years in prison.	verurteilen
fine *n* [faɪn]	the money you have to pay as a punishment	Strafgebühr
prison *n* ['prɪzn]	a place where criminals are locked up	Gefängnis
prisoner *n* ['prɪznə]	Several ~s tried to escape.	Gefangener
regulation *n* [regjʊ'leɪʃn]	a rule that has the force of a law	Vorschrift
as a rule [ru:l]	▶▶ usually	in der Regel
exceptional *adj* [ɪk'sepʃənl]	▶▶ unusual	außergewöhnlich
principle *n* ['prɪnsəpl]	a general truth or a rule for living	Prinzip
standard *n* ['stændəd]	Japan has a high ~ of living.	Standard
tradition *n* [trə'dɪʃn]	a custom that is passed on from one generation to another	Tradition
traditional *adj* [trə'dɪʃənl]	The ~ English breakfast consists of three courses.	traditionell, herkömmlich
bill *n* [bɪl]	a plan for a new law	Gesetzesvorlage
act *n* [ækt]	▶▶ a law	Gesetz
constitution *n* [kɒnstɪ'tju:ʃn]	The United States has a written ~. (⋙ set of elementary laws)	Verfassung

constitutional *adj* [kɒnstɪˈtjuːʃənl]	allowed by the constitution	verfassungsmäßig
amendment *n* [əˈmendmənt]	≫ a change e.g. to a law	Zusatz *(Verfassung)*
to pass *v* [pɑːs]	Parliament has ~ed two new **laws.** (▶▶ approved)	verabschieden *(Gesetz)*
to maintain *v* [meɪnˈteɪn]	≫ to keep in good condition	aufrechterhalten, instand halten
to abolish *v* [əˈbɒlɪʃ]	≫ to bring to an end	abschaffen
to break *v* [breɪk]	Her brother is constantly ~ing **the law.** (≫ going against)	brechen *(Gesetz)*
to commit *v* [kəˈmɪt]	He has ~ted five robberies.	begehen *(Verbrechen)*
justice *n* [ˈdʒʌstɪs]	fairness in the treatment of other people	Gerechtigkeit
injustice *n* [ɪnˈdʒʌstɪs]	unfair treatment	Ungerechtigkeit
legislature *n* [ˈledʒɪsleɪtʃə]	Parliament is the British ~. (≫ group of people who can make laws)	Gesetzgebung
law and order *n* [lɔː, ˈɔːdə]	peaceful behaviour and respect for the law	Recht und Ordnung
legal *adj* [ˈliːgl]	≫ allowed by the law	legal, rechtlich
illegal *adj* [ɪˈliːgl]	≫ against the law	illegal, ungesetzlich
voluntary *adj* [ˈvɒləntrɪ]	Their offer was ~. Nobody asked them to help.	freiwillig
to permit *v* [pəˈmɪt]	▶▶ to allow	erlauben, zulassen
to grant *v* [grɑːnt]	They ~ed him permission to leave the country.	gewähren
to deny *v* [dɪˈnaɪ]	They ~ied their children nothing. (▶▶ refused)	abschlagen, versagen, ablehnen
to forbid *v* [fəˈbɪd] **forbad(e)** [fəˈbæd] **forbidden** [fəˈbɪdn]	▶◀ to allow	verbieten, untersagen
to prohibit *v* [prəˈhɪbɪt]	▶▶ to forbid, ▶◀ to allow	verbieten
permission *n* [pəˈmɪʃn]	The teacher gave him ~ to leave the classroom.	Erlaubnis

Read the words out loud: same sound but different spelling

[ɪ]	[ʃ]	[ɔː]	[ʊ]	[tʃ]	[ɜː]
h**i**t	wa**sh**	b**ou**ght	p**u**t	wa**tch**	sh**ir**t
Mond**ay**	**s**ure	h**a**ll	w**oo**d	**ch**eerful	h**ur**t
for**eig**n	admi**ss**ion	s**aw**	sh**oul**d	na**tu**re	**ear**n
b**u**sy	transla**ti**on	d**oo**r	w**o**lf	ques**ti**on	conc**er**n
vall**ey**	o**c**ean	s**or**t			w**or**m
w**o**men	physi**ci**an				

7

boycott *n* [ˈbɔɪkɒt]	The bus ~ was a protest against high fares.	Boykott
visa *n* [ˈviːzə]	a stamp in a passport that shows that a person may enter or leave a foreign country	Visum, Visa
magistrate *n* [ˈmædʒɪstreɪt]	a kind of judge in a lower court	richterlicher Beamter
coroner *n* [ˈkɒrənə]	A ~ tries to find out the causes of a sudden, unnatural death.	Coroner
cop *n informal* [kɒp]	▶▶ a policeman	Polizist, „Bulle“
jury *n* [ˈdʒʊərɪ]	a group of 12 people who decide questions in a law court	Geschworene, Jury

v verb · *AE* American English · *BE* British English · ☒ a word you have learnt · ~ entry · ▶◀ opposite · ▶▶ synonym · ≫ paraphrase

solicitor *n* [sə'lɪsɪtə]	a lawyer who gives advice and appears in lower courts	Rechtsanwalt
Supreme Court *n* [su:'pri:m]	**The** ~ is the highest court in the USA.	Oberster Gerichtshof
to accuse *v* [ə'kju:z]	The police ~d the woman **of** murder.	anklagen, beschuldigen
to plead *v* [pli:d]	He ~ed not guilty.	plädieren
case *n* [keɪs]	⩾ a legal affair	Fall, Sache
trial *n* ['traɪəl]	the examination of a case in a law court	Prozeß
to defend *v* [dɪ'fend]	The man's lawyer ~ed him in court. (⩾ spoke for the case of)	verteidigen
defence *n* [dɪ'fens] **defense** *n AE*	The murderer's ~ was rather weak.	Verteidigung
witness *n* ['wɪtnɪs]	a person who tells a law court what he/she saw	Zeuge
to witness *v* ['wɪtnɪs]	to see as something happens	Zeuge sein von
to testify *v* ['testɪfaɪ]	to give information to a court She couldn't ~ **against** her husband. (⩾ act as a witness)	bezeugen aussagen gegen
evidence *n* ['evɪdəns]	▶▶ proof	Beweis(mittel)
responsible *adj* [rɪ'spɒnsəbl]	He is not ~ for the accident.	verantwortlich
responsibility *n* [rɪspɒnsə'bɪlətɪ]	It's your ~ if anything happens to her.	Verantwortung
guilt *n* [gɪlt]	responsibility for a crime	Schuld
innocent *adj* ['ɪnəsnt]	▶◀ guilty	unschuldig
conditional discharge *n* [kən'dɪʃənl 'dɪstʃɑ:dʒ]	He was given a ~ by the magistrate.	Freispruch auf Bewährung
will *n* [wɪl]	The lawyer read out the old lady's ~.	letzter Wille
to inherit *v* [ɪn'herɪt]	to receive e.g. money from someone after his/her death	erben
inheritance *n* [ɪn'herɪtəns]	the things that you get after another person has died	Erbschaft
heir *n* [eə]	The prince was ~ to the throne.	Erbe
sergeant *n* ['sɑ:dʒənt]	a rank in the police	Wachtmeister
guardian *n* ['gɑ:dɪən]	a person who acts as a parent and cares for a child	Vormund, Hüter
warden *n* ['wɔ:dn]	e.g. a **traffic** ~	Politesse, Verkehrsaufseher
to guard *v* [gɑ:d]	A big dog ~ed the house. (▶▶ protected)	bewachen
offence *n* [ə'fens] **offense** *n AE*	▶▶ a crime	Vergehen
to offend *v* [ə'fend]	People who ~ against the law will be punished.	verstoßen gegen
criminal *n, adj* ['krɪmɪnl]	He committed lots of ~ acts before the police caught him.	Verbrecher, kriminell
thief *n* [θi:f] *pl* **thieves** [θi:vz]	A ~ has stolen my wallet.	Dieb
robber *n* ['rɒbə]	R~s have taken all his money.	Räuber
burglar *n* ['bɜ:glə]	A ~ breaks into houses to steal.	Einbrecher
kidnapper *n* ['kɪdnæpə] **kidnaper** *n AE*	The ~s demanded $70 000 from the child's family.	Entführer
murderer *n* ['mɜ:dərə] **murderess** *n* ['mɜ:dərɪs]	a man/woman who has killed another person	Mörder(in)

tʃ	dʒ	θ	ð	ʃ	ʒ	ŋ	w	v
cheap	**j**ump	**th**ing	**th**en	**sh**op	plea**s**ure	sa**ng**	**w**et	**v**oice

to rob *v* [rɒb]	They ~bed him **of** his money. Three gangsters ~bed a bank.	berauben, ausrauben

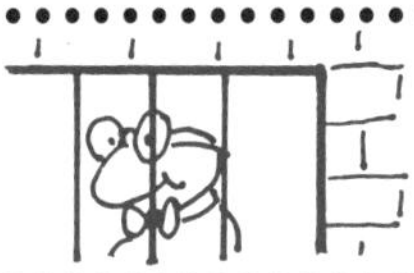

steal: things that do not belong to you.
rob: a person or a place.

to hijack *v* [ˈhaɪdʒæk]	The terrorists ~ed the plane. (⋗ illegally took control of)	entführen *(Flugzeug, Fahrzeug)*
to kidnap *v* [ˈkɪdnæp]	Terrorists ~ped the rich man's daughter.	entführen *(Kinder, Menschen)*
to murder *v* [ˈmɜːdə]	He ~ed his partner to get the money. (⋗ killed . . . on purpose)	umbringen, ermorden
forgery *n* [ˈfɔːdʒərɪ]	This picture is not by Rubens, it's a ~.	Fälschung
theft *n* [θeft]	▶▶ stealing	Diebstahl
vandalism *n* [ˈvændəlɪzəm]	destruction of (public) property	Zerstörungswut
robbery *n* [ˈrɒbərɪ]	He was arrested for armed ~.	Raub, Raubüberfall
suicide *n* [ˈsjuːɪsaɪd]	He **committed** ~ by jumping from the bridge.	Selbstmord
jail *n* [dʒeɪl] **gaol** *n BE* [dʒeɪl]	▶▶ prison	(öffentl.) Gefängnis
punishment *n* [ˈpʌnɪʃmənt]	▶◀ reward	Strafe, Bestrafung
sentence *n* [ˈsentəns]	The ~ was 12 years in prison.	Strafe
to impose *v* [ɪmˈpəʊz]	The magistrate ~d a fine.	verhängen, auferlegen
to let off *v + adv* [let]	I thought I was going to be punished, but the headmaster ~ me ~.	entlassen
to beat *v* [biːt] **beat** [biːt] **beaten** [ˈbiːtn]	to hit hard (e.g. with a stick)	schlagen
to beat up *v + adv* [biːt]	The two hooligans started to ~ the old man.	verprügeln
to hang *v* [hæŋ]	People used to be ~ed for murder.	hängen
to execute *v* [ˈeksɪkjuːt]	The murderer was ~ed at dawn. (⋗ killed as a punishment)	hinrichten

7.6 Entertainment and recreation

hobby *n* [ˈhɒbɪ]	My ~ies are collecting stamps and reading.	Hobby, Steckenpferd
to play *v* [pleɪ]	The children are ~ing in the garden.	spielen
play *n* [pleɪ]	Children must have time for ~.	Spiel, Spielen
party *n* [ˈpɑːtɪ]	A ~ is a meeting of friends to eat, drink, dance and have fun.	Party
fun *n* [fʌn]	They had great ~ at the party. It was very amusing. He did it **for** ~.	Spaß, Scherz zum Spaß
funny *adj* [ˈfʌnɪ] **amusing** *adj* [əˈmjuːzɪŋ]	A ~ story makes you laugh.	lustig
humour *n* [ˈhjuːmə] **humor** *n AE*	The play is full of ~. (⋗ is very funny)	Humor
joke *n* [dʒəʊk]	You tell ~s to make people laugh.	Witz, Spaß
to joke *v* [dʒəʊk]	She didn't mean it seriously; she was only ~ing.	scherzen, Spaß machen

spare time *n* [speə 'taɪm]	▶▶ free time	Freizeit, Muße
leisure *n* ['leʒə]		
activity *n* [æk'tɪvətɪ]	What are your **spare-time** ~ies?	Beschäftigung
music *n* ['mju:zɪk]	Many people are fond of Richard Wagner's ~.	Musik
concert *n* ['kɒnsət]	a musical performance	Konzert
performance *n* [pə'fɔ:məns]	The ~ of Macbeth was very good. (≫ playing)	Aufführung, Vorstellung
to play *v* [pleɪ]	Peter ~s **the** piano.	spielen *(Musik)*
band *n* [bænd]	a group of musicians who play popular music together	Band *(Musik)*
musical instrument *n* ['mju:zɪkl 'ɪnstrʊmənt]	He plays the piano and other ~s.	Musikinstrument
instrument *n*		

piano *n* [pɪ'ænəʊ] ①		Klavier, Flügel
pianist *n* ['pɪənɪst] ②		Pianist
record player *n* ['rekɔ:d pleɪə] ③		Plattenspieler
record *n* ['rekɔ:d] ④		Schallplatte
tape recorder *n* ['teɪp rɪkɔ:də] ⑤		Tonbandgerät
tape *n* [teɪp] ⑥		Tonband
cassette recorder *n* [kə'set rɪ'kɔ:də] ⑦		Kassettenrekorder
cassette *n* [kə'set] ⑧		Musikkassette
to record *v* [rɪ'kɔ:d]	to put on a disc, tape or cassette	aufnehmen
radio (set) *n* ['reɪdɪəʊ (set)]	They bought a new ~.	Radiogerät
song *n* [sɒŋ]	*'Yellow Submarine'* is a ~ by the Beatles.	Lied, Song
to sing *v* [sɪŋ] **sang** [sæŋ] **sung** [sʌŋ]	S~ your brother a song.	singen
singer *n* ['sɪŋə]	a person who sings	Sänger(in)
dance *n* [dɑ:ns]	The waltz is a beautiful ~.	Tanz, Tanzen
to dance *v* [dɑ:ns]	She likes to ~ to pop music.	tanzen
dancer *n* ['dɑ:nsə] ⑨		Tänzer(in)

theatre *n* ['θɪətə] **theater** *n AE*	A ~ is a building where you can see plays.	Theater
show *n* [ʃəʊ]	music and singing or a play in the theatre or on radio or TV	Show, Vorstellung

stage *n* [steɪdʒ]		Bühne
play *n* [pleɪ]	'Macbeth' is a ~ by Shakespeare.	Theaterstück, Schauspiel
to act *v* [ækt]	Roger Moore has ~ed the part of James Bond very often.	spielen, darstellen *(Film, Theater)*
to play *v* [pleɪ]	She's ~ing Eliza Doolittle in 'My Fair Lady'.	spielen, darstellen
scene *n* [si:n]	The first ~ of the play takes place in the Millers' house.	Szene

adj	*adv*	*art*	*conj*	*n*	*pl*	*prep*	*pron*	*sing*
adjective	adverb(ial)	article	conjunction	noun	plural	preposition	pronoun	singular

actor *n* ['æktə]	a person who acts in plays or films	Schauspieler
actress *n* ['æktrɪs]		Schauspielerin
star *n* [stɑ:]	a famous actor, singer etc	Star
director *n* [dɪ'rektə]	The ~ tells the actors what to do.	Regisseur
western *n* ['westən]	Most ~ films are about Red Indians and cowboys.	Western
photograph *n* ['fəʊtəgrɑ:f] **photo** *n* ['fəʊtəʊ]	She **took** some ~s of the castle. (▶▶ pictures)	Photographie, Foto

safe	**Tresor**
photographer	**Photograph**
great	**famos**
stage	**Stadium**
narrow	**schmal**

treasure ['treʒə]	Schatz
photograph ['fəʊtəgra:f]	Foto, Bild
famous ['feɪməs]	berühmt
stadium ['steɪdɪəm]	Stadion
small [smɔ:l]	klein

film *n* [fɪlm]	There was no ~ in his camera.	Film
camera *n* ['kæmərə]	a machine for taking photographs	Fotoapparat, Kamera
to develop *v* [dɪ'veləp]	He ~d the film himself.	entwickeln
print *n* [prɪnt]	a photograph made from a negative	Papierbild, Abzug
to amuse *v* [ə'mju:z]	His jokes ~d everybody. (⩾ made . . . laugh)	belustigen, amüsieren, unterhalten
to entertain *v* [entə'teɪn]	They ~ed us with funny stories. (▶▶ amused)	unterhalten
to celebrate *v* ['selɪbreɪt]	He's having a party to ~ his 18th birthday.	feiern
amusement *n* [ə'mju:zmənt]	To the pupils' ~ the teacher fell from his chair.	Spaß, Unterhaltung
entertainment *n* [entə'teɪnmənt]	Shows, parties, concerts or films are ~.	Unterhaltung
humorous *adj* ['hju:mərəs]	▶▶ funny	humorvoll
celebration *n* [selɪ'breɪʃn]	The team's victory was followed by a great ~.	Feier, Fest
reception *n* [rɪ'sepʃn]	an official party	Empfang
festival *n* ['festɪvl]	We are going to the Edinburgh F~ this year.	Festspiel, Festival
recreation *n* [rekrɪ'eɪʃn]	a way of spending one's free time	Erholung
pastime *n* ['pɑ:staɪm]	Dancing is my favourite ~. (▶▶ recreation, hobby)	Zeitvertreib
to take part in [pɑ:t]	May I ~ your game? (▶▶ join)	teilnehmen an
to participate *v* [pɑ:'tɪsɪpeɪt]	Did he ~ in the match? (▶▶ take part)	teilnehmen
to take up *v + adv* [teɪk]	to begin to take interest in	sich befassen mit
audience *n* ['ɔ:dɪəns]	The ~ **was/were** listening to the show.	Publikum, Zuhörer
spectator *n* [spek'teɪtə]	The ~s enjoyed the tennis match. (⩾ people watching)	Zuschauer
to applaud *v* [ə'plɔ:d]	The audience ~ed her singing.	applaudieren
applause *n* [ə'plɔ:z]	There was long ~ when the performance ended.	Applaus, Beifall
ballet *n* ['bæleɪ]	a dance in which a story is told without speech or singing	Ballett

7

opera *n* ['ɒprə]	a musical play in which actors sing most of the words	Oper
musical *n* ['mjuːzɪkl]	'My Fair Lady' and 'West Side Story' are ~s.	Musical
melody *n* ['melədɪ]	a pleasant piece of music	Melodie
tune *n* [tjuːn]		
composition *n* [kɒmpə'zɪʃn]	a piece of music	Komposition
hit *n* [hɪt]	The song was a ~. (⩾ success)	Hit, Schlager
note *n* [nəʊt]		Note *(Musik)*
harmony *n* ['hɑːmənɪ]	the pleasant arrangement of notes in music	Harmonie
beat *n* [biːt]	a regular repeated sound	Takt
rhythm *n* ['rɪðəm]	a regular beat in music	Rhythmus
classical music *n* ['klæsɪkl 'mjuːzɪk]	e.g. Beethoven's 9th symphony	Klassik, klassische Musik
pop (music) *n* ['pɒp (mjuːzɪk)]	modern music that is popular with lots of people	Pop(musik)
to conduct *v* [kən'dʌkt]	Sir Michael Tippett ~ed the orchestra last year.	dirigieren
to compose *v* [kəm'pəʊz]	to write music	komponieren
orchestra *n* ['ɔːkɪstrə]	a group of people who play musical instruments together	Orchester
group *n* [gruːp]	The Beatles were a well-known ~ of the 60s.	Gruppe *(Musik)*
musician *n* [mjʊ'zɪʃn]	a person who plays music professionally	Musiker
composer *n* [kəm'pəʊzə]	Wagner was a famous German ~.	Komponist
conductor *n* [kən'dʌktə] (1)		Dirigent
trumpet *n* ['trʌmpɪt] (2)		Trompete
bagpipes *n* ['bægpaɪps] (3)		Dudelsack
violin *n* [vaɪə'lɪn] (4)		Geige, Violine
guitar *n* [gɪ'tɑː] (5)		Gitarre
drum *n* [drʌm] (6)		Trommel

He played **the** piano, violin, guitar etc

recording *n* [rɪ'kɔːdɪŋ]	They made a ~ of the speech.	Aufnahme
loudspeaker *n* [laʊd'spiːkə]		Lautsprecher
microphone *n* ['maɪkrəfəʊn]		Mikrophon
mike *n* [maɪk]		
frequency *n* ['friːkwənsɪ]	The BBC World Service broadcasts on several ~ies.	Frequenz
radio ham *n* ['reɪdɪəʊ hæm]	a person whose hobby is sending or receiving radio messages	Funkamateur
volume *n* ['vɒljuːm]	Your radio is too loud. Turn the ~ down.	Lautstärke
disco *n* ['dɪskəʊ] **discotheque** *n* ['dɪskətek]	a club where young people dance to recorded pop music	Discothek
disc jockey *n* ['dɪsk dʒɒkɪ]	A ~ plays and talks about records on the radio or TV.	Diskjockey

tʃ	dʒ	θ	ð	ʃ	ʒ	ŋ	w	v
cheap	jump	thing	then	shop	pleasure	sang	wet	voice

body-popper *n* ['bɒdɪpɒpə]	a person who does 'break-dancing'	Break-dancer
opera house *n* ['ɒprə haʊs]	a theatre for operas	Oper, Opernhaus
drama *n* ['drɑ:mə]	My brother's doing a course on ~. (►► plays)	Schauspiel, Drama
tragedy *n* ['trædʒədɪ]	a serious play that ends sadly	Tragödie
comedy *n* ['kɒmədɪ]	a funny play or film	Komödie
production *n* [prə'dʌkʃn]	I like this ~ of 'Death of a Salesman' very much.	Produktion, Inszenierung
props *n* [prɒps]	the objects needed on a stage	Requisiten
thriller *n* ['θrɪlə]	'The Mousetrap' is a ~ by Agatha Christie. (≫ very exciting play or story)	Thriller, Gruselstück
dramatic *adj* [drə'mætɪk]	The headmaster criticized the programme of the ~ society.	Schauspiel-
tragic *adj* ['trædʒɪk]	≫ very sad, like a tragedy	tragisch
to perform *v* [pə'fɔ:m]	►► to play, to act	aufführen, spielen
part *n* [pɑ:t] **role** *n* [rəʊl]	(the words of) a character in a play	Rolle
character *n* ['kærəktə]	a person in a play or story	Rolle, handelnde Person
hero *n* ['hɪərəʊ] **heroine** *n* ['herəʊɪn]	the most important male/female part in a play	Held Heldin
snapshot *n* ['snæpʃɒt]	a photo taken quickly	Schnappschuß
screen *n* [skri:n]	A picture appeared on the ~.	Bildfläche, Projektionsfläche
to project *v* [prə'dʒekt]	They ~ed the film onto the wall.	projizieren
to enlarge *v* [ɪn'lɑ:dʒ]	He ~d the photograph. (≫ made a large print of)	vergrößern
slide *n* [slaɪd]		Dia(positiv)
music hall *n* ['mju:zɪk hɔ:l]	a place where performances of dancing, singing etc are given	Varietétheater, Konzerthalle
conjuror *n* ['kʌndʒərə] (1)		Zauberkünstler
box office *n* ['bɒks ɒfɪs] **ticket office** *n* ['tɪkɪt ɒfɪs]	a place where tickets are sold in a theatre or cinema	Kasse *(Theater/Kino)*
nightclub *n* ['naɪtklʌb]	They went to a ~ after the film.	Nachtclub, Bar
fair *n* [feə] **funfair** *n* ['fʌnfeə]	a festival in the open air, where you can play games, buy things or eat and drink	(Jahr)Markt; Messe

7.7 Sports and games

7

sport *n* [spɔ:t]	Skiing is a winter ~.	Sport
game *n* [geɪm]	Football and cricket are ~s.	Spiel, Sport
match *n* [mætʃ]	They all went to the football ~.	Spiel, Wettkampf, Match
sportsman *n* ['spɔ:tsmən]	a person who enjoys sports	Sportler
sportswoman *n* ['spɔ:tswʊmən]		Sportlerin
professional *n* [prə'feʃnəl]	A ~ lives on the money he or she earns by sport.	Profi
judge *n* [dʒʌdʒ]	A ~ decides who is the best in a sport or contest.	Kampfrichter
cup *n* [kʌp]	Our team will win the ~ this year.	Pokal, Cup

to hit *v* [hɪt] **hit** [hɪt] **hit** [hɪt]	H~ the ball with the racket, like this.	schlagen, treffen
to miss *v* [mɪs]	He tried to hit the ball but ~ed it.	verfehlen
to run *v* [rʌn] **ran** [ræn] **run** [rʌn]	He always ~s races in summer.	laufen, rennen
run *n* [rʌn]	He went for a ~ in the park.	Lauf
race *n* [reɪs]	We went to a car ~ last weekend.	Rennen, Wettlauf
to bet *v* [bet]	He ~s **on** horses. I ~ he'll win the race.	setzen auf *(Geld)* wetten
to jump *v* [dʒʌmp]	She ~ed into the water.	springen, hüpfen
to ride *v* [raɪd] **rode** [rəʊd] **ridden** ['rɪdn]	Can you ~ a horse? He tried to ~ 18 miles on his bike.	reiten, fahren
to swim *v* [swɪm] **swam** [swæm] **swum** [swʌm]	We went ~ming in the river.	schwimmen
swimming pool *n* ['swɪmɪŋ pu:l] **pool** *n* [pu:l]	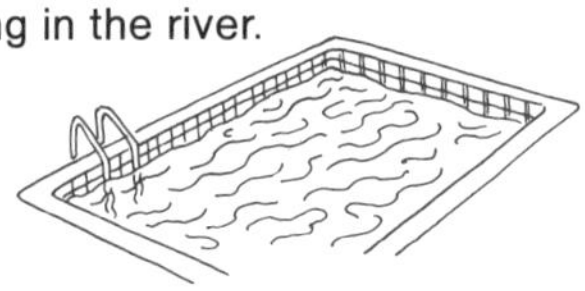	Schwimmbecken
to beat *v* [bi:t] **beat** [bi:t] **beaten** ['bi:tn]	They always ~ us at football. (▶▶ defeat)	schlagen, besiegen übertreffen
to win *v* [wɪn] **won** [wʌn] **won** [wʌn]	▶◀ to lose	gewinnen

beat: a person or a team
win: a game, a war or a prize

result *n* [rɪ'zʌlt]	Peter listened to the football ~s on the radio.	Ergebnis, Resultat
score *n* [skɔ:]	the number of points that you win in a game	Punktzahl
football *n* ['fʊtbɔ:l]	a ball game with two teams of 11 players	Fußball(spiel)
team *n* [ti:m]	A ~ is a group of people who play or work together	Team, Mannschaft
captain *n* ['kæptɪn]	the leader of a team or group	Mannschaftskapitän
football *n* ['fʊtbɔ:l]	 	Fußball
toy *n* [tɔɪ]	Children play with ~s.	Spielzeug
cards *n* [kɑ:dz]	They always play ~ on Friday.	Karten(spiel)
competition *n* [kɒmpə'tɪʃn] **contest** *n* ['kɒntest]	a test to find who is best at a game or sport	Wettkampf, Wettbewerb
championship *n* ['tʃæmpɪənʃɪp]	▶▶ competition	Meisterschaft
challenge *n* ['tʃælɪndʒ]	an invitation to a contest	Herausforderung
to challenge *v* ['tʃælɪndʒ]	She ~d her father to play against her.	herausfordern
Cup Final *n* [kʌp 'faɪnl]	The two teams meet in the ~ on Saturday.	Pokalendspiel
Olympic Games *n* [ə'lɪmpɪk 'geɪmz]	There are ~ every four years.	Olympische Spiele

exercise *n* [ˈeksəsaɪz]	She needs more ~. Jogging would be a good idea.	körperliche Bewegung
to exercise *v* [ˈeksəsaɪz]	You're getting too fat. You aren't ~ing enough.	sich Bewegung verschaffen
training *n* [ˈtreɪnɪŋ]	She is in ~ for the Olympics.	Training
to gamble *v* [ˈgæmbl]	to risk money at games of chance	spielen *(um Geld)*
winner *n* [ˈwɪnə]	a person who wins in a game	Gewinner
loser *n* [ˈlu:zə]	▶◀ winner	Verlierer
athlete *n* [ˈæθli:t]	Many ~s took part in the Olympic Games.	Athlet
player *n* [ˈpleɪə]	a person who plays in a game	Spieler(in)
competitor *n* [kəmˈpetɪtə]	someone who takes part in a competition	Konkurrent(in)
rival *n* [ˈraɪvl]	The two athletes have often competed against each other. They're great ~s.	Rivale, Rivalin
champion *n* [ˈtʃæmpɪən]	the best player at a certain sport	Champion, Meister
coach *n* [kəʊtʃ]	The football ~ makes his team practise every day. (▶▶ trainer)	Trainer
fan *n* [fæn] **supporter** *n* [səˈpɔ:tə]	Thousands of football ~s came to the Cup Final.	Fan, Anhänger
follower *n* [ˈfɒləʊə] ①	▶▶ fan, supporter	Anhänger, Fan
cheerleader *n AE* [ˈtʃɪəli:də] ②		Cheerleader
hooligan *n* [ˈhu:lɪgən]	There are too many ~s at football matches.	(Fußball)Rowdy
sponsor *n* [ˈspɒnsə]	a person or business that pays for a sports event	Sponsor, Förderer
referee *n* [refəˈri:]	A ~ controls football matches.	Schiedsrichter
medal *n* [ˈmedl]	The winner in the Olympic Games will get a **gold** ~.	Medallie
outdoor *adj* [ˈaʊtdɔ:]	The children are fond of ~ games. (⋗ . . . not in a building)	im Freien, draußen
in the open air [eə]	⋗ not in a building, outdoors	im Freien
indoor *adj* [ˈɪndɔ:]	⋗ inside a building	im Haus, Innen-
indoors *adv* [ɪnˈdɔ:z]	⋗ inside a building	drinnen
ground *n* [graʊnd] **field** *n* [fi:ld]	Can you show me the way to the football ~?	Platz, Spielfeld
stadium *n* [ˈsteɪdɪəm]		Stadion
soccer *n* [ˈsɒkə]	▶▶ football	Fußball
rugby *n* [ˈrʌgbɪ] **rugger** *n, informal* [ˈrʌgə]	ball game with two teams of fifteen players.	Rugby
cricket *n* [ˈkrɪkɪt]	C~ is England's national summer sport.	Cricket
hit *n* [hɪt]	He gave the ball a good ~.	Schlag, Treffer
to kick *v* [kɪk]	to hit with the foot	treten, kicken
goal *n* [gəʊl]	He scored six ~s. (▶▶ points)	Tor
goalkeeper *n* [ˈgəʊlki:pə] **goalie** *n, informal* [ˈgəʊlɪ]	the footballer who defends the goal	Torwart, Torhüter
point *n* [pɔɪnt]	A ~ is a mark that you win in a game or sport.	Punkt

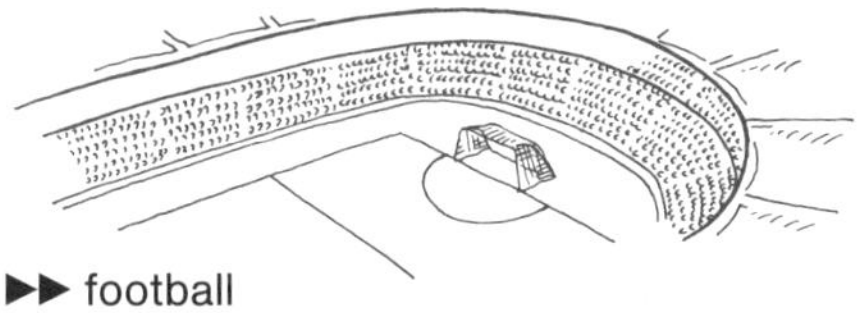

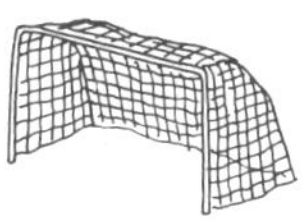

7

v	*AE*	*BE*	☒	~	▶◀	▶▶	⋗
verb	American English	British English	a word you have learnt	entry	opposite	synonym	paraphrase

to score *v* [skɔː]	They ~d five points in the last ten minutes.	(Punkte) erzielen, (Tore) schießen
tennis *n* ['tenɪs] ①		Tennis
racket *n* ['rækɪt] ②		(Tennis)Schläger
golf *n* [gɒlf] ③		Golf
ski *n* [skiː] ④		Ski
skate *n* [skeɪt] ⑤ **ice skate** *n* ['aɪs skeɪt]		Schlittschuh
to ski *v* [skiː]	S~ing is a popular winter sport.	Ski fahren
to skate *v* [skeɪt] **to ice-skate** *v* ['aɪs skeɪt]	Come on! Let's go ~ing.	Schlittschuh laufen
skateboard *n* ['skeɪtbɔːd]		Skateboard
aim *n* [eɪm]	He took ~ and then fired the gun.	Ziel(scheibe)
to aim *v* [eɪm]	She ~ed the gun **at** the cat. (▶▶ pointed)	zielen auf, richten auf
darts *n* [dɑːts]		Wurfpfeilspiel
to jog *v* [dʒɒg]	⪢ to run slowly, for exercise	joggen
to leap *v* [liːp] **leapt** [lept] **leapt** [lept]	He tried to ~ over the fence. (▶▶ jump)	springen, hüpfen
rider *n* ['raɪdə]	a person who rides a horse	Reiter
on horseback ['hɔːsbæk]	He arrived ~. (⪢ riding a horse)	zu Pferd
saddle *n* ['sædl]		Sattel
jockey *n* ['dʒɒkɪ]		Jockey
gymkhana *n* [dʒɪm'kɑːnə]	a local sports meeting (for horseracing and jumping)	(Reit)Sportfest
moto-cross *n* ['məʊtəʊkrɒs]	a race for motorcycles over rough country	Moto-cross
speedway *n* ['spiːdweɪ]	races with cars or motorbikes	Motorrennen, Rennbahn
marathon *n* ['mærəθən]	a long race of 26 miles	Marathon
discus *n* ['dɪskəs]	Throwing the ~ is an Olympic event.	Diskus
swimmer *n* ['swɪmə]		Schwimmer
swimming costume *n* ['swɪmɪŋ kɒstjuːm] **swimming suit** *n* ['swɪmɪŋ suːt] **bathing suit** *n* ['beɪðɪŋ suːt]		Badeanzug
to dive *v* [daɪv]	Suddenly the boy ~d into the water. (⪢ jumped head first)	einen Kopfsprung machen, tauchen
surfing *n* ['sɜːfɪŋ]	riding on top of waves	Surfen
surfboard *n* ['sɜːfbɔːd]		Surfbrett
to row *v* [rəʊ]	She ~ed the boat across the river.	rudern
to sail *v* [seɪl]	Where did she learn to ~ a boat?	segeln
gymnasium *n* [dʒɪm'neɪzɪəm] **gym** *n* [dʒɪm]	We do physical exercises in the school ~.	Turnhalle
basketball *n* ['bɑːskɪtbɔːl]		Basketball
volleyball *n* ['vɒlɪbɔːl]	They're playing ~ in the new gym.	Volleyball
net *n* [net]		Netz
to box *v* [bɒks]	to fight with the fists	boxen
boxer *n* ['bɒksə]	Muhamed Ali was a famous ~.	Boxer

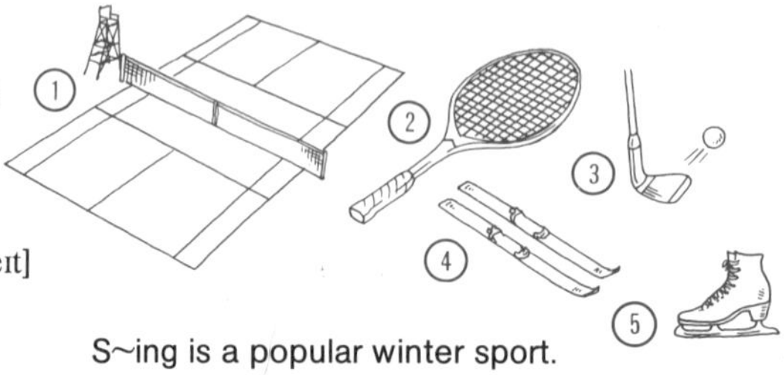

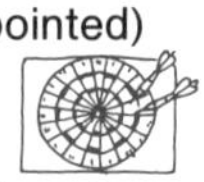

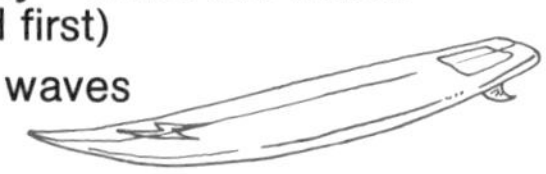

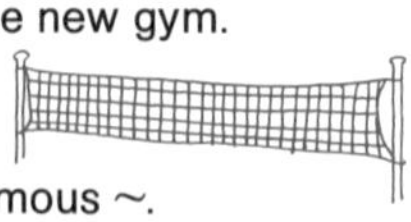

tʃ	dʒ	θ	ð	ʃ	ʒ	ŋ	w	v
cheap	**j**ump	**th**ing	**th**en	**sh**op	plea**s**ure	sa**ng**	**w**et	**v**oice

to punch *v* [pʌntʃ]	Ali ~ed him on the nose.	boxen, einen Hieb versetzen
punch *n* [pʌntʃ]	a strong blow with the fist	Faustschlag
fist *n* [fist]		Faust
judo *n* [ˈdʒu:dəʊ]	a Japanese sport	Judo
dice *n* [daɪs]		Würfel
playground *n* [ˈpleɪgraʊnd]	an area where children can play	Spielplatz
swing *n* [swɪŋ] (1)		Schaukel
roundabout *n* [ˈraʊndəbaʊt] (2)		Karussell
merry-go-round *n* [ˈmerɪgəʊraʊnd]		
pet *n* [pet]	an animal that you keep in the house or garden, e.g. a dog or cat	Heimtier, Haustier
doll *n* [dɒl] (1)		Puppe
puppet *n* [ˈpʌpɪt] (2)		Puppe, Marionette
puzzle *n* [ˈpʌzl]	a difficult problem which you must think hard about in order to answer	Rätsel
riddle *n* [ˈrɪdl]	Here's a ~: What goes up and never comes down? *(your age)*	Rätsel
quiz *n* [kwɪz] *pl* **quizzes** [ˈkwɪzɪz]	Five people took part in the TV ~.	Quiz, Fragespiel
crossword (puzzle) *n* [ˈkrɒswɜ:d (pʌzl)]		Kreuzworträtsel
tongue twister *n* [ˈtʌŋ twɪstə]	'Sister Susie's sewing shirts for sailors' is a ~.	Zungenbrecher

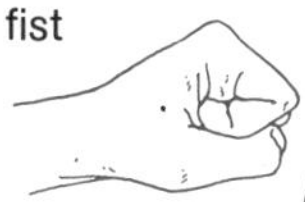

(1)

(2)

(1)

(2)
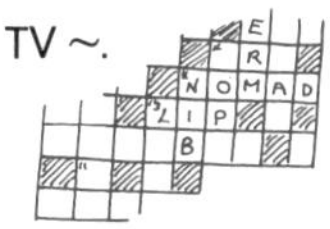

tʃ	dʒ	θ	ð	ʃ	ʒ	ŋ	w	v
cheap	**j**ump	**th**ing	**th**en	**sh**op	plea**s**ure	sa**ng**	**w**et	**v**oice

8 Working life
8.1 Arts, science and technology

art *n* [ɑːt]	That painting by Picasso is a great work of ~.	Kunst

kind, sort, way	**Art**
so, thus, therefore	**also**
something like this	**so was**
now	**jetzt**

art [ɑːt]	Kunst
also [ˈɔːlsəʊ]	auch
so what	na und?
yet [jet]	noch, schon

picture *n* [ˈpɪktʃə]	There are many ~s on the walls of his house.	Bild, Gemälde
to draw *v* [drɔː] **drew** [druː] **drawn** [drɔːn]	to make a picture with a pencil/pen	zeichnen
paint *n* [peɪnt]	Wet ~! Please do not touch!	Farbe
to paint *v* [peɪnt]	I'd like to ~ a picture of you.	(be)malen
museum *n* [mjuːˈzɪəm]	You can see old, interesting or beautiful things in a ~.	Museum
science *n* [ˈsaɪəns]	the study of nature	(Natur)Wissenschaft
scientist *n* [ˈsaɪəntɪst]	a person whose work is in a branch of science	Wissenschaftler(in)
engineer *n* [endʒɪˈnɪə]	An ~ plans and makes machines, roads, bridges etc.	Ingenieur
expert *n* [ˈekspɜːt]	He's an ~ **in/at** repairing computers.	Experte, Spezialist
specialist *n* [ˈspeʃəlɪst]	(⩾ a person with special training)	
practical *adj* [ˈpræktɪkl]	He has a ~ knowledge of the language. (▶▶ useful)	praktisch
technical *adj* [ˈteknɪkl]	We've had a few ~ problems with the machine.	technisch
automatic *adj* [ɔːtəˈmætɪk]	The machine is ~. It works by itself.	automatisch
mechanical *adj* [mɪˈkænɪkl]	moved or produced by machinery	mechanisch
method *n* [ˈmeθəd]	A ~ is how a thing is done.	Methode
means *n* [miːnz]	The telephone is **a** ~ **of** communication. (▶▶ way, method)	Mittel
by means of [miːnz]	She entered the house ~ a ladder. (▶▶ by using)	mittels, mit Hilfe
to produce *v* [prəˈdjuːs]	The factory ~s motorbikes. (▶▶ makes)	herstellen, produzieren
product *n* [ˈprɒdʌkt]	something that is produced	Produkt, Erzeugnis
to form *v* [fɔːm]	The idea began to ~ in his mind. (▶▶ develop)	(sich) bilden
change *n* [tʃeɪndʒ]	There was a ~ in the programme.	Wechsel, Änderung
to change *v* [tʃeɪndʒ]	Paul has ~d the colour of his hair. (⩾ made . . . different)	verändern
	In the bookshop I ~d the paperback for another.	umtauschen
to copy *v* [ˈkɒpɪ]	Please ~ this letter for me.	kopieren
copy *n* [ˈkɒpɪ]	I've made a ~ of the plan.	Kopie, Abschrift
real *adj* [rɪəl]	Is your watch ~ gold?	echt, wirklich

to destroy *v* [dɪ'strɔɪ]	A big fire ~ed the pub.	zerstören, vernichten
ruin *n* ['ru:ɪn]	After the war the town was **in** ~s. (≫ destroyed)	Ruine, Zerstörung
to ruin *v* ['ru:ɪn]	▶▶ to destroy	ruinieren, zerstören
to waste *v* [weɪst]	She ~d all her money **on** sweets.	vergeuden, verschwenden
to repair *v* [rɪ'peə]	If the watch can't be ~ed, I'll have to buy a new one.	reparieren
repair *n* [rɪ'peə]	The ~s to this house are not yet finished.	Reparatur(arbeiten)
to fix *v* [fɪks] **to mend** *v* [mend]	I must get my bike ~ed. (▶▶ repaired)	reparieren
to sew *v* [səʊ] **sewed** [səʊd] **sewn** [səʊn]	She was ~ing a button on her blouse.	nähen
shape *n* [ʃeɪp]	They bought a house in the ~ of an L.	Form, Gestalt
to use *v* [ju:z]	I always ~ this pen for writing letters.	benutzen, verwenden
to serve *v* [sɜ:v]	The box over there will ~ **as** a table.	dienen als
to do *v* [du:]	This will ~ for our purpose. (≫ be suitable)	genügen, ausreichen
way *n* [weɪ] **manner** *n* ['mænə]	He looked at me in a very strange ~.	Art und Weise
style *n* [staɪl]	He writes with a ~ all his own.	Stil, Stilrichtung
process *n* ['prəʊses]	a series of actions leading to a particular result	Verfahren
painting *n* ['peɪntɪŋ]	a painted picture	Gemälde
drawing *n* ['drɔ:ɪŋ]	a picture made with a pencil or pen	Zeichnung
portrait *n* ['pɔ:trɪt]	a picture of a person	Portrait
sketch *n* [sketʃ]	a quick drawing without many details	Skizze
cartoon *n* [kɑ:'tu:n]	a funny drawing	Karikatur, Cartoon
outline *n* ['aʊtlaɪn]	a picture showing the shape of something	Umriß, Silhouette
image *n* ['ɪmɪdʒ]	a picture in the mind or on a screen	Bild, Vorstellung, Abbild
hologram *n* ['hɒləgræm]	a special kind of picture that looks very real	Holographie
tapestry *n* ['tæpɪstrɪ]	The Bayeux T~ shows the Battle of Hastings.	Wandteppich
background *n* ['bækgraʊnd]	things in the back of a picture	Hintergrund
to sketch *v* [sketʃ]	to make a quick drawing (of)	skizzieren
to illustrate *v* ['ɪləstreɪt]	A famous artist ~d his book. (≫ drew the pictures in)	illustrieren, veranschaulichen
piece *n* [pi:s]	She has written a new ~ of music.	Stück, Werk
masterpiece *n* ['mɑ:stəpi:s]	This book is his ~. It's his greatest work.	Meisterwerk
statue *n* ['stætʃu:] ①		Statue
column *n* ['kɒləm] ②		Säule
carving *n* ['kɑ:vɪŋ]	Something cut in wood is a ~.	Schnitzarbeit
artist *n* ['ɑ:tɪst]	someone who paints pictures	Künstler
painter *n* ['peɪntə]	Rembrandt and Picasso were ~s.	Maler
china *n* ['tʃaɪnə]	Most cups and plates are made from ~.	Porzellan
to knit *v* [nɪt] **knitted/knit** ['nɪtɪd/nɪt] **knitted/knit** ['nɪtɪd/nɪt]	She's ~ting a pullover.	stricken
gallery *n* ['gælerɪ] **art gallery** *n* ['ɑ:t gælərɪ]	a place where works of art are shown	Kunstgalerie

8

v verb · *AE* American English · *BE* British English · ☒ a word you have learnt · ~ entry · ▶◀ opposite · ▶▶ synonym · ≫ paraphrase

waxworks *n* ['wæksw3:ks]	models of human beings in wax	Wachsfiguren(kabinett)
studies *n* ['stʌdɪz]	He's continuing his ~ at university.	Studium
to research *v* [rɪ's3:tʃ]	to carry out a close study, to find out new information	nachforschen, recherchieren
research *n* [rɪ's3:tʃ]	His work is medical ~. (≽ scientific study)	Forschung
proof *n* [pru:f]	a piece of evidence showing that something is true	Beweis
to prove *v* [pru:v] **proved** [pru:vd] **proven** ['pru:vn]	It may be true, but can you ~ it?	beweisen
technology *n* [tek'nɒlədʒɪ]	the scientific study of practical things	Technik, Technologie
technological *adj* [teknə'lɒdʒɪkl]	≽ of technology	technologisch
engineering *n* [endʒɪ'nɪərɪŋ]	E~ is the job of an engineer.	Technik
theoretical *adj* [θɪə'retɪkl]	▶◀ practical	theoretisch
mechanic *n* [mɪ'kænɪk]	a person who repairs machines	Mechaniker
technician *n* [tek'nɪʃn]	an expert who works with machines	Techniker
scientific *adj* [saɪən'tɪfɪk]	A microscope is a ~ instrument.	wissenschaftlich
medicine *n* ['medsɪn]	the study of health and illness	Medizin
psychology *n* [saɪ'kɒlədʒɪ]	the study of the mind and how it works	Psychologie
sociology *n* [səʊsɪ'ɒlədʒɪ]	the study of human behaviour in groups	Soziologie
experiment *n* [ɪk'sperɪmənt]	They did a chemical ~. (▶▶ test)	Experiment
to experiment *v* [ɪk'sperɪmənt]	He ~ed **with** the new medicine.	experimentieren

Lerntip

Sachgruppen und Unbekanntes

Neue Wörter mit den dazugehörigen *synonyms, opposites* oder *paraphrases* kannst Du 1. im Lernwörterbuch am Ende jeder Hauptgruppe oder 2. in einem Ringbuch (z. B. A5) eintragen, das nach den Sachgruppen des Lernwörterbuchs unterteilt ist. Eine Aufteilung in drei gleichgroße Spalten hat sich bewährt:

englische Vokabel	englische Erklärung	deutsche Entsprechung

Auch unbekannte Wörter aus dem Unterricht sollten notiert und in einem zweisprachigen Wörterbuch nachgeschlagen werden. Bei Unklarheiten bitte Deinen Lehrer fragen.

laboratory *n* [lə'bɒrətrɪ] **lab** *n informal* [læb]	Scientists work in ~ies.	Labor, Laboratorium
workshop *n* ['w3:kʃɒp]	a room or place where you repair or make things	Werkstatt
to manufacture *v* [mænjʊ'fæktʃə]	to produce in large quantities	herstellen
to assemble *v* [ə'sembl]	The calculator was ~d in Italy. (▶▶ put together)	zusammensetzen, montieren
production *n* [prə'dʌkʃn]	The ~ of cars has increased. (▶▶ making)	Produktion
output *n* ['aʊtpʊt]	the number of things that are made by a factory, etc	Produktionsmenge
form *n* [fɔ:m]	▶▶ shape	Form
pattern *n* ['pætn]	a plan that you can copy when you want to make something	Muster, Vorlage
model *n* ['mɒdl]	a small copy of something	Modell, Muster

design *n* [dɪ'zaɪn]	a plan or pattern	Entwurf, Muster
invention *n* [ɪn'venʃn]	The ~ of the telephone made Alexander Graham Bell famous.	Erfindung
inventor *n* [ɪn'ventə]	Alexander Graham Bell was the ~ of the telephone.	Erfinder
to invent *v* [ɪn'vent]	James Watt ~ed the steam engine.	erfinden
to think up *v + adv* [θɪŋk]	▶▶ invent	sich ausdenken
to design *v* [dɪ'zaɪn]	He ~s dresses for a famous shop in Paris.	entwerfen, planen
to imitate *v* ['ɪmɪteɪt]	▶▶ to copy	imitieren, nachahmen
false *adj* [fɔ:ls]	My grandmother has ~ teeth.	falsch
destruction *n* [dɪ'strʌkʃn]	He wrote a book about the ~ of the city in the war. (⪢ destroying)	Zerstörung
to recycle *v* [ri:'saɪkl]	The glass from bottles is ~d. (⪢ used again to make something else)	wiederaufbereiten
to prepare *v* [prɪ'peə]	The teacher ~d his lessons for Monday. Mike ~d to go out.	vorbereiten sich bereit machen
to get ready [get 'redɪ]	We must ~ for the party. (▶▶ prepare)	vorbereiten, (sich) fertigmachen
preparation *n* [prepə'reɪʃn]	Has she made all the ~s for her trip? (▶▶ arrangements)	Vorbereitung
to apply *v* [ə'plaɪ]	His invention was ~ied to new production methods. (▶▶ used for)	anwenden auf
to function *v* ['fʌŋkʃn]	My phone isn't ~ing at the moment. (⪢ working)	funktionieren
use *n* [ju:s]	A knife has a lot of ~s. You can do a lot of different things with it.	Nutzen, Gebrauch, Anwendungsmöglichkeit
function *n* ['fʌŋkʃn]	What ~ does this new machine have? (▶▶ use)	Funktion; Aufgabe
application *n* [æplɪ'keɪʃn]	He talked about the ~ of new scientific discoveries.	Anwendung
usage *n* ['ju:zɪdʒ]	Given careful ~, the product should last many years.	Gebrauch

8.2 Work and production

work *n* [wɜ:k]	Jane has started ~. (⪢ a paid job)	Arbeit
effort *n* ['efət]	John **made** a big ~ to finish his work. (▶▶ attempt) We need more ~ on this job. (▶▶ hard work)	Anstrengung, Mühe
to work *v* [wɜ:k]	Peter ~s in a factory.	arbeiten
to be busy *v* ['bɪzɪ]	He's ~ repair**ing** his radio. Sabine is ~ **with** her homework.	damit beschäftigt sein
worker *n* ['wɜ:kə]	A person who works is a ~.	Arbeiter
workman *n* ['wɜ:kmən] *pl* **workmen** ['wɜ:kmən]	A ~ works with his hands or with machines.	Arbeiter, Handwerker
industry *n* ['ɪndəstrɪ]	The making of goods in factories is called ~.	Industrie
industrial *adj* [ɪn'dʌstrɪəl]	He lives in an ~ area. (⪢ with lots of factories)	industriell, Industrie-
factory *n* ['fæktərɪ]	A ~ is a building where things are made in great quantities.	Fabrik
business *n* ['bɪznɪs]	He sold his ~ to a friend. (▶▶ firm)	Geschäft, Unternehmen
company *n* ['kʌmpənɪ]	Esso is an oil ~.	Gesellschaft, Firma

i:	ɪ	e	æ	ɑ:	ɒ	ɔ:	ʊ	u:	ʌ	ɜ:	ə
eat	bit	ten	bad	fast	got	saw	sure	too	cut	bird	about

Words for people: -er; -or [ə]

teach**er**	hunt**er**	work**er**	camp**er**	box**er**	edit**or**
teach	hunt	work	camp	box	edit
manag**er**	driv**er**	writ**er**	beginn**er**	winn**er**	runn**er**
manage	drive	write	begin	win	run

department *n* [dɪˈpɑːtmənt]	a part of a company, shop etc	Abteilung
office *n* [ˈɒfɪs]	He sat at his desk in the ~.	Büro, Amt
firm *n* [fɜːm]	a business company	Firma
branch *n* [brɑːntʃ]	The bank has ~es all over the city.	Filiale, Zweigstelle
employer *n* [ɪmˈplɔɪə]	An ~ pays other people to do work for him.	Arbeitgeber(in)
manager *n* [ˈmænɪdʒə]	A ~ is a person who controls a business.	Manager, Leiter, Geschäftsführer
director *n* [dɪˈrektə]	the chief manager	Direktor, Leiter
boss *n* [bɒs]	►► employer, manager	Boss, Arbeitgeber
employee *n* [emplɔɪˈiː]	An ~ is paid to work for a firm.	Arbeitnehmer(in)
clerk *n* [klɑːk] **office worker** *n* [ˈɒfɪs wɜːkə]	A ~ works in an office.	Büroangestellte(r)
secretary *n* [ˈsekrətrɪ]	A ~ types letters, answers the phone and arranges meetings.	Sekretär(in)
typist *n* [ˈtaɪpɪst]	A ~ uses a typewriter.	Stenotypistin, Schreibkraft

Words for people: -ist; -ian; -ent/-ant

typ**ist** [ˈtaɪpɪst]	Maschinenschreiber(in)	resid**ent** [ˈrezɪdənt]	Bewohner(in)
motor**ist** [ˈməʊtəɪst]	Autofahrer(in)	stud**ent** [ˈstjuːdnt]	Student(in)
tour**ist** [tʊəɪst]	Tourist(in)	par**ent** [ˈpeərənt]	Elternteil
cycl**ist** [ˈsaɪklist]	Radfahrer(in)		
pian**ist** [ˈpɪənɪst]	Klavierspieler(in)		
guard**ian** [ˈgɑːdɪən]	Vormund	assist**ant** [əˈsɪstənt]	Mitarbeiter(in)
music**ian** [mjuːˈzɪʃn]	Musikant(in)	inhabit**ant** [inˈhæbɪtənt]	Einwohner(in)
librar**ian** [laɪˈbreərɪən]	Bibliothekar(in)		

job *n* [dʒɒb]	Her boyfriend has got a ~ in her father's firm.	Job, Stellung, Arbeit
profession *n* [prəˈfeʃn]	He's a teacher **by** ~.	Beruf *(akademisch)*
trade *n* [treɪd]	He's a plumber **by** ~.	Beruf *(handwerklich)*
to apply *v* [əˈplaɪ]	He ~ied (**to** the manager) **for** the job.	sich bewerben um
application *n* [æplɪˈkeɪʃn]	The firm got six ~s for the job.	Bewerbung
to join *v* [dʒɔɪn]	Her brother ~ed the company. (≫ became a member of)	eintreten in, sich anschließen
to fire *v* [ˈfaɪə]	The boss ~d him for being late.	entlassen, feuern
employment *n* [ɪmˈplɔɪmənt]	She found ~ in a car factory.	Beschäftigung, Stelle
unemployment *n* [ʌnɪmˈplɔɪmənt]	When the factory had to close, it caused a lot of ~.	Arbeitslosigkeit
unemployed *adj* [ʌnɪmˈplɔɪd] **out of work** [wɜːk]	≫ without a job	arbeitslos

adj	*adv*	*art*	*conj*	*n*	*pl*	*prep*	*pron*	*sing*
adjective	adverb(ial)	article	conjunction	noun	plural	preposition	pronoun	singular

to earn *v* [ɜːn]	She ~s $ 3,000 a year.	verdienen *(Geld)*
living *n* [ˈlɪvɪŋ]	Teaching is her ~. (▶▶ job)	Lebensunterhalt
pay *n* [peɪ]	I get my ~ at the end of the week.	Bezahlung
salary *n* [ˈsæləri]	the money you receive every month for work	Gehalt
wages *n* [ˈweɪdʒɪz]	weekly payments for work done	Lohn, Löhne
trade union *n* [treɪd ˈjuːnɪən]	an organization of workers to represent their interests	Gewerkschaft
union *n* [ˈjuːnɪən]		
strike *n* [straɪk]	All the steel workers were **on** ~.	Streik
holiday *n* [ˈhɒlədeɪ]	a time when we don't go to work	Urlaub, Ferien
off *adv* [ɒf]	Jenny has **a day** ~ today.	frei *(Tag, Woche)*

farm *n* [fɑːm]		Bauernhof
field *n* [fiːld]	a piece of land on a farm	Feld, Acker
rich *adj* [rɪtʃ]	e.g. ~ land	fruchtbar
to grow *v* [grəʊ] **grew** [gruː] **grown** [grəʊn]	The farmers here ~ vegetables.	anbauen, züchten
to plant *v* [plɑːnt]	We've ~ed a tree in the garden.	pflanzen
farmer *n* [ˈfɑːmə]	a person who runs a farm	Bauer, Landwirt
gardener *n* [ˈgɑːdnə]	A ~ works in a garden.	Gärtner(in)
to fish *v* [fɪʃ]	They are ~ing in the river.	angeln, fischen
occupation *n* [ɒkjʊˈpeɪʃn]	▶▶ job, employment	Beruf
post *n* [pəʊst]	He held the ~ of headmaster for ten years. (▶▶ job)	Posten, Stellung
career *n* [kəˈrɪə]	She's having a successful ~ in banking. (▶▶ profession)	Laufbahn, Beruf, Karriere
task *n* [tɑːsk]	a piece of work which must be done	Aufgabe
housework *n* [ˈhaʊswɜːk]	the work of looking after a house	Hausarbeit
to employ *v* [ɪmˈplɔɪ]	The firm ~s 120 men.	beschäftigen
staff *n* [stɑːf]	a group of people who work together, e.g. for a company	Personal, Stab
personnel *n* [pɜːsəˈnel]		
temporary *adj* [ˈtemprəri]	for a short time, ▶◀ permanent	vorübergehend
full-time *adj, adv* [fʊlˈtaɪm]	Jane is a ~ worker. She works from nine to five.	Ganztags-
part-time *adj, adv* [pɑːtˈtaɪm]	Karen has a ~ job from nine to one.	Teilzeit-
overtime *adv* [ˈəʊvətaɪm]	He's **working** ~ to earn some extra money.	Überstunden
to quit *v AE* [kwɪt] **quit/quitted** [kwɪt/ˈkwɪtɪd] **quit/quitted** [kwɪt/ˈkwɪtɪd]	I had to ~ my job because of ill health. (▶▶ leave, give up)	aufgeben, verlassen
to retire *v* [rɪˈtaɪə]	Her father wants to ~ at the age of 62. (≫ give up working)	in Pension gehen
vacancy *n* [ˈveɪkənsi]	a place for a new worker	freie Stelle
vacant *adj* [ˈveɪkənt]	There are no ~ positions in our firm. (▶▶ free)	frei, unbesetzt

8

v	*AE*	*BE*	☒	~	▶◀	▶▶	≫
verb	American English	British English	a word you have learnt	entry	opposite	synonym	paraphrase

to go *v* [gəʊ] **to run** *v* [rʌn]	The machine won't ~. (▶▶ work)	funktionieren, gehen
to operate *v* ['ɒpəreɪt]	Is it difficult to ~ this camera? (▶▶ use) The machine ~s day and night. (▶▶ works)	bedienen, handhaben arbeiten
to co-operate *v* [kəʊ'ɒpəreɪt] **to cooperate** *v*	They don't ~ **with** us. (▶▶ work together)	zusammenarbeiten
occupied *adj* ['ɒkjʊpaɪd]	▶▶ busy	beschäftigt mit
idle *adj* ['aɪdl]	▶◀ busy, working	untätig, müßig
without effort ['efət]	≫ without trying hard	mühelos
appointment *n* [ə'pɔɪntmənt]	They talked about the ~ of a new general manager.	Ernennung
to appoint *v* [ə'pɔɪnt]	They ~ed him manager.	ernennen
retirement *n* [rɪ'taɪəmənt]	the time when an old person gives up work	Pensionierung
to gain *v* [geɪn]	He ~ed $ 8 by selling his old hat. (▶▶ won, made a profit of)	gewinnen, erlangen, verdienen
to profit *v* ['prɒfɪt]	I hope you'll ~ from the experience. (▶▶ gain)	profitieren, nützen
to get *v* [get]	How much does she ~ a week? (▶▶ earn)	verdienen
to earn one's living [ɜːn, 'lɪvɪŋ]	She wants to ~ her ~ by playing the guitar.	seinen Lebensunterhalt verdienen

EARN	... **a living**	seinen Lebensunterhalt verdienen	... **money**	Geld verdienen
	... **a salary**	ein Gehalt empfangen	... **wages**	Lohn empfangen
FIND	... **an answer** (to a question)	eine Antwort (auf eine Frage) finden		
	... **a solution** (to a problem)	eine Lösung (für ein Problem) finden		
	... **time** (for something)	Zeit (für etwas) finden		

income *n* ['ɪŋkʌm]	She had to pay a lot of ~ **tax**.	Einkommen
earnings *n* ['ɜːnɪŋz]	money which is earned by working	Einkünfte
fee *n* [fiː]	money paid for a service	Honorar, Gebühr
pocket-money *n* ['pɒkɪt mʌnɪ]	money that children get from their parents to buy small things	Taschengeld
pension *n* ['penʃn] **old age pension** *n* ['əʊld eɪdʒ 'penʃn]	When you're old and do not work any longer, you get a(n) ~ from the government or a company.	Pension, Rente
allowance *n* [ə'laʊəns]	a sum of money that you get regularly	Zuwendung *(Geld)*
expenses *n* [ɪk'spensɪz]	▶▶ costs	Ausgaben, (Un)Kosten
rise *n* [raɪz]	She got a £5 ~ last month. (≫ increase in pay)	Gehaltserhöhung, Erhöhung
cut *n* [kʌt]	They've had to accept ~s in their wages. (▶▶ reductions)	Kürzung
agency *n* ['eɪdʒənsɪ]	an office that handles business for others	Agentur, Vertretung
agent *n* ['eɪdʒənt]	a person who handles business for others	Beauftragter
headquarters *n* [hed'kwɔːtəz]	the main offices of a large organization	Zentrale, Hauptquartier
management *n* ['mænɪdʒmənt]	the control of a business or factory	Management
manufacturer *n* [mænjʊ'fæktʃərə]	a person or firm that produces goods	Hersteller, Fabrikant

supervisor *n* ['su:pəvaɪzə]	A ~ watches to see if people are working correctly.	Aufseher(in)
apprentice *n* [ə'prentɪs]	a young worker who is learning his/her trade or job	Lehrling, Auszubildende(r)
apprenticeship *n* [ə'prentɪʃɪp]	He is **serving his** ~ as a butcher.	Lehrzeit, Lehre
master *n* ['mɑ:stə]	A ~ is a skilled workman with his own business.	Meister *(Handwerk)*
carpenter *n* ['kɑ:pɪntə]	A ~ makes things from wood.	Zimmermann, Schreiner
plumber *n* ['plʌmə]	A ~ can fit and repair water pipes.	Installateur
electrician *n* [ɪlek'trɪʃn]	An ~ does electrical work.	Elektriker
watchmaker *n* ['wɒtʃmeɪker]	A ~ makes or repairs watches and clocks.	Uhrmacher(in)
bookkeeper *n* ['bʊkki:pə]	A ~ looks after the accounts of a firm.	Buchhalter(in)
bookkeeping *n* ['bʊkki:pɪŋ]	the keeping of accounts	Buchhaltung, Buchführung
working conditions *n* ['wɜ:kɪŋ kən'dɪʃnz]	the environment in which work is done	Arbeitsbedingungen
working hours *n* ['wɜ:kɪŋ aʊəz]	the times of day between which one is at work	Arbeitsstunden, Arbeitszeit
shift *n* [ʃɪft]	He works on the **night** ~.	Schicht
to strike *v* [straɪk]	They were ~ing **for** better working conditions.	streiken
vacation *n AE* [və'keɪʃn]	▶▶ holidays	Urlaub, Ferien
agriculture *n* ['ægrɪkʌltʃə]	▶▶ farming, the growing of crops	Landwirtschaft
agricultural *adj* [ægrɪ'kʌltʃərəl]	The farmer employed 10 ~ workers.	landwirtschaftlich
gardening *n* ['gɑ:dnɪŋ]	working in a garden	Gartenarbeit
ranch *n* [rɑ:ntʃ]	a large farm (in North America) with e.g. cattle	Ranch, Rinderfarm
cowboy *n* ['kaʊbɔɪ]	A ~ looks after cattle on a ranch.	Cowboy
plantation *n* [plæn'teɪʃn]	He bought a tea ~ in Sri Lanka.	Plantage
meadow *n* ['medəʊ]	a field of grass	Weide, Wiese
cornfield *n* ['kɔ:nfi:ld]	a field where corn is grown	Getreidefeld
crop *n* [krɒp]	e.g. a good ~ of apples a type of plant, e.g. wheat	Ernte, Ertrag Nutzpflanze
harvest *n* ['hɑ:vɪst]	▶▶ crops	Ernte
farmhouse *n* ['fɑ:mhaʊs]	the main house on a farm	Bauernhaus

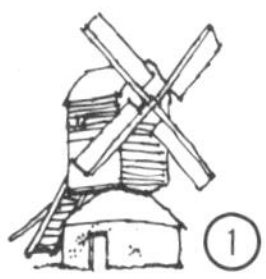

stable *n* ['steɪbl]	a building where horses are kept	Pferdestall
miller *n* ['mɪlə]	a person who works a mill	Müller
windmill *n* ['wɪndmɪl] ①		Windmühle
hedge *n* [hedʒ] ②		Hecke
cattle grid *n* ['kætl grɪd] ③		Viehrost
hay *n* [heɪ]	dried grass used as cattle food	Heu

tractor *n* ['træktə]		Traktor, Schlepper
plough *n* [plaʊ]		Pflug
plow *n AE* [plaʊ]		
to cultivate *v* ['kʌltɪveɪt]	They tried to ~ land which didn't seem very fertile.	kultivieren, anbauen

i:	ɪ	e	æ	ɑ:	ɒ	ɔ:	ʊ	u:	ʌ	ɜ:	ə
eat	bit	ten	bad	fast	got	saw	sure	too	cut	bird	about

8

to dig *v* [dɪg] **dug** [dʌg] **dug** [dʌg]	They were ~ging a hole in the ground.	graben
to harvest *v* ['hɑ:vɪst]	to gather a crop	ernten
labourer *n* ['leɪbərə] **laborer** *n AE*	A ~ does heavy work with his hands.	Hilfsarbeiter, Schwerarbeiter

8.3 Money and trade

money *n* ['mʌnɪ]	You need ~ to buy things.	Geld
coin *n* [kɔɪn]	a round piece of metal money	Münze
change *n* [tʃeɪndʒ] **small change** *n* [smɔ:l 'tʃeɪndʒ]	Can you give me ~ for a £5 note?	Wechselgeld, Kleingeld
cheque *n* [tʃek] **check** *n AE* [tʃek]	I'd like to pay **by** ~, not in cash.	Scheck

traveller's cheque *n* ['trævləz tʃek]

Reisescheck

pound *n* [paʊnd]	**penny** *n* ['penɪ]	**dollar** *n* ['dɒlə]	**cent** *n* [sent]
Pfund Sterling	Penny	Dollar	Cent

pence *n* [pens]	That'll cost a few ~ only.	Pence, Pennies
note *n* [nəʊt] **bill** *n AE* [bɪl]	She gave her a pound ~. She gave her a dollar ~. (⋗ piece of paper money)	Banknote, Geldschein
cash *n* [kæʃ]	I have no ~ on me! (⋗ money in coins and notes)	Bargeld
bank *n* [bæŋk]	He sold his house and put the money **in** the ~.	Bank, Geldinstitut
to change *v* [tʃeɪndʒ]	I'd like to ~ my French money **for** German money.	tauschen, wechseln
to save *v* [seɪv]	I'm ~ing **for** a new camera.	sparen
account *n* [ə'kaʊnt]	Mike has opened an ~ with the local bank.	Konto
to owe *v* [əʊ]	I ~ Tom £1 that he lent me last week. (⋗ have to pay)	schulden
economic *adj* [i:kə'nɒmɪk]	There was a discussion about the country's ~ problems.	Wirtschafts-, ökonomisch
rich *adj* [rɪtʃ]	Her father has a lot of money. He is a ~ man.	reich, wohlhabend
poor *adj* [pʊə]	▶◀ rich	arm
to cost *v* [kɒst] **cost** [kɒst] **cost** [kɒst]	The book ~s $4. You have to pay $4 for it.	kosten
to charge *v* [tʃɑ:dʒ]	He ~d $20 for his work.	berechnen als
charge *n* [tʃɑ:dʒ]	the price you have to pay for an article or service	Kosten
worth *adj* [wɜ:θ]	Our house is ~ much more than we paid for it.	wert

to afford *v* [ə'fɔ:d]	We can't ~ a new car.	sich leisten (können)
to spend *v* [spend] **spent** [spent] **spent** [spent]	They ~ a lot of **money on** their holidays every year.	ausgeben *(Geld)*

pension	**Rente**	**rent** [rent]	Miete
to give	**spenden**	**to spend** [spend]	ausgeben, verbrauchen
to save	**sparen**	**to spare** [speə]	schonen; übrig sein
to get, to obtain, to receive	**bekommen**	**to become** [bɪ'kʌm]	werden

to pay *v* [peɪ] **paid** [peɪd] **paid** [peɪd]	You have to ~ $7 to go in.	(be)zahlen
to settle a bill ['setl, bɪl]	to pay a bill	Rechnung begleichen
to lend *v* [lend] **lent** [lent] **lent** [lent]	Can you ~ me your pen?	leihen, ausborgen
to borrow *v* ['bɒrəʊ]	▶◀ to lend	ausleihen, borgen
to hire *v* ['haɪə]	They ~d the car for three weeks.	mieten
to rent *v* [rent]	His daughter ~ed a room from an old lady. (⪢ paid money to use)	mieten
	The farmer ~s the field to the cricket club.	vermieten
rent *n* [rent]	money paid for the use of a house or room	Miete
to let *v* [let] **let** [let] **let** [let]	He ~s his flat to holiday-makers in winter.	vermieten

for hire [fə 'haɪə]	**to let** [tə 'let]	**for sale** [fə 'seɪl]	**sold** [səʊld]
zu vermieten *(Autos/Boote usw.)*	zu vermieten *(Häuser/Wohnungen)*	zu verkaufen	verkauft

price *n* [praɪs]	What's the ~ of that radio? How much must I pay for it?	Preis
value *n* ['vælju:]	the worth of something in money	Wert
cost *n* [kɒst]	What is the ~ of this project?	Kosten, Preis
tax *n* [tæks]	money which must be paid to the government	Steuer
V.A.T. [vi: eɪ 'ti:, væt]	value added tax	Mehrwertsteuer
customs *n* ['kʌstəmz]	e.g. the ~ officer	Zoll
duty *n* ['dju:tɪ]	taxes paid on certain goods coming into a country	Zoll
duty-free *adj* [dju:tɪ'fri:]	You can buy a great number of ~ articles on board this ship.	zollfrei
insurance *n* [ɪn'ʃʊərəns]	His car ~ is £40 a year.	Versicherung
to insure *v* [ɪn'ʃʊə]	Our house is ~d **against** fire.	versichern

8

v	*AE*	*BE*	☒	~	▶◀	▶▶	⪢
verb	American English	British English	a word you have learnt	entry	opposite	synonym	paraphrase

bill *n* [bɪl]	A ~ shows you how much money you have to pay.	Rechnung
receipt *n* [rɪ'si:t]	a piece of paper showing that money has been received	Quittung
expensive *adj* [ɪk'spensɪv]	That dress is very ~. It costs a lot of money.	teuer
dear *adj* [dɪə]		

high *adj* [haɪ]	▶◀ low	hoch *(Preis)*
valuable *adj* ['væljʊəbl]	worth a lot of money	wertvoll
cheap *adj* [tʃi:p]	▶◀ expensive	billig, preiswert
low *adj* [ləʊ]	Prices are very ~ here.	niedrig *(Preis)*
free *adj* [fri:]	How much does it cost? – Nothing, it's ~.	gratis, umsonst
trade *n* [treɪd]	the business of buying and selling goods e.g. between countries	Handel
business *n* ['bɪznɪs]	B~ is good before Christmas.	Geschäft, Handel
salesman *n* ['seɪlzmən]	A ~ sells goods to homes or businesses.	Handlungsreisender, Verkäufer
order *n* ['ɔ:də]	The shop assistant took my ~ for 10 bottles of wine. The plants are **on** ~. They will be here soon.	Bestellung, Auftrag bestellt
to order *v* ['ɔ:də]	They ~ed two chairs from the shop.	bestellen
to have *v* [hæv] **had** [hæd] **had** [hæd]	That shop won't ~ any dairy products. (≫ keep in stock)	vorrätig haben
to sell *v* [sel] **sold** [səʊld] **sold** [səʊld]	I tried to ~ my old car. The new book doesn't ~.	verkaufen, sich verkaufen lassen
sale *n* [seɪl]	The ~ of the pictures raised several thousand pounds. (▶▶ selling) a time when a shop sells goods at lower prices than usual	Verkauf Verkauf, Ausverkauf, Schlußverkauf
to buy *v* [baɪ] **bought** [bɔ:t] **bought** [bɔ:t]	▶◀ to sell	kaufen
shop *n* [ʃɒp]	A ~ is a room or building where you can buy things.	Laden, Geschäft
store *n* [stɔ:] *AE*	≫ a large shop ▶▶ a shop	Geschäft, Laden
department store *n* [dɪ'pɑ:tmənt stɔ:]	Harrods and Selfridges are London ~s.	Kaufhaus
self-service *n* [self 'sɜ:vɪs]	We had lunch in a ~ restaurant.	Selbstbedienung
market *n* ['mɑ:kɪt]	a place where people meet to buy and sell goods	Markt, Marktplatz
supermarket *n* ['su:pəmɑ:kɪt]	≫ a large self-service store	Supermarkt

shelf *n pl* **shelves** [ʃelf, ʃelvz]		Verkaufsregal
shopping *n* ['ʃɒpɪŋ]	She always **does her** ~ after work. (≫ buys the things she needs)	Einkäufe, Einkauf
shop assistant *n* ['ʃɒp əsɪstənt]	A ~ serves customers in a shop.	Verkäufer(in)
customer *n* ['kʌstəmə]	a person who buys things from a shop	Kunde, Kundin

tʃ	dʒ	θ	ð	ʃ	ʒ	ŋ	w	v
cheap	jump	thing	then	shop	pleasure	sang	wet	voice

grocer *n* ['grəʊsə]	A ~ sells e.g. coffee, tea, sugar and tinned food.	Lebensmittelhändler
butcher *n* ['bʊtʃə]	A ~ sells meat.	Fleischer, Metzger
baker *n* ['beɪkə]	A ~ makes bread and cakes.	Bäcker
banknote *n* ['bæŋknəʊt]	a piece of paper money	Banknote
currency *n* ['kʌrənsɪ]	the money in use in a country, e.g. pounds, francs	Währung
profit *n* ['prɒfɪt] **gain** *n* [geɪn]	money gained from business	Profit, Gewinn
loss *n* [lɒs]	▶◀ gain, profit	Verlust
wealthy *adj* ['welθɪ]	▶▶ rich	reich, wohlhabend
luxurious *adj* [lʌg'ʒʊərɪəs]	Sheila is wearing ~ clothes. (≫ expensive)	luxuriös
wealth *n* [welθ]	a lot of money and possessions	Reichtum
luxury *n* ['lʌkʃərɪ]	A millionaire can live in ~.	Luxus
fortune *n* ['fɔ:tʃu:n]	a great amount of money, wealth	Vermögen
treasure *n* ['treʒə]	(a collection of) gold, silver, jewels and other valuable things	Schatz
bankrupt *adj* ['bæŋkrʌpt]	The firm **went** ~ because it couldn't sell its products.	bankrott
poverty *n* ['pɒvətɪ]	▶◀ wealth	Armut
budget *n* ['bʌdʒɪt]	a plan of how to spend money	Budget, Haushalt
savings *n* ['seɪvɪŋz]	money saved	Ersparnisse
economical *adj* [i:kə'nɒmɪkl]	My new car is very ~ **on** petrol. (≫ doesn't use much petrol)	sparsam, wirtschaftlich
financial *adj* [faɪ'nænʃl]	concerning money	finanziell
safe *n* [seɪf]	a strong metal box for keeping money etc safely	Safe, Tresor
due *adj* [dju:]	The rent is ~ next week.	fällig
debt *n* [det]	the money that you must pay to somebody	Schuld, Schulden
loan *n* [ləʊn]	He asked his bank for a ~ of £500.	Darlehen, Anleihe
stock market *n* ['stɒk mɑ:kɪt]	a place where shares are bought and sold	Börse
to purchase *v* ['pɜ:tʃəs]	▶▶ to buy	kaufen
to acquire *v* [ə'kwaɪə]	They ~d the caravan very cheaply. (▶▶ obtained)	erwerben, kaufen
to bargain *v* ['bɑ:gɪn]	He will sell it more cheaply if you ~ with him about the price.	handeln, feilschen
to swap *v* [swɒp] **to swop** *v*	Keith ~ped his record **for** a thriller. (▶▶ exchanged)	tauschen, austauschen
bargain *n* ['bɑ:gɪn]	something bought for less than its real value	gutes Geschäft, gute Gelegenheit
purchase *n* ['pɜ:tʃəs]	He **made** several ~s in the toy shop.	Einkauf, Kauf
payment *n* ['peɪmənt]	She got £20 in ~ for her work. They made 5 monthly ~s of £9.	Bezahlung Zahlung(en)
cost of living [kɒst, 'lɪvɪŋ]	the costs of goods and services in the family budget	Lebenshaltungskosten
fare *n* [feə]	money paid for a journey	Fahrgeld
precious *adj* ['preʃəs]	▶▶ valuable	wertvoll
invaluable *adj* [ɪn'væljʊəbl]	too precious to be measured	unschätzbar, sehr wertvoll
worthless *adj* ['wɜ:θlɪs]	of no value	wertlos
to trade *v* [treɪd]	His uncle ~s **in** corn. (≫ buys and sells)	handeln mit
to export *v* [ɪk'spɔ:t]	to sell to another country	exportieren

i:	ɪ	e	æ	ɑ:	ɒ	ɔ:	ʊ	u:	ʌ	ɜ:	ə
eat	bit	ten	bad	fast	got	saw	sure	too	cut	bird	about

to import *v* [ɪm'pɔːt]	▶◀ to export	importieren
export *n* ['ekspɔːt]	selling things to another country	Export, Ausfuhr
import *n* ['ɪmpɔːt]	▶◀ export	Import, Einfuhr
contract *n* ['kɒntrækt]	▶▶ a business agreement	Vertrag
deal *n* [diːl]	Well, it's a ~.	Geschäftsabschluß
commerce *n* ['kɒmɜːs]	▶▶ trade	Handel
businessman *n* ['bɪznɪsmən]	A ~ is involved in buying and selling goods.	Geschäftsmann
businesswoman *n* ['bɪznɪswʊmən]	▶◀ businessman	Geschäftsfrau
on business ['bɪznɪs]	I'm here ~, not on holidays.	geschäftlich

ON

... on business geschäftlich	**... on duty** im Dienst	**... on foot** zu Fuß	**... on horseback** zu Pferd	**... on purpose** absichtlich
... on holiday im Urlaub	**... on time** pünktlich	**... on sale** zu verkaufen		

economy *n* [ɪ'kɒnəmɪ]	a country's industry and trade	Wirtschaft
economics *n* [iːkə'nɒmɪks]	the science of national economy	Wirtschaftswissenschaften
to charter *v* ['tʃɑːtə]	▶▶ to hire (a plane, boat or bus)	mieten, chartern
to estimate *v* ['estɪmeɪt]	It's impossible to ~ the costs of the project. (▶▶ calculate)	abschätzen
to negotiate *v* [nɪ'gəʊʃɪeɪt]	They ~d a new contract.	verhandeln, aushandeln
negotiation *n* [nɪgəʊsɪ'eɪʃn]	a discussion in order to reach agreement	Verhandlung
goods *n* [gʊdz]	articles that you sell or buy	Waren
stock *n* [stɒk]	the goods in a shop or factory	Vorrat, Lager
in stock [stɒk]	▶▶ available	vorrätig, auf Lager
load *n* [ləʊd]	The lorry was carrying a ~ of vegetables.	Ladung, Last
to deal in *v + prep* [diːl]	This shop doesn't ~ groceries. (≫ buy and sell)	handeln mit
invoice *n* ['ɪnvɔɪs]	▶▶ bill	Warenrechnung
to tax *v* [tæks]	Alcohol and tobacco are heavily ~ed in Britain.	besteuern
discount *n* ['dɪskaʊnt]	The shop will give you a 10% ~ if you pay at once.	Preisnachlaß
shopping centre *n* ['ʃɒpɪŋ sentə]	part of a town where there are a number of shops together	Einkaufszentrum
grocery *n* ['grəʊsərɪ]	a grocer's shop	Lebensmittelgeschäft
stall *n* [stɔːl] **stand** *n* [stænd]	a small open shop in a street or a table in a market	Stand, Marktstand
jumble sale *n* ['dʒʌmbl seɪl]	a sale of used goods to raise some money e.g. for charity	Wohltätigkeitsbazaar
wholesale *n* ['həʊlseɪl]	the selling of goods in large amounts to shopkeepers	Großhandel
to shop *v* [ʃɒp]	She was ~ping **for** clothes.	einkaufen
consumer *n* [kən'sjuːmə]	▶◀ producer	Verbraucher
dealer *n* ['diːlə]	Her uncle is a **car** ~.	Händler
greengrocer *n* ['griːngrəʊsə]	A ~ sells vegetables and fruit.	Obst-/Gemüsehändler

milkman *n* [ˈmɪlkmən]	A ~ takes milk to people's houses.	Milchmann
trolley *n* [ˈtrɒlɪ]		Einkaufswagen
cash-desk *n* [ˈkæʃdesk]	the place in a shop where you pay for the	Kasse
checkout *n* [ˈtʃekaʊt]	goods you want to buy	
till *n* [tɪl]	There was no money in the ~.	(Laden)Kasse
cashier *n* [kəˈʃɪə]	A ~ works at the cash-desk.	Kassierer(in)
opening hours *n* [ˈəʊpənɪŋ aʊəz]	the time when a shop, business etc is open for customers	Öffnungszeiten

8.4 Numbers and measurements

number *n* [ˈnʌmbə]	a word or figure like 1, 2, 3, . . . or one, two, three, . . .	Zahl, Anzahl
figure *n* [ˈfɪgə]	Write the number in ~s, not in words.	Ziffer, Zahl
rate *n* [reɪt]	The birth ~ is higher in Africa than in Europe.	Rate, Ziffer

Numbers

1,000,000,000,000	one/a billion [ˈbɪlɪən]	
1,000,000,000	one/a billion *AE*	
1,000,000	one/a million [ˈmɪlɪən]	

one/a thousand	1,000	*(th)*	the/a	thousandth [ˈθaʊznd, -θ]
one/a hundred	100	*(th)*	the/a	hundredth [ˈhʌndrəd, -θ]
fifty	50	*(th)*	the/a	fift**ieth**
forty	40	*(th)*	the/a	fort**ieth** [ˈfɔːtɪ, -əθ]
twenty	20	*(th)*	the/a	twent**ieth** [ˈtwentɪ, -əθ]
nineteen	19	*(th)*	the/a	nineteenth [naɪnˈtiːn, -θ]
eighteen	18	*(th)*	the/a	eighteenth [eɪˈtiːn, -θ]
seventeen	17	*(th)*	the/a	seventeenth [sevnˈtiːn, -θ]
sixteen	16	*(th)*	the/a	sixteenth [sɪksˈtiːn, -θ]
fifteen	15	*(th)*	the/a	fifteenth [fɪfˈtiːn, -θ]

fourteen	14	*(th)*	the/a	fourteenth [fɔːˈtiːn, -θ]
thirteen	13	*(th)*	the/a	thirteenth [θɜːˈtiːn, -θ]
twelve	12	*(th)*	the/a	**twelf**th [twelv, twelfθ]
eleven	11	*(th)*	the/an	eleventh [ɪˈlevn, -θ]
ten	10	*(th)*	the/a	tenth [ten, -θ]
nine	9	*(th)*	the/a	**nin**th [naɪn, -θ]
eight	8	*(th)*	the/an	eigh**t**h [eɪt, -θ]
seven	7	*(th)*	the/a	seventh [ˈsevn, -θ]
six	6	*(th)*	the/a	sixth [sɪks, -θ]
five	5	*(th)*	the/a	**fif**th [faɪv, fɪfθ]
four	4	*(th)*	the/a	fourth [fɔː, -θ]
three	3	*(rd)*	the/a	**third** [θriː, θɜːd]
two	2	*(nd)*	the	**second** [tuː, ˈsekənd]
one	1	*(st)*	the	**first** [wʌn, fɜːst]
nought/zero/oh	0			[nɔːt/ˈzɪərəʊ/əʊ]

the fifth – der fünfte a fifth – ein Fünftel

once *adv* [wʌns]	▶▶ one time [ˈwʌn taɪm]	einmal
twice *adv* [twaɪs]	▶▶ two times, 2x [ˈtuː taɪmz]	zweimal
times *prep* [taɪmz]	How many ~ do I have to tell you?	mal
only *adj* [ˈəʊnlɪ]	Peter is the ~ young man who wants the job. There are no others.	einzig, alleinig
alone *adj* [əˈləʊn]	▶▶ without others	allein
single *adj* [ˈsɪŋgl]	▶▶ only one	einzeln
double *adj* [ˈdʌbl]	▶▶ twice as much	doppelt

half *n* [hɑːf] *pl* **halves** [hɑːvz]	one of two equal parts	Hälfte
half *adv* [hɑːf]	The glass is only ~ full. (⩾ 50 per cent)	halb
quarter *n* ['kwɔːtə]	one of four equal parts	Viertel
pair *n* [peə]	Two things of the same kind that are together are a ~.	Paar
zero *n* ['zɪərəʊ]	the number 0	Null
not *adv* [nɒt]	We did ~ see him.	nicht
not at all [nɒt ət 'ɔːl]	It was ~ windy. (⩾ There was absolutely no wind.)	nicht im geringsten, überhaupt nicht
none *pron* [nʌn]	N~ of the prisoners was caught. (⩾ Not one)	keine(r, s)
total *n* ['təʊtl]	If you add up 3 and 8, the ~ is 11.	Summe
to add *v* [æd]	If you ~ 8 to 9 you get 17. She ~ed the numbers up/together.	zusammenzählen, addieren
calculator *n* ['kælkjʊleɪtə]	a machine that can add, subtract etc	Rechenmaschine
pocket calculator *n* ['pɒkɪt] ①		Taschenrechner
computer *n* [kəm'pjuːtə] ②		Computer
computer operator *n* ['ɒpəreɪtə] ③		Programmierer

to count *v* [kaʊnt]	The little boy can already ~ to 100. (⩾ say the numbers) The shopkeeper ~ed the money. (⩾ added up)	zählen
per *prep* [pɜː]	▶▶ for each	per, pro
per cent *n* [pɜː 'sent]	%	Prozent
problem *n* ['prɒbləm]	The teacher explained the mathematical ~ to the pupils.	Aufgabe, Problem
line *n* [laɪn]		Linie, Gerade
row *n* [rəʊ]	A ~ is a line of people or things.	Reihe
point *n* [pɔɪnt]		Punkt *(Geometrie)*
circle *n* ['sɜːkl]		Kreis
square *n* [skweə]		Quadrat
cross *n* [krɒs]		Kreuz

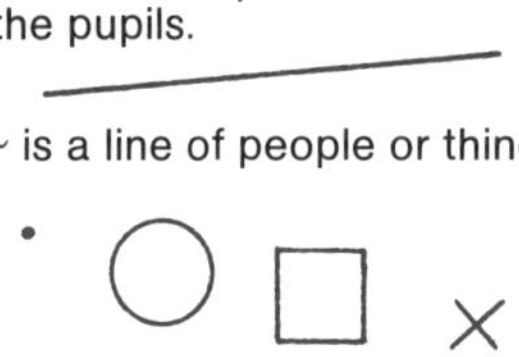

round *adj* [raʊnd]	shaped like a circle or ball	rund
square *adj* [skweə]	in the shape of a square	quadratisch
central *adj* ['sentrəl]	being in the middle of	zentral
straight *adj* [streɪt] *adv*	He drew a ~ line. Go ~ on.	gerade
direct *adj* [dɪ'rekt]	as straight as possible	direkt
to measure *vi, vt* ['meʒə]	He ~d the length of his house. The room ~s seventeen feet in length.	messen, abmessen
to weigh *vt, v* [weɪ]	She ~ed herself. The box ~s 6 pounds.	wiegen
weight *n* [weɪt]	▶▶ heaviness	Gewicht
balance *n* ['bæləns]	He **lost his** ~ and fell down.	Gleichgewicht
long *adj* [lɒŋ] ①		lang
wide *adj* [waɪd] ②		breit
broad *adj* [brɔːd] ③		breit
narrow *adj* ['nærəʊ] ④		eng

tʃ	dʒ	θ	ð	ʃ	ʒ	ŋ	w	v
cheap	**j**ump	**th**ing	**th**en	**sh**op	plea**s**ure	sa**ng**	**w**et	**v**oice

high *adj* [haɪ] ⑤		hoch
low *adj* [ləʊ] ⑥		niedrig
tall *adj* [tɔ:l] ⑦		groß *(Personen)*
short *adj* [ʃɔ:t] ⑧		klein, kurz
deep *adj* [di:p] ⑨		tief
shallow *adj* [ˈʃæləʊ] ⑩		seicht, flach
thick *adj* [θɪk] ⑪		dick
thin *adj* [θɪn] ⑫		dünn
depth *n* [depθ]	How deep is this lake? It has a ~ of 100 metres.	Tiefe

Weights and measures

1 inch *(in) n* [ɪntʃ] = 2.54 cm 1 Inch	**1 foot** *(ft) n* [fʊt] = 30.46 cm 1 Fuß	**1 yard** *(yd) n* [jɑ:d] = 91 cm (3 feet) 1 Yard	**1 mile** *n* [maɪl] = 1609 m 1 Meile	
1 millimetre *(mm) n* **millimeter** *n AE* [ˈmɪlɪmi:tə] = 0.03937 in 1 Millimeter	**1 centimetre** *(cm) n* **centimeter** *n AE* [ˈsentɪmi:tə] = 10 mm 1 Centimeter	**1 metre** *(m) n* **meter** *n AE* [ˈmi:tə] = 100 cm 1 Meter	**1 kilometre** *(km) n* **kilometer** *n AE* [ˈkɪləmi:tə] = 1000 m 1 Kilometer	
1 fluid ounce *n* [ˈflu:ɪd aʊns] = 28.41 cm 1 Flüssigunze	**1 pint** *(pt) n* [paɪnt] = 0.57 litres 1 Pint	**1 gallon** *(gal) n* [ˈgælən] = 3.785 litres = 8 pt 1 Gallone	**1 millilitre** *n* **milliliter** *n AE* [ˈmɪlɪli:tə] = 0.0176 pint 1 Milliliter	**1 litre** *(l) n* **liter** *n AE* [ˈli:tə] = 1.75 pints 1 Liter
1 ounce *(oz) n* [aʊns] = 28.35 g 1 Unze	**1 pound** *(lb) n* [paʊnd] = 16 ounces = 0.454 kg 1 Pfund	**1 ton** [tʌn] = 1.016 kilograms 1 Tonne	**1 gram** *(g) n* [græm] = 0.035 oz 1 Gramm	**1 kilo** *(kg) n* **kilogram** *n* [ˈki:lə] [ˈkɪləgræm] = 2.205 pound 1 Kilogramm

multiple *adj* [ˈmʌltɪpl]	The accident victim had ~ injuries.	mehrfach, vielfach
dozen *n* [ˈdʌzn]	a group of twelve	Dutzend
sum *n* [sʌm]	►► total	Summe
unit *n* [ˈju:nɪt]	a single item complete in itself	Einheit
arithmetic *n* [əˈrɪθmətɪk]	Working with numbers is called ~.	Rechnen, Arithmetik
to subtract *v* [səbˈtrækt]	The pupils ~ed 12 from 25 and got 13.	abziehen, subtrahieren
to take away *v + adv* [teɪk]	►► to subtract	abziehen
to multiply *v* [ˈmʌltɪplaɪ]	If you ~ 3 by 3 you get 9.	multiplizieren
to divide *v* [dɪˈvaɪd]	D~ 16 by 4 and you get 4. D~ 4 into 16 and you get 4.	dividieren, teilen
addition *n* [əˈdɪʃn]	adding up numbers	Addition
division *n* [dɪˈvɪʒn]	The ~ of 16 by 4 gives you 4.	Division

8

i:	ɪ	e	æ	ɑ:	ɒ	ɔ:	ʊ	u:	ʌ	ɜ:	ə
eat	**bit**	**ten**	**bad**	**fast**	**got**	**saw**	**sure**	**too**	**cut**	**bird**	**about**

to calculate *v* ['kælkjʊleɪt]	The teacher ~d the result. They ~d that they would arrive at four in the afternoon.	berechnen, ausrechnen, rechnen mit
to program *v* ['prəʊgræm]	They ~med the new computer. (⪢ gave instructions to)	programmieren
code number *n* ['kəʊd nʌmbə]	You'll only understand the message if you know the right ~.	Kennziffer
plus *n* [plʌs]	+	Plus
minus *n* ['maɪnəs]	–	Minus
to amount to *v + prep* [ə'maʊnt]	The bills ~ £15.50.	sich belaufen auf
average *n* ['ævərɪdʒ]	The ~ of 7, 8, and 9 is 8. (⪢ middle number)	Durchschnitt
	He gets 7 phone calls **on** ~.	im Durchschnitt
series *n* ['sɪəri:z]	a number of things coming one after another	Serie
diagram *n* ['daɪəgræm] ①		Diagramm
degree *n* [dɪ'gri:]	A right angle has 90° ~s.	Grad
zigzag *n, adv* ['zɪgzæg] ②		zickzack
oval *adj* ['əʊvl]	shaped like an egg	oval
indirect *adj* [ɪndɪ'rekt]	▶◀ direct	indirekt
measurement *n* ['meʒəmənt]	the length or height of something	Maß, Maße
length *n* [leŋθ]	The ~ of the room is 4 metres. It's four metres long.	Länge
width *n* [wɪtθ]	the size from side to side	Breite
height *n* [haɪt]	What's her ~? She's 5 feet tall.	Höhe, Größe
volume *n* ['vɒlju:m]	What's the ~ of that container?	Rauminhalt, Volumen
capacity *n* [kə'pæsətɪ]	The ~ of the barrel is 60 litres.	Kapazität, Inhalt

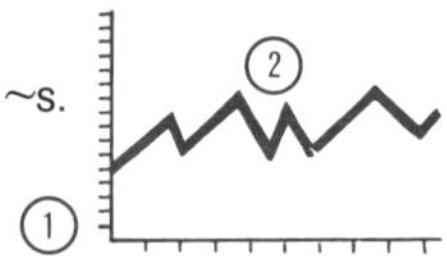

8.5 Materials and objects

material *n* [mə'tɪərɪəl]	Wood and stones are building ~s.	Material, Rohstoff
stuff *n informal* [stʌf]	▶▶ material	Zeug
atom *n* ['ætəm]	An ~ is the smallest piece of a chemical element.	Atom
atomic *adj* [ə'tɒmɪk] **nuclear** *adj* ['nju:klɪə]	Politicians often discuss ~ energy.	Atom-, atomar, nuklear
thing *n* [θɪŋ] **object** *n* ['ɒbdʒɪkt]	What's that ~ on the table?	Sache, Ding, Gegenstand
set *n* [set]	a number of things that go together	Satz, Garnitur
piece *n* [pi:s]	Would you like a ~ of cake?	Stück
part *n* [pɑ:t]	▶◀ whole	Teil
detail *n* ['di:teɪl]	I can't remember every little ~.	Einzelheit, Detail
bit *n* [bɪt]	a small amount	kleines Stück
ball *n* [bɔ:l]	The Earth is a ~.	Ball
ring *n* [rɪŋ]		Ring
wheel *n* [wi:l]	Cars run on ~s.	Rad
gas *n* [gæs]	Air contains lots of ~es.	Gas
metal *n, adj* ['metl]	Silver and gold are ~s.	Metall
gold *n, adj* [gəʊld]	She bought a ~ watch.	Gold
silver *n, adj* ['sɪlvə]	Her mother has a ~ teapot.	Silber
iron *n, adj* ['aɪən]	It was a heavy ~ gate.	Eisen

steel *n, adj* [sti:l]	Knives are made of ~.	Stahl
stone *n* [stəʊn]	Some houses are built of ~.	Stein
rock *n* [rɒk]	a large piece of stone	Felsen
sand *n* [sænd]	You find lots of ~ in the Sahara.	Sand
glass *n* [glɑ:s]	Windows are made of ~.	Glas
wood *n* [wʊd]	the material we get from trees	Holz
wooden *adj* [ˈwʊdn]	≫ made of wood	hölzern
board *n* [bɔ:d]	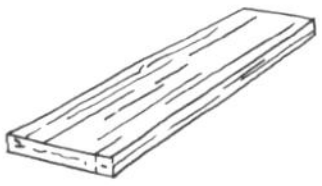	Brett
stick *n* [stɪk]		Stock
water *n* [ˈwɔ:tə]	We find ~ in rivers, lakes and the sea, and it comes down as rain.	Wasser
drop *n* [drɒp]		Tropfen
pipe *n* [paɪp]	The workmen are laying water ~s.	Rohr
tube *n* [tju:b]	a thin pipe of e.g. metal or glass	Röhre
energy *n* [ˈenədʒɪ]	the power which does work and drives machines	Energie
power *n* [ˈpaʊə]	People plan to use wind ~ to produce energy.	Kraft
coal *n* [kəʊl]	a hard, black material which gives heat when you burn it	Kohle
steam *n* [sti:m]	S~ was coming from the tea pot.	Dampf
fire *n* [ˈfaɪə]	A ~ burns and gives light and heat.	Feuer, Brand
to burn *v* [bɜ:n] **burnt** [bɜ:nt] **burnt** [bɜ:nt]	Our house is ~ing! He is ~ing the old leaves.	brennen verbrennen
to light *v* [laɪt] **lighted/lit** [ˈlaɪtɪd/lɪt] **lighted/lit** [ˈlaɪtɪd/lɪt]	'L~ the fire behind the house, please.'	anzünden
to put out *v + adv* [pʊt]	to stop (e.g. a fire) from burning	auslöschen
oil *n* [ɔɪl]	We use ~ for heating and car engines.	Öl
petrol *n* [ˈpetrəl] **gasoline** *n AE* [ˈgæsəli:n]	Please fill up the car with ~ at the next filling station.	Benzin
smoke *n* [sməʊk]	the cloud that goes up from a fire	Rauch
electricity *n* [ɪlekˈtrɪsətɪ]	E~ can produce heat, light and sound and can move things.	Elektrizität
electric *adj* [ɪˈlektrɪk]	producing or using electricity	elektrisch
electrical *adj* [ɪˈlektrɪkl]	His mother is an ~ engineer.	Elektro-, elektrisch
electronics *n* [ɪlekˈtrɒnɪks]	He's studying ~.	Elektronik
current *n* [ˈkʌrənt]	electricity running through a wire	Strom
cotton *n, adj* [ˈkɒtn]	She likes wearing ~ shirts.	Baumwolle
wool *n* [wʊl]	He took a new ball of ~ and started knitting.	Wolle
woollen *adj* [ˈwʊlən]	≫ made of wool	wollen, aus Wolle
string *n* [strɪŋ]	A ~ is a long, thin line used for tying things up.	Bindfaden, Schnur
wire *n* [ˈwaɪə]	thin metal like a string	Draht
leather *n, adj* [ˈleðə]	Most shoes are made of ~.	Leder
plastic *n, adj* [ˈplæstɪk]	Put all the things into a ~ bag.	Plastik
soap *n* [səʊp]	We use ~ to wash things.	Seife
ink *n* [ɪŋk]	Sometimes she writes her letters **in** ~.	Tinte
tool *n* [tu:l]	I need the right ~s for the job.	Werkzeug

machine *n* [məˈʃiːn]	Computers and cassette recorders are ~s.	Maschine
motor *n* [ˈməʊtə]	A washing-machine has an electric ~.	Motor
engine *n* [ˈendʒɪn]	An ~ makes things move.	Maschine, Motor
lamp *n* [læmp] ①		Lampe
spade *n* [speɪd] ②		Spaten
bell *n* [bel] ③		Glocke
glasses *n* [ˈglɑːsɪz] ④		Brille
match *n* [mætʃ] ⑤		Streichholz
lock *n* [lɒk] ⑥		Türschloß, Schloß
key *n* [kiː] ⑦		Schlüssel
handle *n* [ˈhændl] ⑧		Türklinke, Griff
knob *n* [nɒb] ⑨		(Dreh)Knopf
knife *n, pl* **knives** [naɪf, naɪvz] ⑩		Messer
pin *n* [pɪn] ⑪		Stecknadel
needle *n* [ˈniːdl] ⑫		Nähnadel
screw *n* [skruː] ⑬		Schraube

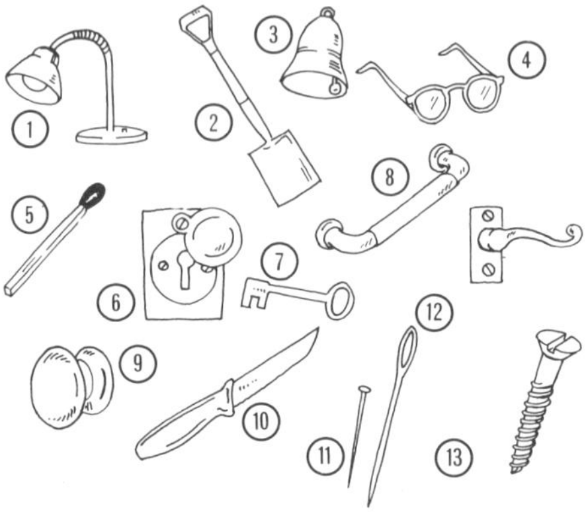

to stick *v* [stɪk] **stuck** [stʌk] **stuck** [stʌk]	S~ the stamp on the envelope. Don't ~ the needle into your finger.	kleben stechen
sharp *adj* [ʃɑːp]	He uses a ~ knife to cut the vegetables.	scharf
fridge *n* [frɪdʒ] ①		Kühlschrank
basket *n* [ˈbɑːskɪt] ②		Korb
box *n* [bɒks] *pl* **boxes** [ˈbɒksɪz] ③		Schachtel, Behälter
case *n* [keɪs]	a large box	Kiste
tin *n* [tɪn] **can** *n AE* [kæn]	She bought a ~ of soup.	Dose, Büchse
tinned *adj* [tɪnd]	I don't like ~ food.	aus der Dose

tube *n* [tjuːb]		Tube
packet *n* [ˈpækɪt]	He lost a ~ of cigarettes.	Päckchen
suitcase *n* [ˈsuːtkeɪs]		Koffer
luggage *n BE* [ˈlʌgɪdʒ] **baggage** *n AE* [ˈbægɪdʒ]	suitcases, bags etc taken on a journey	Gepäck
bag *n* [bæg]	Put everything in that paper ~.	Tüte, Tasche
to pick up *v + prep* [pɪk]	to take something up from the ground	aufheben
to pack *v* [pæk]	He ~ed his clothes into a suitcase.	einpacken
to wrap *v* [ræp]	W~ the books in paper, please.	einwickeln
to contain *v* [kənˈteɪn]	The box ~s 6 bottles of beer.	enthalten
to include *v* [ɪnˈkluːd]	The class of twenty-five ~s 8 girls.	enthalten, einschließen
waste *n* [weɪst]	Put the ~ in the dustbin.	Abfall
resources *n* [rɪˈsɔːsɪz]	Africa has great **natural** ~ such as oil, coal and water.	Rohstoffe, Bodenschätze
element *n* [ˈelɪmənt]	The ~s of water are hydrogen and oxygen.	Element
item *n* [ˈaɪtəm]	a single thing in a list	Punkt, Posten
solid *n, adj* [ˈsɒlɪd]	Metals are ~s.	Feststoff; fest, solid
liquid *n, adj* [ˈlɪkwɪd]	Water and oil are ~s.	Flüssigkeit, flüssig
chemical *adj* [ˈkemɪkl]	The scientists watched a ~ reaction.	chemisch
article *n* [ˈɑːtɪkl]	▶▶ thing, object, item of goods	Artikel, Gegenstand

Only one sound is different

	NOUN **c** [s]:	advi**c**e [əd'vaɪs]	practi**c**e ['præktɪs]	
	VERB **s** [z]:	advi**s**e [əd'vaɪz]	practi**s**e ['præktɪs]	
NOUN **f** [f]:	li**f**e [laɪf]	sa**f**ety ['seɪftɪ]	proo**f** [pru:f]	belie**f** [bɪ'li:f]
VERB **v** [v]:	li**v**e [lɪv]	sa**v**e [seɪv]	pro**v**e [pru:v]	belie**v**e [bɪ'li:v]

slice *n* [slaɪs]	She took another ~ of meat. (≫ thin, flat piece)	Scheibe
mass *n* [mæs]	a large quantity or number	Masse
heap *n* [hi:p] **pile** *n* [paɪl]	a mass of things one on top of the other	Haufen
bunch *n* [bʌntʃ]	He sent her a ~ of flowers.	Bund, Strauß
section *n* ['sekʃn]	a part of an object, group or place	Abteilung, Sektion
soil *n* [sɔɪl] **earth** *n* [ɜ:θ]	S~ is the material in which plants can grow.	Erdboden, Erde
powder *n* ['paʊdə]	P~ is material in very small pieces, e.g. washing ~.	Pulver, Puder
mud *n* [mʌd]	soft, wet earth	Schlamm
muddy *adj* ['mʌdɪ]	The earth was ~ after the rain.	schlammig
rocky *adj* ['rɒkɪ]	≫ full of rocks	felsig
concrete *n* ['kɒŋkri:t]	a hard, grey building material	Beton
quarry *n* ['kwɒrɪ]	a place where stone is dug out	Steinbruch
block *n* [blɒk]	a solid piece of e.g. stone or wood	Block
brick *n* [brɪk]	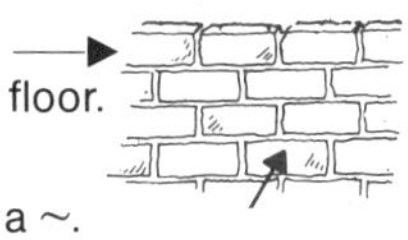	Ziegel, Backstein
bar *n* [bɑ:]	The **gold** ~s lay on the floor.	Stange, Stück, Barren
jewel *n* ['dʒu:əl]	a precious stone	Edelstein, Juwel
diamond *n* ['daɪəmənd]	You can cut glass with a ~.	Diamant
pearl *n* [pɜ:l]		Perle
tin *n* [tɪn]	a soft white metal	Zinn
lead *n* [led]	a heavy grey metal	Blei
copper *n* ['kɒpə]	a red-brown metal	Kupfer
uranium *n* [jʊ'reɪnɪəm]	U~ is used to produce nuclear power.	Uran
log *n* [lɒg]	a thick piece of wood	(Holz-)Klotz, (gefällter) Baumstamm
pole *n* [pəʊl]	The little boy tried to climb up the telegraph ~.	Mast, Stange, Pfahl
rubber *n* ['rʌbə]	Tyres are made of ~.	Gummi
oyxgen *n* ['ɒksɪdʒən]	Climbers need ~ when they reach a certain height.	Sauerstoff
spark *n* [spɑ:k]	a tiny bit of burning material	Funke
fuel *n* ['fju:əl]	Wood, oil, coal and gas are kinds of ~.	Brennstoff
power station *n* ['paʊə steɪʃn]	a place where electricity is produced	Kraftwerk
pipeline *n* ['paɪplaɪn]	The firm built an oil ~ across the desert.	Pipeline, Ölleitung
textiles *n* ['tekstaɪlz]	materials made of wool, nylon etc	Textilien
silk *n* [sɪlk]	He bought a green ~ scarf.	Seide
canvas *n* ['kænvəs]	the strong material used for tents and sails	Segeltuch, Leinwand
linen *n* ['lɪnɪn]	material made from flax	Leinen
denim *n* ['denɪm]	a kind of cotton material used for making jeans or overalls	Jeansstoff

8

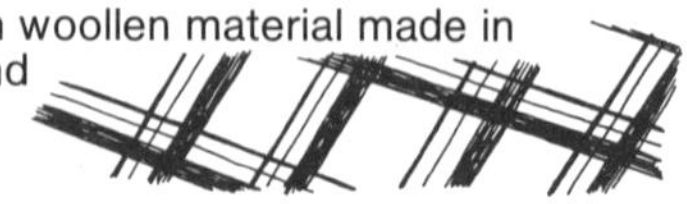

tweed *n* [twi:d]	a rough woollen material made in Scotland	Tweed
tartan *n* ['tɑ:tn]		Schottenmuster, Schottenstoff
band *n* [bænd]	They kept the box together with a rubber ~.	Band
tape *n* [teɪp]	He closed the envelope with a piece of ~.	Band, Klebeband
ribbon *n* ['rɪbən]	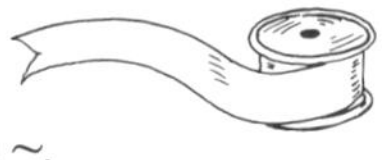	Band, Farbband
strip *n* [strɪp]	a long, narrow piece	Streifen
strip of paper *n* [strɪp, 'peɪpə]	He wrote the lines on a ~.	Papierstreifen
thread *n* [θred]		Faden
rope *n* [rəʊp]	People climbing mountains have to use ~s.	Seil
cable *n* ['keɪbl]	a thick rope made of metal wires	Kabel
chain *n* [tʃeɪn]		Kette
line *n* [laɪn]	Mum is putting the wet clothes on the ~.	Leine, Wäscheleine
glue *n* [glu:]	G~ is used for joining things together.	Klebstoff, Leim
sticky *adj* ['stɪkɪ]	The boy's hands were ~ with marmalade.	klebrig
to sweep *v* [swi:p] **swept** [swept] **swept** [swept]	to clean with a brush	fegen, säubern
to polish *v* ['pɒlɪʃ]	You must ~ your boots with a brush.	polieren
polish *n* ['pɒlɪʃ]	What kind of **shoe** ~ does she use?	Politur
equipment *n* [ɪ'kwɪpmənt]	the things needed to do something	Ausrüstung
instrument *n* ['ɪnstrʊmənt]	The doctor carried his ~s in his bag.	Instrument, Werkzeug
gadget *n* ['gædʒɪt]	a small, useful machine	Gerät, Vorrichtung
robot *n* ['rəʊbɒt]	a machine that can work nearly like a person	Roboter
slot machine *n* ['slɒtməʃi:n]	A ~ sells you e.g. sweets or drinks if you put a coin into it.	Automat
machinery *n* [mə'ʃi:nərɪ]	The Chinese factory bought a lot of new ~.	Maschinen
turbine *n* ['tɜ:baɪn] 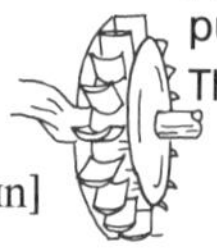		Turbine
pump *n* [pʌmp]		Pumpe
to pump *v* [pʌmp]	He ~ed the water out of his cellar.	pumpen
globe *n* [gləʊb]	an object in the shape of a ball such as a model of the earth	Kugel, Globus
sphere *n* [sfɪə]	a globe or ball	Kugel
structure *n* ['strʌktʃə]	The scientist studied the ~ of the cell.	Struktur
system *n* ['sɪstəm]	The solar ~ consists of the sun and nine planets.	System
systematic *adj* [sɪstə'mætɪk]	⋙ well-organized	systematisch
network *n* ['netwɜ:k]	A large railway ~ covers the British Isles. (⋙ system of lines)	Netz
frame *n* [freɪm]	The walls of the building are fixed to a steel ~.	Rahmen
panel *n* ['pænl]	Alternative technology uses solar ~s, windmills etc.	Platte, Tafel
candle *n* ['kændl] 		Kerze
battery *n* ['bætərɪ]		Batterie
electronic *adj* [ɪlek'trɒnɪk]	He bought a new ~ typewriter.	elektronisch

heater *n* [ˈhiːtə]	a machine to warm up e.g. air or water	Heizgerät
oven *n* [ˈʌvn] (1)	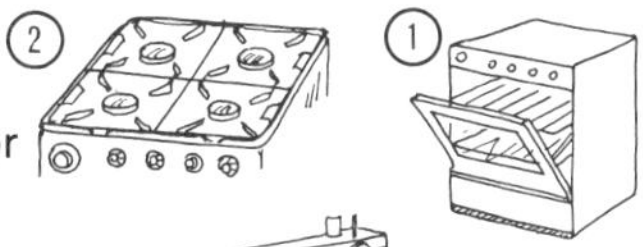	Bratröhre, Backofen
cooker *n* [ˈkʊkə] (2)		Herd
stove *n* [stəʊv]	a cooker or heater	Ofen
radiator *n* [ˈreɪdɪeɪtə] (3)	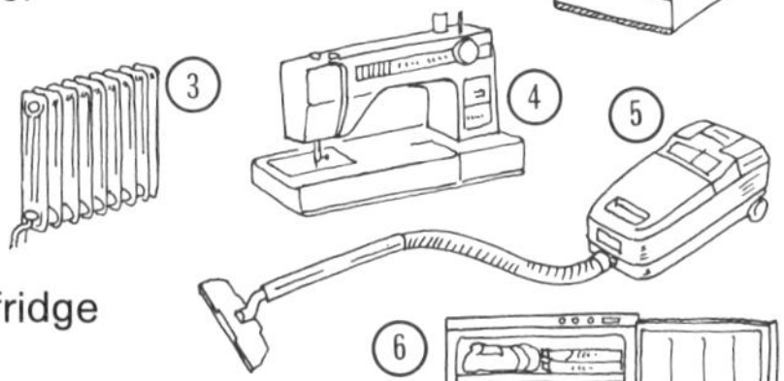	Heizkörper
sewing machine *n* [ˈsəʊɪŋ məʃiːn] (4)		Nähmaschine
vacuum cleaner *n* [ˈvækjʊəm kliːnə] (5)		Staubsauger
refrigerator *n* [rɪˈfrɪdʒəreɪtə]	▶▶ fridge 	Kühlschrank
freezer *n* [ˈfriːzə] (6)		Gefrierschrank
scales *n* [skeɪlz] **pair of scales** *n* [peər əv ˈskeɪlz] (7)		Waage
spectacles *n* [ˈspektəklz]	▶▶ glasses	Brille
thermometer *n* [θəˈmɒmɪtə]	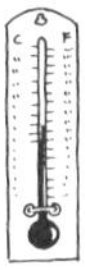	Thermometer
lens *n* [lenz]		Linse
contact lens *n* [ˈkɒntækt lenz]	Jane doesn't like wearing glasses. She prefers ~es.	Kontaktlinse
keyhole *n* [ˈkiːhəʊl]	the hole for the key in a lock	Schlüsselloch
scissors *n* [ˈsɪzəz]		Schere
to sharpen *v* [ˈʃɑːpən]	▶▶ to make sharp	schärfen
blunt *adj* [blʌnt]	▶◀ sharp	stumpf
saw *n* [sɔː]		Säge
to saw *v* [sɔː] **sawed** [sɔːd] **sawn/sawed** [sɔːn/sɔːd]	to cut with a saw	sägen, zersägen
nail *n* [neɪl]		Nagel
to nail *v* [neɪl]	to fasten with a nail	annageln
flag *n* [flæg]	The British ~ is called the Union Jack.	Flagge
poster *n* [ˈpəʊstə]	His bedroom is full of beautiful ~s.	Poster, Plakat
badge *n* [bædʒ]		Abzeichen, Button
vase *n* [vɑːz]	a container for holding flowers	Vase
barrel *n* [ˈbærəl]		Faß
bin *n* [bɪn]	a large container with a lid	Behälter
chest *n* [tʃest]	a large wooden box for storing	Kiste
cage *n* [keɪdʒ] (1)	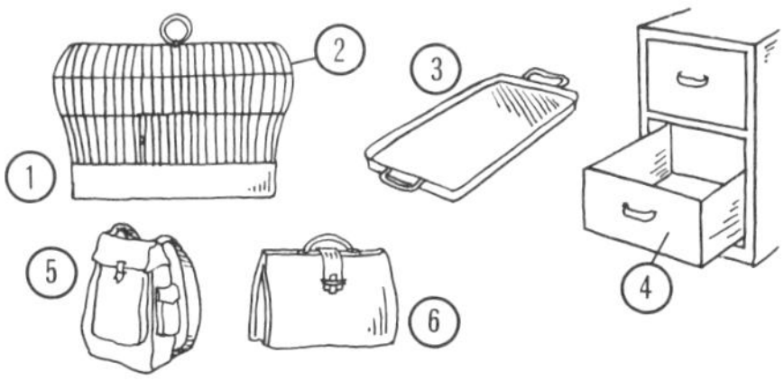	Käfig
wire netting *n* [ˈwaɪə netɪŋ] (2)		Drahtgeflecht
tray *n* [treɪ] (3)		Tablett
drawer *n* [drɔː] (4)		Schubfach
rucksack *n* [ˈrʌksæk] (5)		Rucksack
briefcase *n* [ˈbriːfkeɪs] (6)		Aktentasche
package *n* [ˈpækɪdʒ]	a parcel, a number of things packed together	Packung
cover *n* [ˈkʌvə]	Put the ~ on the pot.	Deckel
lid *n* [lɪd]		Deckel
cap *n* [kæp]		Kappe, Schraubkappe

8

☐	**to consist of** *v + prep* [kən'sɪst]	The United Kingdom ~s ~ England, Wales, Scotland and Northern Ireland.	bestehen aus
☐	**to put in** *v + adv* [pʊt]	Take the box and ~ as many books as possible.	hineinlegen
☐	**to insert** *v* [ɪn'sɜːt]	He ~ed some coins into the slot machine.	einwerfen, einfügen
☐	**to take out** *v + adv* [teɪk]	▶▶ to remove	entfernen, herausnehmen
☐	**exclusive** *adj* [ɪk'skluːsɪv]	not shared by others	ausschließlich, exklusiv
☐	**to cover** *v* ['kʌvə]	Someone ~ed the body with a blanket.	bedecken
☐	**to surround** *v* [sə'raʊnd]	A high wall ~s the house.	umgeben
☐	**to enclose** *v* [ɪn'kləʊz]	She ~d a photo with the letter.	einlegen, einschließen
☐	**to gather** *v* ['gæðə]	A big crowd ~ed in the marketplace. (▶▶ came together)	zusammenkommen
		They ~ed some roses. (▶▶ picked)	sammeln, pflücken
☐	**to collect** *v* [kə'lekt]	My brother ~s stamps and old bus tickets.	sammeln
☐	**collection** *n* [kə'lekʃn]	Peter has a good ~ of French stamps.	Sammlung
☐	**rubbish** *n* ['rʌbɪʃ]	what you throw away because it is no longer useful	Abfall, Müll
☐	**refuse** *n* ['refjuːs]	▶▶ rubbish	Abfall, Müll
☐	**litter** *n* ['lɪtə]	The streets were covered with ~ after the demonstration.	Abfall
☐	**to get rid of** [get 'rɪd]	Please ~ those old newspapers. (▶▶ throw away)	loswerden
☐	**to shed** *v* [ʃed] **shed** [ʃed] **shed** [ʃed]	Most trees ~ their leaves in autumn. (⩾ let . . . fall)	abwerfen, fallen lassen; vergießen

My own notes

tʃ	dʒ	θ	ð	ʃ	ʒ	ŋ	w	v
cheap	**j**ump	**th**ing	**th**en	**sh**op	plea**s**ure	sa**ng**	**w**et	**v**oice

9 General and abstract expressions
9.1 General actions

to make *v* [meɪk] **made** [meɪd] **made** [meɪd]	The car ~s a loud noise. The teacher ~s the pupils write a test.	machen, erzeugen veranlassen
to cause *v* [kɔ:z]	What ~d the accident?	verursachen
to force *v* [fɔ:s]	He ~d them to leave. (⩾ made them leave)	zwingen
to deal with *v + prep* [di:l]	I'll ~ this problem later. (▶▶ take care of, handle)	sich befassen mit
to realize *v* [ˈrɪəlaɪz]	He ~d all his plans. (▶▶ carried out)	verwirklichen
reason *n* [ˈri:zn]	What was the ~ **for** his anger?	Grund, Ursache
cause *n* [kɔ:z]	What was the ~ **of** the fire?	Grund, Ursache
effect *n* [ɪˈfekt]	▶▶ a result, an influence	Wirkung
result *n* [rɪˈzʌlt]	His illness is the ~ of an accident.	Ergebnis
must *v* [mʌst]	It's late. I ~ go now.	müssen
have *v* [hæv] **have got** *v* [həv ˈgɒt]	I ~ to go at nine.	müssen
ought to *v* [ˈɔ:t tə] **should** *v* [ʃʊd]	You ~ do your homework.	sollte
to need *v* [ni:d]	You ~n't tell me if you don't want to. You don't ~ to tell me.	brauchen

must [mʌst]: it is necessary
needn't [ni:dnt]: it is not necessary
mustn't [mʌsnt]: it is not allowed

to be supposed to [səˈpəʊzd]	He is ~ wear a school uniform. (▶▶ expected to) You are **not** ~ smoke here. (▶▶ allowed to)	sollen nicht dürfen
to control *v* [kənˈtrəʊl]	She couldn't ~ her feelings. The pilot ~s the plane.	kontrollieren
control *n* [kənˈtrəʊl]	Parents have no ~ **over** their children any longer.	Kontrolle
influence *n* [ˈɪnflʊəns]	The Press has a strong ~ **on** people.	Einfluß
organization *n* [ɔ:gənaɪˈzeɪʃn] **-isation** *n*	They're all busy with the ~ of the conference. (▶▶ planning, arranging)	Organisation
to organize *v* [ˈɔ:gənaɪz]	She ~d a trip to Cambridge. (⩾ planned and arranged)	organisieren
to do *v* [du:] **did** [dɪd] **done** [dʌn]	The girl is ~ing her homework.	tun, machen
to act *v* [ækt]	You must ~ now! (▶▶ take action) He ~ed very strangely. (▶▶ behaved)	handeln sich benehmen
to manage *v* [ˈmænɪdʒ]	Hugh ~d to carry the heavy box alone.	fertigbringen, schaffen
to try *v* [traɪ]	They ~ied the new soup. He ~ied to repair his car.	probieren versuchen
to do well *v + adv* [dʊ ˈwel]	▶▶ to be successful	erfolgreich sein
to pass *v* [pɑ:s]	Did you ~ the test? (▶▶ succeed in)	bestehen
success *n* [səkˈses]	a good result	Erfolg
successful *adj* [səkˈsesfʊl]	She's a ~ actress.	erfolgreich

i:	ɪ	e	æ	ɑ:	ɒ	ɔ:	ʊ	u:	ʌ	ɜ:	ə
eat	bit	ten	bad	fast	got	saw	sure	too	cut	bird	about

to improve *v* [ɪmˈpruːv]	▶▶ to make/get better	(sich) verbessern
to fail *v* [feɪl]	Unfortunately, he ~ed his final examination. (⪢ didn't pass)	durchfallen, scheitern, versagen
to repeat *v* [rɪˈpiːt]	▶▶ to do again	wiederholen
to practise *v* [ˈpræktɪs] **-ice**	Helen ~d her English. (⪢ did . . . many times in order to get better at it)	üben
practice *n* [ˈpræktɪs]	The team met regularly for ~. (▶▶ training)	Übung

Lerntip

Vokabelkartei

Viele Schüler arbeiten mit einer Vokabelkartei. Sie hat den Vorteil, daß sich schwer zu merkende Vokabeln leicht aussortieren und gezielt wiederholen lassen. Eine Karteikarte könnte etwa wie folgt aufgebaut sein:

Vorderseite (englische Vokabel)

clean (adj)
opp?
def?

Rückseite (deutsche Entsprechung)

rein, sauber
dirty
free from dirt

to fasten *v* [ˈfɑːsn]	The farmer ~ed the gate.	befestigen
to fix *v* [fɪks]	▶▶ to fasten (firmly)	befestigen
to tie *v* [taɪ]	They ~d the prisoner's arms. (▶▶ bound)	binden, festbinden
to open *v* [ˈəʊpən]	Jenny ~ed the door and went in.	öffnen
to shut *v* [ʃʌt] **shut** [ʃʌt] **shut** [ʃʌt]	▶◀ to open	schließen
to close *v* [kləʊz]	▶▶ to shut	schließen, zumachen
to lock *v* [lɒk]	Please ~ the door. (⪢ fasten . . . with a lock)	zusperren
open *adj* [ˈəʊpən]	Leave the door ~.	offen, geöffnet
shut *adj* [ʃʌt]	The window was ~. (▶◀ open)	geschlossen
closed *adj* [kləʊzd]	▶▶ shut	geschlossen
to join *v* [dʒɔɪn]	▶▶ to link, to put together	zusammenfügen
to connect *v* [kəˈnekt]	A new road ~s the two villages.	verbinden
connection *n* [kəˈnekʃn]	The telephone ~ with Japan was very good.	Verbindung
relationship *n* [rɪˈleɪʃnʃɪp] **relation** *n* [rɪˈleɪʃn]	The two countries have a friendly ~. (▶▶ connection)	Verbindung, Beziehung
united *adj* [juːˈnaɪtɪd]	▶▶ joined together, ▶◀ divided	vereinigt
to separate *v* [ˈsepəreɪt]	She ~d the good strawberries **from** the bad ones.	trennen
	We ~d near the marketplace.	sich trennen
separate *adj* [ˈseprət]	▶◀ joined	getrennt
detached *adj* [dɪˈtætʃt]	The Hills have a ~ **house**.	freistehend, getrennt
to exchange *v* [ɪksˈtʃeɪndʒ]	to give one thing for another	austauschen
exchange *n* [ɪksˈtʃeɪndʒ]	I'll give you my comic **in** ~ **for** your poster.	Austausch
to press *v* [pres]	The minister ~ed the button and started the new machine.	drücken, pressen
to damage *v* [ˈdæmɪdʒ]	A storm ~d our car.	beschädigen

adj	*adv*	*art*	*conj*	*n*	*pl*	*prep*	*pron*	*sing*
adjective	adverb(ial)	article	conjunction	noun	plural	preposition	pronoun	singular

to spoil *v* [spɔɪl] **spoilt** [spɔɪlt] **spoilt** [spɔɪlt]	▶▶ to make useless	zunichte machen, verderben
to hurt *v* [hɜːt] **hurt** [hɜːt] **hurt** [hɜːt]	She ~ her leg when she fell.	verletzen
to harm *v* [hɑːm]	▶▶ to damage, to hurt	schaden, verletzen
damage *n* ['dæmɪdʒ]	The big fire caused a lot of ~ to the factory.	Schaden, Beschädigung
to show *v* [ʃəʊ] **showed** [ʃəʊd] **shown** [ʃəʊn]	S~ me your new records. (≫ let me see)	zeigen
to hide *v* [haɪd] **hid** [hɪd] **hidden** ['hɪdn]	She ~s the stolen goods in her garage. The murderer is ~ing **from** the police.	verstecken, verbergen sich verstecken
to find *v* [faɪnd] **found** [faʊnd] **found** [faʊnd]	I can't ~ my purse anywhere.	finden
to check *v* [tʃek]	The mechanic ~ed the motor. (▶▶ examined)	überprüfen
to discover *v* [dɪ'skʌvə]	Columbus ~ed America in 1492.	entdecken
to find out *v + adv* [faɪnd]	▶▶ to discover	herausfinden, entdecken
to look for *v + prep* [lʊk]	I'm ~ing ~ my glasses. (≫ trying to find)	suchen
search *n* [sɜːtʃ]	They made a ~ for the stolen cars.	Suche
help *n* [help]	Thank you for your ~.	Hilfe
to help *v* [help]	He ~ed his friend to climb over the fence. She **couldn't** ~ cry**ing**. **It can't be** ~**ed**. (≫ We must accept it.) **I can't** ~ **it**.	helfen nicht umhin können Es läßt sich nicht ändern. Ich kann nichts dafür.
assistant *n* [ə'sɪstənt]	An ~ is a person who helps a more important person.	Assistent
to prevent (from) *v + prep* [prɪ'vent]	I couldn't ~ him ~ entering the nightclub. (≫ keep . . . from)	abhalten (von), verhindern
to save *v* [seɪv]	The doctors ~d the boy's life.	retten
to protect *v* [prə'tekt]	Helen ~ed her friend from the attacks of the others.	schützen vor, beschützen
safety *n* ['seɪftɪ]	freedom from danger	Sicherheit
care *n* [keə]	They left the baby in the ~ of their neighbours. (▶▶ protection) He always does his work with ~.	Schutz, Sorge Sorgfalt
careful *adj* ['keəfʊl]	Nicola is a very ~ driver; she never takes any risks.	vorsichtig
careless *adj* ['keəlɪs]	This is a ~ piece of work. It's full of silly mistakes.	unvorsichtig
safe *adj* [seɪf]	≫ out of danger	sicher

hurt: animals or persons
damage: things
harm: animals, persons or things

to get *v* [get] **got** [gɒt] **got** [gɒt]	Try to ~ the machine going. (≫ bring . . . to a start) He'll soon ~ caught.	bringen zu werden
to bring about *v + adv* [brɪŋ]	Computers will ~ many changes in our way of life. (▶▶ cause)	zustande bringen

9

v	*AE*	*BE*	☒	~	▶◀	▶▶	≫
verb	American English	British English	a word you have learnt	entry	opposite	synonym	paraphrase

to carry out *v + adv* ['kærɪ]	They can't ~ the plan.	ausführen
to involve *v* [ɪn'vɒlv]	The job ~s a lot of travelling. Don't ~ me **in** your problems.	nach sich ziehen verwickeln in
realization *n* **-isation** [rɪəlaɪ'zeɪʃn]	Winning the Cup was the ~ of his hopes.	Verwirklichung
effective *adj* [ɪ'fektɪv]	The new medicine is very ~. It produces good results.	wirkungsvoll
efficient *adj* [ɪ'fɪʃnt]	Peter is an ~ worker; he gets his work done quickly.	tüchtig, wirksam
inefficient *adj* [ɪnɪ'fɪʃənt]	not producing good results	unrationell, nicht wirkungsvoll
efficiency *n* [ɪ'fɪʃənsɪ]	The ~ of the new system impressed us all.	Wirksamkeit
basis *n* ['beɪsɪs]	What is the ~ **for/of** your opinion?	Grundlage, Ausgangspunkt
consequence *n* ['kɒnsɪkwəns]	You should think about **the ~s of** your plans. (▶▶ results)	Folge, Auswirkung
in consequence (of) ['kɒnsɪkwəns] **as a result (of)** [rɪ'zʌlt]	▶▶ because of	infolge
to be obliged to *v* [ə'blaɪdʒd]	▶▶ to be forced to	gezwungen sein
force *n* [fɔːs]	The burglars used ~ to get into the flat.	Gewalt
to be to *v* ['biː tə]	All classes **are to** take part in the fire practice.	müssen
to encourage *v* [ɪn'kʌrɪdʒ]	I ~d him to try again.	ermutigen
encouragement *n* [ɪn'kʌrɪdʒmənt]	help and support	Ermutigung
to establish *v* [ɪ'stæblɪʃ]	The state ~ed a new school for handicapped children.	einrichten
to found *v* [faʊnd]	The cricket club was ~ed in 1949.	gründen
to influence *v* ['ɪnflʊəns]	Mass media ~ people's opinions. (≫ have an effect on)	beeinflussen
to interfere *v* [ɪntə'fɪə]	She never ~s **in** my affairs. These noisy parties ~ **with** my work.	sich einmischen stören
to react *v* [rɪ'ækt]	How did he ~ **to** your proposal?	reagieren
reaction *n* [rɪ'ækʃn]	What was his ~ **to** your proposal?	Reaktion
repetition *n* [repɪ'tɪʃn]	doing or saying something again	Wiederholung
echo *n* ['ekəʊ]	a sound that comes back when it strikes a surface	Echo, Widerhall
to echo *v* ['ekəʊ]	Their voices ~ed when they shouted in the mountains.	widerhallen
to cope *v* [kəʊp]	She wasn't able to ~ **with** all her problems.	fertigwerden mit
to tackle *v* ['tækl]	He tried to ~ the problem. (▶▶ deal with)	anpacken
to attempt *v* [ə'tempt]	He ~ed to lift the box. (▶▶ tried)	versuchen
attempt *n* [ə'tempt]	They **made an** ~ **to** help us.	Versuch
try *n* [traɪ]	Come on; **have a** ~. (≫ make an attempt)	Versuch

MAKE	**... an attempt**	versuchen	**... a noise**	ein Geräusch verursachen
	... a decision	eine Entscheidung treffen	**... a proposal**	vorschlagen
	... a journey	eine Reise unternehmen	**... a request**	bitten um
	... a mistake	einen Fehler machen	**... a suggestion**	vorschlagen

tʃ	dʒ	θ	ð	ʃ	ʒ	ŋ	w	v
cheap	**j**ump	**th**ing	**th**en	**sh**op	plea**s**ure	sa**ng**	**w**et	**v**oice

to succeed *v* [səkˈsiːd]	He ~ed **in** passing his driving test.	Erfolg haben
to flourish *v* [ˈflʌrɪʃ]	His business is ~ing.	blühen, gedeihen
to do one's best [best]	He's ~ing his ~ to help us.	sein Bestes geben
to achieve *v* [əˈtʃiːv]	to reach successfully	erringen, erreichen
to fulfil *v* [fʊlˈfɪl] **to fulfill** *v AE* [fʊlˈfɪl]	He didn't ~ his promises. (⪢ keep, carry out)	erfüllen
improvement *n* [ɪmˈpruːvmənt]	The pupils' work shows some ~.	(Ver)Besserung
achievement *n* [əˈtʃiːvmənt]	something successfully carried out	Leistung, Erfolg
failure *n* [ˈfeɪljə]	▶◀ success	Scheitern, Mißerfolg, Versagen
to bind *v* [baɪnd] **bound** [baʊnd] **bound** [baʊnd]	to fasten with e.g. rope or string	binden, anbinden
to knot *v* [nɒt]	He ~ted the two ropes together.	verknoten, knoten
knot *n* [nɒt]		Knoten
to split *v* [splɪt] **split** [splɪt] **split** [splɪt]	Which scientist first ~ the atom?	aufteilen, spalten
to disconnect *v* [dɪskəˈnekt]	Mr Harriet ~ed the caravan **from** his car.	abhängen, trennen
to lose contact [luːz ˈkɒntækt]	Don't ~ **with** all your friends.	Kontakt verlieren
to combine *v* [kəmˈbaɪn]	The two shops ~d. (▶▶ joined)	vereinen, sich vereinen, verbinden
to unite *v* [juːˈnaɪt]	The two countries ~d to form a single state.	sich vereinigen
to be in contact [ˈkɒntækt]	Have you been ~ with your family recently? (⪢ in communication)	in Kontakt sein, Kontakt haben zu
link *n* [lɪŋk]	Something that connects is a ~.	Bindeglied, Glied
unity *n* [ˈjuːnətɪ]	U~ is strength.	Einigkeit, Einheit
separation *n* [sepəˈreɪʃn]	She was sad about the ~ **from** her husband.	Trennung, Scheidung
to dissolve *v* [dɪˈzɒlv]	Salt ~s in water.	(sich) auflösen
to tear *v* [teə] **tore** [tɔː] **torn** [tɔːn]	to break by pulling hard	zerreißen, reißen

One word form, two different pronunciations

tear — [tɪə] Träne / [teə] zerreißen	**bow** — [baʊ] sich verbeugen / [bəʊ] Bogen	**live** — [lɪv] leben / [laɪv] lebendig

to smash *v* [smæʃ]	A group of boys ~ed the shop window. (⪢ broke . . . into pieces)	zertrümmern, zerschlagen
to squeeze *v* [skwiːz]	She ~d the lemon. (⪢ pressed . . . hard)	drücken, auspressen
to strike *v* [straɪk] **struck** [strʌk] **struck** [strʌk]	▶▶ to hit	schlagen
to explode *v* [ɪkˈspləʊd]	The bomb ~d and destroyed the house.	explodieren
explosion *n* [ɪkˈspləʊʒn]	The ~ of an atomic bomb destroyed Hiroshima.	Explosion
harm *n* [hɑːm]	▶▶ damage, injury	Schaden
harmless *adj* [ˈhɑːmlɪs]	causing no damage	harmlos

puncture *n* ['pʌŋktʃə]	a small hole in a tyre	Reifenpanne, Loch im Reifen
exhibition *n* [eksɪ'bɪʃn]	a public show of paintings etc	Ausstellung
display *n* [dɪ'spleɪ]	▶▶ showing	Ausstellung, Auslage
to display *v* [dɪ'spleɪ]	The greengrocer ~s oranges in his window.	ausstellen, zeigen
to point *v* [pɔɪnt]	He ~ed **to/at** the cat on the tree.	zeigen, zielen auf
to indicate *v* ['ɪndɪkeɪt]	▶▶ to show, to point to	anzeigen, angeben
to search *v* [sɜːtʃ]	She ~ed her pockets for some coins.	durchsuchen, durchforsten
to seek *v* [siːk]	▶▶ to try to find, to look for	suchen
to come across *v + prep* [kʌm ə'krɒs]	to find or meet by chance	treffen auf, zufällig finden
to trace *v* [treɪs]	The police have ~d the stolen jewels.	aufspüren
to explore *v* [ɪk'splɔː]	Livingstone ~d Africa in the 19th century.	erforschen
discovery *n* [dɪ'skʌvərɪ]	He wrote a book about the ~ of America by Columbus.	Entdeckung
trace *n* [treɪs]	The cat left a ~ in the snow.	Spur
exploration *n* [eksplə'reɪʃn]	The ~ of all the unknown parts of the world is not yet complete.	Erforschung
check *n* [tʃek]	At the airport we went through a security ~.	Überprüfung
explorer *n* [ɪk'splɔːrə]	Livingstone was a famous ~.	Forscher, Erforscher
discoverer *n* [dɪ'skʌvərə]	Columbus was the ~ of America.	Entdecker
boy scout *n* [bɔɪ 'skaʊt]		Pfadfinder
girl guide *n* [gɜːl 'gaɪd] **girl scout** *n AE* [gɜːl 'skaʊt]		Pfadfinderin
hunter *n* ['hʌntə]	a person who hunts animals	Jäger
aid *n* [eɪd]	▶▶ help	Hilfe
to rescue *v* ['reskjuː]	to save from danger	retten
protection *n* [prə'tekʃn]	A raincoat gives ~ against the rain.	Schutz
security *n* [sɪ'kjʊərətɪ]	▶▶ safety	Sicherheit
preservation *n* [prezə'veɪʃn]	The ~ of wild life is very important.	Erhaltung
shelter *n* ['ʃeltə]	a place where you can be safe from danger or bad weather	Schutz, Unterschlupf, Obdach
to shelter *v* ['ʃeltə]	The old hut ~ed him from the storm. (▶▶ protected)	schützen, Schutz gewähren
reserve *n* [rɪ'zɜːv]	He kept $100 in ~. They visited a **nature** ~.	Reserve, Reservat
to look out *v + adv* [lʊk]	▶▶ to be careful	achten auf
carelessness *n* ['keəlɪsnɪs]	being careless	Unachtsamkeit
secure *adj* [sɪ'kjʊə]	▶▶ safe	sicher
proof *adj* [pruːf]	This material is ~ **against** water. (≫ protected)	geschützt
waterproof *adj* ['wɔːtəpruːf]	Raincoats must be ~.	wasserdicht

9.2 Quantity and size

amount *n* [ə'maʊnt]	She bought a large ~ of sugar.	Menge
size *n* [saɪz]	What is the ~ of your shoes? (≫ How big are your shoes?)	Größe

adj	*adv*	*art*	*conj*	*n*	*pl*	*prep*	*pron*	*sing*
adjective	adverb(ial)	article	conjunction	noun	plural	preposition	pronoun	singular

great *adj* [greɪt]	She took ~ care.	groß
big *adj* [bɪg]	An elephant is a ~ animal.	groß
large *adj* [lɑːdʒ]	We have a ~ living-room.	groß
small *adj* [smɔːl]	A mouse is a ~ animal. (▶◀ big)	klein
little *adj* [ˈlɪtl]	≫ small	klein
much *adj* [mʌtʃ] *adv*	I don't have ~ time. Thank you very ~.	viel sehr
more *adv* [mɔː] *adj*	The second text was ~ difficult than the first. I need ~ time. This house has ~ rooms.	mehr
most *adv* [məʊst] *adj*	She's the ~ beautiful girl in the group. M~ families have got a TV.	meist-, am meisten die meisten
many *adj* [ˈmenɪ]	Were there ~ people at the party?	viele
a lot of [lɒt] **lots of** [lɒts]	He bought ~ pop records. (≫ a large number of)	viel, viele

much/many — *negative sentences, questions*

positive sentences — lots of/a lot of/(many)

under *prep* [ˈʌndə]	The book cost ~ $8. (≫ less than)	unter, weniger als
over *prep* [ˈəʊvə]	≫ more than	über, mehr als
very *adv* [ˈverɪ]	It's ~ cold today.	sehr
far *adv* [fɑː]	His essay is ~ better than I thought. (≫ very much)	weit, bei weitem
extreme *adj* [ɪkˈstriːm]	He handled the matter with ~ care. (▶▶ very great)	äußerst
extremely *adv* [ɪkˈstriːmlɪ]	▶▶ very much, very	äußerst, höchst
about *prep* [əˈbaʊt]	There were ~ 50 people at the party.	ungefähr
little *adv* [ˈlɪtl]	The pupils understood ~ of what the teacher explained. (▶▶ not much)	wenig
a little [ˈlɪtl]	≫ some, but not much	ein wenig
less *adv* [les]	▶◀ more	weniger
least *adv* [liːst]	▶◀ most	am wenigsten
few *adj, pron* [fjuː] **fewer** [ˈfjuːə] **fewest** [ˈfjuːɪst]	~ pupils knew the answer. (▶▶ Not many)	wenige weniger am wenigsten
a few [fjuː]	a small number	ein paar
several *adj* [ˈsevrəl]	≫ some, but not many	mehrere

Amount words

uncountable		**countable**	
all most much some a little little no	▲ more / less ▼	▲ more / less/fewer ▼	all most many some several a few few no

main *adj* [meɪn]	▶▶ most important	Haupt-, hauptsächlich
to increase *v* [ɪnˈkriːs]	▶▶ to get more; ▶◀ to decrease, to reduce	anwachsen

9

v	*AE*	*BE*	☒	~	▶◀	▶▶	≫
verb	American English	British English	a word you have learnt	entry	opposite	synonym	paraphrase

only *adv* [ˈəʊnlɪ]	O~ five people attended the meeting.	nur
just *adv* [dʒʌst]	He ~ stood there, without doing anything. (▶▶ only)	nur
	It's ~ three o'clock. (▶▶ exactly)	genau, gerade
besides *adv* [bɪˈsaɪdz]	He doesn't want to come, and ~ he's rather tired. (▶▶ in addition)	außerdem
prep	There were 200 people ~ us.	außer
by the way [weɪ] **incidentally** *adv* [ɪnsɪˈdentlɪ]	B~, what do you think of the new James Bond film?	übrigens
apart from *prep* [əˈpɑːt]	▶▶ except for	abgesehen von, außer
otherwise *adv* [ˈʌðəwaɪz]	▶▶ apart from that	sonst, ansonsten
hardly *adv* [ˈhɑːdlɪ]	She could ~ speak. (⪢ almost not)	kaum

ziemlich

not	**fairly**	**quite**	**rather/pretty**	very
tired	tired	tired	tired	tired

too *adv* [tuː]	The question is ~ difficult.	zu
	I speak English. Do you speak English, ~?	auch
also *adv* [ˈɔːlsəʊ] **as well** *adv* [əz ˈwel]	▶▶ too	auch
else *adv* [els]	What ~ do you want? (⪢ more)	sonst
anything else [ˈenɪθɪŋ els]	Do you want ~? (▶▶ anything more)	sonst noch etwas
what else [wɒt ˈels]	▶▶ what more	was noch
even *adv* [ˈiːvn]	Mr West always gets up early, ~ on Sundays.	sogar, selbst
not even *adv* [nɒt ˈiːvn]	N~ the teacher noticed the mistake.	nicht einmal
both *adj, pron* [bəʊθ]	B~ policemen knew the burglar. (⪢ the two)	beide
both . . . and *conj* [bəʊθ . . . ənd]	She's a champion at ~ tennis ~ golf. (⪢ not only . . . but also)	sowohl . . . als auch
every *adj* [ˈevrɪ]	She understood ~ word he said although he was whispering.	jede(r, s)
each *adj, pron* [iːtʃ]	E~ of you take an apple.	beide, jede(r, s)
either *adj, pron* [ˈaɪðə]	Take a seat on ~ chair. (⪢ one of the two)	einer von beiden
	There was a lamp on ~ side of the sofa. (⪢ both sides)	beide
not . . . either [nɒt . . . ˈaɪðə]	You don't like him and I do ~ like him ~.	auch nicht
either . . . or *conj* [ˈaɪðə . . . ɔː]	E~ shut up ~ leave the classroom.	entweder . . . oder
or *conj* [ɔː]	You can come with me ~ watch TV.	oder
neither *adj, pron* [ˈnaɪðə]	N~ film was very good. They were both awful.	keiner von beiden
neither *adv* [ˈnaɪðə]	I can't sing. – N~ can I. (⪢ I can't either)	auch nicht
nor *conj* [nɔː]	He doesn't want to see the play. N~ do I. (⪢ And I don't either)	auch nicht
enough *adj* [ɪˈnʌf]	Have we got ~ money for the tickets?	genug, ausreichend
adv	She didn't run fast ~ to catch the bus.	
plenty *pron* [ˈplentɪ]	more than enough	reichlich, viel

full *adj* [fʊl]	The bus is ~. There are no seats left.	voll
full up *adj* ['fʊl ʌp]	completely full	vollbesetzt
completely *adv* [kəm'pli:tlɪ]	in every way	vollständig
whole *adj* [həʊl]	He told me the ~ story.	ganz, vollständig
all *adj, pron* [ɔ:l] *adv*	A~ my friends like pop records. She's ~ alone. (▶▶ completely)	alle ganz
spare *adj* [speə]	Cars have four wheels and a ~ wheel.	extra, zusätzlich
extra *adj, adv* ['ekstrə]	▶▶ additional, more than usual	extra, zusätzlich
crowded *adj* ['kraʊdɪd]	The store was ~. (▶▶ full)	voll, vollgestopft
occupied *adj* ['ɒkjʊpaɪd]	You can't use the toilet; it's ~.	besetzt
complete *adj* [kəm'pli:t]	Our work is ~ now. (▶▶ fully finished)	vollständig
total *adj* ['təʊtl]	The new film was a ~ success. (▶▶ complete)	vollständig
rest *n* [rest]	Take what you want and throw away the ~.	Rest
empty *adj* ['emptɪ]	▶◀ full	leer
to fill *v* [fɪl]	He ~ed the basket with apples.	(sich) füllen
to fill in *v + adv* [fɪl] **to complete** *v* [kəm'pli:t]	Please ~ the form. (≫ write what is necessary into)	ausfüllen
to empty *v* ['emptɪ]	▶◀ to fill	leeren

These words have different meanings

present ['preznt] — Gegenwart / Geschenk	**fine** [faɪn] — fein, gut, schön / Geldstrafe	**match** [maetʃ] — Wettspiel / Streichholz
rest [rest] — Rest / Rast, Ruhe	**porter** ['pɔ:tə] — Gepäckträger / Portier	**lie** [laɪ] — Lüge, lügen / liegen
last [la:st] — dauern / zuletzt	**bank** [bænk] — Flußufer / Bankhaus	**case** [keɪs] — Kasten / Fall, Angelegenheit

quantity *n* ['kwɒntətɪ]	▶▶ amount	Menge
grand *adj* [grænd]	≫ big and fine	großartig
immense *adj* [ɪ'mens]	▶▶ very large	unermeßlich, riesig
enormous *adj* [ɪ'nɔ:məs]	▶▶ very big	riesig, gewaltig
vast *adj* [vɑ:st]	Australia is a ~ continent. (≫ very large and wide)	weit, riesig
huge *adj* [hju:dʒ]	▶▶ very big	riesig
gigantic *adj* [dʒaɪ'gæntɪk]	≫ unusually big	riesenhaft, gigantisch
terrific *adj* [tə'rɪfɪk]	There was a ~ storm during the night. (▶▶ very great) Your party was ~.	furchtbar, schrecklich großartig, toll
considerable *adj* [kən'sɪdərəbl]	He earned a ~ sum of money.	beträchtlich
tiny *adj* ['taɪnɪ]	a ~ animal (▶▶ very small)	winzig

9

i:	ɪ	e	æ	ɑ:	ɒ	ɔ:	ʊ	u:	ʌ	ɜ:	ə
eat	bit	ten	bad	fast	got	saw	sure	too	cut	bird	about

major *adj* ['meɪdʒə]	The ~ part of the work is done now. (▶▶ greater)	größer
minor *adj* ['maɪnə]	▶▶ unimportant	kleiner
principal *adj* ['prɪnsəpl]	▶▶ main	Haupt-, hauptsächlich
chief *adj* [tʃi:f]	Do you know the ~ cities of England? (▶▶ main)	Haupt-, wichtigst
mainly *adv* ['meɪnlɪ] **largely** *adv* ['lɑ:dʒlɪ]	▶▶ mostly	hauptsächlich
superior *adj* [su:'pɪərɪə]	better or more important	überlegen, höherstehend
inferior *adj* [ɪn'fɪərɪə]	▶◀ superior	minderwertig, unterlegen
advanced *adj* [əd'vɑ:nst]	He's taking an ~ course in English. (▶◀ elementary)	fortgeschritten
maximum *n* ['mæksɪməm]	the largest number or amount	Maximum
minimum *n* ['mɪnɪməm]	the smallest number or amount	Minimum
to reduce *v* [rɪ'dju:s]	▶◀ to increase	verringern
to shrink *v* [ʃrɪŋk] **shrank/shrunk** [ʃræŋk/ʃrʌŋk] **shrunk** [ʃrʌŋk]	Woollen pullovers ~ in hot water. (▶▶ become smaller)	schrumpfen, einlaufen
growth *n* [grəʊθ]	It's interesting to watch the ~ of a pet.	Wachsen, Wachstum
increase *n* ['ɪŋkri:s]	There has been an ~ in traffic.	Anwachsen, Zunahme
reduction *n* [rɪ'dʌkʃn]	▶◀ increase	Verringerung, Ermäßigung
a great deal [greɪt 'di:l] **a good deal** [gʊd 'di:l]	▶▶ very much, a lot	viel
numerous *adj* ['nju:mərəs]	The diplomat had ~ friends. (▶▶ very many)	zahlreich
innumerable *adj* [ɪ'nju:mərəbl]	too many to be counted	unzählig
many a ['menɪ]	I've met him ~ time. (⩾ many times)	manch
quite a few [kwaɪt ə 'fju:]	▶▶ several, a number of	mehrere
at least *adv* [ət 'li:st]	It costs ~ $30. (⩾ not less than) The coffee wasn't good, but ~ it was hot.	mindestens wenigstens
not least [nɒt 'li:st]	▶▶ especially	besonders
not in the least [li:st]	I do ~ want to know about it. (▶▶ not at all)	nicht im geringsten
scarcely *adv* ['skeəslɪ]	▶▶ hardly	kaum, mit Mühe
in addition [ə'dɪʃn]	I~ to a dog, we have two cats and an alligator.	außer
as well as [əz 'wel əz]	▶▶ in addition to	außer, zusätzlich zu, sowie
likewise *adv* ['laɪkwaɪz]	▶▶ similarly, in the same way	ebenso, gleichfalls
additionally *adv* [ə'dɪʃənəlɪ]	She said, ~, that she'd like to meet you. (▶▶ too)	noch dazu, außerdem
moreover *adv* [mɔ:'rəʊvə]	▶▶ besides	außerdem, weiterhin
furthermore *adv* [fɜ:ðə'mɔ:]		
except *prep* [ɪk'sept]	All the pupils came ~ Peter, who was ill.	außer
aside from [ə'saɪd]	▶▶ apart from	abgesehen von
or else [ɔ:r 'els]	Hurry up, ~ you'll be late. (▶▶ if not)	ansonsten
mutual *adj* ['mju:tʃʊəl]	He's our ~ friend; we both like him.	gemeinsam, gegenseitig
available *adj* [ə'veɪləbl]	There are no rooms ~ in this hotel. (⩾ ready to be used)	verfügbar, zur Verfügung
sufficient *adj* [sə'fɪʃnt]	▶▶ enough	ausreichend, genug
insufficient *adj* [ɪnsə'fɪʃnt]	▶▶ not enough	ungenügend

adj	*adv*	*art*	*conj*	*n*	*pl*	*prep*	*pron*	*sing*
adjective	adverb(ial)	article	conjunction	noun	plural	preposition	pronoun	singular

Opposites ▶◀

un-	in-	im-	ir-	non-	dis-
unhappy	**in**correct	**im**patient	**ir**regular	**non**sense	**dis**agree
unable	**in**convenient	**im**polite			**dis**appear
unconscious	**in**dependent	**im**possible			**dis**like
unemployed	**in**direct				**dis**connect
unfair	**in**efficient				
unfriendly	**in**formal				
unlucky	**in**sufficient				
unpleasant					

additional *adj* [ə'dɪʃənl]	▶▶ extra	zusätzlich
surplus *adj, n* ['sɜ:pləs]	▶▶ additional	überzählig, Überfluß
overcrowded *adj* [əʊvə'kraʊdɪd]	completely full, too full of people	überfüllt
absolute *adj* ['æbsəlu:t]	▶▶ complete	vollständig, völlig
entire *adj* [ɪn'taɪə]	▶▶ whole, total	gesamt, ganz, vollständig
thorough *adj* ['θʌrə]	They gave the house a ~ cleaning. (▶▶ complete)	gründlich
entirely *adv* [ɪn'taɪəlɪ] **totally** *adv* ['təʊtəlɪ]	▶▶ completely	völlig
incomplete *adj* [ɪnkəm'pli:t]	not fully finished	unvollständig

9.3 Quality

heavy *adj* ['hevɪ]	I can't carry this box. It's too ~. His father is a ~ **smoker**. He smokes 40 cigarettes a day.	schwer stark
light *adj* [laɪt]	▶◀ heavy	leicht
flat *adj* [flæt]	The earth is round, not ~.	flach
hard *adj* [hɑ:d]	Rocks are ~.	hart
stiff *adj* [stɪf]	The paper is ~; you can't very easily bend it.	steif
smooth *adj* [smu:ð]	The table was ~. It had a surface like glass.	glatt
soft *adj* [sɒft]	▶◀ hard	weich
rough *adj* [rʌf]	The sea was ~ and stormy.	rauh
tight *adj* [taɪt]	My trousers are too ~. I can hardly get into them. The rope was ~. (▶▶ stretched)	eng gespannt, straff
loose *adj* [lu:s]	▶◀ tight	locker, lose
general *adj* ['dʒenrəl]	without details	allgemein
altogether *adv* [ɔ:ltə'geðə]	≫ on the whole I can't agree with you ~. (▶▶ completely)	im ganzen völlig
normal *adj* ['nɔ:ml]	▶▶ usual, regular	normal
ordinary *adj* ['ɔ:dɪnrɪ]	▶▶ usual, common	gewöhnlich
usual *adj* ['ju:ʒl]	She arrived at the ~ time.	gewöhnlich, normal
as usual [əz 'ju:ʒl]	You're late, ~.	wie gewöhnlich
usually *adv* ['ju:ʒəlɪ]	I ~ go to bed at 10 o'clock.	normalerweise
regular *adj* ['regjʊlə]	The doctor told him to have ~ meals.	regelmäßig
irregular *adj* [ɪ'regjʊlə]	▶◀ regular	unregelmäßig

9

to be used to [ˈjuːst tə]	My father is ~ walking to his office.	gewöhnt sein an
to be accustomed to [əˈkʌstəmd tə]	(▶▶ familiar with)	
particular *adj* [pəˈtɪkjʊlə]	I like this author, but I didn't enjoy this ~ book.	besondere(r, s)
especially *adv* [ɪˈspeʃəlɪ]	I like all kinds of music, ~ rock and soul music.	besonders
in particular [pəˈtɪkjʊlə]		
particularly *adv* [pəˈtɪkjʊləlɪ]		
easy *adj* [ˈiːzɪ]	This question is ~ to answer.	leicht
simple *adj* [ˈsɪmpl]	The job is quite ~.	einfach, leicht
difficult *adj* [ˈdɪfɪkəlt]	English isn't ~ to learn, is it?	schwierig, schwer
hard *adj* [hɑːd]		
special *adj* [ˈspeʃl]	You must have ~ shoes for climbing.	speziell, besondere(r, s)
strange *adj* [streɪndʒ]	They heard a ~ noise.	seltsam, ungewöhnlich
trouble *n* [ˈtrʌbl]	▶▶ difficulty	Schwierigkeit
to be in trouble [ˈtrʌbl]	to have problems	in Schwierigkeiten sein

Don't mix them up.

also [ˈɔːlsəʊ] auch	**pri c e** [praɪs] Preis	**how** [haʊ] wie	**had** [hæd] hatte
although [ɔːlˈðəʊ] obwohl	**pri z e** [praɪz] Belohnung	**who** [huː] wer	**head** [hed] Kopf
		where [weə] wo	**hat** [hæt] Hut
country [ˈkʌntrɪ] Land	**pupil** [ˈpjuːpl] Schüler(in)	**because** [bɪˈkɒz] weil, da	
county [ˈkaʊntɪ] Grafschaft	**people** [ˈpiːpl] Leute	**of course** [əvˈkɔːs] natürlich	

right *adj* [raɪt]	What is the ~ answer?	richtig
correct *adj* [kəˈrekt]		
proper *adj* [ˈprɒpə]	You must have the ~ tools to do this job. (▶▶ right)	richtig, geeignet
suitable *adj* [ˈsuːtəbl]	This man isn't ~ for the job.	geeignet, passend
exact *adj* [ɪgˈzækt]	What is the ~ time of the course? (▶▶ correct)	korrekt, richtig, genau
exactly *adv* [ɪgˈzæktlɪ]	The match started at ~ three o'clock. (≫ just) ▶◀ roughly	genau
perfect *adj* [ˈpɜːfɪkt]	Her English is almost ~.	perfekt, vollkommen
ideal *adj* [aɪˈdɪəl]	(≫ as good as it can be)	
wrong *adj* [rɒŋ]	▶◀ right	falsch
false *adj* [fɔːls]	▶▶ wrong	falsch
mistake *n* [mɪˈsteɪk]	Your dictation is full of ~s.	Fehler
fault *n* [fɔːlt]	His only ~ is laziness. (▶▶ weak point)	Fehler, Schwachstelle
it's my fault [fɔːlt]	▶▶ I'm responsible, I'm to blame	es ist meine Schuld
broken *adj* [ˈbrəʊkən]	The machine is ~ .	kaputt
out of order [ˈɔːdə]	My telephone is ~. (▶▶ not working)	kaputt
fair *adj* [feə] *adv*	Taking all the money isn't ~. He always plays ~.	fair
reasonable *adj* [ˈriːznəbl]	They sold us the car at a ~ price. (▶▶ fair)	vernünftig
strong *adj* [strɒŋ]	Hercules was a very ~ man.	stark

powerful *adj* ['paʊəfʊl]	▶▶ very strong	kraftvoll
weak *adj* [wi:k]	▶◀ strong	schwach
to be able *v* ['eɪbl]	Are you ~ to come? (≫ Can you come?)	in der Lage sein, können
can *n* [kæn]	C~ you open the box, please?	können
could *v* [kʊd]	He ~ not translate the text. (≫ wasn't able to)	konnte
unable *adj* [ʌn'eɪbl]	▶▶ not able	unfähig, nicht in der Lage
in order to ['ɔ:də]	▶▶ so that	um, um zu
useful *adj* ['ju:sfʊl]	▶▶ helpful	nützlich, von Nutzen
useless *adj* ['ju:slɪs]	▶▶ of no use	sinnlos, zwecklos
ready *adj* ['redɪ]	He's always ~ to help.	bereit, fertig
lightweight *adj, n* ['laɪtweɪt]	He's a ~ boxer.	leicht, leichtgewichtig
mild *adj* [maɪld]	We had ~ weather.	mild
to shorten *v* ['ʃɔ:tn]	▶▶ to make shorter	verkürzen
to stretch *v* [stretʃ]	Try to ~ that rope. (≫ pull . . . to make it longer)	strecken, dehnen
on the whole [həʊl]	O~, he's a good teacher. (▶▶ Generally speaking)	im ganzen
relatively *adv* ['relətɪvlɪ]	My grandfather walks ~ fast for a man of 80. (▶▶ quite)	relativ
familiar *adj* [fə'mɪlɪə]	I'm ~ with the problem. (≫ I know the problem well.)	vertraut mit, bekannt
to get used to ['ju:st tə] **to get accustomed to** [ə'kʌstəmd tə]	She must try to ~ her new situation. (≫ become familiar with)	sich gewöhnen an
moderate *adj* ['mɒdərət]	▶◀ extreme	gemäßigt
by far [baɪ 'fɑ:]	He is ~ the best man.	bei weitem
above all [ə'bʌv ɔ:l]	most important of all	vor allem
unusual *adj* [ʌn'ju:ʒl]	It is ~ to see him without his girlfriend. (▶▶ strange)	ungewöhnlich
fancy *adj* ['fænsɪ]	He has many ~ ideas. (▶▶ unusual)	fantastisch, ausgefallen
fantastic *adj* [fæn'tæstɪk]	What ~ ideas she has! (▶▶ very strange)	fantastisch
specific *adj* [spə'sɪfɪk]	▶▶ particular, very special	besondere(r, s) spezifisch
extraordinary *adj* [ɪk'strɔ:dnrɪ]	Does anyone believe this ~ story? (▶▶ remarkable, very unusual)	außergewöhnlich
remarkable *adj* [rɪ'mɑ:kəbl]	▶▶ unusual	bemerkenswert
overwhelming *adj* [əʊvə'welmɪŋ]	The victory was ~.	überwältigend
odd *adj* [ɒd] **curious** *adj* ['kjʊərɪəs]	▶▶ strange	seltsam, sonderbar
suspicious *adj* [sə'spɪʃəs]	The policeman became ~ when he saw the man climbing through a window.	mißtrauisch
	The man's behaviour was ~.	verdächtig
monster *n* ['mɒnstə]	Frankenstein created a ~.	Monster
Martian *n* ['mɑ:ʃn]	a person from the planet Mars	Marsmensch
elementary *adj* [elɪ'mentərɪ]	▶▶ simple, ▶◀ advanced	elementar
difficulty *n* ['dɪfɪkəltɪ]	She had ~ (in) answering his questions. (▶▶ problems)	Schwierigkeit
hardship *n* ['hɑ:dʃɪp]	difficult conditions of life	Mühsal, Bedrängnis

i:	ɪ	e	æ	ɑ:	ɒ	ɔ:	ʊ	u:	ʌ	ɜ:	ə
eat	bit	ten	bad	fast	got	saw	sure	too	cut	bird	about

to simplify *v* [ˈsɪmplɪfaɪ]	to make easier or simpler	vereinfachen
to regulate *v* [ˈregjʊleɪt]	A policeman was ~ing the traffic. (▶▶ controlling)	regulieren
valid *adj* [ˈvælɪd]	Your train ticket is no longer ~. Get a new one.	gültig
precise *adj* [prɪˈsaɪs]	▶▶ exact	präzise, genau
accurate *adj* [ˈækjərət]	▶▶ correct, free of mistakes	richtig, genau
incorrect *adj* [ɪnkəˈrekt]	▶◀ correct	falsch
defective *adj* [dɪˈfektɪv]	▶▶ with faults	fehlerhaft
error *n* [ˈerə]	▶▶ mistake	Fehler, Irrtum
slip *n* [slɪp]	a slight mistake	Fehler, Schnitzer
to mix up *v + adv* [mɪks]	It's easy to ~ her ~ with her twin sister.	verwechseln
just *adj* [dʒʌst]	The judge is a very ~ man. (▶▶ fair)	gerecht
fairness *n* [ˈfeənɪs]	The teacher always acted with ~.	Gerechtigkeit, Ehrlichkeit
unfair *adj* [ʌnˈfeə]	His decision was rather ~.	ungerecht, unfair
use *n* [juːs]	This old bike is of no ~. You can throw it away.	Verwendung, Zweck
sensible *adj* [ˈsensəbl]	▶▶ reasonable	vernünftig

sensitive	**sensibel**
liking	**Sympathie**
vulgar	**ordinär**
personnel, staff	**Personal**

sensible [ˈsensəbl]	vernünftig
sympathy [ˈsɪmpəθɪ]	Mitleid, Mitgefühl
ordinary [ˈɔːdɪnrɪ]	normal, gewöhnlich
personal [ˈpɜːsənl]	persönlich

worthwhile *adj* [wɜːθˈwaɪl]	The visit to the castle was ~.	lohnend, die Mühe wert
rewarding *adj* [rɪˈwɔːdɪŋ]		
it's no use [juːs]	I~ complaining! Nobody will listen to you.	es hat keinen Sinn
in vain *adv* [veɪn]	▶▶ without success	vergebens
vain *adj* [veɪn]	It was a ~ attempt. (▶▶ unsuccessful)	vergeblich
aimless *adj* [ˈeɪmlɪs]	▶▶ useless, with no aim/purpose	ziellos, sinnlos
inconvenient *adj* [ɪnkənˈviːnɪənt]	▶◀ convenient	unbequem
inconvenience *n* [ɪnkənˈviːnɪəns]	▶▶ trouble	Unannehmlichkeit
to enable *v* [ɪˈneɪbl]	Our help ~d her to pass the exam. (≫ made it possible for)	ermöglichen, befähigen
to strengthen *v* [ˈstreŋθn]	to make/become strong(er)	stärken
to weaken *v* [ˈwiːkən]	to make/become weak(er)	schwächen
tough *adj* [tʌf]	▶▶ strong	zäh
strength *n* [streŋθ]	My neighbour is a man of great ~; he's very strong.	Stärke
might *n* [maɪt]	▶▶ power, strength	Macht
weakness *n* [ˈwiːknɪs]	▶◀ strength	Schwäche

9.4 Having and getting

to belong to *v + prep* [bɪˈlɒŋ]	These books ~ her; they're hers.	gehören
about *prep* [əˈbaʊt]	He wrote a book ~ German history.	über

adj	*adv*	*art*	*conj*	*n*	*pl*	*prep*	*pron*	*sing*
adjective	adverb(ial)	article	conjunction	noun	plural	preposition	pronoun	singular

concerning *prep* [kən'sɜːnɪŋ]	His mother got a letter ~ his behaviour at school. (≫ about)	betreffend
as far as [əz 'fɑː əz]	A~ I know she is leaving today.	soweit
of *prep* [əv]	Who is the owner ~ this car?	von
to have *v* [hæv] **to have got** [həv 'gɒt]	They ~ a French car.	haben, besitzen
own *adj, pron* [əʊn]	I saw the accident with my ~ eyes.	eigen
owner *n* ['əʊnə]	Do you know the ~ of this house? (≫ person who owns)	Eigentümer(in)
to own *v* [əʊn]	He ~s a small car.	besitzen
things *n* [θɪŋz]	They packed their ~ for the trip.	Sachen
property *n* ['prɒpətɪ]	what belongs to you	Besitz

to take *v* [teɪk] **took** [tʊk] **taken** ['teɪkən]	T~ the money and go away.	nehmen
to keep *v* [kiːp] **kept** [kept] **kept** [kept]	You can ~ the book. I don't need it.	behalten
to choose *v* [tʃuːz] **chose** [tʃəʊz] **chosen** ['tʃəʊzn]	Please ~ one of the books.	auswählen
choice *n* [tʃɔɪs]	There are so many things. It's difficult to **make a** ~.	Wahl, Auswahl
to get *v* [get] **got** [gɒt] **got** [gɒt]	You'll ~ a lot of presents for your birthday. I'll ~ you something to eat.	bekommen, erhalten holen, besorgen
to receive *v* [rɪ'siːv]	Mary ~d a love letter yesterday.	erhalten, empfangen
to bring back *v + adv* [brɪŋ]	He must ~ the money I gave him.	zurückbringen
to get back *v + adv* [get]	I must ~ the money ~.	zurückbekommen
to hold *v* [həʊld] **held** [held] **held** [held]	He was ~ing the glass in his hand. (≫ keeping)	halten
to catch *v* [kætʃ] **caught** [kɔːt] **caught** [kɔːt]	Try to ~ the ball.	fangen
to give *v* [gɪv] **gave** [geɪv] **given** ['gɪvn]	The cake is really good. G~ me another piece, please.	geben
to let . . . have [let . . . hæv]	L~ me ~ the other half.	geben, überlassen
to offer *v* ['ɒfə]	He ~ed me a lot of money for my sports car.	anbieten, bieten
to deserve *v* [dɪ'zɜːv]	I ~ a holiday because I've worked extremely hard.	verdienen
to put back *v + adv* [pʊt]	Let's ~ the books ~ on the shelf.	zurücklegen
instead of *prep* [ɪn'sted əv]	You should work ~ sleeping.	statt zu
present *n* ['preznt]	He opened his birthday ~s.	Geschenk
offer *n* ['ɒfə]	He had six ~s for his car.	Angebot
to supply *v* [sə'plaɪ]	The firm ~ies gas **to** private houses. The company ~ied the explorers **with** special equipment.	liefern an beliefern mit

9

v	*AE*	*BE*	☒	~	▶◀	▶▶	≫
verb	American English	British English	a word you have learnt	entry	opposite	synonym	paraphrase

to provide *v* [prəˈvaɪd]	The shop ~s us **with** vegetables. (▶▶ supplies) It ~s vegetables for us.	versorgen mit liefern
to do . . . for *v + prep* [duː]	I'll ~ it ~ you.	für jemanden tun
to serve *v* [sɜːv]	He joined the army to ~ his country.	dienen
service *n* [ˈsɜːvɪs]	The hotel ~ was bad.	Service, Bedienung
to hand out *v + adv* [hænd]	▶▶ to give out	austeilen
to pass *v* [pɑːs]	She ~ed me the salt.	reichen, überreichen
to share *v* [ʃeə]	The children ~d the cake between them.	teilen, sich teilen
share *n* [ʃeə]	That's my ~.	Anteil
common *adj* [ˈkɒmən]	Europe has a C~ Market.	gemeinsam
to put away *v + adv* [pʊt]	P~ the shoes, please. (⋙ put . . . in the correct place e.g. a cupboard)	wegräumen
to possess *v* [pəˈzes]	She ~es two cars. (▶▶ has)	besitzen
of one's own [əʊn]	Our son wants a car ~ his ~.	eigen
possession *n* [pəˈzeʃn]	▶▶ property	Besitz
to pick *v* [pɪk]	He ~ed a rose.	pflücken
to pick out *v + adv* [pɪk]	▶▶ to choose	auswählen
to select *v* [sɪˈlekt]	She ~ed some oranges. (▶▶ chose)	auswählen
selection *n* [sɪˈlekʃn]	a group of things from which you can choose	Auswahl
to obtain *v* [əbˈteɪn]	▶▶ to get, to acquire	erhalten, erlangen
to return *v* [rɪˈtɜːn]	I'll ~ the paper to him. (▶▶ give . . . back)	zurückgeben
to replace *v* [rɪˈpleɪs]	She ~d the vase on the table. (▶▶ put back) I had to ~ him. (⋙ take his place)	zurückstellen ersetzen
instead *adv* [ɪnˈsted]	She's ill, so I came ~.	stattdessen
to seize *v* [siːz]	to take with force	ergreifen
to grasp *v* [grɑːsp]	to seize and hold firmly	fassen, ergreifen
to grip *v* [grɪp]	▶▶ to hold tightly	greifen, packen
to snatch *v* [snætʃ]	The thief ~ed my purse and ran off. (▶▶ took . . . quickly)	schnappen, packen
to grab *v* [græb]	▶▶ to snatch	packen, ergreifen
trap *n* [træp]	e.g. a mouse ~	Falle
trapped *adj* [træpt]	caught in a trap	gefangen, in der Falle
hold *n* [həʊld]	He **took** ~ **of** the racket.	Griff, ergreifen
grip *n* [grɪp]	a very tight, strong hold	Griff
supply *n* [səˈplaɪ]	The shop got a fresh ~ of food.	Lieferung, Vorrat, Versorgung
store *n* [stɔː]	▶▶ supply	Vorrat
to store *v* [stɔː]	to keep something for future use	speichern, lagern
to fit *v* [fɪt]	You must ~ a new lock on the door. (▶▶ put in) The trousers don't ~. (⋙ aren't the right size)	einbauen passen
facilities *n* [fəˈsɪlətɪz]	The club has good ~ for a variety of sports.	Einrichtungen, Möglichkeiten
gift *n* [gɪft]	▶▶ present	Geschenk, Gabe
reward *n* [rɪˈwɔːd]		Belohnung
to reward *v* [rɪˈwɔːd]	The Government ~ed him with $5,000.	belohnen
souvenir *n* [suːvəˈnɪə]	This plate is a ~ of my trip to Japan.	Souvenir, Andenken

tʃ	dʒ	θ	ð	ʃ	ʒ	ŋ	w	v
cheap	jump	thing	then	shop	pleasure	sang	wet	voice

Words for people: policewoman, policeman — postwoman, postman — businesswoman, businessman — landlady, landlord

to distribute *v* [dɪˈstrɪbjuːt]	The teacher ~d the test papers. (▶▶ handed out)	verteilen
to clear *v* [klɪə]	Please ~ the snow away. (⪢ remove the snow)	wegräumen
disposal *n* [dɪˈspəʊzl]	Waste ~ is very important in a big city.	Beseitigung
at your disposal [dɪˈspəʊzl]	These £20 are ~.	Verfügung, zu Ihrer Verfügung

9.5 Being, reality and possibility

to be [biː] **was/were** [wəz/wə] **been** [biːn]	'To ~ or not to ~, that is the question.'	sein
to seem *v* [siːm]	The story doesn't ~ very likely. He ~ed to like the show.	scheinen
condition *n* [kənˈdɪʃn]	The hotel is **in good** ~.	Zustand
situation *n* [sɪtʃʊˈeɪʃn]	The ~ was very difficult.	Situation, Lage
quality *n* [ˈkwɒlətɪ]	e.g. goods of the best ~	Eigenschaft, Qualität
kind *n* [kaɪnd] **sort** *n* [sɔːt] **type** *n* [taɪp]	What ~ of people are here?	Art, Sorte
example *n* [ɪgˈzɑːmpl]	Let me give you an ~ of what I mean.	Beispiel
fact *n* [fækt]	Something that is true is a ~.	Tatsache
in fact [ɪn ˈfækt]	I thought he was at home, but ~ he was at work.	tatsächlich
truth *n* [truːθ]	Don't tell lies, tell me the ~.	Wahrheit, Wirklichkeit
real *adj* [rɪəl]	What is the ~ reason for his absence? (▶▶ true)	wirklich, echt
actually *adv* [ˈæktʃʊlɪ] **really** *adv* [ˈrɪəlɪ]	▶▶ in fact	tatsächlich, eigentlich, wirklich
true *adj* [truː]	concrete, ▶◀ false	wahr, wirklich
to get *v* [get] **got** [gɒt] **got** [gɒt]	It's ~ting cold.	werden
to become *v* [bɪˈkʌm] **became** [bɪˈkeɪm] **become** [bɪˈkʌm]	My sister wants to ~ a doctor.	werden
to turn *v* [tɜːn]	The headmaster ~ed red with anger.	werden (lassen)
to grow *v* [grəʊ] **grew** [gruː] **grown** [grəʊn]	Your father is ~ing old, you know. (▶▶ becoming)	werden
to happen *v* [ˈhæpən]	A strange thing ~ed to me yesterday.	geschehen, passieren
to take place *v + n* [pleɪs]	When will the test ~? (▶▶ happen)	stattfinden
to be on *v + adv* [ɒn]		
to go on *v + adv* [gəʊ]	What's ~ing ~ here? (▶▶ happening)	vor sich gehen, stattfinden
event *n* [ɪˈvent]	an important happening	Ereignis
adventure *n* [ədˈventʃə]	an exciting or dangerous journey or series of events	Abenteuer

9

to look like *v + prep* [lʊk]	He ~s ~ his grandfather.	aussehen wie
to be like *v + prep* [laɪk]		
like *prep* [laɪk]	She can swim ~ a fish.	wie
alike *adj, adv* [ə'laɪk]	The two sisters are very ~.	gleich
same *adj* [seɪm]	She went to the ~ school as I did.	gleich
pron	He said **the** ~.	dasselbe
all the same [seɪm]	Shall I do it or not? – It's ~ to me.	egal, gleich
similar *adj* ['sɪmɪlə]	▶▶ almost the same	ähnlich
equal *adj* ['i:kwəl]	the same in size, number or value	gleich
as...as *conj* [əz...əz]	I can run ~ fast ~ John.	so . . . wie *(Vergleich)*
such *adj* [sʌtʃ]	S~ things are expensive. (≥ . . . of that sort)	solch(e)
such a [sʌtʃ]	He's ~ fool.	solch ein, so ein
different *adj* ['dɪfrənt]	Paul is ~ **from** his brother.	verschieden von
various *adj* ['veərɪəs]	▶▶ different	verschiedenartig
opposite *adj, adv*	e.g. words of ~ meaning	entgegengesetzt
prep	She lives in the flat ~.	gegenüber
other *adj* ['ʌðə]	Let's go to the ~ side of the street. (≥ opposite)	anderer, -e, -es
other *pron* ['ʌðə]	I'll take this book and you take the ~.	der, die, das andere
another *adj* [ə'nʌðə]	That's ~ story. (≥ a different)	ein(e) andere(r,s)
pron	Take ~ piece of cake. (≥ one more)	noch ein(e,es)
difference *n* ['dɪfrəns]	What is the ~ between soccer and rugby?	Unterschied
opposite *n* ['ɒpəzɪt]	'Hot' is the ~ of 'cold'.	Gegenteil
to compare *v* [kəm'peə]	If you ~ the two colours, you'll see they aren't quite the same.	vergleichen mit
perhaps *adv* [pə'hæps]	P~ she'll go tomorrow.	vielleicht
maybe *adv* ['meɪbi:]	(≥ It may be that)	
possibly *adv* ['pɒsəblɪ]	▶▶ perhaps	möglicherweise
may *n* [meɪ]	It ~ rain tomorrow. (≥ will perhaps)	kann, wird vielleicht
	M~ I go to the toilet? (≥ am I allowed to go)	darf
might *v* [maɪt]	She ~ do it tomorrow. (≥ will perhaps)	könnte vielleicht
	M~ I come in? (≥ am I allowed to)	dürfte
it/that depends [dɪ'pendz]	Will you come? – I~./T~. I may have to babysit. (≥ it's not certain)	das kommt darauf an, je nachdem
in this case [keɪs]	if this happens	in diesem Fall
should *v* [ʃʊd]	The guests ~ arrive in a few minutes. (≥ will probably)	sollte(n)
possible *adj* ['pɒsəbl]	It is ~ to leave a little earlier.	möglich
impossible *adj* [ɪm'pɒsəbl]	▶◀ possible	unmöglich
certain *adj* ['sɜ:tn]	I think so but I'm not ~.	sicher
sure *adj* [ʃʊə]		
certainly *adv* ['sɜ:tnlɪ]	She can't go today but she will ~ go tomorrow.	bestimmt, sicher
of course *adv* [əv 'kɔ:s]	▶▶ naturally	natürlich, klar
probable *adj* ['prɒbəbl]	≥ almost certain	wahrscheinlich
probably *adv* ['prɒbəblɪ]	≥ almost certainly	wahrscheinlich
chance *n* [tʃɑ:ns]	We met her **by** ~. It was not planned.	Zufall
	They have **no** ~ **of** winning.	Chance, Gelegenheit
luck *n* [lʌk]	▶▶ chance	Glück
opportunity *n* [ɒpə'tju:nətɪ]	The fine weather was a good ~ to do some gardening.	günstige Gelegenheit

adj	*adv*	*art*	*conj*	*n*	*pl*	*prep*	*pron*	*sing*
adjective	adverb(ial)	article	conjunction	noun	plural	preposition	pronoun	singular

advantage *n* [əd'vɑ:ntɪdʒ]	It's an ~ for a basketball player to be tall.	Vorteil
it's my turn [tɜ:n]	Let me try. I~ now. (⪢ it's my chance/duty)	ich bin an der Reihe
lucky *adj* ['lʌkɪ]	You got the first prize; you're ~.	vom Glück begünstigt
fortunately *adv* ['fɔ:tʃənətlɪ]	▶▶ luckily, through good luck	glücklicherweise
danger *n* ['deɪndʒə]	The steamer was **in** ~ **of** sinking.	Gefahr
risk *n* [rɪsk]	▶▶ danger	Risiko
dangerous *adj* ['deɪndʒərəs]	The terrorist is a ~ person.	gefährlich
important *adj* [ɪm'pɔ:tnt]	It's ~ that you come early.	wichtig
serious *adj* ['sɪərɪəs]	▶◀ joking, funny	ernst, ernsthaft
seriously *adv* ['sɪərɪəslɪ]	She was ~ injured in the accident. (▶▶ very badly)	ernstlich
importance *n* [ɪm'pɔ:tns]	We have a matter of the greatest ~ to discuss.	Bedeutung, Wichtigkeit
necessary *adj* ['nesəsərɪ]	Food and water are ~ for life.	notwendig
matter *n* ['mætə]	You've been crying. **What's the** ~?	Was ist los?
to matter *v* ['mætə]	It doesn't ~ to her. (⪢ isn't important)	von Bedeutung sein
shall *v* [ʃæ, ʃl]	What ~ we do now?	sollen
to appear *v* [ə'pɪə]	▶▶ to seem	scheinen
characteristic *n* [kærəktə'rɪstɪk]	a typical quality	Kennzeichen, Eigenschaft
instance *n* ['ɪnstəns]	an example or occasion	Beispiel
sample *n* ['sɑ:mpl]	an item or piece that shows what the rest is like	Muster
specimen *n* ['spesɪmɪn]	▶▶ sample	Muster
a sort of [sɔ:t]	His brother is ~ social worker. (⪢ something like)	eine Art
form *n* [fɔ:m]	What ~ of payment does he want? (▶▶ kind)	Art, Form

No problem for me: **i** before **e** except after **c**.

bel**ie**ve [bɪ'li:v] BUT de**cei**ve [dɪ'si:v] AND s**ei**ze [si:z]
ch**ie**f [tʃi:f] re**cei**ve [rɪ'si:v]
th**ie**f [θi:f] re**cei**pt [rɪ'si:t]
p**ie**ce [pi:s] **cei**ling ['si:lɪŋ]

to represent *v* [reprɪ'zent]	The sign $ ~s the word 'dollar'. (▶▶ stands for)	darstellen, stehen für
typical *adj* ['tɪpɪkl]	We asked for a ~ English breakfast.	typisch
characteristic *adj* [kærəktə'rɪstɪk]	It is ~ that she didn't come to such a meeting. (▶▶ typical)	kennzeichnend
reality *n* [rɪ'ælətɪ]	what is real, things as they actually are	Wirklichkeit, Realität
realistic *adj* [rɪə'lɪstɪk]	like the real thing	realistisch
as a matter of fact ['mætə, fækt]	▶▶ really, actually	in der Tat, nebenbei bemerkt
actual *adj* ['æktʃʊəl]	What were her ~ words?	tatsächlich, eigentlich
to tend *v* [tend]	Prices ~ to go up. (⪢ are likely to)	neigen zu
tendency *n* ['tendənsɪ]	Some pupils have a ~ to forget things.	Tendenz, Neigung
to occur *v* [ə'kɜ:]	The railway accident ~red in India. (▶▶ happened)	passieren, sich ereignen

v verb · *AE* American English · *BE* British English · ☒ a word you have learnt · ~ entry · ▶◀ opposite · ▶▶ synonym · ⪢ paraphrase

affair *n* [əˈfeə]	That's a strange ~.	Angelegenheit
incident *n* [ˈɪnsɪdənt]	an unimportant event	Vorfall
incidental *adj* [ɪnsɪˈdentl]	happening by chance	zufällig
coincidence *n* [kəʊˈɪnsɪdəns]	It was a ~ that she was in Wales at the same time as you.	Zufall

BY

... by accident zufällig	**... by chance** zufällig	**... by day** bei Tag	**... by heart** auswendig
... by mistake aus Versehen	**... by name** mit Namen	**... by sight** vom Sehen	

circumstances *n* [ˈsɜːkəmstənsɪz]	**in the** ~ (≥ in the situation)	Umstände
emergency *n* [ɪˈmɜːdʒənsɪ]	a sudden, dangerous happening	Notfall
to resemble *v* [rɪˈzembl]	▶▶ to look like	ähneln, gleichen
identical *adj* [aɪˈdentɪkl]	▶▶ exactly alike, the same	identisch
even *adj* [ˈiːvn]	No one is really winning; it's been a very ~ game so far.	gleich
contrary *adj* [ˈkɒntrərɪ]	She holds a ~ opinion. (▶▶ completely different)	entgegengesetzt, gegenteilig
on the contrary [ˈkɒntrərɪ]	You're not late. O~, you're early.	im Gegenteil
similarity *n* [sɪməˈlærətɪ]	▶◀ difference	Ähnlichkeit
identity *n* [aɪˈdentətɪ]	Where is your ~ card?	Identität
to vary *v* [ˈveərɪ]	Cars ~ in size. (≥ are different)	sich ändern, sich unterscheiden
variety *n* [vəˈraɪətɪ]	a number of different things	Vielfalt
alternative *n* [ɔːlˈtɜːnətɪv]	We have to do it; there's no ~.	Alternative
alternative *adj* [ɔːlˈtɜːnətɪv]	More and more people are getting interested in ~ technology.	alternativ
to distinguish *v* [dɪˈstɪŋgwɪʃ]	It's difficult to ~ right from wrong. I can't ~ between the two sisters. (≥ see the difference)	unterscheiden
to grade *v* [greɪd]	≥ to separate into different levels	stufen, sortieren
grade *n AE* [greɪd]	What ~ did she get in the last test?	Stufe, Note
stage *n* [steɪdʒ]	The plans are still at an early ~.	Stadium
likely *adv* [ˈlaɪklɪ]	They'll quite ~ come tonight. (▶▶ probably)	wahrscheinlich
to be likely [ˈlaɪklɪ]	She's ~ to be late. It's ~ that he didn't understand you.	wahrscheinlich
possibility *n* [pɒsəˈbɪlətɪ]	Something that can happen is a ~.	Möglichkeit
probability *n* [prɒbəˈbɪlətɪ]	a probable event	Wahrscheinlichkeit
in case [keɪs]	Take your umbrella ~ it rains.	für den Fall, daß
can *v* [kæn]	It ~ be very hot in Japan.	kann *(Möglichkeit)*
could *v* [kʊd]	She ~ go today. (▶▶ might)	könnte
ought to *v* [ˈɔːt tə]	She ~ arrive soon. (≥ will probably)	sollte
will *v* [wɪl]	These things ~ happen. (≥ are likely to)	können
would *v* [wʊd]	Why don't we have a picnic. Yes, that ~ be nice.	wäre

tʃ	dʒ	θ	ð	ʃ	ʒ	ŋ	w	v
cheap	**j**ump	**th**ing	**th**en	**sh**op	plea**s**ure	sa**ng**	**w**et	**v**oice

definite *adj* ['definət]	I want a ~ answer. (▶▶ clear)	genau, bestimmt
definitely *adv* ['definətlɪ]	▶▶ certainly, of course	bestimmt, gewiß
surely *adv* ['ʃʊəlɪ]		sicherlich
undoubtedly *adv* [ʌn'daʊtɪdlɪ]		zweifellos
must *v* [mʌst]	He ~ know about it.	muß
to be bound [baʊnd]	This is ~ to happen. (≫ certain)	muß, wird bestimmt
to ensure *v* [ɪn'ʃʊə]	to make something certain to happen	sicherstellen
in any case [keɪs]	≫ whatever may happen	auf jeden Fall,
at any rate [reɪt]		jedenfalls
fortune *n* ['fɔːtʃuːn]	▶▶ luck	Glück
unfortunate *adj* [ʌn'fɔːtʃʊnət]	▶◀ fortunate	unglücklich
unlucky *adj* [ʌn'lʌkɪ]	▶▶ unfortunate	unglücklich
disadvantage *n* [dɪsəd'vɑːntɪdʒ]	▶◀ advantage	Nachteil
essential *adj* [ɪ'senʃl]	Food and drink are ~ for life. (▶▶ necessary)	wesentlich, notwendig
vital *adj* ['vaɪtl]	▶▶ very necessary	lebenswichtig
vitally *adv* ['vaɪtəlɪ]	The decision was ~ important.	grundlegend
solemn *adj* ['sɒləm]	He has a ~ expression on his face. (▶▶ serious)	ernst, feierlich
fundamental *adj* [fʌndə'mentl]	These questions are ~. (▶▶ basic)	grundlegend
necessity *n* [nɪ'sesətɪ]	something that is necessary	Notwendigkeit
unnecessary *adj* [ʌn'nesəsrɪ]	▶◀ necessary	nicht notwendig
not necessarily [nesə'serəlɪ]	The most expensive restaurant is ~ the best.	nicht notwendigerweise
unimportant *adj* [ʌnɪm'pɔːtnt]	▶◀ important	unwichtig
slight *adj* [slaɪt]	She made a ~ mistake. (▶▶ an unimportant)	unbedeutend
mere *adj* [mɪə]	The new queen is a ~ child. (≫ nothing more than)	bloß
merely *adv* ['mɪəlɪ]	▶▶ only	bloß

iː	ɪ	e	æ	ɑː	ɒ	ɔː	ʊ	uː	ʌ	ɜː	ə
eat	bit	ten	bad	fast	got	saw	sure	too	cut	bird	about

9

Index Englisch

87 a *art*
151 a few
154 a good deal
154 a great deal
151 a little
151 a lot of
24 a quarter of an hour
163 a sort of
25 a.m. *adv*
20 abandon *vt+o*
103 abbey *n*
90 abbreviation *n*
67 ability *n*
67 able *adj (to inf)*
11 aboard *adv*
111 abolish *vt+o*
13 about *adv*
151 ~ *prep*
158 ~
14 above *prep,adv*
157 above all
6 abroad *adv*
16 absence *n*
13 absent *adj (from)*
155 absolute *adj*
69 abstract *adj*
83 accent *n*
72 accept *vt+o (as)*
107 ~ *vt+that*
75 acceptable *adj*
8 accident *n*
49 accommodation *n*
21 accompany *vt+o*
74 according to *prep*
130 account *n*
158 accurate *adj*
112 accuse *vt+o (of)*
156 accustomed *adj (to)*
39 ache *n*
39 ache *vi*
~ *vi+to inf*
149 achieve *vt+o*
149 achievement *n*
95 acquaintance *n*
95 acquainted with
133 acquire *vt+o*
14 across *prep,adv*
110 act *n*
145 act *vi*
~ *vi+adv*
114 act *vt+o*
~ *vi*
54 action *n*
36 active *adj*
85 ~ *adj,n*
56 ~
114 activity *n*
115 actor *n*
115 actress *n*
163 actual *adj*
23 ~
161 actually *adv*
80 ad *n*
136 add *vt+o*
~ *vi*
40 addicted *adj (to)*
137 addition *n*
155 additional *adj*
154 additionally *adv*
44 additive *n*
76 address *n*
82 adjective *n*
106 administration *n*
61 admiration *n*
61 admire *vt+o*
19 admission *n*
17 admit *vt+o*
72 ~ *vt+v-ing*
~ *vt+that*
75 adopt *vt+o*
94 ~
91 adult *n,adj*
20 advance *n*
154 advanced *adj*
163 advantage *n*
161 adventure *n*
82 adverb *n*
82 advertise *vt+o*
~ *vt+that*
~ *vi*
80 advertisement *n*
72 advice *n*
75 advise *vt+o (on)*
~ *vt+v-ing*
~ *vt+that*
~ *vt+indir o+that*
~ *vt+indir o+wh*
~ *vt+o+to inf*
9 aeroplane *n*
164 affair *n*
131 afford *vt+o*
107 ~ *vt+to inf*
59 afraid *adj (of)*
13 after *prep*
24 ~ *prep,adv*
28 ~
89 after all *conj*
110 ~
23 afternoon *n*
28 afterwards *adv*
28 again *adv*
15 against *prep*
23 age *n*
27 ~
27 aged *adj*
128 agency *n*
128 agent *n*
108 agent (secret) *n*
29 ago *adv*
72 agree *vi (with+indir o) (on+dir o)*
~ *vi+to inf*
~ *vi+that*
72 agreement *n*
129 agricultural *adj*
129 agriculture *n*
90 ah! *interj*
14 ahead *adv (of)*
150 aid *n*
66 aim *n*
120 ~
120 aim *vt+o (at)*
~ *vi (at)*
158 aimless *adj*
3 air *n*
9 air hostess *nBE*
51 air-conditioned *adj*
9 aircraft *n*
9 airline *n*
80 airmail *n*
9 airplane *nAE*
9 airport *n*
24 alarm clock *n*
41 alcohol *n*
44 ale *n*
162 alike *adj,adv*
31 alive *adj*
151 all *adj,pron*
153 ~
28 all day
16 all over *adv*
37 all right
162 all the same
97 alliance *n*
33 alligator *n*
109 allow *vt+o*
~ *vt+v-ing*
~ *vt+o+to inf*
~ *vt+indir o+dir o*
128 allowance *n*
28 almost *adv*
135 alone *adj*
15 along *prep,adv*
64 aloud *adv*
77 alphabet *n*
28 already *adv*
152 also *adv*
122 ~
156 ~
164 alternative *adj*
164 ~ *n*
88 although *conj*
156 ~
155 altogether *adv*
28 always *adv*
63 amaze *vt+o*
63 amazement *n*
63 amazing *adj*
107 ambassador *n*
69 ambition *n*
69 ambitious *adj*
40 ambulance *n*
111 amendment *n*
14 among *prep*
150 amount *n*
138 amount to *vt prep+o*
115 amuse *vt+o*
115 amusement *n*
113 amusing *adj*
87 an *art*
94 ancestor *n*
27 ancient *adj*
88 and *conj*
90 and so on
103 angel *n*
60 anger *n*
59 angry *adj (with)*
~ *(about)*
31 animal *n*
36 ankle *n*
73 announce *vt+o*
~ *vi*
73 announcement *n*
82 announcer *n*
60 annoy *vt+o*
60 annoying *adj*
25 annual *adj*
162 another *adj*
71 answer *n*
71 answer *vt+o*
~ *vt+that*
~ *vi*
27 antique *adj*
27 antique *n*
61 anxious *adj (about)*
62 ~
59 ~
86 any *adj*
~ *pron*
87 anybody *pron*
89 anyhow *adv*
87 anyone *pron*
87 anything *pron*
152 anything else
87 anyway *adv*
87 anywhere *adv*
16 apart *adv*
152 apart from *prep*
48 apartment *nAE*
75 apologize *vi (to)(for)*
75 apology *n*
76 apostrophe *n*
16 appear *vi*
163 ~ *vi+to inf*
~ *vi+n*
~ *vi+adj*
~ *vi+adv*
46 appearance *n*
78 appendix *n*
42 appetite *n*
115 applaud *vt+o*
~ *vi*
115 applause *n*
33 apple *n*
125 application *n*
126 ~
126 apply *vi (to)(for)*
~ *vt+o*
125 apply *vt+o*
128 appoint *vt+o+n*
~ *vt+o*
~ *vt+o+to inf*
5 appointment *n*
128 ~
67 appreciate *vt+o*
129 apprenticeship *n*
19 approach *n*
19 approach *vi*
~ *vt+o*
75 approve of *vt prep+o*
~ *vt prep+v-ing*
30 approximately *adv*
24 April *n*
103 archbishop *n*
96 area *n*
59 argue *vi*
71 ~ *vt+o*
~ *vt+that*
~ *vi*
59 argument *n*
71 ~
19 arise *vi*
137 arithmetic *n*
35 arm *n*
51 armchair *n*
105 army *n*
13 around *adv*
~ *prep*
76 arrangement *n*
110 arrest *vt+o*
17 arrival *n*
17 arrive *vi*
101 art *n*
122 ~
123 art gallery *n*
82 article *n*
77 ~
140 ~
123 artist *n*
30 as *conj*
89 ~
162 as . . . as *conj*
163 as a matter of fact
148 as a result (of)
110 as a rule

adj	*adv*	*dir o*	*indir o*	*inf*	*ing*	*n*	*o*
adjective	adverb(ial)	direct object	indirect object	infinitive without to	ing-form	noun	object

15 as far as
159 ~
88 as if
28 as soon as *conj*
88 as though
155 as usual
152 as well *adv*
59 ashamed *adj (of)*
42 ashtray *n*
16 aside *adv*
71 ask *vi*
~ *vt+o*
~ *vt+to inf*
~ *vt+that*
~ *vt+wh*
~ *vt+o+to inf*
~ *vt+indir o+dir o*
~ *vt+indir o+wh*
71 ask for *vt prep+o*
35 asleep *adj*
124 assemble *vt+o*
102 assembly *n*
106 ~
147 assistant *n*
97 association *n*
74 assure *vt+o (of)*
~ *vt+indir o+that*
63 astonish *vt+o*
63 astonishment *n*
12 astronaut *n*
28 at *prep*
13 ~
62 ~
29 at a different time
62 at a loss
88 at all
165 at any rate
28 at first *adv*
63 at first sight
48 at home
30 at last *adv*
29 ~
154 at least *adv*
29 ~
27 at once *adv*
29 at present *adv*
161 at your disposal
27 at the moment *adv*
119 athlete *n*
4 atmosphere *n*
138 atom *n*
138 atomic *adj*
108 attack *n*
105 attack *vt+o*
~ *vi*
148 attempt *n*
148 attempt *vt+o*
~ *vt+to inf*
~ *vt+v-ing*
101 attend *vt+o*
68 attention *n*
53 attitude *n*
56 attract *vt+o*
56 attraction *n*
54 attractive *adj*
115 audience *n*
24 August *n*
92 aunt *n*
78 author *n*
106 authority *n*
122 automatic *adj*
10 automobile *n*
101 autoshop *nAE*
25 autumn *n*
85 auxiliary verb *n*
154 available *adj*
11 avenue *n*
55 average *adj*
138 ~ *n*
18 avoid *vt+o*
~ *vt+v-ing*
35 awake *adj*
67 aware *adj (of)*
13 away *adv*
14 ~
13 away from *prep*
55 awful *adj*

• • • • • • • • • • • • • • • •

91 baby *n*
94 baby-sitting *n*
95 bachelor *n*
13 back *adv*
13 back *n*
35 ~
39 backache *n*
123 background *n*
16 backwards *adv*
43 bacon *n*
37 bad *adj (at)*
55 ~
60 bad-tempered *adj*
143 badge *n*
140 bag *n*
140 baggage *nAE*
116 bagpipes *n*
41 bake *vt+indir o+dir o*
~ *vt+o*
~ *vi*
133 baker *n*
44 baking tin *n*
136 balance *n*
48 balcony *n*
138 ball *n*
55 ~
76 ball pen *n*
115 ballet *n*
33 banana *n*
97 band *n*
114 ~
142 ~
40 bandage *n*
40 bandage *vt+o*
1 bank *n*
130 ~
153 ~
133 banknote *n*
133 bankrupt *adj*
42 bar *n*
141 ~
44 barbecue *n*
46 bare *adj*
46 barefoot *adv*
46 bareheaded *adv*
133 bargain *n*
133 bargain *vi*
32 bark *vi*
99 baron *n*
99 baroness *n*
143 barrel *n*
15 barrier *n*
48 basement *n*
148 basis *n*
140 basket *n*
120 basketball *n*
49 bath *n*
45 bath *vi*
~ *vt+o*
120 bathing suit *n*
49 bathroom *n*
44 batter *n*
142 battery *n*
108 battle *n*
31 be *vi*
161 be *vi*
157 be able *vi+to inf*
30 be about to *vi+inf*
53 be good!
46 be in *vi adv*
95 be in love
162 be like *vt prep+o*
~ *vt prep+v-ing*
164 be likely
161 be on *vi*
26 be over *vi adv*
55 be right *vi*
37 be sick *vi*
148 be to *vi+inf*
55 be wrong *vi*
1 beach *n*
34 beans *n*
32 bear *n*
53 bear *vt+o*
~ *vt+to inf*
~ *vt+v-ing*
35 beard *n*
32 beast *n*
116 beat *n*
113 beat *vt+o*
118 ~
113 beat up *vt adv+o*
54 beautiful *adj*
88 because *conj*
156 ~
88 because of *prep*
161 become *vi+n*
131 ~ *vi+adj*
49 bed *n*
6 bed and breakfast *n*
49 bedroom *n*
50 bedsitter *n*
43 beef *n*
41 beer *n*
33 beetle *n*
24 before *prep*
28 ~
29 before long *adv*
30 before now
74 beg *vt+o*
~ *vi (for)*
~ *vt+that*
~ *vt+o+to inf*
25 begin *vt+o*
~ *vt+to inf*
~ *vt+v-ing*
~ *vi*
26 beginning *n*
53 behave *vi+adv*
~ *vi*
~ *vt+o*
54 behavior *nAE*
54 behaviour *n*
14 behind *adv,prep*
32 being *n*
68 belief *n*
103 ~
76 believe *vt+o*
~ *vt+wh*
~ *vt+that*
103 believe in
~ *vt prep+o*
~ *vt prep+v-ing*
140 bell *n*
158 belong to *vt prep+o*
14 below *prep,adv*
46 belt *n*
51 bench *n*
1 ~
8 bend *n*
21 bend *vt+o*
~ *vi*
16 beneath *prep,adv*
15 beside *prep*
152 besides *adv*
54 best
118 bet *vi (on)*
~ *vt+o*
~ *vt+that*
~ *vt+indir o+dir o*
37 better *adj*
54 ~
14 between *prep,adv*
14 beyond *prep,adv*
8 bicycle *n*
151 big *adj*
8 bike *n*
110 bill *n*
130 ~ *AE*
132 ~
143 bin *n*
149 bind *vt+o*
~ *vt+o+adv*
101 biology *n*
31 bird *n*
31 birth *n*
27 birthday *n*
41 biscuit *n*
138 bit *n*
37 bite *vt+o*
~ *vi*
64 bitter *adj*
44 ~ *n*
4 black *adj,n*
35 ~ *n*
100 blackboard *n*
75 blame *n*
75 blame
vt+dir o+on+indir o
~ *vt+indir o+for+dir o*
49 blanket *n*
36 bleed *vi*
38 blind *adj*
39 blindness *n*
141 block *n*
48 block (of flats) *n*
35 blood *n*
35 bloody *adj*
45 blouse *n*
39 blow *n*
3 blow *vi*
4 blue *adj,n*
143 blunt *adj*
61 blush *vi*
100 board *n*
139 ~
7 boarding-house *n*
9 boat *n*
35 body *n*
117 body-popper *n*
41 boil *vt+o+adj*
~ *vt+o*
~ *vi*
~ *vt+indir o+dir o*
105 bomb *n*
36 bone *n*
77 book *n*

6 book *vt+indir o+dir o*
~ *vt+o*
~ *vi*
7 booking office *n*
129 bookkeeper *n*
129 bookkeeping *n*
79 bookshop *n*
47 boot *n*
12 border *n*
63 bore *vt+o*
~ *vi*
57 bored *adj*
60 boring *adj*
31 born *adj*
98 borough *n*
131 borrow *vt+o (from)*
~ *vi*
126 boss *n*
6 ~
152 both *adj,pron*
152 both . . . and *conj*
59 bother *vt+o*
~ *vi (about)*
~ *vi+to inf*
42 bottle *n*
12 bottom *n*
165 bound *adj (for)*
149 bow *n*
149 bow *vi*
~ *vt+o*
44 bowl *n*
140 box *n*
120 box *vi*
117 box office *n*
120 boxer *n*
91 boy *n*
150 boy scout *n*
111 boycott *n*
95 boy-friend *n*
76 brackets *n*
36 brain *n*
10 brake *n*
20 brake *vi*
~ *vt+o*
34 branch *n*
126 ~
59 brave *adj*
41 bread *n*
22 break *n*
102 ~
38 break *vt+o*
~ *vi*
111 break *vt+o*
~ *vi*
26 break down *vi adv*
26 breakdown *n*
39 ~
40 breakfast *n*
36 breath *n*
36 breathe *vi*
~ *vt+o*
37 breathless *adj*
141 brick *n*
95 bride *n*
95 bridegroom *n*
8 bridge *n*
22 brief *adj*
143 briefcase *n*
1 ~
4 bright *adj*
67 ~
18 bring *vt+o*
~ *vt+indir o+dir o*
147 bring about *vt adv+o*
159 bring back *vt adv+o*
~ *vt adv+indir o+dir o*
92 bring up *vt adv+o*
136 broad *adj*
81 broadcast *n*
81 broadcast *vt+o*
~ *vi*
77 brochure *n*
156 broken *adj*
91 brother *n*
94 brother-in-law *n*
36 brow *n*
4 brown *adj*
45 brush *n*
47 brush *vt+o*
~ *vt+o+adj*
104 Buddhist *n*
133 budget *n*
48 build *vt+o*
~ *vi*
~ *vt+indir o+dir o*
48 building *n*
109 bullet *n*
56 bully *n*
141 bunch *n*
50 bungalow *n*
112 burglar *n*
139 burn *vt+o*
~ *vi*
104 bury *vt+o*
8 bus *n*
10 bus stop *n*
125 business *n*
132 ~
134 businessman *n*
134 businesswoman *n*
20 busy *adj (with)*
125 ~ *(v-ing)*
88 but *conj*
133 butcher *n*
41 butter *n*
33 butterfly *n*
45 button *n*
64 ~
132 buy *vt+o*
~ *vi*
~ *vt+indir o+dir o*
~ *vt+o+adj*
28 by *adv*
9 ~ *prep*
16 ~ *prep,adv*
164 ~
66 by chance
157 by far
69 by heart
122 by means of
152 by the way
80 by word of mouth
94 bye-bye *interj*
107 by-election *n*
11 by-pass *n*

• • • • • • • • • • • • • • • • •

10 cab *nAE*
34 cabbage *n*
11 cabin *n*
50 ~
142 cable *n*
34 cactus *n*
42 café *n*
44 cafeteria *n*
143 cage *n*
41 cake *n*
138 calculate *vt+o*
~ *vt+that*
~ *vt+wh*
136 calculator *n*
25 calendar *n*
32 calf *n*
73 call *n*
80 ~
70 call *vt+o+n*
71 ~ *vt+o+adj*
~ *vt+o+adv*
6 call on *vt prep+o*
81 call up *vt adv+o*
59 calm *adj*
62 calmness *n*
32 camel *n*
115 camera *n*
7 camp *n*
70 camp *vi*
107 campaign *vi (for)*
6 camping *n*
7 camping ground *nAE*
7 camping site *n*
7 camping van *n*
140 can *nAE*
6 ~
157 can *vi*
164 ~ *vi+inf*
2 canal *n*
25 cancel *vt+o*
107 candidate *n*
142 candle *n*
11 canoe *n*
109 cannon *n*
44 canteen *n*
141 canvas *n*
46 cap *n*
143 ~
70 capable *adj (of)*
70 capacity *n*
138 ~
96 capital (city) *n*
76 capital (letter) *n*
12 capsule *n*
9 captain *n*
118 ~
8 car *n*
8 car park *nBE*
7 caravan *n*
76 card *n*
118 cards *n*
147 care *n*
52 care *vi (about)*
~ *vt+wh*
38 care for *vt prep+o*
52 ~
127 career *n*
147 careful *adj (with)*
147 careless *adj (of)(with)*
150 carelessness *n*
49 caretaker *n*
129 carpenter *n*
49 carpet *n*
10 carriage *n*
34 carrot *n*
18 carry *vt+o*
23 carry on *vt adv+o*
~ *vt adv+v-ing*
~ *vi adv*
148 carry out *vt adv+o*
123 cartoon *n*
44 carve *vt+o*
~ *vi*
~ *vt+indir o+dir o*
123 carving *n*
112 case *n*
140 ~
153 ~
130 cash *n*
135 cash-desk *n*
135 cashier *n*
114 cassette *n*
114 cassette recorder *n*
48 castle *n*
58 casual *adj*
32 cat *n*
78 catalog *nAE*
78 catalogue *n*
159 catch *vt+o*
64 ~
38 catch a cold
103 cathedral *n*
104 Catholic *n*
32 cattle *n*
129 cattle grid *n*
145 cause *n*
145 cause *vt+o*
~ *vt+o+to inf*
~ *vt+indir o+dir o*
2 cave *n*
26 cease *vi*
~ *vt+o*
~ *vt+v-ing*
~ *vt+to inf*
48 ceiling *n*
115 celebrate *vt+o*
~ *vi*
115 celebration *n*
50 cellar *n*
130 cent *n*
13 center *nAE*
96 ~
137 centimetre *n*
136 central *adj*
49 central heating *n*
13 centre *n*
96 ~
24 century *n*
103 ceremony *n*
162 certain *adj (about)*
99 certainly *adv*
162 ~
100 certificate *n*
142 chain *n*
49 chair *n*
100 chalk *n*
118 challenge *n*
118 challenge *vt+o*
~ *vt+o+to inf*
119 champion *n*
118 championship *n*
162 chance *n*
106 chancellor *n*
122 change *n*
130 ~
46 change *vi*
122 ~ *vt+o*
130 ~
66 change one's mind
5 changeable *adj*
81 channel *n*
103 chapel *n*
77 chapter *n*
117 character *n*
163 characteristic *adj (of)*
163 ~ *n*
130 charge *n*
130 charge *vt+o*

adj	***adv***	***dir o***	***indir o***	***inf***	***ing***	***n***	***o***
adjective	adverb(ial)	direct object	indirect object	infinitive without to	ing-form	noun	object

58 charity *n*
54 charming *adj*
134 charter *vt+o*
12 charter flight *n*
73 chat *n*
73 chat *vi*
132 cheap *adj*
55 cheat *vt+o*
~ *vi*
150 check *n*
130 ~ *AE*
147 check *vi*
6 check in *vi adv*
134 checkout *n*
36 cheek *n*
57 cheerful *adj*
119 cheerleader *n*
94 cheers *interj*
41 cheese *n*
6 chef *n*
140 chemical *adj*
38 chemist *n*
101 chemistry *n*
130 cheque *nBE*
34 cherry *n*
36 chest *n*
143 ~
34 chestnut *n*
42 chew *vt+o*
~ *vi*
32 chicken *n*
154 chief *adj*
99 chief *n*
91 child *n*
27 childhood *n*
93 childish *adj*
93 childlike *adj*
4 chilly *adj*
50 chimney *n*
36 chin *n*
123 china *n*
43 chips *n*
41 chocolate *n*
159 choice *n*
101 choir *n*
159 choose *vt+o*
~ *vt+to inf*
~ *vt+o+to inf*
~ *vt+indir o+dir o*
104 Christian *n*
94 Christian name *n*
25 Christmas *n*
101 church *n*
103 churchyard *n*
42 cigar *n*
42 cigarette *n*
80 cinema *n*
136 circle *n*
164 circumstances *n*
97 citizen *n*
96 city *n*
98 civil *adj*
106 civil servant *n*
106 civil service *n*
97 civilisation *n*
97 civilization *n*
74 claim *vt+o*
~ *vi*
~ *vt+to inf*
~ *vt+that*
93 clan *n*
97 class *n*
100 ~
78 classical *adj*
116 classical music *n*
100 classroom *n*
82 clause *n*
83 ~
45 clean *adj*
45 clean *vt+o*
~ *vi*
4 clear *adj*
63 ~
161 clear *vt+o*
~ *vi*
126 clerk *n*
67 clever *adj (at)*
70 cleverness *n*
2 cliff *n*
4 climate *n*
17 climb *vt+o*
~ *vi*
50 cloakroom *n*
24 clock *n*
15 close *adj (to)*
146 close *vt+o*
~ *vi*
146 closed *adj*
44 clothes *n*
46 clothing *n*
3 cloud *n*
4 cloudless *adj*
3 cloudy *adj*
96 club *n*
128 co-operate *vi*
10 coach *n*
119 ~
139 coal *n*
1 coast *n*
107 ~
45 coat *n*
78 code *n*
138 code number *n*
41 coffee *n*
44 coffee bar *n*
130 coin *n*
164 coincidence *n*
44 cola *n*
4 cold *adj*
3 ~
96 ~
5 cold *n*
38 ~
47 collar *n*
92 colleague *n*
144 collect *vt+o*
144 collection *n*
99 college *nAE*
102 ~
83 colloquial *adj*
76 colon *n*
105 colonization *n*
105 colonize *vt+o*
105 colony *n*
4 color *n,adjAE*
4 colour *n,adj*
123 column *n*
45 comb *n*
45 comb *vt+o*
149 combine *vt+o (with)*
~ *vi*
16 come *vi*
~ *vi+v-ing*
~ *vi+adv*
150 come across *vt prep+o*
18 come along *vi adv*
6 come and see
16 come from *vi prep*
117 comedy *n*
62 comfort *n*
62 comfort *vt+o*
59 comfortable *adj*
76 comma *n*
73 comment *n*
73 comment *vi (on)*
~ *vt+that*
134 commerce *n*
82 commercial *n*
111 commit *vt+o*
106 committee *n*
99 common *adj*
160 ~
69 common sense *n*
105 commonwealth *n*
73 communicate *vt+o*
~ *vi (with)*
80 communication *n*
97 community *n*
95 company *n*
125 ~
84 comparative *adj,n*
162 compare *vt+o (with)*
10 compartment *n*
70 competence *n*
70 competent *adj*
118 competition *n*
119 competitor *n*
72 complain *vi (about)*
~ *vt+that*
75 complaint *n*
153 complete *adj*
153 complete *vt+o*
153 completely *adv*
73 compliment *n*
73 compliment *vt+o (on)*
116 compose *vt+o*
~ *vi*
116 composer *n*
102 composition *n*
116 ~
69 comprehension *n*
101 comprehensive school *n*
75 compromise *n*
136 computer *n*
136 computer operator *n*
57 conceal *vt+o*
~ *vt+v-ing*
159 concerning *prep*
114 concert *n*
68 conclude *vt+that*
68 conclusion *n*
141 concrete *n*
37 condition *n*
161 ~
85 conditional *n,adj*
112 conditional discharge *n*
54 conduct *n*
116 conduct *vt+o*
10 conductor *n*
116 ~
73 conference *n*
56 confidence *n*
75 confirm *vt+o*
~ *vt+that*
~ *vt+wh*
108 conflict *n*
73 congratulate *vt+o (on)*
94 congratulations *interj,n*
106 Congress *n*
82 conjunction *n*
117 conjuror *n*
146 connect *vt+o (with)*
146 connection *n*
108 conquer *vt+o*
~ *vi*
109 conqueror *n*
56 conscience *n*
36 conscious *adj (of)*
148 consequence *n*
107 conservative *n,adj*
56 consider *vt+o*
66 ~ *vt+that*
~ *vt+wh*
68 consider *vt+o+n*
153 considerable *adj*
68 consideration *n*
144 consist of *vt prep+o*
85 consonant *n*
23 constant *adj*
30 constantly *adv*
107 constituency *n*
110 constitution *n*
111 constitutional *adj*
49 construct *vt+o*
49 construction *n*
134 consumer *n*
65 contact *n*
73 contact *vt+o*
143 contact lens *n*
140 contain *vt+o*
78 contents *n*
118 contest *n*
83 context *n*
1 continent *n*
2 continental *adj*
22 continue *vi*
~ *vt+o*
~ *vt+to inf*
~ *vt+v-ing*
23 continuous *adj*
134 contract *n*
164 contrary *adj (to)*
145 control *n*
145 control *vt+o*
62 convenient *adj (for)*
71 conversation *n*
74 conviction *n*
74 convince *vt+o*
~ *vt+o+to inf*
~ *vt+indir o+that*
42 cook *n*
41 cook *vt+indir o+dir o*
~ *vt+o*
~ *vi*
142 cooker *n*
4 cool *adj*
3 ~
96 ~
128 cooperate *vi (with)*
~ *vi+to inf*
111 cop *n*
148 cope *vi (with)*
141 copper *n*
77 copy *n*
122 ~
76 copy *vt+o*
122 ~ *vt+indir o+dir o*
34 corn *nBE*
8 corner *n*
129 cornfield *n*
43 cornflakes *n*
111 coroner *n*
156 correct *adj*
100 correct *vt+o*
102 correction *n*
81 correspond *vi (with)*

pp	***prep***	***pron***	***that***	***to inf***	***vi***	***vt***	***wh***
past participle	preposition	pronoun	that-clause	infinitive with to	intransitive verb	transitive verb	wh-clause

81 correspondence *n*
50 corridor *n*
64 ~
131 cost *n*
130 cost *v+n*
107 ~ *vt+indir o+dir o*
133 cost of living *n*
46 costume *n*
29 ~
49 cottage *n*
139 cotton *n,adj*
51 couch *n*
38 cough *n*
38 cough *vi*
157 could *vi+inf*
164 ~
106 council *n*
50 Council house *n*
106 counsellor *n*
136 count *vt+o*
~ *vt+wh*
84 countable *adj*
96 country *n*
156 ~
98 countryside *n*
98 county *n*
156 ~
95 couple *n*
61 courage *n*
61 courageous *adj*
42 course *n*
100 ~
50 court *n*
110 court (of law) *n*
50 courtyard *n*
93 cousin *n*
78 cover *n*
142 ~
144 cover *vt+o (with)*
32 cow *n*
61 coward *n*
129 cowboy *n*
11 crash *n*
65 ~
11 crash *vi*
65 ~ *vt+o*
19 crawl *vi*
46 craze *n*
70 crazy *adj (about)*
41 cream *n*
31 create *vt+o*
32 creature *n*
9 crew *n*
119 cricket *n*
110 crime *n*
112 criminal *adj*
110 ~ *n*
69 critic *n*
56 ~
69 critical *adj (of)*
69 criticism *n*
56 ~
68 criticize *vt+o*
~ *vi*
129 crop *n*
136 cross *n*
18 cross *vt+o*
~ *vi*
11 crossing *n*
19 ~
11 crossroads *n*
121 crossword (puzzle) *n*
96 crowd *n*
153 crowded *adj*
106 crown *n*
106 crown *vt+o*
~ *vt+o+n*
59 cruel *adj (to)*
60 cruelty *n*
73 cry *n*
59 cry *vi*
71 ~
129 cultivate *vt+o*
97 cultural *adj*
97 culture *n*
42 cup *n*
117 ~
118 Cup Final *n*
49 cupboard *n*
62 curious *adj (about)*
157 ~
36 curly *adj*
133 currency *n*
139 current *n*
49 curtain *n*
51 cushion *n*
109 custom *n*
29 ~
132 customer *n*
9 customs *n*
131 ~
9 customs officer *n*
37 cut *n*
128 ~
41 cut *vt+o*
37 ~
44 cut up *vt adv+o*
20 cycle *vi*
10 cyclist *n*

••••••••••••••••••

93 dad *n*
25 daily *adj,adv*
80 ~ *n*
43 dairy *n*
147 damage *n*
146 damage *vt+o*
4 damp *adj*
114 dance *n*
114 dance *vi (with)*
~ *vt+o*
~ *vt+o+adv*
114 dancer *n*
163 danger *n*
163 dangerous *adj*
61 dare *vi*
~ *vi+inf*
~ *vt+inf*
~ *vt+to inf*
~ *vt+o+v-ing*
4 dark *adj*
4 dark(ness) *n*
95 darling *n,adj*
120 darts *n*
76 dash *n*
6 date *n*
25 ~
95 date *vt+o*
~ *vi*
91 daughter *n*
23 day *n*
24 ~
24 day after tomorrow, the
24 day before yesterday, the
5 daylight *n*
31 dead *adj*
39 deaf *adj (to)*
39 deafness *n*
134 deal *n*
134 deal in *vt prep+o*
145 deal with *vt prep+o*
134 dealer *n*
77 dear *adj*
132 ~
31 death *n*
71 debate *n*
74 debate *vt+o*
~ *vi (with)(about)*
133 debt *n*
24 December *n*
56 decent *adj*
66 decide *vt+o*
~ *vt+to inf*
~ *vt+that*
~ *vt+wh*
~ *vi (on)(about)*
66 decision *n*
11 deck *n*
73 declaration *n*
73 declare *vt+o*
~ *vt+that*
~ *vt+o+n*
~ *vt+o+adj*
51 decorate *vt+o*
~ *vi*
51 decoration *n*
51 decorative *adj*
137 deep *adj*
32 deer *n*
109 defeat *n*
105 defeat *vt+o*
158 defective *adj*
112 defence *nBE*
108 ~
105 defend *vt+o*
112 ~
108 defense *nAE*
112 ~
72 define *vt+o*
165 definite *adj*
103 definetely *adv*
165 ~
72 definition *n*
83 ~
3 degree *n*
100 ~
138 ~
25 delay *n*
25 delay *vt+o*
~ *vt+v-ing*
~ *vi*
26 delayed *adj*
58 delicate *adj*
65 delicious *adj*
57 delighted *adj (with)*
79 deliver *vt+o*
20 delivery *n*
75 demand *n*
74 demand *vt+o*
~ *vt+to inf*
~ *vt+that*
105 democracy *n*
107 democrat *n*
104 democratic *adj*
108 demonstrate *vi*
108 demonstration *n*
75 denial *n*
141 denim *n*
65 dense *adj*
38 dentist *n*
75 deny *vt+o*
~ *vt+v-ing*
~ *vt+that*
~ *vt+o+to inf*
111 deny *vt+indir o+dir o*
19 depart *vi*
126 department *n*
132 department store *n*
17 departure *n*
57 depend on/upon *vt prep+o*
57 dependent *adj (on)*
137 depth *n*
71 describe *vt+o (to)*
~ *vt+wh*
74 description *n*
2 desert *n*
159 deserve *vt+o*
~ *vt+to inf*
125 design *n*
125 design *vt+o*
~ *vi*
49 desk *n*
53 despair *n*
53 desperate *adj*
89 despite *prep*
42 dessert *n*
19 destination *n*
123 destroy *vt+o*
~ *vi*
125 destruction *n*
146 detached *adj*
138 detail *n*
110 detective *n*
61 determined *adj*
8 detour *n*
27 develop *vt+o*
115 ~
27 development *n*
138 diagram *n*
81 dial *vt+o*
~ *vi*
83 dialect *n*
73 dialog *nAE*
73 dialogue *n*
141 diamond *n*
25 diary *n*
121 dice *n*
102 dictate *vt+o*
~ *vi*
102 dictation *n*
82 dictionary *n*
31 die *vi*
110 ~
162 difference *n*
162 different *adj (from)*
156 difficult *adj*
157 difficulty *n*
130 dig *vi*
~ *vt+o*
49 dining room *n*
40 dinner *n*
33 dinosaur *n*
136 direct *adj*
85 direct object *n*
85 direct speech *n*
1 direction *n*
72 ~
115 director *n*
126 ~
45 dirt *n*
45 dirty *adj*
38 disabled *adj*
165 disadvantage *n*

adj	***adv***	***dir o***	***indir o***	***inf***	***ing***	***n***	***o***
adjective	adverb(ial)	direct object	indirect object	infinitive without to	ing-form	noun	object

60 disagree *vi*
60 disagreement *n*
16 disappear *vi*
55 disappoint *vt+o*
57 disappointment *n*
116 disc jockey *n*
54 discipline *n*
116 disco *n*
149 disconnect *vt+o*
116 discotheque *n*
134 discount *n*
147 discover *vt+o*
~ *vt+that*
~ *vt+wh*
150 discoverer *n*
150 discovery *n*
120 discus *n*
71 discuss *vt+o (with)*
~ *vt+wh*
71 discussion *n*
39 disease *n*
57 disguise *vt+o*
40 dish *n*
57 dishonest *adj*
54 disinterested *adj*
54 dislike *n*
54 dislike *vt+o*
~ *vt+v-ing*
150 display *n*
150 display *vt+o*
161 disposal *n*
149 dissolve *vt+o*
~ *vi*
15 distance *n*
16 distant *adj*
164 distinguish *vt+o (from)*
69 distinguished *adj*
161 distribute *vt+o*
96 district *n*
59 disturb *vt+o*
120 dive *vi*
~ *vi+adv*
137 divide *vt+o*
~ *vt+indir o+dir o*
137 division *n*
95 divorce *n*
92 divorced *adj*
123 do *vi*
145 do *vt+o*
64 ~ *vt+indir o+dir o*
~ *vi*
~ *vi+inf*
160 do . . . for *vt prep+o*
149 do one's best
145 do well *vi adv*
11 docks *n*
38 doctor *n*
78 document *n*
82 documentary *n*
32 dog *n*
121 doll *n*
130 dollar *n*
101 domestic science *n*
105 dominion *n*
32 donkey *n*
94 don't mention it
48 door *n*
50 doorway *n*
78 dot *n*
78 dot *vt+o*
135 double *adj*
6 double room *n*
71 doubt *n*
71 doubt *vt+o*
~ *vt+that*
~ *vt+wh*
74 doubtful *adj (about)*
74 doubtless *adj*
15 down *prep,adv*
48 downstairs *adv*
98 downtown *adv,n*
137 dozen *n*
77 draft *n*
117 drama *n*
62 dramatic *adj*
117 ~
18 draw *vt+o*
122 ~ *vi*
143 drawer *n*
123 drawing *n*
83 drawling *adj*
56 dreadful *adj*
35 dream *n*
35 dream *vt+o*
~ *vt+that*
~ *vi (about)*
44 dress *n*
44 dress *vt+o*
~ *vi*
46 dress up *vt adv+o*
~ *vi adv*
47 dressmaker *n*
41 drink *n*
41 drink *vt+o*
~ *vi*
17 drive *vt+o*
~ *vi*
10 driver *n*
10 driving licence *n*
139 drop *n*
17 drop *vt+o*
~ *vi*
5 drown *vi*
~ *vt+o*
39 drug *n*
38 drugstore *nAE*
116 drum *n*
41 drunk *adj*
3 dry *adj*
3 dry *vi*
~ *vt+o*
5 dry up *vi*
~ *vt+o*
99 duchess *n*
33 duck *n*
133 due *adj (to)*
89 due to *prep*
99 duke *n*
4 dull *adj*
70 dumb *adj AE*
39 ~ *BE*
27 during *prep*
45 dust *n*
47 dust *vt+o*
~ *vi*
47 dusty *adj*
55 duty *n*
131 ~
131 duty-free *adj*

90 e.g.
152 each *adj,pron*
86 each other *pron*
62 eager *adj (for)*
35 ear *n*
99 earl *n*
22 early *adj*
127 earn *vt+o*
128 ~ *vt+indir o+dir o*
128 earn one's living
128 earnings *n*
1 earth *n*
141 ~
3 earthquake *n*
1 east *n,adj*
25 Easter *n*
1 eastern *adj*
156 easy *adj*
40 eat *vt+o*
~ *vi*
148 echo *n*
148 echo *vi*
130 economic *adj*
133 economical *adj*
134 economics *n*
134 economy *n*
16 edge *n*
79 edition *n*
79 editor *n*
101 educate *vt+o*
100 education *n*
145 effect *n*
148 effective *adj*
148 efficiency *n*
148 efficient *adj*
125 effort *n*
107 ~
40 egg *n*
152 either *adj,pron*
152 either . . . or *conj*
93 elder *adj*
27 elderly *adj*
93 eldest *adj*
104 elect *vt+o*
~ *vt+o+n*
104 election *n*
139 electric *adj*
139 electrical *adj*
129 electrician *n*
139 electricity *n*
142 electronic *adj*
139 electronics *n*
46 elegant *adj*
140 element *n*
157 elementary *adj*
101 elementary school *n*
32 elephant *n*
48 elevator *n AE*
152 else *adv*
59 embarrass *vt+o*
62 embarrassing *adj*
107 embassy *n*
164 emergency *n*
53 emotion *n*
53 emotional *adj*
105 emperor *n*
74 emphasis *n*
73 emphasize *vt+o*
~ *vt+that*
105 empire *n*
127 employ *vt+o*
126 employee *n*
126 employer *n*
126 employment *n*
105 empress *n*
153 empty *adj*
153 empty *vt+o*
~ *vi*
158 enable *vt+o+to inf*
~ *vt+o*
144 enclose *vt+o*
148 encourage *vt+o+to inf*
~ *vt+o*
148 encouragement *n*
26 end *n*
26 end *vi*
~ *vt+o*
78 ending *n*
26 endless *adj*
92 enemy *n*
139 energy *n*
92 engaged *adj*
56 ~
95 engagement *n*
10 engine *n*
140 ~
122 engineer *n*
124 engineering *n*
101 English *n*
55 enjoy *vt+o*
~ *vt+v-ing*
57 enjoyable *adj*
117 enlarge *vt+o*
~ *vi*
153 enormous *adj*
152 enough *adj*
74 enquire *vt+o*
~ *vt+wh*
~ *vi*
71 enquiry *n*
165 ensure *vt+o*
~ *vt+that*
~ *vt+indir o+dir o*
17 enter *vt+o*
~ *vi*
115 entertain *vt+o*
~ *vi*
115 entertainment *n*
155 entire *adj*
155 entirely *adv*
48 entrance *n*
76 envelope *n*
98 environment *n*
62 envy *n*
62 envy *vt+indir o+dir o*
~ *vt+o*
162 equal *adj (to)*
142 equipment *n*
78 erase *vt+o*
78 eraser *n*
158 error *n*
50 escalator *n*
20 escape *n*
20 escape *vi (from)*
~ *vt+o*
156 especially *adv*
102 essay *n*
165 essential *adj (to)*
148 establish *vt+o*
~ *vt+that*
~ *vt+wh*
98 establishment *n*
98 Establishment *n*
50 estate *n*
134 estimate *vt+o*
~ *vt+that*
90 etc
164 even *adj*
152 ~ *adv*
89 even so *adv*
88 even though *conj*
23 evening *n*
161 event *n*

pp	***prep***	***pron***	***that***	***to inf***	***vi***	***vt***	***wh***
past participle	preposition	pronoun	that-clause	infinitive with to	intransitive verb	transitive verb	wh-clause

30 eventually *adv*
23 ~
28 ever *adv*
30 ever since *adv*
86 every *adj*
152 ~
87 everbody *pron*
87 everyone *pron*
87 everything *pron*
13 everywhere *adv*
87 ~
112 evidence *n*
65 evident *adj (to)*
106 ex-president *n*
156 exact *adj*
156 exactly *adv*
74 exaggerate *vt+o*
~ *vi*
100 exam *n*
38 examination *n*
100 ~
38 examine *vt+o*
161 example *n*
56 excellent *adj*
154 except *prep*
107 ~
109 exception *n*
110 exceptional *adj*
146 exchange *n*
146 exchange *vt+o (for) (with)*
7 exchange visit *n*
62 excited *adj (about)*
62 excitement *n*
59 exciting *adj*
83 exclamation *n*
76 exclamation mark *n*
144 exclusive *adj*
72 excuse *n*
71 excuse *vt+o*
~ *vt+v-ing*
113 execute *vt+o*
100 exercise *n*
119 ~
119 exercise *vi*
~ *vt+o*
37 exhausted *adj*
150 exhibition *n*
31 exist *vi*
31 existence *n*
48 exit *n*
67 expect *vt+o*
107 ~ *vt+to inf*
~ *vt+that*
~ *vt+o+to inf*
69 expectation *n*
7 expedition *n*
128 expenses *n*
132 expensive *adj*
66 experience *n*
124 experiment *n*
124 experiment *vi (with)*
122 expert *n*
71 explain *vt+o (to)*
~ *vi*
~ *vt+that*
~ *vt+wh*
71 explanation *n*
149 explode *vi*
~ *vt+o*
150 exploration *n*
150 explore *vt+o*
150 explorer *n*
149 explosion *n*
134 export *n*
133 export *vt+o*
~ *vi*
10 express *n*
71 express *vt+o*
~ *vt+wh*
10 express train *n*
82 expression *n*
153 extra *adj,adv*
157 extraordinary *adj*
151 extreme *adj*
151 extremely *adv*
35 eye *n*

• • • • • • • • • • • • • • • • •

103 fable *n*
35 face *n*
63 face *vt+o*
~ *v+adv*
160 facilities *n*
161 fact *n*
125 factory *n*
146 fail *vt+o*
~ *vi+to inf*
~ *vi*
~ *vi+to inf*
149 failure *n*
4 fair *adj*
35 ~
156 ~
117 fair *n*
152 fairly *adv*
158 fairness *n*
103 faith *n*
56 faithful *adj*
25 fall *n*
17 fall *vi*
~ *vi+adv*
35 fall asleep *vi*
39 fall ill
95 fall in love
57 false *adj*
125 ~
156 ~
69 fame *n*
157 familiar *adj*
91 family *n*
92 family name *n*
67 famous *adj*
115 ~
119 fan *n*
157 fancy *adj*
54 fancy *vt+o*
~ *vt+v-ing*
~ *vt+o+v-ing*
68 ~ *vt+that*
46 fancy dress *n*
157 fantastic *adj*
15 far *adv*
151 ~
16 far away *adv*
133 fare *n*
127 farm *n*
127 farmer *n*
129 farmhouse *n*
16 farther *adj,adv*
16 farthest *adj,adv*
46 fashion *n*
46 fashionable *adj*
18 fast *adj*
18 ~ *adv*
146 fasten *vt+o*
~ *vi*
36 fat *adj*
43 fat *n*
23 fate *n*
91 father *n*
94 father-in-law *n*
156 fault *n*
52 favor *n AE*
52 favour *n*
54 favourite *adj*
59 fear *n*
61 fear *vt+o*
~ *vt+that*
59 fearful *adj (of)*
33 feather *n*
2 feature *n*
82 ~
24 February *n*
57 fed up *adj (with)*
105 federal *adj*
128 fee *n*
40 feed *vt+o*
~ *vi (on)*
52 feel *vt+o*
~ *vi+adj*
~ *vt+that*
65 feel *vt+o*
~ *vt+wh*
37 feel sick *vi*
52 feeling *n*
31 female *adj,n*
50 fence *n*
11 ferry *n*
115 festival *n*
18 fetch *vt+o*
39 fever *n*
151 few *adj,pron*
151 fewer *adj,pron*
151 fewest *adj,pron*
95 fiancé *n*
95 fiancée *n*
78 fiction *n*
119 field *n*
127 ~
60 fierce *adj*
104 fight *n*
104 fight *vt+o*
~ *vi (with) (against)*
104 fighting *n*
35 figure *n*
135 ~
78 file *n*
153 fill *vt+o (with)*
~ *vi*
153 fill in *vt adv+o*
11 filling station *n*
80 film *n*
115 ~
47 filthy *adj*
26 final *adj*
102 final examination *n*
28 finally *adv*
133 financial *adj*
147 find *vt+o*
128 ~ *vt+that*
147 find out *vt adv+o*
~ *vi adv*
3 fine *adj*
37 ~
54 ~
153 ~
110 fine *n*
153 ~
35 finger *n*
25 finish *vt+v-ing*
~ *vi+adv*
2 fiord *n*
139 fire *n*
126 fire *vt+o*
105 ~ *vt+o*
~ *vi*
10 fire engine *n*
10 fireman *n*
50 fireplace *n*
59 firm *adj*
168 firm *n*
26 first *adj,adv*
40 first aid *n*
50 first floor *n*
92 first name *n*
26 first of all
31 fish *n*
41 ~
125 fish *vi*
121 fist *n*
37 fit *adj*
160 fit *vi*
~ *vt+o*
123 fix *vt+o*
146 ~
143 flag *n*
5 flash *n*
5 flash *vi*
~ *vt+o*
155 flat *adj*
48 ~ *n*
73 flatter *vt+o*
65 flavor *nAE*
65 flavour *n*
20 flee *vi*
9 flight *n*
19 float *vi*
3 flood *n*
48 floor *n*
64 ~
43 flour *n*
149 flourish *vi*
20 flow *vi*
33 flower *n*
38 flu *n*
83 fluent *adj*
137 fluid ounce *n*
32 fly *n*
17 fly *vi*
~ *vt+o*
3 fog *n*
4 foggy *adj*
47 fold *vi*
~ *vt+o*
93 folk *nBE*
93 folks *nAE*
18 follow *vt+o*
~ *vi*
119 follower *n*
52 fond *adj (of)+n +v-ing*
40 food *n*
67 fool *n*
57 fool *vt+o*
35 foot *n*
137 ~
118 football *n*
29 for *prep*
90 for . . .'s sake
28 for ever *adv*
89 for example
131 for hire
90 for instance

adj	*adv*	*dir o*	*indir o*	*inf*	*ing*	*n*	*o*
adjective	adverb(ial)	direct object	indirect object	infinitive without to	ing-form	noun	object

23 for once
131 for sale
90 for the sake of
30 for the time being
111 forbid vt+o+to inf
~ vt+o
~ vt+v-ing
148 force n
145 force vt+o
~ vt+o+to inf
~ vt+o+adj
4 forecast n
23 ~
97 foreign adj
83 foreign language n
97 foreigner n
2 forest n
28 forever adv
113 forgery n
66 forget vt+o
~ vt+to inf
~ vt+v-ing
~ vt+that
~ vt+wh
~ vi
69 forgetful adj (of)
72 forgive
vt+indir o+dir o
~ vt+indir o+for dir o
~ vt+o
41 fork n
76 form n
100 ~
124 ~
163 ~
122 form vi
~ vt+o+adv
~ vt+o
~ vi+n
~ vi+adv
58 formal adj
26 former adj
50 fort n
25 fortnight n
50 fortress n
163 fortunately adv
133 fortune n
165 ~
13 forward adv
56 foul adj
148 found vt+o
32 fox n
142 frame n
53 frame of mind
56 frank adj
56 frankly adv
97 free adj
132 ~
99 free vt+o (from)
97 freedom n
5 freeze vi
~ vi+adj
~ vt+o
~ vt+o+adj
143 freezer n
4 freezing adj
3 ~
101 French n
43 French fries nAE
116 frequency n
22 frequent adj
27 fresh adj
24 Friday n
140 fridge n
92 friend n
92 friendly adj (to)(with)
95 friendship n
61 frighten vt+o
~ vt+o+adv
61 frightened adj (at)(of)
33 frog n
13 from prep
13 front n
15 frontier n
4 frost n
4 frosty adj
4 frozen adj
33 fruit n
43 fruit juice n
44 fry vt+o
~ vi
~ vt+indir o+dir o
44 frying-pan n
44 fudge n
141 fuel n
149 fulfil vt+o
149 fulfill vt+o
153 full adj
76 full stop n
153 full up adj
127 full-time adj,adv
113 fun n
125 function n
125 function vi
165 fundamental adj
117 funfair n
113 funny adj
32 fur n
60 furious adj
51 furnish vt+o
49 furnished adj
49 furniture n
15 further adv adj
154 furthermore adv
15 furthest adv adj
60 fuss n
26 future adj
22 future n
84 ~
84 future continuous n
84 future perfect n
84 future perfect continuous n
84 future perfect progressive n
84 future progressive n

• • • • • • • • • • • • • • • •

142 gadget n
133 gain n
128 gain vt+o
~ vi
5 gale n
123 gallery n
137 gallon n
119 gamble vi
117 game n
97 gang n
11 gangway n
113 gaol nBE
15 gap n
8 garage n
48 ~
48 garden n
127 gardener n
129 gardening n
138 gas n
11 gas station n
139 gasoline nAE
9 gate n
48 ~
144 gather vi
~ vt+o
68 gather vt+o
~ vt+that
57 gay adj
10 gear n
155 general adj
109 ~ n
94 generation n
58 generosity n
56 generous adj (to)
70 genius n
58 gentle adj (with)
91 gentleman n
2 geography n
101 ~
101 German n
80 gesture n
161 get vi+n
~ vi+adj
~ vi+pp
17 get vi+adv
69 get vt+o
~ vt+wh
128 get vt+o
147 get vt+o+to inf
131 ~ vt+o+v-ing
~ vt+o+adj
~ vt+o+adv
~ vi+pp
159 get vt+o
~ vt+indir o+dir o
157 get accustomed to
17 get back vi adv
159 get back vt+o+adv
95 get divorced
95 get engaged
62 get excited
17 get in vi adv
~ vi prep
92 get married
17 get off vi adv
17 get on vt prep+o
96 get on with
vt adv prep+o
47 get ready vt adv+o
125 ~ vi adv
144 get rid of
95 get to know
17 get up vi adv
157 get used to
20 getaway n
2 geyser n
103 ghost n
70 gift n
160 ~
110 ~
70 gifted adj
153 gigantic adj
43 gingerbread n
99 gipsy n
91 girl n
150 girl guide nBE
150 girl scout nBE
95 girlfriend n
159 give vt+o
72 ~ vt+indir o+dir o
131 ~
105 give in vi adv
8 give a lift
25 give up vi adv
105 ~ vt adv+o
~ vt adv+v-ing
2 glacier n
55 glad adj (of)(about)
63 glance n
63 glance vi+adv (at)
42 glass n
139 ~
140 glasses n
65 glimpse n
142 globe n
61 glory n
47 glove n
142 glue n
16 go vi
17 ~ vi+adv
~ vi+v-ing
128 go vi
22 go ahead vi adv
17 go away vi adv
12 go down vi adv
17 go for . . .
17 go for a walk
161 go on vi adv
119 goal n
119 goalie n
119 goalkeeper n
32 goat n
100 God n
100 god n
138 gold n,adj
120 golf n
54 good adj (at)
59 ~
67 ~
94 good-bye interj,n
90 Good heavens!
54 good-looking adj
60 good-tempered adj
134 goods n
33 goose n
34 gooseberry n
56 gorgeous adj
80 gossip n
106 govern vt+o
~ vi
104 government n
46 gown n
160 grab vt+o
102 grade n
164 ~
164 grade vt+o
23 gradually adv
137 gram n
83 grammar n
101 grammar school n
102 ~
153 grand adj
91 grandchild n
92 granddaughter n
91 grandfather n
91 grandmother n
92 grandparents n
92 grandson n
111 grant vt+o
~ vt+indir o+dir o
~ vt+indir o+that
34 grape n
34 grapefruit n
160 grasp vt+o
33 grass n
56 grateful adj (to)(for)
58 gratitude n

pp	prep	pron	that	to inf	vi	vt	wh
past participle	preposition	pronoun	that-clause	infinitive with to	intransitive verb	transitive verb	wh-clause

103 graveyard *n*
43 gravy *n*
4 gray *adj,n*
54 great *adj*
151 ~
107 ~
115 ~
58 greedy *adj*
4 green *adj,n*
134 greengrocer *n*
94 greet *vt+o*
107 ~
4 grey *adj,n*
32 greyhound *n*
44 grill *n*
60 grin *n*
60 grin *vi*
160 grip *n*
160 grip *vt+o*
39 groan *vi*
133 grocer *n*
134 grocery *n*
48 ground *n*
119 ~
50 ground floor *n*
96 group *n*
116 ~
161 grow *vi*
27 ~
127 grow *vt+o*
~ *vi*
32 growl *vi*
91 grown-up *n,adj*
154 growth *n*
75 grumble *vi*
75 guarantee *n*
75 guarantee *vt+o*
~ *vt+to inf*
~ *vt+that*
~ *vt+indir o+dir o*
110 guard *n*
112 guard *vt+o*
112 guardian *n*
68 guess *n*
67 guess *vt+o*
~ *vt+that*
6 guest *n*
6 guesthouse *n*
64 ~
6 guide *n*
20 guide *vt+o*
112 guilt *n*
110 guilty *adj (of)*
116 guitar *n*
2 gulf *n*
105 gun *n*
109 gunpowder *n*
93 guy *nAE*
120 gym *n*
120 gymkhana *n*
120 gymnasium *n*
102 ~
99 gypsy *n*

109 habit *n*
35 hair *n*
46 haircut *n*
46 hairdresser *n*
136 half *adv*
136 half *n*
24 half an hour
16 halfway down
49 hall *n*
50 ~
88 hallo *interj*
17 halt *n*
26 ~
26 halt *vi*
~ *vt+o*
43 ham *n*
42 hamburger *n*
35 hand *n*
160 hand out *vt adv+o*
~ *vt adv+indir o+dir o*
46 handbag *n*
38 handicapped *adj*
45 handkerchief *n*
140 handle *n*
64 ~
64 handle *vt+o*
94 handshake *n*
56 handsome *adj*
77 handwriting *n*
12 hang *vi+adv*
~ *vt+o*
113 hang *vt+o*
81 hang on *vi adv*
81 hang up *vi adv*
51 hanger *n*
45 hankie *n*
161 happen *vi (to)*
~ *vi+to inf*
~ *vi+that*
57 happiness *n*
55 happy *adj (about)*
94 Happy birthday
11 harbor *nAE*
11 harbour *n*
155 hard *adj*
156 ~
152 hardly *adv*
157 hardship *n*
32 hare *n*
149 harm *n*
147 harm *vt+o*
149 harmless *adj*
116 harmony *n*
129 harvest *n*
130 harvest *vt+o*
~ *vi*
20 hasten *vt+o*
~ *vi+adv (to)*
45 hat *n*
156 ~
54 hate *n*
52 hate *vt+o*
~ *vt+v-ing*
~ *vt+to inf*
~ *vt+o+v-ing*
~ *vt+o+to inf*
54 hatred *n*
159 have *vi+to inf*
41 ~ *vt+inf*
45 ~ *vt+o+pp*
132 ~ *vt+o*
145 ~
71 ~
63 have a look
159 have got *vt+o*
145 ~
129 hay *n*
86 he *pron*
35 head *n*
99 ~
156 ~
38 headache *n*
77 heading *n*
78 headline *n*
101 headmaster *n*
101 headmistress *n*
128 headquarters *n*
40 heal *vi*
~ *vt+o*
37 health *n*
38 healthy *adj*
140 heap *n*
64 hear *vi*
~ *vt+o*
~ *vt+o+inf*
~ *vt+o+v-ing*
35 heart *n*
3 heat *n*
143 heater *n*
49 heating *n*
155 heavy *adj*
129 hedge *n*
33 hedgehog *n*
36 heel *n*
47 ~
138 height *n*
112 heir *n*
12 helicopter *n*
100 hell *n*
88 hello *interj*
46 helmet *n*
147 help *n*
147 help *vt+o*
~ *vt+v-ing*
~ *vt+o+inf*
~ *vt+o+to inf*
~ *vi*
42 help to *vt+dir o+prep*
56 helpful *adj*
42 helping *n*
33 hen *n*
86 her *pron*
106 Her Majesty
34 herb *n*
32 herd *n*
13 here *adv*
59 hero *n*
117 ~
40 heroin *n*
117 heroine *n*
86 hers *pron*
86 herself *pron*
22 hesitate *vi*
~ *vi+to inf*
90 hey! *interj*
89 hi *interjAE*
89 hi there *interjAE*
147 hide *vt+o (from)*
~ *vi*
132 high *adj*
137 ~
101 high school *nAE*
102 ~
2 highland(s) *n,adj*
11 highway *nAE*
113 hijack *vt+o*
1 hill *n*
2 hilly *adj*
86 him *pron*
86 himself *pron*
74 hint *n*
74 hint *vt+o*
~ *vt+that*
131 hire *vt+o*
86 his *pron*
106 His Majesty
23 historic *adj*
23 historical *adj*
101 history *n*
116 hit *n*
119 ~
118 hit *vt+o*
19 hitchhike *vi*
113 hobby *n*
160 hold *n*
159 hold *vt+o*
1 hole *n*
127 holiday *n*
100 holidays *n*
123 hologram *n*
103 holy *adj*
48 home *n*
101 home economics *n*
100 homework *n*
55 honest *adj (about)*
56 honesty *n*
43 honey *n*
95 honeymoon *n*
61 honor *nAE*
61 honor *vt+o (for) AE*
61 honour *n*
61 honour *vt+o (for)*
119 hooligan *n*
52 hope *n*
52 hope *vi (for)*
~ *vt+to inf*
~ *vt+that*
53 hopeful *adj (about)*
53 hopefully *adv*
53 hopeless *adj (at)*
2 horizon *n*
2 horizontal *adj*
56 horrible *adj*
32 horse *n*
38 hospital *n*
7 hospitality *n*
7 host *n*
7 host family *n*
108 hostage *n*
7 hostess *n*
3 hot *adj*
65 ~
43 hot dog *n*
6 hotel *n*
24 hour *n*
25 hourly *adj,adv*
48 house *n*
106 House of Commons *n*
106 House of Lords *n*
106 House of Representatives *n*
106 Houses of Parliament *n*
93 household *n*
92 housewife *n*
127 housework *n*
11 hovercraft *n*
87 how *adv*
156 ~
94 How do you do?
88 however *conj*
153 huge *adj*
88 hullo *interj*
91 human *adj*
93 ~ *n*
93 human being *n*
98 humanity *n*
62 humble *adj*
113 humor *nAE*
115 humorous *adj*
113 humour *n*

adj	*adv*	*dir o*	*indir o*	*inf*	*ing*	*n*	*o*
adjective	adverb(ial)	direct object	indirect object	infinitive without to	ing-form	noun	object

32 hump *n*
42 hunger *n*
40 hungry *adj*
20 hunt *vt+o*
~ *vi*
150 hunter *n*
5 hurricane *n*
18 hurry *n*
18 hurry *vi*
~ *vt+o*
38 hurt *vi*
147 ~ *vt+o*
92 husband *n*
49 hut *n*
76 hyphen *n*

• • • • • • • • • • • • • • • •

86 I *pron*
52 I had rather
52 I would rather
90 i.e.
3 ice *n*
41 ice-cream *n*
120 ice skate *n*
120 ice-skate *vi*
4 icy *adj*
66 idea *n*
156 ideal *adj*
164 identical *adj*
164 identity *n*
83 idiom *n*
128 idle *adj*
90 ie
88 if *conj*
70 ignorance *n*
70 ignore *vt+o*
37 ill *adj*
111 illegal *adj*
37 illness *n*
5 illuminate *vt+o*
123 illustrate *vt+o*
123 image *n*
68 imagination *n*
67 imagine *vt+o*
~ *vt+o+v-ing*
~ *vt+that*
~ *vt+wh*
125 imitate *vt+o*
22 immediate *adj*
22 immediately *adv*
153 immense *adj*
7 immigrant *n*
7 immigration *n*
63 impatience *n*
62 impatient *adj*
108 impeach *vt+o*
85 imperative *n,adj*
58 impolite *adj*
134 import *n*
134 import *vt+o*
~ *vi*
163 importance
163 important *adj (for)*
113 impose *vt+o (on)*
162 impossible *adj*
68 impression *n*
61 impressive *adj*
146 improve *vt+o*
~ *vi*
149 improvement *n*
28 in *prep*
14 ~ *prep,adv*
61 ~
28 in a minute
154 in addition
30 in advance
165 in any case
164 in case
148 in consequence (of)
149 in contact
161 in fact
66 in favour of
14 in front (of) *prep*
100 in God's name
95 in love
157 in order to
90 in other words
156 in particular
98 in public
63 in sight
19 in single file
88 in spite of *prep*
134 in stock
96 in the country
30 in the end *adv*
30 in the meantime *adv*
29 in the near future
119 in the open air
162 in this case
22 in time
156 in trouble
158 in vain *adv*
90 in view of
77 in writing
70 incapable *adj (of)*
137 inch *n*
164 incident *n*
164 incidental *adj*
152 incidentally *adv*
140 include *vt+o (in)*
90 including *prep*
128 income *n*
155 incomplete *adj*
158 inconvenience *n*
158 inconvenient *adj*
158 incorrect *adj*
154 increase *n*
151 increase *vt+o*
~ *vi*
68 incredible *adj*
90 indeed *adv*
105 independence *n*
57 independent *adj (of)*
150 indicate *vt+o*
~ *vt+that*
~ *vi*
62 indifferent *adj (to)*
138 indirect *adj*
85 indirect object *n*
85 indirect speech *n*
85 individual *n*
119 indoor *adj*
119 indoors *adv*
125 industrial *adj*
125 industry *n*
148 inefficient *adj*
23 inevitable *adj*
154 inferior *adj (to)*
85 infinitive *n*
145 influence *n*
148 influence *vt+o*
~ *vt+o+to inf*
38 influenza *n*
73 inform *vt+o (of)*
(about)
~ *vt+indir o+that*
58 informal *adj*
79 information *n*
7 information office *n*
44 ingredient *n*
49 inhabitant *n*
112 inherit *vt+o*
~ *vi*
112 inheritance *n*
39 injure *vt+o*
39 injury *n*
111 injustice *n*
139 ink *n*
16 inner *adj*
112 innocent *adj (of)*
154 innumerable *adj*
74 inquire *vt+o*
~ *vt+wh*
~ *vi*
71 inquiry *n*
70 insane *adj*
32 insect *n*
144 insert *vt+o*
14 inside *adv,prep*
14 ~ *n*
73 insist *vi (on)*
~ *vt+that*
163 instance *n*
160 instead *adv*
159 instead of *prep*
97 institution *n*
102 instruct *vt+o (in)*
~ *vt+o+to inf*
~ *vt+that*
~ *vt+indir o+that*
~ *vt+indir o+wh*
72 instruction *n*
102 ~
114 instrument *n*
142 ~
154 insufficient *adj (for)*
131 insurance *n*
131 insure *vt+o (against)*
70 intelligence *n*
67 intelligent *adj*
69 intend *vt+to inf*
~ *vt+v-ing*
~ *vt+o+to inf*
~ *vt+o+adv*
69 intention *n*
52 interest *n*
52 interest *vt+o*
52 interested *adj (in)*
53 interesting *adj*
148 interfere *vi (with)*
82 interjection *n*
97 international *adj*
84 interpret *vt+o*
~ *vi*
84 interpreter *n*
85 interrogative *n*
71 interrupt *vt+o*
~ *vi*
11 intersection *nAE*
22 interval *n*
6 interview *n*
6 interview *vt+o*
14 into *prep*
83 intonation *n*
85 intransitive verb *n*
92 introduce *vt+o (to)*
94 introduction *n*
78 ~
108 invade *vt+o*
133 invaluable *adj*
30 invariably *adv*
108 invasion *n*
125 invent *vt+o*
~ *vi*
125 invention *n*
125 inventor *n*
5 invitation *n*
5 invite *vt+o (to)*
134 invoice *n*
148 involve *vt+o*
16 inward(s) *adv*
47 iron *n*
138 ~
47 iron *vi*
~ *vt+o*
155 irregular *adj*
85 irregular verb *n*
1 island *n*
79 issue *n*
79 issue *vt+o*
86 it *pron*
29 ~
156 it's my fault
163 it's my turn
158 it's no use
162 it/that depends
77 italics *n*
140 item *n*
86 its *pron*
29 ~
86 itself *pron*

• • • • • • • • • • • • • • • •

45 jacket *n*
113 jail *n*
41 jam *n*
6 ~
24 January *n*
42 jar *n*
62 jealous *adj (of)*
62 jealousy *n*
43 jelly *n*
46 jersey *n*
12 jet *n*
104 Jew *n*
141 jewel *n*
47 jewellery *n*
47 jewelry *nAE*
126 job *n*
120 jockey *n*
120 jog *vi*
146 join *vt+o*
126 ~ *vi (in)*
113 joke *n*
113 joke *vi (about)*
81 journalist *n*
6 journey *n*
57 joy *n*
57 joyful *adj*
68 judg(e)ment *n*
110 judge *n*
117 ~
68 judge *vt+o*
~ *vt+that*
~ *vt+o+n*
~ *vt+o+adj*
~ *vi (by)(from)*
121 judo *n*
41 juice *n*
24 July *n*
134 jumble sale *n*
118 jump *vi*
~ *vt+o*
24 June *n*

pp	***prep***	***pron***	***that***	***to inf***	***vi***	***vt***	***wh***
past participle	preposition	pronoun	that-clause	infinitive with to	intransitive verb	transitive verb	wh-clause

2 jungle *n*
27 junior *adj*
111 jury *n*
158 just *adj*
152 ~ *adv*
111 justice *n*
74 justify *vt+o*
~ *vt+v-ing*

••••••••••••••••

34 kauri *n*
33 kea *n*
59 keen *adj (on)*
52 ~
159 keep *vt+o*
~ *vt+o+n*
~ *vt+o+adj*
~ *vt+o+adv*
23 keep going
44 kettle *n*
140 key *n*
64 ~
143 keyhole *n*
119 kick *vt+o*
~ *vi*
93 kid *n*
113 kidnap *vt+o*
112 kidnaper *nAE*
112 kidnapper *n*
31 kill *vt+o*
~ *vi*
137 kilo *n*
137 kilometre *n*
46 kilt *n*
55 kind *adj (to)*
161 kind *n*
55 ~
122 ~
58 kindness *n*
104 king *n*
105 kingdom *n*
37 kip *n*
43 kipper *n*
92 kiss *n*
92 kiss *vt+o*
~ *vt+indir o+dir o*
~ *vi*
49 kitchen *n*
33 kiwi *n*
35 knee *n*
19 kneel *vi*
41 knife *n*
140 ~
99 knight *n*
123 knit *vt+o*
~ *vi*
~ *vt+indir o+dir o*
140 knob *n*
65 knock *vt+o*
~ *vi*
149 knot *n*
149 knot *vt+o+adv*
~ *vt+o*
66 know *vt+o*
~ *vt+that*
~ *vt+wh*
~ *vt+o+to inf*
~ *vi*
63 know . . . by sight
66 knowledge *n*

••••••••••••••••

124 lab *n*
78 label *n*
124 laboratory *n*
130 laborer *nAE*
130 labourer *n*
53 lack *n*
53 lack *vt+o*
50 ladder *n*
91 lady *n*
99 ~
39 lady doctor *n*
100 lady teacher *n*
44 lager *n*
6 ~
1 lake *n*
32 lamb *n*
140 lamp *n*
1 land *n*
9 land *vt+o*
~ *vi*
12 landing *n*
48 landlady *n*
48 landlord *n*
2 landscape *n*
11 lane *n*
82 language *n*
151 large *adj*
154 largely *adv*
33 lark *n*
26 last *adj,adv*
153 ~
22 last *vi+adv*
153 ~ *vi*
24 last night
22 late *adj (for)*
29 lately *adv*
26 later *adj,adv*
30 later on *adv*
26 latest *adj*
101 Latin *n*
26 latter *adj*
60 laugh *n*
58 laugh *vi (at)(about)*
60 laughter *n*
26 launch *vt+o*
47 laundry *n*
51 lavatory *n*
109 law *n*
111 law and order *n*
110 law court
50 lawn *n*
110 lawyer *n*
31 lay *vt+o*
18 ~ *vi*
37 laziness *n*
36 lazy *adj*
56 ~
141 lead *n*
18 lead *vt+o*
31 ~ *vi+adv (to)*
~ *vt+o+adv*
97 leader *n*
33 leaf *n*
78 leaflet *n*
21 lean *vi+adv*
~ *vt+o+adv*
~ *vi*
120 leap *vi+adv*
~ *vi*
~ *vt+o*
67 learn *vi*
~ *vt+o*
~ *vt+to inf*
~ *vt+wh*
~ *vt+that*
69 learning *n*
151 least *adv*
139 leather *n,adj*
17 leave *vt+o*
69 leave out *vt prep+o*
73 lecture *n*
102 ~
13 left *adj,adv,n*
35 leg *n*
111 legal *adj*
103 legend *n*
111 legislature *n*
114 leisure *n*
34 lemon *n*
131 lend *vt+indir o+dir o*
~ *vt+o*
138 length *n*
143 lens *n*
151 less *adv*
100 lesson *n*
109 let *vt+o+inf*
131 ~
159 let . . . have
113 let off *vt adv+o*
76 letter *n*
81 letterbox *n*
34 lettuce *n*
50 level *n*
99 lib *n*
107 liberal *n,adj*
99 liberation *n*
99 liberty *n*
79 librarian *n*
77 library *n*
109 licence *n*
109 license *nAE*
143 lid *n*
57 lie *n*
153 ~
12 lie *vi*
153 ~
57 lie *vi (to)(about)*
12 lie down *vi adv*
31 life *n*
48 lift *nBE*
17 lift *vt+o*
5 light *adj*
155 ~
4 light *n*
139 light *vt+o*
5 lightning *n*
157 lightweight *adj,n*
163 like *prep*
52 like *vt+o*
55 ~ *vt+to inf*
~ *vt+v-ing*
~ *vt+o+to inf*
164 likely *adv (to inf)*
154 likewise *adv*
158 liking *n*
36 limb *n*
78 limerick *n*
15 limit *n*
136 line *n*
142 ~
141 linen *n*
149 link *n*
82 linking word *n*
32 lion *n*
32 lioness *n*
36 lip *n*
140 liquid *n*
76 list *n*
64 listen *vi (to)*
78 literature *n*
137 litre *n*
144 litter *n*
151 little *adj*
151 ~ *adv*
31 live *adj*
149 ~
47 live *vi*
31 ~
149 ~
37 lively *adj*
36 liver *n*
31 living *adj*
127 ~ *n*
49 living room *n*
134 load *n*
41 loaf *n*
133 loan *n*
33 lobster *n*
97 local *adj*
15 located *adj*
2 loch *n*
140 lock *n*
146 lock *vt+o*
~ *vi*
10 locomotive *n*
50 lodge *n*
49 lodgings *n*
141 log *n*
69 logic *n*
96 loneliness *n*
92 lonely *adj*
22 long *adj*
136 ~
46 long-sleeved *adj*
63 look *n*
63 look *vi (at)*
~ *vi+pp*
38 look after *vt prep+o*
147 look for *vi prep*
67 look forward to *vt adv prep+o*
162 look like *vi prep+adv*
150 look out *vi adv*
74 look up *vt adv+o*
155 loose *adj*
107 ~
107 Lord Mayor *n*
8 lorry *n*
105 lose *vt+o*
107 ~ *vi*
149 lose contact
60 lose one's temper
19 lose one's way
119 loser *n*
133 loss *n*
7 lost property office
151 lots of
77 lots of love
64 loud *adj*
116 loudspeaker *n*
12 lounge *n*
52 love *n*
77 ~
52 love *vt+o*
~ *vt+to inf*
~ *vt+v-ing*
~ *vt+o+to inf*
~ *vi*
54 lovely *adj*
132 low *adj*
137 ~
97 lower class, the *n*
56 loyal *adj (to)*
57 loyalty *n*

adj	***adv***	***dir o***	***indir o***	***inf***	***ing***	***n***	***o***
adjective	adverb(ial)	direct object	indirect object	infinitive without to	ing-form	noun	object

162 luck *n*
163 lucky *adj*
140 luggage *nBE*
40 lunch *n*
36 lungs *n*
133 luxurious *adj*
133 luxury *n*

••••••••••••••••

140 machine *n*
142 machinery *n*
60 mad *adj (at)*
67 ~ *(about)*
91 Madam *n*
91 madam *n*
70 madness *n*
80 magazine *n*
103 magic *n*
111 magistrate *n*
56 magnificent *adj*
99 maid *n*
81 mail *nAE*
151 main *adj*
42 main course *n*
8 main road *n*
154 mainly *adv*
111 maintain *vt+o*
61 majesty *n*
154 major *adj*
137 ~
107 majority *n*
145 make *vt+o*
148 ~ *vt+indir o+dir o*
~ *vt+o+n*
~ *vt+o+adj*
~ *vt+o+inf*
92 make friends
71 make sure *vt adj+that*
~ *vt adj+wh*
47 make-up *n*
66 make up one's mind
31 male *adj,n*
91 man *n*
145 manage *vt+o*
~ *vt+to inf*
~ *vi*
128 management *n*
126 manager *n*
98 mankind *n*
123 manner *n*
53 manners *n*
50 mansion (house) *n*
124 manufacture *vt+o*
128 manufacturer *n*
151 many *adj*
154 many a
1 map *n*
120 marathon *n*
24 March *n*
19 march *n*
19 march *vi*
43 margarine *n*
102 mark *n*
102 mark *vt+o*
~ *vt+o+adj*
132 market *n*
43 marmalade *n*
6 ~
95 marriage *n*
92 married *adj (to)*
95 married couple *n*
92 marry *vi*
~ *vt+o*
157 Martian *n*
56 marvellous *adj*
57 mask *n*
57 mask *vt+o*
141 mass *n*
81 mass media *n*
97 master *n*
129 ~
123 masterpiece *n*
51 mat *n*
117 match *n*
140 ~
153 ~
138 material *n*
101 math *nAE*
101 mathematics *n*
101 maths *nBE*
83 matter *n*
163 ~
163 matter *vi*
51 mattress *n*
27 mature *adj*
154 maximum *n*
24 May *n*
162 may *vi*
~ *vi+inf*
162 maybe *adv*
106 mayor *n*
107 ~
86 me *pron*
129 meadow *n*
40 meal *n*
58 mean *adj*
79 mean *vt+o*
~ *vt+that*
~ *vt+wh*
~ *vt+to inf*
~ *vt+o+to inf*
79 meaning *n*
122 means *n*
10 means of transport *n*
30 meanwhile *adv*
136 measure *vt+o*
~ *vi*
~ *vi+n*
138 measurement *n*
40 meat *n*
124 mechanic *n*
122 mechanical *adj*
119 medal *n*
81 media *n*
38 medical *adj*
38 medicine *n*
124 ~
5 meet *vt+o*
~ *vi*
5 meeting *n*
116 melody *n*
5 melt *vi*
~ *vt+o*
107 Member of Parliament *n*
92 member *n*
97 membership *n*
69 memory *n*
123 mend *vt+o*
69 mental *adj*
71 mention *vt+o (to)*
~ *vt+that*
42 menu *n*
58 mercy *n*
165 mere *adj*
165 merely *adv*
2 meridian *n*
121 merry-go-round *n*
47 mess *n*
60 mess about *vi adv*
79 message *n*
80 messenger *n*
138 metal *n,adj*
122 method *n*
137 metre *n*
116 microphone *n*
25 mid-
23 midday *n*
13 middle *n*
97 middle class, the *n*
23 midnight *n*
158 might *n*
162 might *vi*
~ *vi+inf*
116 mike *n*
157 mild *adj*
3 ~
137 mile *n*
109 military *n*
41 milk *n*
135 milkman *n*
129 miller *n*
137 millilitre *n*
137 millimetre *n*
43 mince *nBE*
66 mind *n*
72 mind *vt+o*
~ *vi*
~ *vt+v-ing*
~ *vt+that*
~ *vt+wh*
~ *vt+o+v-ing*
55 mine *n*
86 mine *pron*
10 minibus *n*
154 minimum *n*
104 minister *n*
154 minor *adj*
107 minority *n*
43 mint *n*
138 minus *n*
24 minute *n*
63 miracle *n*
49 mirror *n*
57 miserable *adj*
57 misery *n*
57 mislead *vt+o*
91 Miss *n*
91 miss *n*
118 miss *vt+o*
52 ~ *vt+v-ing*
109 missile *n*
13 missing *adj*
103 missionary *n*
4 mist *n*
156 mistake *n*
4 misty *adj*
69 misunderstand *vt+o*
~ *vi*
41 mix *vt+o*
~ *vi*
~ *vt+indir o+dir o*
158 mix up *vt adv+o*
43 mixture *n*
10 mobile *adj*
85 modal verb *n*
46 model *n*
124 ~
157 moderate *adj*
26 modern *adj*
62 modest *adj*
93 mom *nAE*
22 moment *n*
105 monarch *n*
105 monarchy *n*
104 monastery *n*
24 Monday *n*
130 money *n*
103 monk *n*
32 monkey *n*
157 monster *n*
24 month *n*
25 monthly *adj*
104 monument *n*
52 mood *n*
1 moon *n*
151 more *adv*
154 moreover *adv*
104 Mormon *n*
23 morning *n*
104 mosque *n*
151 most *adv*
7 motel *n*
91 mother *n*
83 mother tongue *n*
94 mother-in-law *n*
19 motion *n*
120 moto-cross *n*
140 motor *n*
8 motorbike *n*
10 motorcycle *n*
10 motorist *n*
8 motorway *n*
1 mountain *n*
33 mouse *n*
36 moustache *n*
35 mouth *n*
16 move *vt+o*
~ *vi*
19 movement *n*
82 movie *nAE*
82 movies *nAE*
107 MP *n*
91 Mr *n*
91 Mrs *n*
151 much *adj*
141 mud *n*
141 muddy *adj*
98 multi-national *adj*
137 multiple *adj*
137 multiply *vt+o*
~ *vi*
93 mum *n*
110 murder *n*
113 murder *vt+o*
112 murderer *n*
112 murderess *n*
73 murmur *vi*
~ *vt+o*
~ *vt+that*
36 muscle *n*
122 museum *n*
34 mushroom *n*
101 music *n*
114 ~
117 music hall *n*
116 musical *n*
114 musical instrument *n*
116 musician *n*
104 Muslim *n*
145 must *vi+inf*
165 ~
36 mustache *nAE*
43 mustard *n*
43 mutton *n*
154 mutual *adj*
86 my *pron*

pp	*prep*	*pron*	*that*	*to inf*	*vi*	*vt*	*wh*
past participle	preposition	pronoun	that-clause	infinitive with to	intransitive verb	transitive verb	wh-clause

86 myself *pron*
63 mysterious *adj*
63 mystery *n*

143 nail *n*
143 nail *vt+o*
46 naked *adj*
82 name *n*
70 name *vt+o+n*
~ *vt+o*
73 named *adj*
90 namely *adv*
37 nap *n*
44 napkin *n*
136 narrow *adj*
115 ~
20 narrow escape *n*
55 nasty *adj*
96 nation *n*
97 national *adj,n*
98 nationality *n*
98 native *adj*
98 ~ *n*
83 native language *n*
31 natural *adj*
31 natural history *n*
1 nature *n*
56 naughty *adj*
109 navy *n*
15 near *adv*
15 near *prep*
28 nearly *adv*
47 neat *adj*
163 necessary *adj (for)*
165 necessity *n*
35 neck *n*
47 necklace *n*
53 need *n*
145 need *vi*
~ *vi+inf*
52 need *vt+o*
~ *vt+to inf*
~ *vt+v-ing*
~ *vt+o+pp*
~ *vt+o+to inf*
140 needle *n*
101 needlework *n*
85 negative *n,adj*
40 neglect *vt+o*
~ *vt+v-ing*
134 negotiate *vt+o*
~ *vi*
134 negotiation *n*
36 negro *n*
96 neighbor *nAE*
98 neighborhood *nAE*
96 neighbour *n*
98 neighbourhood *n*
152 neither *adj,pron*
152 neither *adv*
93 nephew *n*
36 nerve *n*
59 nervous *adj*
32 nest *n*
120 net *n*
142 network *n*
28 never *adv*
89 nevertheless *conj*
26 new *adj (to)*
25 New Year's Day *n*
79 news *n*
81 newsagent *n*
80 newspaper *n*
15 next *adj,adv*
15 next to *prep*
54 nice *adj*
94 nickname *n*
93 niece *n*
23 night *n*
117 nightclub *n*
37 nightmare *n*
86 no *adj*
89 ~ *interj*
74 no doubt
87 no one *pron*
99 noble *adj*
99 nobleman *n*
99 noblewoman *n*
87 nobody *pron*
64 noise *n*
64 noisy *adj*
107 nominate *vt+o*
~ *vt+o+n*
107 nomination *n*
136 none *pron*
79 nonsense *n*
23 noon *n*
152 nor *conj*
67 normal *adj*
155 ~
1 north *n,adj*
1 northern *adj*
35 nose *n*
135 not *adv*
94 not at all
135 ~
152 not even *adv*
154 not in the least
154 not least
165 not necessarily
152 not . . . either
76 note *n*
116 ~
130 ~ *BE*
75 note down *vt adv+o*
76 notebook *n*
89 nothing (. . .) but
87 nothing *pron*
64 notice *n*
64 notice *vt+o*
~ *vi*
~ *vt+that*
~ *vt+wh*
~ *vt+o+inf*
~ *vt+o+v-ing*
135 nought *n*
82 noun *n*
42 nourish *vt+o*
78 novel *n*
24 November *n*
27 now
30 now and then *adv*
29 nowadays *adv*
87 nowhere *adv*
138 nuclear *adj*
60 nuisance *n*
84 number *n*
135 ~
154 numerous *adj*
103 nun *n*
38 nurse *n*
40 nursing *n*
34 nut *n*

25 o'clock *adv*
75 obey *vt+o*
~ *vi*
138 object *n*
75 object *vi (to)*
~ *vt+that*
75 objection *n*
148 obliged *adj (to)*
2 observatory *n*
64 observe *vt+o*
~ *vt+that*
~ *vt+wh*
~ *vt+o+inf*
~ *vt+o+v-ing*
15 obstacle *n*
160 obtain *vt+o*
131 ~
65 obvious *adj*
65 obviously *adv*
22 occasion *n*
23 occasional *adj*
30 occasionally *adv*
108 occupation *n*
127 ~
128 occupied *adj*
153 ~
47 occupy *vt+o*
105 ~
163 occur *vi*
1 ocean *n*
24 October *n*
157 odd *adj*
159 of *prep*
99 of course *adv*
156 ~
162 ~
160 of one's own
13 off *adv*
127 ~
109 off duty
62 offence *n*
112 ~
112 offend *vt+o*
62 ~ *vi (against)*
62 offense *nAE*
112 ~
159 offer *n*
159 offer *vt+o*
~ *vt+indir o+dir o*
~ *vt+to inf*
126 office *n*
126 office worker *n*
105 officer *n*
110 ~
106 official *adj*
109 ~ *n*
28 often *adv*
41 oil *n*
139 ~
37 okay / OK *adj*
26 old *adj*
27 old age *n*
128 old age pension *n*
27 old-fashioned *adj*
118 Olympic Games *n*
43 omelette *n*
69 omit *vt+o*
~ *vt+to inf*
~ *vt+v-ing*
28 on *prep*
13 ~ *prep, adv*
134 ~
89 on account of *prep*
11 on board *adv*
134 on business
88 on condition (that)
109 on duty
120 on horseback
66 on purpose
164 on the contrary
157 on the whole
23 on time
12 on top (of)
27 once *adv*
135 ~
28 once again *adv*
28 once more *adv*
30 once upon a time
89 one *pron*
89 one another *pron*
9 one-way-ticket *n*
34 onion *n*
135 only *adj*
152 ~ *adv*
13 onto *prep*
56 open *adj*
146 ~
146 open *vt+o*
~ *vi*
15 opening *n*
135 opening hours *n*
116 opera *n*
117 opera house *n*
40 operate *vi (on)*
128 ~ *vt+o*
~ *vi*
40 operation *n*
81 operator *n*
67 opinion *n*
79 ~
107 opinion poll *n*
95 opponent *n*
162 opportunity *n*
108 oppose *vt+o*
108 Opposition *n*
162 opposite *adj,adv*
83 ~ *n*
162 ~ *n*
108 opposition *n*
152 or *conj*
154 or else
83 oral *adj*
83 orally *adv*
4 orange *adj*
33 ~ *n*
2 orbit *n*
2 orbit *vt+o*
~ *vi*
116 orchestra *n*
75 order *n*
132 ~
132 order *vt+o*
72 ~ *vt+o+to inf*
~ *vt+that*
155 ordinary *adj*
158 ~
31 organic *adj*
145 organization *n*
145 organize *vt+o*
~ *vt+o+to inf*
~ *vi*
26 origin *n*
26 original *adj*
26 originally *adv*
162 other *adj*
162 ~ *pron*
152 otherwise *adv*
90 ouch! *interj*
145 ought to *vi+inf*
164 ~ *vi*
137 ounce *n*

adj	***adv***	***dir o***	***indir o***	***inf***	***ing***	***n***	***o***
adjective	adverb(ial)	direct object	indirect object	infinitive without to	ing-form	noun	object

86 our pron
86 ours pron
86 ourselves pron
14 out adv
14 out of prep
63 ~
156 out of order
15 out of reach
37 out of shape
63 out of sight
126 out of work
27 out-of-date adj
119 outdoor adj
46 outfit n
123 outline n
124 output n
14 outside adv,prep
14 ~ n
98 outskirts n
69 outstanding adj
46 outward appearance
138 oval adj
142 oven n
151 over prep
14 ~ prep,adv
46 overcoat n
155 overcrowded adj
102 overhead projector n
7 oversea adj
7 overseas adv
37 oversleep vi
20 overtake vt+o
~ vi
127 overtime adv
157 overwhelming adj
130 owe vt+indir o+dir o
~ vt+o (for)
89 owing to prep
33 owl n
159 own adj
159 own vt+o
159 owner n
32 ox n
141 oxygen n

• • • • • • • • • • • • • • • •

25 p.m. adv
140 pack vt+o
~ vi
~ vt+indir o+dir o
143 package n
7 package tour n
140 packet n
78 pad n
76 page n
37 pain n
38 painful adj
122 paint n
122 paint vt+o
~ vt+o+adj
~ vi
123 painter n
123 painting n
45 pair n
135 ~
143 pair of scales n
50 palace n
5 pale adj
36 ~
142 panel n
45 pants nAE
76 paper n
80 ~
78 papers n
12 parachute n
103 paradise n
78 paragraph n
83 paraphrase n
79 parcel n
72 pardon interj
~ n
91 parents n
48 park n
8 park vt+o
~ vi
~ vt+o+adv
8 parking lot nAE
106 parliament n
33 parrot n
34 parsley n
117 part n
138 ~
19 part vt+o
~ vi
127 part-time adj,adv
115 participate vi (in)
156 particular adj
156 particularly adv
92 partner n
96 party n
104 ~
113 ~
22 pass vi
16 ~ vt+o
160 ~ vt+indir o+dir o
145 pass vi
111 pass vt+o
~ vi
19 passage n
50 ~
83 ~
6 passenger n
53 passion n
85 passive adj,n
109 passport n
22 past n
24 ~ prep
15 ~ prep,adv
84 past continuous n
85 past participle n
84 past perfect n
84 past perfect continuous n
84 past perfect progressive n
84 past progressive n
115 pastime n
44 pastry n
95 pat n
95 pat vt+o
8 path n
62 patient adj (with)
40 ~ n
124 pattern n
22 pause n
22 pause
11 pavement n
127 pay n
131 pay vt+o
68 ~ vt+indir o+dir o
~ vt+o+to inf
~ vi (for)
68 pay attention
133 payment n
34 pea n
62 peace n
104 ~
62 peaceful adj
34 peach n
33 pear n
141 pearl n
10 pedestrian n
44 peel vt+o
76 pen n
95 pen-friend n
95 pen-pal n
130 pence n
76 pencil n
130 penny n
128 pension n
64 ~
131 ~
91 people n
96 ~
156 ~
43 pepper n
136 per prep
136 per cent n
156 perfect adj
117 perform vt+o
~ vi
114 performance n
65 perfume n
162 perhaps adv
23 ~
22 period n
76 ~
81 periodical n
109 periscope n
23 permanent adj
111 permission n
111 permit vt+o
~ vt+v-ing
~ vt+o+to inf
~ vi
84 person n
91 ~
91 personal adj
158 ~
93 personality n
127 personnel n
158 ~
74 persuade vt+o
~ vt+o+to inf
~ vt+indir o+that
121 pet n
139 petrol n
11 petrol station n
46 petticoat n
90 phew! interj
69 philosopher n
69 philosophy n
80 phone n
80 phone vt+o
~ vt+indir o+dir o
~ vt+indir o+that
~ vi
81 phone booth n
115 photo n
115 photograph n
115 photographer n
86 phrasal verb n
83 phrase n
35 physical adj
101 physical education n
39 physician n
101 physics n
114 pianist n
114 piano n
160 pick vt+o
~ vt+indir o+dir o
160 pick out vt adv+o
140 pick up vt prep+o
40 picnic n
122 picture n
82 pictures n
43 pie n
123 piece n
138 ~
32 pig n
33 pigeon n
141 pile n
103 pilgrim n
39 pill n
81 pillar-box n
12 pilot n
140 pin n
34 pinapple n
65 pinch vt+o
~ vi
34 pine n
4 pink adj,n
137 pint n
49 pioneer n
42 pipe n
139 ~
141 pipeline n
109 pistol n
55 pity n
55 pity vt+o (for)
8 place n
12 ~
18 place vt+o+adv
2 plain n
66 plan n
66 plan vt+o
~ vt+to inf
~ vi
9 plane n
2 planet n
33 plant n
127 plant vt+o
~ vi
129 plantation n
139 plastic n,adj
41 plate n
47 plated adj
9 platform n
113 play n
114 ~
113 play vi
114 ~ vt+o
119 player n
121 playground n
112 plead vi (for) (against)
~ vi+adj
54 pleasant adj
56 please interj
57 please vt+o
~ vi
55 pleased adj (with)
55 pleasure n
152 plenty pron
108 plot n
129 plough n
129 plow nAE
34 plum n
43 plum pudding n
129 plumber n
84 plural n,adj
138 plus n
45 pocket n
136 pocket calculator n
128 pocket-money n

pp	prep	pron	that	to inf	vi	vt	wh
past participle	preposition	pronoun	that-clause	infinitive with to	intransitive verb	transitive verb	wh-clause

77 poem *n*
79 poet *n*
78 poetry *n*
76 point *n*
119 ~
136 ~
150 point *vi*
~ *vt+o*
39 poison *n*
110 ~
39 poisonous *adj*
32 polar bear *n*
2 pole *n*
141 ~
110 police *n*
110 police station *n*
110 policeman *n*
110 policewoman *n*
107 policy *n*
142 polish *n*
142 polish *vt+o*
~ *vt+o+adj*
56 polite *adj*
58 politeness *n*
104 political *adj*
104 political party *n*
104 politician *n*
104 politics *n*
47 pollute *vt+o*
47 pollution *n*
103 poltergeist *n*
101 polytechnic *n*
2 pond *n*
32 pony *n*
118 pool *n*
55 poor *adj*
130 ~
116 pop (music) *n*
19 pop in *vi adv*
19 pop up *vi adv*
103 Pope *n*
103 pope *n*
53 popular *adj*
54 popularity *n*
97 population *n*
43 pork *n*
43 porridge *n*
9 port *n*
20 portable *adj*
9 porter *n*
153 ~
42 portion *n*
123 portrait *n*
15 position *n*
98 ~
85 positive *adj,n*
84 ~
160 possess *vt+o*
160 possession *n*
164 possibility *n*
162 possible *adj*
162 possibly *adv*
23 ~
127 post *n*
79 ~ *BE*
79 post *vt+o*
~ *vt+indir o+dir o*
79 post office *n*
79 postage *n*
81 postal *adj*
76 postcard *n*
81 postcode *nBE*
81 poste restante *n*
143 poster *n*
79 postman *n*
26 postpone *vt+o*
~ *vt+v-ing*
79 postwoman *n*
41 pot *n*
6 ~
34 potato *n*
130 pound *n*
137 ~
3 pour *vi*
~ *vi+adv*
19 pour *vt+o*
~ *vt+indir o+dir o*
133 poverty *n*
141 powder *n*
139 power *n*
141 power station *n*
157 powerful *adj*
122 practical *adj*
146 practice *n*
146 practise *vt+o*
~ *vt+v-ing*
~ *vi*
2 prairie *n*
73 praise *n*
73 praise *vt+o (for)*
10 pram *n*
103 pray *vi*
103 prayer *n*
19 precede *vt+o*
~ *vi*
133 precious *adj*
158 precise *adj*
107 predecessor *n*
85 predicate *n*
23 prediction *n*
52 prefer *vt+o*
~ *vt+to inf*
~ *vt+v-ing*
~ *vt+o+to inf*
54 preferable *adj (to)*
54 preference *n*
86 prefix *n*
31 pregnant *adj*
54 prejudice *n*
102 prep *n*
102 preparation *n*
125 ~
41 prepare
vt+indir o+dir o
~ *vt+o*
125 prepare *vt+o*
~ *vt+to inf*
82 preposition *n*
86 prepositional *adj*
40 prescription *n*
79 ~
16 presence *n*
68 presence of mind *n*
13 present *adj*
27 ~
22 present *n*
159 ~
153 ~
84 present continuous *n*
85 present participle *n*
84 present perfect *n*
84 present perfect
continuous *n*
84 present perfect
progressive *n*
84 present
progressive *n*
150 preservation *n*
104 president *n*
60 press *n*
146 press *vt+o*
~ *vi*
57 pretend *vt+o*
~ *vi*
~ *vt+to inf*
~ *vt+that*
54 pretty *adj*
152 pretty *adv*
147 prevent (from) *vt+o*
~ *vt+o+v-ing*
~ *vt+o+prep+v-ing*
26 previous *adj*
30 previously *adv*
131 price *n*
156 ~
62 pride *n*
103 priest *n*
101 primary school *nBE*
104 prime minister *n*
105 prince *n*
105 princess *n*
154 principal *adj*
101 ~ *n*
110 principle *n*
76 print *n*
115 ~
79 print *vt+o*
~ *vi*
110 prison *n*
110 prisoner *n*
91 private *adj*
99 privilege *n*
103 prize *n*
156 ~
164 probability *n*
162 probable *adj*
162 probably *adv*
59 problem *n*
136 ~
123 process *n*
122 produce *vt+o*
~ *vi*
122 product *n*
117 production *n*
124 ~
125 profession *n*
117 professional *n*
101 professor *n*
133 profit *n*
128 profit *vi (by)*
~ *vt+o*
~ *vt+indir o+dir o*
80 program *nAE*
138 programme *vt+o*
~ *vt+o+to inf*
80 programme *n*
18 progress *n*
27 progressive *adj*
111 prohibit *vt+o*
~ *vt+v-ing*
69 project *n*
117 project *vt+o*
~ *vi*
05 prominent *adj*
72 promise *n*
72 promise *vt+o*
~ *vt+to inf*
~ *vt+that*
~ *vt+o+to inf*
~ *vt+indir o+dir o*
~ *vt+indir o+that*
82 pronoun *n*
82 pronounce *vt+o*
~ *vt+o+adv*
~ *vi+adv*
83 pronunciation *n*
150 proof *adj*
125 ~ *n*
156 proper *adj*
159 property *n*
74 proposal *n*
74 propose *vt+o*
~ *vt+v-ing*
~ *vt+that*
95 propose to *vi prep*
~ *vt+o+prep*
117 props *n*
147 protect *vt+o (from)*
150 protection *n*
108 protest *n*
104 protest *vi*
104 Protestant *n*
59 proud *adj (of)*
124 prove *vt+o*
~ *vt+that*
~ *vt+wh*
83 proverb *n*
160 provide
vt+dir o(+for indir o)
~ *vt+indir o(+with dir o*
89 provided (that) *conj*
98 province *n*
39 psychiatrist *n*
124 psychology *n*
42 pub *n*
97 public *adj,n*
68 public opinion *n*
101 public school *nBE*
79 publication *n*
79 publish *vt+o*
~ *vi*
79 publisher *n*
42 pudding *n*
2 puddle *n*
18 pull *n*
18 pull *vt+o*
~ *vi*
61 pull together *vt+o+adv*
45 pullover *n*
36 pulse *n*
142 pump *n*
142 pump *vt+o*
121 punch *n*
121 punch *vt+o*
~ *vi*
23 punctual *adj*
150 puncture *n*
110 punish *vt+o (for)*
113 punishment *n*
100 pupil *n*
156 ~
121 puppet *n*
133 purchase *n*
133 purchase *vt+o*
45 pure *adj*
104 Puritan *n*
4 purple *adj,n*
66 purpose *n*
45 purse *n*
18 push *n*
18 push *vt+o*
~ *vi*
~ *vt+o+adj*
18 put *vt+o+adv*
160 put away *vt adv+o*
159 put back *vt adv+o*

adj	*adv*	*dir o*	*indir o*	*inf*	*ing*	*n*	*o*
adjective	adverb(ial)	direct object	indirect object	infinitive without to	ing-form	noun	object

75 put down vt adv+o
144 put in vt adv+o
26 put off vt adv+o
~ vt adv+v-ing
45 put on vt adv+o
139 put out vt adv+o
48 put up vt adv+o
49 ~
53 put up with
vt adv prep+o
63 puzzle n
121 ~
46 pyjamas n

104 Quaker n
103 qualification n
103 qualify vi (for)
~ vi+to inf
~ vt+o+to inf
161 quality n
153 quantity n
59 quarrel n
59 quarrel vi (with)
~ vi (about)
141 quarry n
98 quarter n
135 ~
104 queen n
71 question n
74 question vt+o (about)
~ vt+wh
76 question mark n
83 question tag n
16 queue n
16 queue vi
18 quick adj (at)
59 quiet adj
64 ~
29 ~
62 quiet(ness) n
127 quit vt+o
~ vt+v-ing
~ vi
152 quite adv
29 ~
154 quite a few
121 quiz n
74 quotation n
76 quotation marks n
74 quote vt+o
~ vi

32 rabbit n
96 race n
118 ~
55 ~
98 racial adj
120 racket n
142 radiator n
80 radio n
114 radio (set) n
116 radio ham n
60 rage n
5 rage vi
108 raid n
108 raid vt+o
~ vi
8 rail n
9 railroad nAE
9 railway n
9 railway station n
3 rain n
3 rain vi
4 rainbow n
46 raincoat n
4 rainy adj
17 raise vt+o
74 ~
94 ~
73 raise one's voice
34 raisin n
50 ramp n
15 range n
129 ranch n
98 rank n
20 rapid adj
30 rarely adv
135 rate n
152 rather adv
54 rather than adv
42 raw adj
15 reach n
17 reach vi+adv
~ vt+o
~ vt+o+to inf
~ vi
148 react vi (to)
148 reaction n
76 read vt+o
~ vi (about)
~ vt+indir o+dir o
~ vt+that
~ vt+wh
76 reader n
77 reading n
102 ~
157 ready adj (for)
122 real adj
161 ~
163 realistic adj
163 reality
148 realization n
67 realize vt+o
145 ~ vt+that
~ vt+wh
161 really adv
66 reason n
145 ~
156 reasonable adj
108 rebel n
108 rebellion n
69 recall vt+o
~ vt+v-ing
~ vt+that
~ vt+wh
131 receipt n
79 ~
81 receive vt+o
95 ~
159 ~
131 ~
81 receiver n
27 recent adj
27 recently adv
6 reception n
115 ~
44 recipe n
79 ~
69 recognition n
67 recognize vt+o
~ vt+that
72 recommend
vt+indir o+dir o
~ vt+o
~ vt+v-ing
~ vt+o+inf
~ vt+that
75 recommendation n
77 record n
114 ~
114 record vt+o
~ vt+wh
~ vi
114 record player n
116 recording n
40 recover vi
40 recovery n
115 recreation n
125 recycle vt+o
~ vi
4 red adj,n
154 reduce vt+o (to)
~ vi
154 reduction n
74 refer to vt prep+o
119 referee n
74 reference n
108 reform n
108 reform vt+o
42 refreshments n
143 refrigerator n
75 refusal n
144 refuse n
72 refuse vt+o
~ vt+to inf
~ vt+indir o+dir o
68 regard vt+o+adv
94 regards n
98 region n
98 regional adj
78 register n
78 register vt+o
~ vi
58 regret n
55 regret vt+o
~ vt+v-ing
~ vt+that
~ vt+to inf
155 regular adj
85 regular verb n
158 regulate vt+o
110 regulation n
106 reign n
106 reign vi
93 related adj (to)
92 relation n
146 ~
146 relationship n
92 relative n
157 relatively adv
37 relax vi
57 reliability n
56 reliable adj
100 religion n
103 religious adj
101 religious education n
57 rely on/upon vt prep+o
~ vt prep+o+to inf
47 remain vi
~ vi+n
~ vi+adj
~ vi+adv
73 remark n
73 remark vt+that
157 remarkable adj (for)
40 remedy n
66 remember vt+o
~ vt+v-ing
~ vt+inf
~ vi
~ vt+wh
66 remind vt+o
~ vt+o+to inf
~ vt+indir o+that
66 remind of
vt+indir o+prep+o
16 remote adj (from)
18 remove vt+o
131 rent n
131 rent vt+o
~ vt+indir o+dir o
123 repair n
123 repair vt+o
~ vi
71 repeat vt+o
146 ~ vt+that
148 repetition n
160 replace vt+o
71 reply n
71 reply vi
~ vt+that
77 report n
102 ~
80 report vt+o
~ vt+that
~ vt+v-ing
81 reporter n
163 represent vt+o
~ vt+o+v-ing
107 representative n
105 republic n
105 republican adj
99 reputation n
75 request n
74 request vt+o
~ vt+that
~ vt+o+to inf
53 require vt+o
53 requirement n
150 rescue vt+o (from)
124 research n
124 research vi
~ vt+o
164 resemble vt+o
7 reservation n
150 reserve n
6 reserve vt+o
49 residence n
49 resident n
108 resist vt+o
~ vt+v-ing
~ vi
108 resistance n
69 resolution n
7 resort n
140 resources n
61 respect n
61 respect vt+o
74 respond vi (to)
~ vt+that
74 response n
112 responsibility n
112 responsible adj (for)
35 rest n
153 ~
35 rest vi
42 restaurant n
6 ~
118 result n
145 ~
127 retire vi (from)
128 retirement n
17 return vi (from)

pp	prep	pron	that	to inf	vi	vt	wh
past participle	preposition	pronoun	that-clause	infinitive with to	intransitive verb	transitive verb	wh-clause

160 return vt+o
~ vt+indir o+dir o
~ vi
9 return ticket n
57 reveal vt+o
54 revenge n
68 review n
68 review vt+o
108 revolution n
108 revolutionary adj
109 revolver n
160 reward n
160 reward vt+o (for)
158 rewarding adj
78 rhyme n
78 rhyme vi (with)
116 rhythm n
142 ribbon n
34 rice n
127 rich adj (in)
130 ~
121 riddle n
17 ride n
118 ride vt+o
~ vi
~ vi+adv
120 rider n
70 ridiculous adj
109 rifle n
55 right adj
156 ~
13 ~ adj,adv,n
55 ~ n
16 rim n
80 ring n
138 ~
80 ring (up) vt+o
~ vi
64 ring vt+o
~ vi
80 ring back vi adv
~ vt adv+o
27 ripe adj
128 rise n
19 rise vi
163 risk n
59 risk vt+o
~ vt+v-ing
119 rival n
1 river n
8 road n
44 roast vt+o
~ vi
43 roast meat n
113 rob vt+o (of)
112 robber n
113 robbery n
142 robot n
139 rock n
12 rocket n
141 rocky adj
117 role n
41 roll n
48 roof n
6 room n
12 ~
49 ~
34 root n
142 rope n
33 rose n
155 rough adj
30 roughly adv
136 round adj
13 ~ adv
13 ~ prep
11 roundabout n
121 ~
9 round-trip ticket n
11 route n
136 row n
120 row vi
~ vt+o
106 royal adj
21 rub vt+o
~ vt+o+adj
~ vt+o+adv
21 rub off vi adv
21 rub out vt adv+o
~ vi adv
78 rubber n
141 ~
144 rubbish n
143 rucksack n
58 rude adj (to)
51 rug n
119 rugby n
119 rugger n
123 ruin n
123 ruin vt+o
106 rule n
109 ~
104 rule vt+o
~ vi
78 ruler n
104 ~
80 rumor nAE
80 rumour n
118 run n
128 run vi
118 run vt+o
~ vi
18 rush vi
~ vi+adv
~ vt+o
~ vt+o+adv
8 rush hour n

• • • • • • • • • • • • • • • • •

103 sacrifice n
103 sacrifice vt+o (for)
~ vi
55 sad adj (about)
120 saddle n
7 safari n
147 safe adj (from)
133 safe n
115 ~
147 safety n
18 sail vi
~ vt+o
9 sail vi
120 ~ vt+o
9 sailor n
103 saint n
41 salad n
127 salary n
132 sale n
132 salesman n
41 salt n
162 same adj
163 sample n
139 sand n
41 sandwich n
70 sane adj
2 satellite n
57 satisfaction n
56 satisfactory adj
55 satisfied adj (with)
55 satisfy vt+o
24 Saturday n
43 sauce n
44 saucepan n
44 saucer n
41 sausage n
147 save vt+o (from)
~ vt+o
130 save vi
131 ~ vt+o (for)
~ vt+indir o+dir o
133 savings n
143 saw vt+o
143 saw n
70 say vt+o (to)
~ vt+that
~ vt+wh
83 saying n
143 scales n
39 scar n
154 scarcely adv
61 scared adj (of)
46 scarf n
21 scatter vt+o
~ vi
1 scene n
114 ~
2 scenery n
65 scent n
11 schedule nAE
69 scheme n
102 scholar n
102 scholarship n
99 school n
100 school holidays n
100 schoolboy n
100 schoolgirl n
122 science n
78 science fiction n
124 scientific adj
122 scientist n
143 scissors n
118 score n
120 score vi
~ vt+o
71 scream n
71 scream vi
~ vt+o
~ vt+that
117 screen n
140 screw n
47 scrub vt+o
~ vt+o+adj
1 sea n
32 seal n
78 ~
78 seal vt+o
147 search n
150 search vt+o
~ vi (for)
1 seaside n
7 seaside resort n
25 season n
49 seat n
24 second n
50 second floor n
26 second-hand adj
101 secondary school n
102 ~
57 secrecy n
55 secret adj
55 ~ n
108 secret agent n
126 secretary n
141 section n
150 secure adj (from)
150 security n
63 see vi
67 ~ vt+o
~ vt+that
~ vt+wh
~ vt+o+inf
~ vt+o+to inf
~ vt+o+v-ing
~ vt+o+adv
90 seeing that conj
150 seek vt+o
~ vi
161 seem vi+to inf
~ vi+n
~ vi+adj
~ vi+adv
160 seize vt+o
28 seldom adv
160 select vt+o
~ vt+o+to inf
160 selection n
61 self-confident adj
61 self-conscious adj
54 self-control n
132 self-service n
132 sell vt+o
~ vt+indir o+dir o
~ vt+o+adj
~ vi
102 semester nAE
50 semi-detached house n
76 semicolon n
106 Senate n
106 senator n
79 send vt+o
~ vt+o+adv
~ vt+indir o+dir o
~ vt+o+to inf
20 send for vt prep+o
27 senior adj
53 sensation n
63 ~
56 sensational adj
78 sense n
52 sense of humour n
64 senses n
158 sensible adj (about)
63 sensitive adj (to)
158 ~
82 sentence n
113 ~
110 sentence vt+o (to)
53 sentimental adj
146 separate adj
146 separate vt+o (from)
~ vi
149 separation n
24 September n
109 sergeant n
112 ~
138 series n
163 serious adj (about)
163 seriously adv
41 serve vt+o
~ vi
~ vt+indir o+dir o
~ vt+o+n
123 serve vi
160 ~ vt+o (as)
~ vt+o+adv

adj	adv	dir o	indir o	inf	ing	n	o
adjective	adverb(ial)	direct object	indirect object	infinitive without to	ing-form	noun	object

8 service n
103 ~
160 ~
138 set n
19 set off vi adv
98 setting n
49 settle vi+adv
~ vt+o
~ vt+o+adv
131 settle a bill
49 settle down vt adv+o
~ vi adv
98 settlement n
49 settler n
151 several adj
39 severe adj
58 ~
79 ~
123 sew vt+o
~ vi
143 sewing machine n
31 sex n
46 shabby adj
4 shade n
4 shadow n
21 shake n
19 shake vi
~ vt+o
~ vt+o+adj
29 shall vi+inf
163 ~
137 shallow adj
62 shame n
123 shape n
160 share n
160 share vt+o (with)
~ vi
140 sharp adj
143 sharpen vt+o
~ vi
45 shave vi
~ vt+o
45 shaver n
86 she pron
49 shed n
144 shed vt+o
32 sheep n
49 sheet n
76 ~
132 shelf n
33 shell n
150 shelter n
150 shelter vt+o (from)
129 shift n
4 shine vi
5 shiny adj
9 ship n
10 shipping company n
45 shirt n
29 ~
59 shock n
59 shock vt+o
~ vi
45 shoe n
105 shoot vt+o (at)
~ vi+adv
~ vi
132 shop n
134 shop vi
132 shop assistant n
132 shopping n
134 shopping centre n
22 short adj
137 ~
157 shorten vt+o
~ vi
77 shorthand n
29 shortly adv
45 shorts n
109 shot n
145 should vi+inf
162 ~ vi
35 shoulder n
71 shout n
71 shout vi
~ vt+o
114 show n
20 show vi
~ vt+o
147 show vt+indir o+dir o
~ vt+o
~ vt+wh
~ vt+o+to inf
~ vt+o+v-ing
20 show (a)round
vt+o+adv
vt+o+prep
61 show off vi adv
~ vt adv+o
3 shower n
45 ~
33 shrimp n
154 shrink vi
~ vt+o
21 shrug vi
~ vt+o
146 shut adj
146 shut vi
~ vt+o
50 shutter(s) n
61 shy adj
59 ~
37 sick adj (of)
39 sickness n
13 side n
13 side by side
11 sidewalk n AE
39 sigh n
39 sigh vi
6 sight n
63 ~
6 sightseeing tour n
79 sign n
80 sign vt+o
76 ~ vi
79 signal n
80 signal vi
~ vt+o+to inf
~ vt+indir o+that
~ vt+that
~ vt+to inf
76 signature n
80 signify vt+o
~ vt+that
65 silence n
64 silent adj
141 silk n
67 silly adj (about)
138 silver n,adj
162 similar adj (to)
164 similarity n
156 simple adj
84 simple past n
84 simple present n
158 simplify vt+o
88 since conj
29 since prep
56 sincere adj (about)
77 sincerely yours
114 sing vt+o
~ vi
~ vt+o+adv
~ vt+indir o+dir o
114 singer n
92 single adj
135 ~
6 single room n
9 single ticket n
84 singular n,adj
9 sink vt+o
~ vi
44 sip vt+o
91 Sir n
99 ~
91 sir n
91 sister n
94 sister-in-law n
12 sit vi+adv
~ vt+o+adv
~ vi
12 sit down vi adv
15 situated adj
12 situation n
161 ~
150 size n
120 skate n
120 skate vi
120 skateboard n
123 sketch
123 sketch vt+o
~ vi
120 ski n
120 ski vi
67 skilful adj (at)
67 skill n
70 skilled adj (in)
67 skillful adj (at) AE
35 skin n
69 skip vt+o
~ vi
45 skirt n
29 ~
3 sky n
50 skyline n
50 skyscraper n
46 slacks n
82 slang n
99 slave n
99 slavery n
35 sleep n
35 sleep vi
36 sleepy adj
47 sleeve n
37 slender adj
141 slice n
117 slide n
19 slide vi
~ vt+o
165 slight adj
36 slim adj
37 slim vi
158 slip n
18 slip vi
~ vi+adv
82 slogan n
2 slope n
15 slot n
142 slot machine n
18 slow adj (at)
70 ~
20 slow vt+o
~ vi
20 slow down vi adv
~ vt adv+o
98 slum n
151 small adj
115 ~
130 small change n
47 smart adj
69 ~
149 smash vt+o
~ vi
64 smell n
64 smell vi
~ vt+o
~ vt+v-ing
~ vt+that
~ vt+wh
~ vt+o+v-ing
~ vi+adj
~ vi+adv
58 smile n
58 smile vi (at)
139 smoke n
42 smoke vt+o
~ vi
155 smooth adj
42 snack n
42 snack bar n
33 snake n
117 snapshot n
160 snatch vt+o
39 sneeze vi
3 snow n
3 snow vi
88 so conj
122 ~
89 so as to
30 so far adv
88 so that
122 so what
90 so-called adj
139 soap n
29 ~
82 soap opera n
44 sober adj
119 soccer n
96 social adj
106 social worker n
107 socialist n,adj
96 society n
97 ~
124 sociology n
45 sock n
51 sofa n
155 soft adj
43 soft drink n
141 soil n
2 solar adj
105 soldier n
165 solemn adj
112 solicitor n
140 solid n,adj
68 solution n
66 solve vt+o
86 some adj
~ pron
29 some other time
87 somebody pron
87 somehow adv
87 someone pron
87 something pron
28 sometimes adv
89 somewhat adv
87 somewhere adv
91 son n

pp	prep	pron	that	to inf	vi	vt	wh
past participle	preposition	pronoun	that-clause	infinitive with to	intransitive verb	transitive verb	wh-clause

114 song *n*
28 soon *adv*
40 soothe *vt+o*
37 sore *adj*
58 sorrow *n*
94 sorry *adj,interj*
161 sort *n*
122 ~
103 soul *n*
64 sound *n*
65 sound *vi+n*
~ *vi+adj*
~ *vi*
~ *vt+o*
40 soup *n*
29 ~
64 sour *adj*
2 source *n*
26 ~
1 south *n,adj*
1 southern *adj*
160 souvenir *n*
1 space *n*
12 ~
12 spacecraft *n*
12 spaceship *n*
140 spade *n*
153 spare *adj*
131 spare *vt+o*
114 spare time *n*
141 spark *n*
70 speak *vi (about)(of)*
~ *vt+o*
71 speak to *vt prep+o*
73 speaker *n*
156 special *adj*
122 specialist *n*
157 specific *adj*
163 specimen *n*
65 spectacle *n*
143 spectacles *n*
115 spectator *n*
71 speech *n*
18 speed *n*
11 speed limit *n*
120 speedway *n*
76 spell *vt+o*
~ *vi*
77 spelling *n*
131 spend *vt+o (on)*
22 ~ *vt+o*
142 sphere *n*
43 spice *n*
33 spider *n*
34 spinach *n*
33 spine *n*
103 spirit *n*
43 spirits *n*
103 spiritual *adj*
36 spit *vi*
~ *vt+o*
56 splendid *adj*
149 split *vt+o*
~ *vi*
147 spoil *vt+o*
47 sponge *n*
119 sponsor *n*
41 spoon *n*
117 sport *n*
117 sportsman *n*
117 sportswoman *n*
15 spot *n*
45 ~
21 spray *n*
21 spray *vt+o+adv*
~ *vt+o*
19 spread *vi*
~ *vt+o*
2 spring *n*
25 ~
21 sprinkle *vt+o+adv*
~ *vt+o*
108 spy *n*
108 spy *vi*
136 square *adj*
8 ~ *n*
136 ~ *n*
149 squeeze *vt+o*
~ *vt+o+adv*
33 squirrel *n*
129 stable *n*
119 stadium *n*
115 ~
127 staff *n*
158 ~
101 staff room *n*
114 stage *n*
164 ~
115 ~
50 staircase *n*
40 stairs *n*
134 stall *n*
76 stamp *n*
79 ~
102 ~
76 stamp *vt+o*
134 stand *n*
12 stand *vi*
~ *vi+adv*
53 stand *vt+o*
~ *vt+to inf*
~ *vt+v-ing*
110 standard *n*
19 standstill *n*
1 star *n*
115 ~
65 stare *vi (at)*
26 start *n*
25 start *vt+o*
~ *vi*
~ *vt+to inf*
~ *vt+v-ing*
42 starter *n*
63 startle *vt+o*
42 starvation *n*
42 starve *vi*
110 ~ *vt+o*
96 state *n*
73 statement *n*
9 station *n*
81 ~
78 stationery *n*
123 statue *n*
19 stay *n*
47 stay *vi+n*
~ *vi+adj*
~ *vi+adv*
~ *vi*
23 steady *adj*
40 steak *n*
110 steal *vt+o (from)*
~ *vi*
139 steam *n*
11 steamer *n*
139 steel *n,adj*
1 steep *adj*
20 steer *vt+o*
10 steering wheel *n*
34 stem *n*
16 step *n*
17 step *vi+adv*
9 steward *n*
9 stewardess *n*
139 stick *n*
140 stick *vi+adv (to)*
~ *vt+o+adv*
~ *vi*
142 sticky *adj*
155 stiff *adj*
28 still *adv*
28 still not *adv*
62 stimulate *vt+o*
39 sting *vt+o*
~ *vi*
44 stir *vt+o*
134 stock *n*
133 stock market *n*
45 stocking *n*
35 stomach *n*
34 stone *n*
139 ~
17 stop *n*
26 ~
25 stop *vi*
~ *vt+o*
~ *vt+v-ing*
~ *vt+o+v-ing*
132 store *n*
160 ~
6 ~
160 store *vt+o*
3 storm *n*
77 story *n*
143 stove *n*
136 straight *adj*
156 strange *adj*
97 stranger *n*
34 strawberry *n*
32 stray *adj*
1 stream *n*
8 street *n*
158 strength *n*
158 strengthen *vt+o*
~ *vi*
74 stress *n*
73 stress *vt+o*
157 stretch *vt+o*
~ *vi*
58 strict *adj*
127 strike *n*
129 strike *vi*
149 ~ *vt+o*
~ *vt+o+adv*
139 string *n*
142 strip *n*
142 strip of paper *n*
32 stripe *n*
32 striped *adj*
19 stroll *n*
19 stroll *vi*
156 strong *adj (in)*
79 ~
142 structure *n*
105 struggle *n*
108 struggle *vi (with) (against)*
~ *vi+to inf*
61 stubborn *adj*
100 student *nBE*
124 studies *n*
50 study *n*
67 study *vt+o*
~ *vi*
138 stuff *n*
19 stumble *vi*
67 stupid *adj*
123 style *n*
109 sub *n*
82 subject *n*
85 ~
102 ~
109 submarine *n*
70 subtle *adj*
137 subtract *vt+o*
96 suburb *n*
9 subway *nAE*
11 ~ *nBE*
149 succeed *vi (in +o)*
~ *(in +v-ing)*
145 success *n*
145 successful *adj (in)*
107 successor *n*
162 such *adj*
162 such a
89 such as
22 sudden *adj*
22 suddenly *adv*
38 suffer from *vt prep+o*
154 sufficient *adj*
86 suffix *n*
41 sugar *n*
72 suggest *vt+o*
~ *vt+v-ing*
~ *vt+that*
~ *vt+wh*
72 suggestion *n*
113 suicide *n*
45 suit *n*
45 suit *vt+o*
156 suitable *adj (for)*
140 suitcase *n*
137 sum *n*
78 sum up *vt adv+o*
~ *vi adv*
78 summary *n*
25 summer *n*
1 sun *n*
47 sunbathe *vi*
24 Sunday *n*
1 sunny *adj*
23 sunrise *n*
23 sunset *n*
4 sunshine *n*
54 super *adj*
154 superior *adj*
85 superlative *n,adj*
132 supermarket *n*
12 supersonic *adj*
103 superstition *n*
129 supervisor *n*
40 supper *n*
160 supply *n*
159 supply
vt+dir o+to+indir o
vt+indir o+with+dir o
72 support *n*
72 support *vt+o*
119 supporter *n*
67 suppose *vt+that*
~ *vt+o+to inf*
~ *vt+o+adj*
~ *vt+o+adv*
145 supposed to
112 Supreme Court *n*
162 sure *adj (of)(about)*

adj	***adv***	***dir o***	***indir o***	***inf***	***ing***	***n***	***o***
adjective	adverb(ial)	direct object	indirect object	infinitive without to	ing-form	noun	object

103 surely *adv*
165 ~
13 surface *n*
120 surfboard *n*
120 surfing *n*
94 surname *n*
155 surplus *adj,n*
60 surprise *n*
60 surprise *vt+o*
59 ~
109 surrender *vi*
~ *vt+o*
144 surround *vt+o*
98 surroundings *n*
65 survey *n*
31 survival *n*
31 survive *vi*
~ *vt+o*
74 suspect *vt+o (of)*
~ *vt+o+to inf*
~ *vt+that*
11 suspension bridge *n*
74 suspicion *n*
157 suspicious *adj (of)*
33 swallow *n*
42 swallow *vt+o*
~ *vi*
133 swap *vt+o*
72 swear *vi (at)*
75 swear *vt+o*
~ *vt+to inf*
~ *vt+that*
36 sweat *n*
36 sweat *vi*
29 ~ *vt+o*
45 sweater *n*
142 sweep *vt+o*
~ *vt+o+adv*
~ *vt+o+adj*
64 sweet *adj*
29 ~
95 sweetheart *n*
41 sweets *n*
20 swift *adj*
118 swim *vi*
~ *vt+o*
120 swimmer *n*
120 swimming costume *n*
118 swimming pool *n*
120 swimming suit *n*
121 swing *n*
82 switch off *vt adv+o*
82 switch on *vt adv+o*
133 swop *vt+o*
85 syllable *n*
80 symbol *n*
80 symbolic *adj*
58 sympathy *n*
158 ~
83 synonym *n*
142 system *n*
142 systematic *adj*

49 table *n*
44 tablespoon *n*
40 tablet *n*
148 tackle *vt+o*
70 tact *n*
70 tactful *adj*
70 tactless *adj*
33 tail *n*
47 tailor *n*
22 take *vt+dir o+for+indir o*
~ *vi+n*
18 take *vt+indir o+dir o*
68 ~ *vt+o (to)*
159 take *vt+o (from)*
18 take away *vt adv+o*
137 ~
63 take a look
38 take care of
37 take it easy
9 take off *vi adv*
143 take out *vt adv+o*
115 take part in
161 take place *vi*
60 take sides with
115 take up *vt adv+o*
~ *vt adv+v-ing*
12 take-off *n*
70 talent *n*
70 talented *adj*
71 talk *n*
71 talk *vi (to)*
~ *vt+o*
71 talk about *vi prep*
137 tall *adj*
109 tank *n*
51 tap *n*
114 tape *n*
142 ~
114 tape recorder *n*
123 tapestry *n*
43 tart *n*
142 tartan *n*
127 task *n*
64 taste *n*
64 taste *vt+o*
~ *v+adj*
~ *v+adv*
65 tasteful *adj*
65 tasteless *adj*
65 tasty *adj*
131 tax *n*
134 tax *vt+o*
8 taxi *n*
41 tea *n*
100 teach *vt+indir o+dir o*
~ *vt+o*
~ *vt+o+to inf*
~ *vt+o+v-ing*
~ *vt+that*
~ *vt+wh*
~ *vi*
100 teacher *n*
118 team *n*
36 tear *n*
149 ~
149 tear *vt+o*
~ *vt+o+adv*
60 tease *vt+o*
~ *vi*
122 technical *adj*
101 technical drawing *n*
124 technician *n*
124 technological *adj*
124 technology *n*
93 teenage *adj*
93 teenager *n*
80 telegram *n*
80 telephone *n*
80 telephone *vt+o*
~ *vt+indir o+dir o*
~ *vt+o+to inf*
~ *vi*
81 telephone booth *n*
81 telephone box *n*
81 telephone number *n*
80 television *n*
80 television (set) *n*
70 tell *vt+indir o+dir o*
~ *vt+indir o+that*
~ *vt+indir o+wh*
~ *vt+o*
~ *vt+o+to inf*
60 temper *n*
3 temperature *n*
104 temple *n*
127 temporary *adj*
163 tend *vt+to inf*
~ *vi+adv*
163 tendency *n*
58 tender *adj*
120 tennis *n*
59 tense *adj*
63 tension *n*
6 tent *n*
102 term *n*
12 terminal *n*
50 terrace *n*
55 terrible *adj*
153 terrific *adj*
61 terrify *vt+o*
2 territory *n*
61 terror *n*
108 terrorism *n*
108 terrorist *n*
38 test *n*
100 ~
38 test *vt+o*
112 testify *vt+that*
~ *vi*
82 text *n*
78 textbook *n*
141 textiles *n*
29 ~
88 than *conj*
56 thank *vt+o (for)*
94 thank you *interj*
58 thankful *adj (to)*
94 thanks *interj*
87 that *pron*
88 ~ *pron,adj*
90 that is to say
87 the *art*
29 the day after
23 the following day
29 the next day
23 ~
29 the other day
23 ~
114 theater *nAE*
114 theatre *n*
113 theft *n*
86 their *pron*
86 theirs *pron*
86 them *pron*
83 theme *n*
86 themselves *pron*
27 then *adv*
28 ~
29 ~
124 theoretical *adj*
68 theory *n*
13 there *adv*
88 therefore *adv*
122 ~
143 thermometre *n*
88 these *pron,adj*
29 these days
86 they *pron*
137 thick *adj*
112 thief *n*
36 thin *adj*
137 ~
138 thing *n*
159 things *n*
66 think *vi (about)*
79 ~ *vt+that*
~ *vt+wh*
69 think of *vt prep+o*
66 think over *vt adv+o*
125 think up *vt adv+o*
42 thirst *n*
40 thirsty *adj*
88 this *pron,adj*
24 this evening
24 this morning
155 thorough *adj*
88 those *pron,adj*
88 though *conj*
68 thought *n*
142 thread *n*
75 threat *n*
72 threaten *vt+o (with)*
~ *vt+to inf*
24 three quarters of an hour
117 thriller *n*
62 thrilling *adj*
35 throat *n*
106 throne *n*
14 through *adv,prep*
30 ~ *prep*
30 throughout *prep*
18 throw *vt+o+adv*
~ *vt+o*
~ *vi*
36 thumb *n*
3 thunder *n*
5 thunderstorm *n*
24 Thursday *n*
89 thus *adv*
122 ~
9 ticket *n*
117 ticket office *n*
2 tide *n*
45 tidy *adj*
45 tidy *vi*
~ *vt+o*
45 tie *n*
146 tie *vt+o+adv*
~ *vt+o*
~ *vi*
32 tiger *n*
155 tight *adj*
45 tights *n*
135 till *n*
28 ~ *prep,conj*
22 time *n*
135 times *prep*
9 timetable *n*
100 ~
61 timid *adj*
59 ~
140 tin *n*
141 ~
140 tinned *adj*
153 tiny *adj*
16 tip *n*
42 ~
44 tip *vt+o*
~ *vt+indir o+dir o*
8 tire *nAE*

pp	***prep***	***pron***	***that***	***to inf***	***vi***	***vt***	***wh***
past participle	preposition	pronoun	that-clause	infinitive with to	intransitive verb	transitive verb	wh-clause

36 tired *adj (of)*
36 tissue *n*
77 title *n*
24 to *prep*
13 ~ *prep*
131 to let
43 toast *n*
43 toast *vt+o*
42 tobacco *n*
23 today *n,adv*
36 toe *n*
15 together *adv*
49 toilet *n*
58 tolerance *n*
58 tolerant *adj*
53 tolerate *vt+o*
34 tomato *n*
24 tomorrow *n,adv*
137 ton *n*
36 tongue *n*
83 ~
121 tongue twister *n*
24 tonight *n,adv*
152 too *adv*
139 tool *n*
35 tooth *n*
38 toothache *n*
45 toothbrush *n*
39 toothpaste *n*
1 top *n*
12 ~
83 topic *n*
23 topical *adj*
107 Tory *n*
153 total *adj*
136 ~ *n*
155 totally *adv*
64 touch *n*
64 touch *vt+o*
~ *vi*
158 tough *adj*
6 tour *n*
8 tourism *n*
6 tourist *n*
28 towards *prep*
49 towel *n*
48 tower *n*
96 town *n*
107 town hall *n*
118 toy *n*
150 trace *n*
150 trace *vt+o*
129 tractor *n*
126 trade *n*
132 ~
64 ~
133 trade *vi (with)*
~ *vt+o*
127 trade union *n*
110 tradition *n*
110 traditional *adj*
8 traffic *n*
11 traffic circle *n*
8 traffic lights *n*
117 tragedy *n*
117 tragic *adj*
10 trailer *n*
8 train *n*
69 train *vt+o*
~ *vt+o+to inf*
~ *vt+indir o+wh*
~ *vt+to inf*
~ *vi*
119 training *n*
8 tram *n*
99 tramp *n*
85 transitive verb *n*
82 translate *vt+o (from) (into)*
~ *vi*
83 translation *n*
102 transparency *n*
65 transparent *adj*
10 transport *n*
20 transport *vt+o*
160 trap *n*
160 trapped *adj*
6 travel *n*
6 travel *vi (from)(to)*
70 travel agency *n*
9 travel guide *n*
130 traveller's check *nAE*
130 traveller's cheque *n*
143 tray *n*
133 treasure *n*
115 ~
38 treat *vt+o*
40 treatment *n*
33 tree *n*
112 trial *n*
93 tribe *n*
55 trick *n*
57 trick *vt+o*
47 trim *adj*
47 trim *vt+o*
6 trip *n*
135 trolley *n*
109 troops *n*
59 trouble *n*
156 ~
61 trouble *vt+o*
~ *vi*
~ *vi+to inf*
45 trousers *n*
8 truck *nAE*
161 true *adj*
116 trumpet *n*
57 trust *n*
55 trust *vt+o*
~ *vt+o+to inf*
161 truth *n*
148 try *n*
145 try *vt+o*
~ *vt+to inf*
~ *vt+v-ing*
45 try on *vt adv+o*
139 tube *n*
140 ~
9 ~ *BE*
24 Tuesday *n*
116 tune *n*
11 tunnel *n*
142 turbine *n*
33 turkey *n*
161 turn *n*
19 turn *vt+o*
72 turn down *vt adv+o*
80 turn off *vt adv+o*
80 turn on *vt adv+o*
21 turn round *vt adv+o*
~ *vi adv*
19 turn up *vi adv*
8 turning *n*
80 TV *n*
142 tweed *n*
135 twice *adv*
93 twin *n*
21 twist *vi*
~ *vt+o*
~ *vt+o+adv*
161 type *n*
76 type (out) *vt+o*
~ *vt adv+o*
76 typewriter *n*
163 typical *adj (of)*
126 typist *n*
8 tyre *n*

• • • • • • • • • • • • • • • •

90 ugh! *interj*
55 ugly *adj*
45 umbrella *n*
157 unable *adj (+to inf)*
23 unavoidable *adj*
92 uncle *n*
37 unconscious *adj*
84 uncountable *adj*
14 under *prep*
151 ~ *prep,adv*
46 underclothes *n*
9 underground *n*
74 underline *vt+o*
16 underneath *prep,adv*
67 understand *vt+o*
~ *vi*
~ *vt+that*
~ *vt+wh*
46 underwear *n*
103 undoubtedly *adv*
165 ~
46 undress *vi*
~ *vt+o*
70 uneducated *adj*
126 unemployed *adj*
126 unemployment *n*
62 unexpected *adj*
158 unfair *adj*
165 unfortunate *adj*
96 unfriendly *adj*
57 unhappy *adj*
46 uniform *n*
165 unimportant *adj*
97 union *n*
105 ~
127 ~
137 unit *n*
149 unite *vt+o*
~ *vi*
146 united *adj*
149 unity *n*
2 universe *n*
99 university *n*
102 ~
88 unless *conj*
165 unlucky *adj*
165 unnecessary *adj*
56 unpleasant *adj*
54 unpopular *adj*
57 unreliable *adj*
28 until *prep,conj*
157 unusual *adj*
15 up *prep,adv*
30 up to *adv*
15 ~ *prep*
30 up to now *adv*
27 up-to-date *adj*
13 upon *prep*
97 upper class, the *n*
59 upset *adj*
60 upset *vt+o*
48 upstairs *adv*
98 uptown *adv*
141 uranium *n*
23 urgency *n*
22 urgent *adj*
86 us *pron*
125 usage *n*
125 use *n*
158 ~
123 use *vt+o (for)*
156 used to
157 useful *adj (for)*
157 useless *adj (for)*
155 usual *adj*
155 usually *adv*

• • • • • • • • • • • • • • • •

131 V.A.T.
127 vacancy *n*
127 vacant *adj*
102 vacation *nAE*
129 ~
143 vacuum cleaner *n*
158 vain *adj*
158 valid *adj*
1 valley *n*
132 valuable *adj*
131 value *n*
10 van *n*
113 vandalism *n*
164 variety *n*
162 various *adj*
164 vary *vi*
~ *vt+o*
143 vase *n*
153 vast *adj*
43 veal *n*
40 vegetable *n*
10 vehicle *n*
82 verb *n*
85 ~
83 verbal *adj*
78 verse *n*
83 version *n*
151 very *adv*
108 veto *n*
108 veto *vt+o*
16 via *prep*
106 vice-president *n*
40 victim *n*
109 victory *n*
81 video *n,adj*
81 video recorder *n*
63 view *n*
67 ~
79 ~
82 viewer *n*
96 village *n*
43 vinegar *n*
60 violence *n*
60 violent *adj*
116 violin *n*
111 visa *n*
65 visible *adj*
64 vision *n*
5 visit *n*
5 visit *vt+o*
~ *vi*
6 visitor *n*
56 vital *adj*
165 ~
165 vitally *adv*
83 vocabulary *n*
82 voice *n*
85 ~

adj	*adv*	*dir o*	*indir o*	*inf*	*ing*	*n*	*o*
adjective	adverb(ial)	direct object	indirect object	infinitive without to	ing-form	noun	object

85 voiced *adj*
85 voiceless *adj*
3 volcano *n*
120 volleyball *n*
78 volume *n*
116 ~
138 ~
111 voluntary *adj*
109 volunteer *n*
107 vote *n*
104 vote *vi (for)(against)*
85 vowel *n*
7 voyage *n*
58 vulgar *adj*
158 ~

••••••••••••••••

127 wages *n*
10 waggon *n*
10 wagon *n*
36 waist *n*
12 wait *vi (for)*
42 waiter *n*
10 waiting room *n*
42 waitress *n*
35 wake (up) *vi (adv)*
~ *vt (adv)+o*
17 walk *n*
17 walk *vt+o*
~ *vi*
48 wall *n*
45 wallet *n*
53 want *n*
52 want *vt+o*
~ *vt+to inf*
~ *vt+o+to inf*
~ *vt+v-ing*
104 war *n*
112 warden *n*
51 wardrobe *n*
3 warm *adj*
96 ~
5 warmth *n*
72 warn *vt+o (of)*
~ *vt+that*
~ *vt+indir o+that*
~ *vt+o+to inf*
72 warning *n*
45 wash *vt+o*
~ *vi*
51 wash basin *n*
41 wash up *vi adv*
140 waste *n*
123 waste *vt+o*
25 watch *n*
63 watch *vt+o*
~ *vi*
~ *vt+o+inf*
~ *vt+o+v-ing*
129 watchmaker *n*
139 water *n*
34 watermelon *n*
150 waterproof *adj*
46 ~ *n*
2 wave *n*
21 wave *vi*
~ *vt+o*
124 waxworks *n*
8 way *n*
123 ~
50 way in *n*
97 way of life
50 way out *n*
51 WC *n*
86 we *pron*
157 weak *adj (in)*
158 weaken *vt+o*
~ *vi*
158 weakness *n*
133 wealth *n*
133 wealthy *adj*
105 weapon *n*
44 wear *vt+o*
~ *vt+o+adj*
3 weather *n*
95 wedding *n*
95 wedding anniversary *n*
24 Wednesday *n*
24 week *n*
24 weekday *n*
24 weekend *n*
25 weekly *adj,adv*
80 ~ *n*
60 weep *vt+o*
~ *vi*
136 weigh *vt+o*
~ *v+n*
136 weight *n*
92 welcome *n*
94 welcome *vt+o*
39 welfare *n*
37 well *adj*
54 ~ *adv*
89 ~ *interj*
59 well-behaved *adj*
67 well-known *adj*
1 west *n,adj*
1 western *adj*
115 ~ *n*
3 wet *adj*
87 what *pron,adj*
90 What a . . .!
152 what else
89 whatever *adj,pron*
34 wheat *n*
138 wheel *n*
39 wheelchair *n*
28 when *adv*
87 ~
28 ~ *conj,adv*
89 whenever *conj*
30 ~
87 where *adv*
156 ~
89 whereas *conj*
89 wherever *adv,conj*
88 whether *conj*
87 which *pron*
89 whichever *adj,pron*
27 while *conj*
22 ~ *n*
44 whiskey *nAE*
44 whisky *nBE*
73 whisper *vt+o (to)*
~ *vi*
60 whistle *n*
60 whistle *vt+o*
~ *vi*
25 Whit(sun) *n*
4 white *adj,n*
87 who *pron*
29 ~
156 ~
89 whoever *pron*
153 whole *adj*
134 wholesale *n*
87 whose *pron*
29 ~
87 why *adv*
136 wide *adj*
95 widow *n*
95 widower *n*
138 width *n*
92 wife *n*
31 wild *adj*
54 will *n*
112 ~
164 will *vi+inf*
29 ~
52 willing *adj (+to inf)*
118 win *vt+o*
~ *vi*
3 wind *n*
21 wind *vt+o*
129 windmill *n*
48 window *n*
3 windy *adj*
41 wine *n*
33 wing *n*
50 ~
119 winner *n*
25 winter *n*
47 wipe *vt+o*
139 wire *n*
143 wire netting *n*
81 wireless (set) *n*
70 wisdom *n*
67 wise *adj*
52 wish *n*
52 wish *vt+that*
~ *vt+indir o+dir o*
~ *vt+to inf*
~ *vt+o+to inf*
~ *vt+o+adj*
~ *vt+o+adv*
14 with *prep*
14 within *prep*
15 within reach
14 without *prep*
74 without doubt
128 without effort
112 witness *n*
112 witness *vt+o*
32 wolf *n*
91 woman *n*
60 wonder *n*
60 wonder *vt+wh*
59 ~ *vi*
54 wonderful *adj*
2 wood *n*
139 ~
139 wooden *adj*
101 woodwork *n*
139 wool *n*
139 woollen *adj*
82 word *n*
125 work *n*
125 work *vi*
125 worker *n*
97 working class, the *n*
129 working conditions *n*
129 working hours *n*
125 workman *n*
124 workshop *n*
1 world *n*
2 worldwide *adj*
33 worm *n*
61 worried *adj (about)*
59 worry *vt+o*
~ *vi (about)*
55 worse *adj*
103 worship *n*
103 worship *vt+o*
~ *vi*
55 worst *adj*
130 worth *adj*
133 worthless *adj*
158 worthwhile *adj*
164 would *vi+inf*
52 would like *vt+o*
~ *vt+to inf*
39 wound *n*
39 wound *vt+o*
140 wrap *vt+o*
12 wreck *n*
36 wrist *n*
25 wristwatch *n*
75 write *vt+o*
~ *vi (about)*
~ *vt+indir o+dir o*
~ *vt+to inf*
~ *vt+v-ing*
~ *vt+indir o+that*
75 write down *vt adv+o*
77 writer *n*
77 writing *n*
55 wrong *adj (about)*
156 ~

••••••••••••••••

138 yard *n*
48 ~
55 ~
37 yawn *vi*
24 year *n*
25 yearly *adj,adv*
4 yellow *adj,n*
89 yes *interj*
24 yesterday *n,adv*
28 yet *adv*
43 yogurt *n*
86 you *pron*
75 you had better
94 you're welcome
27 young *adj*
92 youngster *n*
86 your *pron*
106 Your Majesty
77 yours *pron*
86 ~
77 yours faithfully
77 yours sincerely
86 yourself *pron*
86 yourselves *pron*
27 youth *n*
92 ~
7 youth hostel *n*
31 youthful *adj*

••••••••••••••••

33 zebra *n*
11 zebra crossing *n*
135 zero *n*
138 zigzag *n,adv*
46 zip *n*
81 zip code *nAE*
98 zone *n*
32 zoo *n*

Index Deutsch

123 Abbild
20 abbremsen
23 Abend
40 Abendessen
161 Abenteuer
88 aber
103 Aberglaube
19 abfahren
18 abfahren *(Schiff)*
17 Abfahrt
140 Abfall
144 ~
12 Abfertigungsgebäude
16 abgelegen
107 Abgeordnete(r)
107 Abgeordnete(r) des Unterhauses
152 abgesehen von
154 ~
57 abhängen von
149 ~
40 abhängig (von)
57 ~
147 abhalten von
2 Abhang
9 abheben
18 abholen
72 ablehnen
111 ~
75 Ablehnung
76 Abmachung
136 abmessen
37 abnehmen
54 Abneigung
17 Abreise
47 Absatz *(Schuh)*
78 Absatz *(Text)*
134 abschätzen
111 abschaffen
79 abschicken
111 abschlagen
102 Abschlußprüfung
41 abschneiden
76 abschreiben
122 Abschrift
66 Absicht
69 ~
66 absichtlich
12 Abstand
47 abstauben
69 abstrakt
75 abstreiten
103 Abteikirche
10 Abteil
126 Abteilung
141 ~
3 abtrocknen
5 ~
72 abweisen
75 Abweisung
144 abwerfen
13 abwesend
16 Abwesenheit
21 abwischen
47 ~
143 Abzeichen
137 abziehen
115 Abzug
8 Abzweigung
61 achten
150 achten auf
61 Achtung
127 Acker
136 addieren
137 Addition
99 adlig
99 Adlige(r)
94 adoptieren
76 Adresse
164 ähneln
162 ähnlich
164 Ähnlichkeit
27 älter
93 älter *(Familienmitglied)*
93 ältest(er,-e,-es)
122 ändern
122 Änderung
61 ängstlich
59 ~
60 Ärger
59 ärgerlich
60 ~
60 ärgern
60 Ärgernis
47 Ärmel
39 Ärztin
46 äußere Erscheinung
71 äußern
151 äußerst
32 Affe
128 Agentur
67 ahnen
66 Ahnung
100 akademischer Grad
78 Aktenordner
143 Aktentasche
36 aktiv
85 ~
85 Aktiv
85 Aktiv oder Passiv
23 aktuell
83 Akzent
75 akzeptabel
72 akzeptieren
63 alarmieren
67 albern
44 Ale *(Bier)*
41 Alkohol
43 alkoholfreies Getränk
153 alle
11 Allee
92 allein
135 ~
135 alleinig
87 alles
89 alles was
155 allgemein
61 ~
33 Alligator
77 Alphabet
37 Alptraum
28 als
30 ~
88 ~
88 als ob
122 also
26 alt
27 ~
27 Alter
164 alternativ
164 Alternative
27 altertümlich
27 altmodisch
23 am anderen Tag
54 am besten
29 am folgenden Tag
31 am Leben bleiben
151 am meisten
97 am Ort
55 am schlechtesten
15 am weitesten
16 ~
151 am wenigsten
8 Ampel
126 Amt
107 Amtsvorgänger
115 amüsieren
13 an
11 an Bord
94 an Kindesstatt annehmen
15 an . . . vorbei
16 ~
34 Ananas
127 anbauen
129 ~
103 anbeten
159 anbieten
149 anbinden
1 Anblick
65 ~
22 andauern
160 Andenken
162 anderer
74 andeuten
69 Anerkennung
26 Anfang
22 anfangen
25 ~
97 Anführer
76 Anführungszeichen
61 angeben
150 ~
159 Angebot
83 Angelegenheit
153 ~
164 ~
127 angeln
54 angenehm
89 angesichts
59 angespannt
105 angreifen
108 Angriff
59 Angst
59 Angst haben (vor)
61 ~
44 anhaben
26 anhalten
10 Anhänger
119 ~
26 anhalten
78 Anhang
17 anheben
94 an Kindesstatt annehmen
112 anklagen
6 ankommen
17 ~
73 ankündigen
73 Ankündigung
17 Ankunft
22 Anlaß
133 Anleihe
73 anmerken
143 annageln
75 annehmbar
67 annehmen
68 ~
72 ~
75 ~
107 ~
25 annullieren
72 anordnen
75 Anordnung
148 anpacken
45 anprobieren
62 anregen
59 anregend
80 Anruf
80 anrufen
81 ~
71 anschreien
63 ansehen
71 ~
49 ansiedeln
152 ansonsten
154 ~
74 Anspielung
56 anständig
65 anstarren
51 anstreichen
125 Anstrengung
107 ~
51 Anstrich
160 Anteil
27 antik
27 Antiquität
17 antreiben
71 Antwort
74 ~
128 Antwort finden
72 Antwort geben
71 antworten
74 ~
71 antworten auf
151 anwachsen
154 Anwachsen
110 Anwalt
72 Anweisung
125 anwenden auf
125 Anwendung
125 Anwendungsmöglichkeit
13 anwesend
16 Anwesenheit
135 Anzahl
80 Anzeige
150 anzeigen
44 anziehen, (sich)
45 ~
56 ~
56 Anziehungskraft
139 anzünden
45 Anzug
33 Apfel
33 Apfelsine
76 Apostroph
38 Apotheke
38 Apotheker
42 Appetit
115 applaudieren
115 Applaus
24 April
125 Arbeit
126 ~
125 arbeiten
128 ~
125 Arbeiter
97 Arbeiterklasse
126 Arbeitgeber(in)
126 Arbeitnehmer(in)
129 Arbeitsbedingungen
126 arbeitslos
63 ~
126 Arbeitslosigkeit
11 Arbeitsplan
129 Arbeitsstunden
129 Arbeitszeit
50 Arbeitszimmer
71 Argument
71 argumentieren
137 Arithmetik
35 Arm
55 arm
130 ~
93 arm wie eine Kirchenmaus
25 Armbanduhr
105 Armee
133 Armut
65 Aroma
161 Art
163 ~
122 ~
123 Art und Weise
82 Artikel
140 ~
38 Arznei
39 Arznei(mittel)
38 Arzt
39 ~
42 Aschenbecher
147 Assistent
34 Ast
12 Astronaut
36 Atem(zug)
37 atemlos
119 Athlet
36 atmen
4 Atmosphäre
138 Atom
138 Atom-
138 atomar
54 attraktiv
152 auch
122 ~
156 ~
89 auch immer
152 auch nicht
12 auf
13 ~
15 ~
96 auf dem Land
63 auf den ersten Blick
16 auf halbem Wege unten
13 auf . . . hinauf
87 auf jeden Fall
165 ~
134 auf Lager
5 Aufblitzen
5 aufblitzen
19 aufbrechen
57 aufdecken
17 Aufenthalt
19 ~
113 auferlegen
65 auffallend
5 auffordern
71 ~
117 aufführen
114 Aufführung
125 Aufgabe
127 ~
136 ~
20 aufgeben
25 ~
105 ~
127 ~
26 aufgeschoben
67 aufgeweckt
88 aufgrund
12 aufhängen
140 aufheben
25 aufhören
26 ~
25 aufhören mit
78 Aufkleber
79 Auflage
81 auflegen
149 auflösen, (sich)
68 Aufmerksamkeit
116 Aufnahme
114 aufnehmen
68 aufpassen
45 aufräumen
111 aufrechterhalten

59 aufregend
62 Aufregung
55 aufrichtig
56 ~
56 Aufrichtigkeit
108 Aufrührer
59 aufs Spiel setzen
102 Aufsatz
26 aufschieben
63 aufschrecken
75 aufschreiben
25 Aufschub
56 aufsehenerregend
129 Aufseher(in)
9 aufsetzen
150 aufspüren
17 aufstehen *(Bett)*
17 aufsteigen
107 aufstellen
19 aufstreichen
16 auftauchen
19 ~
149 aufteilen
132 Auftrag
35 aufwachen
35 aufwecken
77 Aufzeichnung
92 aufziehen
94 ~
48 Aufzug
35 Auge
22 Augenblick
27 augenblicklich
36 Augenbraue
24 August
13 aus
14 ~
140 aus der Dose
14 aus hinaus
164 aus Versehen
139 aus Wolle
26 aus zweiter Hand
80 aus/abschalten
101 ausbilden
69 ausbilden, (sich) (lassen)
131 ausborgen
82 Ausdruck
71 ausdrücken
16 auseinander
59 Auseinander-setzung
69 ausfallen lassen
6 Ausflug
148 ausführen
153 ausfüllen
134 Ausfuhr
79 Ausgabe
128 Ausgaben
48 Ausgang
50 ~
148 Ausgangspunkt
131 ausgeben *(Geld)*
157 ausgefallen
59 ausgeglichen
70 ausgeklügelt
37 ausgezeichnet
56 ~
69 ~
134 aushandeln
81 ausharren
96 auskommen mit
7 Auskunftsbüro
97 Ausländer
97 ausländisch
150 Auslage
17 auslassen
69 ~
131 ausleihen
139 auslöschen
109 Ausnahme
149 auspressen
21 ausradieren
78 ~
113 ausrauben
138 ausrechnen
123 ausreichen
152 ausreichend
154 ~
46 Ausrüstung
142 ~
82 Ausruf
83 ~
76 Ausrufezeichen
35 ausruhen
18 ausrutschen
73 Aussage
112 aussagen gegen
80 ausschalten
82 ~
144 ausschließlich
51 ausschmücken
106 Ausschuß
63 aussehen
162 aussehen wie
98 Außenbezirke
152 außer
154 ~
107 ~
37 außer Atem
63 außer Gefahr
15 außer Reichweite
63 außer Sicht
88 außer wenn
152 außerdem
154 ~
110 außergewöhnlich
157 ~
14 außerhalb
98 außerhalb des Zentrums
63 Aussicht
108 ausspionieren
83 Aussprache
82 aussprechen
36 ausspucken
51 ausstatten
46 Ausstattung
17 aussteigen
17 aussteigen lassen
150 ausstellen
150 Ausstellung
146 Austausch
133 austauschen
146 ~
160 austeilen
79 austragen
5 austrocknen
132 Ausverkauf
159 auswählen
160 ~
159 Auswahl
160 ~
78 Ausweispapiere
69 auswendig
164 ~
148 Auswirkung
103 Auszeichnung
46 ausziehen, (sich)
8 Auto
10 Auto(mobil)
8 Autobahn
17 Autofahren
126 Autofahrer(in)
142 Automat
122 automatisch
78 Autor
106 Autorität

• • • • • • • • • • • • •

91 Baby
94 Babysitten
1 Bach
36 Backe
41 backen
44 Backform
143 Backofen
141 Backstein
49 Bad
120 Badeanzug
45 baden
71 ~
49 Badewanne
49 Badezimmer
133 Bäcker
32 Bär
9 Bahnhof
9 Bahnsteig
28 bald
48 Balkon
138 Ball
55 ~
115 Ballett
33 Banane
78 Band
142 ~
114 Band *(Musik)*
97 Bande
130 Bank(haus)
1 ~
153 ~
130 Banknote
133 ~
133 bankrott
42 Bar
117 ~
46 barfuß
130 Bargeld
99 Baron
99 Baronin
141 Barren
15 Barriere
35 Bart
93 Base
120 Basketball
142 Batterie
49 Bau
48 Bau(werk)
35 Bauch
48 bauen
49 ~
127 Bauer
129 Bauernhaus
127 Bauernhof
33 Baum
141 Baumstamm
139 Baumwolle
79 beabsichtigen
69 beabsichtigen (als)
68 beachten
64 Beachtung
106 Beamter
106 Beamter (im öff. Dienst)
106 Beamtin
74 beanspruchen
71 beantworten
128 Beauftragter
59 bedacht auf
53 Bedarf
75 ~
55 bedauern
58 Bedauern
144 bedecken
66 bedenken
75 Bedenken
79 bedeuten
80 ~
79 Bedeutung
163 ~
41 bedienen
128 ~
160 Bedienung
53 Bedingung
157 Bedrängnis
72 bedrohen
53 Bedürfnis
61 beeindruckend
148 beeinflussen
25 beenden
104 beerdigen
158 befähigen
67 Befähigung
103 ~
61 befangen
75 Befehl
72 befehlen
85 Befehlsform
146 befestigen
18 befördern
20 ~
10 Beförderung
99 befreien
99 Befreiung
55 befriedigen
57 Befriedigung
67 begabt
70 Begabung
111 begehen *(Verbrechen)*
62 begeistert (von)
59 begierig
62 ~
26 Beginn
25 beginnen
18 begleiten
21 ~
95 Begleitung
73 beglückwünschen
104 begraben
67 begreifen
94 begrüßen
92 Begrüßung
140 Behälter
143 ~
62 Behaglichkeit
159 behalten
38 behandeln
40 Behandlung
73 behaupten
104 beherrschen
61 Beherztheit
39 behindert
106 Behörde
36 bei Bewußtsein
62 bei der Arbeit
164 bei Tag
151 bei weitem
157 ~
152 beide
115 Beifall
62 beim Frühstück
35 Bein
28 beinahe
16 beiseite
161 Beispiel
163 ~
38 beißen
104 bekämpfen
157 bekannt
95 bekannt sein mit
95 Bekannte(r)
73 Bekanntmachung
159 bekommen
131 ~
59 belästigen
20 belebt
62 beleidigen
62 Beleidigung
5 beleuchten
53 beliebt bei
54 Beliebtheit
159 beliefern mit
32 bellen
160 belohnen
160 Belohnung
156 ~
57 belügen
115 belustigen
122 bemalen
64 bemerken
67 ~
73 ~
157 bemerkenswert
73 Bemerkung
55 bemitleiden
55 bemitleidenswert
54 Benehmen
70 benennen
53 Benimm dich
52 benötigen
53 ~
18 benutzen
123 ~
139 Benzin
63 beobachten
64 ~
59 bequem
62 ~
75 beraten
106 Berater(in)
113 berauben
138 berechnen
130 berechnen als
157 bereit
28 bereits
1 Berg
2 Bergland
55 Bergwerk
77 Bericht
80 berichten über
56 berücksichtigen
65 berühmt
67 ~
69 ~
115 ~
64 berühren
65 ~
64 Berührung
127 Beruf
126 Beruf *(akademisch)*
126 Beruf *(handwerklich)*
40 beruhigen
9 Besatzung
146 beschädigen
147 Beschädigung
127 beschäftigen
125 beschäftigt (sein) (mit)
128 beschäftigt mit
114 Beschäftigung
126 ~
59 beschämt
62 bescheiden
71 beschreiben
74 Beschreibung
147 beschützen
112 beschuldigen
161 Beseitigung
104 besetzen
153 besetzt
56 ~

108 Besetzung
5 besichtigen
49 besiedeln
118 besiegen
159 Besitz
160 ~
159 besitzen
160 ~
156 besonderer
157 ~
154 besonders
156 ~
61 ~
159 besorgen
61 besorgt
59 ~
68 besprechen
68 Besprechung
21 besprühen
37 besser
54 ~
73 besser als
149 Besserung
23 beständig
30 ~
75 bestätigen (lassen)
145 bestehen
73 bestehen (auf)
144 bestehen aus
17 besteigen
132 bestellen
132 bestellt
132 Bestellung
134 besteuern
162 bestimmt
103 ~
165 ~
19 Bestimmungswort
110 bestrafen
113 Bestrafung
62 bestrebt
59 bestürzt
5 Besuch
5 besuchen
6 ~
68 ~
101 besuchen *(Schule)*
6 Besucher
65 betasten
103 beten
141 Beton
73 betonen
74 Betonung
153 beträchtlich
159 betreffend
17 betreten
55 betrügen um
41 betrunken
49 Bett
49 Bettdecke
74 betteln
49 Bettlaken
59 beunruhigen
60 ~
61 ~
68 beurteilen
97 Bevölkerung(szahl)
28 bevor
112 bewachen
19 Bewegung
19 Bewegungsart
124 Beweis
112 Beweis(mittel)
124 beweisen
126 Bewerbung
102 bewerten
3 bewölkt
47 bewohnen
49 Bewohner
126 ~
61 bewundern
61 Bewunderung
36 bewußt
37 bewußtlos
131 bezahlen
127 Bezahlung
133 ~
54 bezaubernd
80 bezeichnen
112 bezeugen
146 Beziehung
96 Bezirk
98 ~
71 bezweifeln
77 Bibliothek
79 Bibliothekar(in)
126 ~
20 biegen
8 Biegung
41 Bier
159 bieten
1 Bild
122 ~
115 ~
123 ~
122 bilden, (sich)
117 Bildfläche
100 Bildung
132 billig
75 billigen
149 Bindeglied
146 binden
149 ~
45 Binder
76 Bindestrich
82 Bindewort
139 Bindfaden
101 Biologie
33 Birne
28 bis
30 ~
28 bis (spätestens)
30 bis jetzt
15 bis zu
56 Bitte
75 ~
74 bitten
71 bitten um
74 ~
148 ~
64 bitter
44 Bitter *(Bier)*
44 Blätterteig
3 blasen
5 blaß
36 ~
33 Blatt
76 ~
4 blau
141 Blei
47 bleiben
5 bleich
36 ~
76 Bleistift
63 Blick
63 blicken auf
38 blind
39 Blindheit
5 Blitz
78 Block
141 ~
50 Blockhütte
35 blond
46 bloß
165 ~
149 blühen
33 Blüte
33 Blume
45 Bluse
35 Blut
36 bluten
35 blutig
43 Bockwurst
13 Boden
48 ~
140 Bodenschätze
133 Börse
2 Böschung
59 böse
149 Bogen
34 Bohnen
105 Bombe
9 Boot
131 borgen
126 Boss
80 Bote
79 Botschaft
107 Botschaft(sgebäude)
107 Botschafter
120 boxen
121 ~
120 Boxer
111 Boykott
95 Bräutigam
139 Brand
43 Braten
44 braten
43 Bratensaft
44 Bratpfanne
143 Bratröhre
22 brauchen
52 ~
53 ~
145 ~
4 braun
95 Braut
59 brav
38 brechen
111 brechen *(Gesetz)*
136 breit
138 Breite
11 breite Straße
10 Bremse
139 brennen
141 Brennstoff
139 Brett
76 Brief
95 Brieffreund
81 Briefkasten
79 Briefmarke
78 Briefordner
79 Briefporto
45 Brieftasche
79 Briefträger(in)
76 Briefumschlag
81 Briefwechsel
140 Brille
143 ~
18 bringen
20 ~
147 bringen zu
41 Brötchen
77 Broschüre
78 ~
41 Brot
91 Bruder
8 Brücke
36 Brust(korb)
91 Bub
77 Buch
78 ~
6 buchen
129 Buchführung
129 Buchhalter
129 Buchhaltung
79 Buchhandlung
76 Buchstabe
76 buchstabieren
77 Buchstabieren
7 Buchung
104 Buddhist
133 Budget
140 Büchse
47 Bügeleisen
47 bügeln
114 Bühne
97 Bündnis
97 Bürger
98 Bürger-
98 bürgerlich
106 Bürgermeister
107 ~
126 Büro
126 Büroangestellte(r)
45 Bürste
47 bürsten
111 „Bulle“
19 Bummel
141 Bund
105 Bundes-
96 Bundesland
50 Bungalow
48 Burg
93 Bursche
64 Bus erreichen
10 Bushaltestelle
41 Butter

• • • • • • • • • • • • •

44 Cafeteria
7 Camp
7 campen
6 Camping
7 Campingplatz
123 Cartoon
130 Cent
137 Centimeter
119 Champion
162 Chance
12 Charterflug
134 chartern
99 Chef
6 ~
101 Chemie
140 chemisch
101 Chor(singen)
93 Clan
44 Cola
136 Computer
43 Cornflakes
51 Couch
93 Cousin
93 Cousine
129 Cowboy
41 Creme
9 Crew
119 Cricket

• • • • • • • • • • • • •

10 D-Zug
90 d.h.
88 da
89 ~
156 ~
91 dafür sein
14 dazwischen
48 Dach
88 daher
89 ~
27 damals
29 ~
91 Dame
47 Damenschneiderin
139 Dampf
11 Dampfer
56 dankbar
58 ~
58 Dankbarkeit
94 Danke
56 danken
28 dann
29 ~
66 daran denken
28 darauf
162 darf
133 Darlehen
163 darstellen
114 darstellen *(Film, Theater)*
87 das
14 das Äußere
52 das Gefühl haben
90 das heißt
14 das Innere
162 das kommt darauf an
161 dasselbe
25 Datum
23 dauerhaft
22 dauern
153 ~
36 Daumen
71 Debatte
74 debattieren
11 Deck
48 Decke
49 ~
143 Deckel
74 definieren
74 Definition
157 dehnen
86 dein
86 deines
51 dekorativ
51 dekorieren
51 Dekorierung
107 Demokrat(in)
105 Demokratie
104 demokratisch
108 Demonstration
108 demonstrieren
28 den ganzen Tag
66 denken
67 ~
68 Denken
104 Denkmal
89 dennoch
87 der
162 der andere
87 deren
29 ~
88 deshalb
87 dessen
29 ~
138 Detail
110 Detektiv
63 deutlich
101 Deutsch
24 Dezember
102 Dia(positiv)
117 ~
138 Diagramm
83 Dialekt
73 Dialog
141 Diamant
65 dicht
79 Dichter
78 Dichtung
36 dick
137 ~

45 dicke Wolljacke
87 die
21 die Achseln zucken
151 die meisten
158 die Mühe wert
112 Dieb
113 Diebstahl
160 dienen
123 dienen als
24 Dienstag
109 dienstfrei
99 Dienstmädchen
88 diese
88 dieser
23 dieses eine Mal
102 Diktat
102 diktieren
138 Ding
33 Dinosaurier
86 dir
136 direkt
85 direkte Rede
85 direktes Objekt
101 Direktor
126 ~
101 Direktorin
116 Dirigent
116 dirigieren
116 Discothek
116 Diskjockey
120 Diskus
71 Diskussion
71 diskutieren
96 Distrikt
54 Disziplin
137 dividieren
137 Division
78 Dokument
82 Dokumentarfilm
130 Dollar
84 dolmetschen
84 Dolmetscher
3 Donner
24 Donnerstag
50 Doppelhaushälfte
76 Doppelpunkt
135 doppelt
6 Doppelzimmer
96 Dorf
13 dort
13 dorthin
140 Dose
6 ~
39 Dragee
139 Draht
143 Drahtgeflecht
117 Drama
62 dramatisch
119 draußen
45 Dreck
96 Dreckarbeit
47 dreckig
19 drehen
20 ~
140 Drehknopf
22 dringend
53 dringend benötigen
23 Dringlichkeit
41 Drink
119 drinnen
39 Droge
38 Drogerie
38 Drogist
72 drohen
75 Drohung
76 Druck
79 drucken
65 drücken
146 ~
149 ~
2 Dschungel
86 du
75 Du solltest lieber
116 Dudelsack
36 dünn
137 ~
162 dürfte
55 dürftig
36 dürr
12 Düsenflugzeug
65 Duft
53 dulden
58 Duldsamkeit
67 dumm
70 ~
67 Dummkopf
39 dumpfer Schmerz
4 dunkel
4 Dunkelheit
4 Dunst
4 dunstig
14 durch
146 durchfallen
150 durchforschen
23 durchhalten
138 Durchschnitt
55 durchschnittlich
65 durchsichtig
150 durchsuchen
42 Durst
40 durstig
45 Duschbad
45 Dusche
45 duschen
137 Dutzend

• • • • • • • • • • • • • •

2 Ebbe und Flut
2 Ebene
50 ~
154 ebenso
148 Echo
122 echt
161 ~
8 Ecke
99 edel
141 Edelstein
47 Edelsteine
162 egal
28 ehe
95 Ehe
92 Ehefrau
26 ehemalig
92 Ehemann
95 Ehepaar
61 Ehre
61 ehren
69 Ehrgeiz
69 ehrgeizig
55 ehrlich
56 ~
158 Ehrlichkeit
40 Ei
33 Eichhörnchen
44 Eierteig
62 Eifersucht
62 eifersüchtig
59 eifrig
62 ~
159 eigen
160 ~
161 Eigenschaft
163 ~
82 Eigenschaftswort
161 eigentlich
163 ~
159 Eigentümer(in)
18 Eile
20 eilen
22 eilig
87 ein
29 ein andermal
45 ein Bad nehmen
151 ein paar
47 ein Sonnenbad nehmen
151 ein wenig
162 ein(e) andere(r)
86 einander
78 Einband(deckel)
160 einbauen
65 Einblick
112 Einbrecher
6 einchecken
108 eindringen in
68 Eindruck
61 eindrucksvoll
87 eine
163 eine Art
24 eine Dreiviertelstunde
17 eine Fahrt machen
24 eine halbe Stunde
105 eine Niederlage zufügen
26 eine Panne haben
24 eine Viertelstunde
63 einen Blick werfen auf
95 einen Heiratsantrag machen
121 einen Hieb versetzen
95 einen Klaps geben
120 einen Kopfsprung machen
152 einer von beiden
108 eines Amtsvergehens anklagen
156 einfach
145 Einfluß
144 einfügen
92 einführen
94 Einführung
134 Einfuhr
48 Eingang
50 ~
48 Eingangshalle
98 Eingeborene(r)
98 ein geboren(er)...
35 eingeschlafen
72 eingestehen
81 einhängen
98 Einheimischer
137 Einheit
149 ~
20 einholen
86 einige
149 Einigkeit
132 Einkäufe
132 Einkauf
133 ~
134 einkaufen
17 einkaufen gehen
135 Einkaufswagen
134 Einkaufszentrum
65 einklemmen
128 Einkommen
128 Einkünfte
5 einladen
5 Einladung
17 einlassen
154 einlaufen
144 einlegen
78 Einleitung
27 einmal
135 ~
140 einpacken
21 einreiben
51 einrichten
148 ~
160 Einrichtungen
93 einsam
96 Einsamkeit
80 einschalten
82 ~
35 einschlafen
140 einschließen
144 ~
90 einschließlich
15 Einschränkung
67 einsehen
75 Einspruch
108 ~
27 einst
17 einsteigen
53 Einstellung
27 einstig
78 eintragen
17 eintreten
126 eintreten in
19 Eintritt
72 einverstanden sein
75 Einwand
7 Einwanderer
7 Einwanderung
144 einwerfen
140 einwickeln
49 Einwohner(in)
126 ~
84 Einzahl
9 Einzelfahrkarte
138 Einzelheit
135 einzeln
93 Einzelperson
6 Einzelzimmer
135 einzig
65 einzwicken
3 Eis
32 Eisbär
138 Eisen
8 Eisenbahn
9 ~
4 eisig
32 Elefant
46 elegant
47 ~
129 Elektriker
139 elektrisch
139 Elektrizität
139 Elektro-
139 Elektronik
142 elektronisch
140 Element
157 elementar
57 elend
57 Elend
98 Elendsviertel
91 Eltern
126 ~
81 Empfänger
6 Empfang
115 ~
79 ~
81 empfangen
95 ~
159 ~
72 empfehlen
75 Empfehlung
63 empfindlich
53 empfindsam
53 Empfindung
26 Ende
78 Ende *(Geschichte/ Film)*
25 enden
26 ~
26 endigen
30 endlich
26 endlos
139 Energie
136 eng
155 ~
56 engagiert
103 Engel
101 Englisch
91 Enkelkind
92 Enkelsohn
92 Enkeltochter
147 entdecken
150 Entdecker
150 Entdeckung
33 Ente
144 entfernen
14 entfernt
16 ~
13 entfernt von
15 Entfernung
113 entführen *(Flugzeug, Fahrzeug)*
113 entführen *(Kinder/ Menschen)*
112 Entführer
162 entgegengesetzt
164 ~
140 enthalten
57 enthüllen
20 entkommen
15 entlang
113 entlassen
126 ~
66 entscheiden
66 Entscheidung
64 Entscheidung erreichen
148 Entscheidung treffen
61 entschlossen
69 Entschluß
71 entschuldigen
72 Entschuldigung
75 ~
37 entspannen, (sich)
81 entsprechen, (sich)
19 entstehen
55 enttäuschen
57 Enttäuschung
152 entweder...oder
125 entwerfen
27 entwickeln, (sich)
115 ~
27 Entwicklung
66 Entwurf
77 ~
125 ~
57 entzückt
37 entzündet
86 er
48 erbauen
112 Erbe
112 erben
112 Erbschaft
34 Erbse
3 Erdbeben

34 Erdbeere
48 Erdboden
141 ~
1 Erde
48 ~
141 ~
50 Erdgeschoß
2 Erdkunde
101 ~
1 Erdteil
161 Ereignis
67 erfahren
66 Erfahrung
125 erfinden
125 Erfinder
125 Erfindung
145 Erfolg
149 ~
149 Erfolg haben
145 erfolgreich
145 erfolgreich sein
22 erfordern *(Zeit)*
150 erforschen
150 Erforscher
150 Erforschung
74 erfragen
57 erfreuen
57 erfreulich
57 erfreut
55 erfreut (über)
4 erfrischend
42 Erfrischungen
149 erfüllen
118 Ergebnis
145 ~
160 ergreifen
159 erhalten
160 ~
150 Erhaltung
1 Erhebung
128 Erhöhung
52 erhoffen
115 Erholung
66 erinnern an
69 Erinnerung
38 Erkältung
69 Erkennen
67 erkennen
71 erklären
73 ~
71 Erklärung
73 ~
72 Erklärung geben
39 erkranken
39 Erkrankung
71 Erkundigung
128 erlangen
160 ~
109 erlauben
111 ~
109 Erlaubnis
111 ~
154 Ermäßigung
67 ermessen
158 ermöglichen
113 ermorden
148 ermutigen
148 Ermutigung
40 ernähren
42 ~
128 ernennen
107 Ernennung
128 ~
163 ernst
165 ~
163 ernsthaft
163 ernstlich
129 Ernte
130 ernten
109 Eroberer
108 erobern
74 erörtern
31 Erotik
67 erraten
87 erregend
17 erreichen
149 ~
48 errichten
49 ~
149 erringen
61 erröten
31 erschaffen
16 erscheinen
19 ~
46 Erscheinungsbild
105 erschießen
36 erschöpft
37 ~
61 erschrecken
160 ersetzen
133 Ersparnisse
60 Erstaunen
63 ~
63 erstaunen
60 erstaunt sein über
40 Erste Hilfe
26 erste(r/s)
50 erster Stock
75 Ersuchen
65 ertönen (lassen)
5 ertränken
129 Ertrag
53 ertragen
5 ertrinken
91 erwachsen
91 Erwachsener
60 erwägen
68 Erwägung
71 erwähnen
74 Erwähnung
67 erwarten
107 ~
69 Erwartung
53 erwartungsvoll
133 erwerben
70 erzählen
103 Erzbischof
145 erzeugen
122 Erzeugnis
69 erziehen
92 ~
94 ~
101 ~
100 Erziehung
86 es
29 es ist
158 es hat keinen Sinn
156 es ist meine Schuld
147 es läßt sich nicht ändern
37 es leicht nehmen
88 es sei denn
30 es war einmal . . .
32 Esel
40 Essen
40 essen
43 Essig
44 Eßlöffel
49 Eßzimmer
78 Etikette
30 etwa
86 etwas
87 ~
89 ~
72 etwas dagegen haben
75 ~
60 etwas verärgert
86 euch
86 euer
33 Eule
106 Eure Majestät
86 eures
23 eventuell
77 Exemplar
31 Existenz
31 existieren
144 exklusiv
7 Expedition
124 Experiment
124 experimentieren
122 Experte
149 explodieren
149 Explosion
134 Export
133 exportieren
106 Expräsident
153 extra

• • • • • • • • • • • • •

103 Fabel
125 Fabrik
128 Fabrikant
102 Fach
65 fade
142 Faden
70 fähig (zu)
67 Fähigkeit
70 ~
11 Fähre
11 Fährschiff
133 fällig
113 Fälschung
10 fahrbar
16 fahren
17 ~
118 ~
10 Fahrer
6 Fahrgast
133 Fahrgeld
9 Fahrkarte
9 Fahrplan
11 ~
8 Fahrrad
11 Fahrspur
6 Fahrt
17 ~
10 Fahrzeug
156 fair
112 Fall
153 ~
160 Falle
17 fallen
17 fallen lassen
144 ~
88 falls
12 Fallschirm
55 falsch
125 ~
156 ~
158 ~
47 falten
91 Familie
82 Familienserie
115 famos
119 Fan
159 fangen
157 fantastisch
142 Farbband
4 Farbe
122 ~
35 Farbige(r)
143 Faß
160 fassen
28 fast
36 faul
56 ~
37 Faulheit
121 Faust
121 Faustschlag
24 Februar
33 Feder
76 Federhalter
142 fegen
53 Fehlen
13 fehlend
156 Fehler
158 ~
148 Fehler machen
158 fehlerhaft
103 Feier
115 ~
165 feierlich
115 feiern
61 Feigling
133 feilschen
153 fein
92 Feind
58 feinfühlig
127 Feld
109 Feldwebel
8 Feldweg
11 ~
107 Feldzug
32 Fell
139 Felsen
141 felsig
48 Fenster
50 Fensterladen
100 Ferien
102 ~
127 ~
129 ~
7 Ferienort
80 Fernsehen
80 Fernsehgerät
82 Fernseh-zuschauer
81 Fernsprechzelle
36 Ferse
157 fertig
47 fertig machen, (sich)
125 ~
145 fertigbringen
148 fertig werden mit
115 Fest
140 fest
146 festbinden
95 feste Freundin
95 fester Freund
115 Festival
1 Festland
2 Festland-
115 Festspiel
140 Feststoff
50 Festung
43 Fett
36 fett
93 fett wie ein Schwein
3 feucht
4 ~
139 Feuer
105 feuern
126 ~
105 Feuerwaffe
10 Feuerwehrauto
10 Feuerwehrmann
39 Fieber
39 Fieberzustand
35 Figur
126 Filiale
80 Film
115 ~
82 Film *(Kino)*
133 finanziell
147 finden
35 Finger
125 Firma
126 ~
31 Fisch
41 ~
31 Fischarten
127 fischen
17 fischen gehen
37 fit
2 Fjord
155 flach
143 Flagge
42 Flasche
45 Fleck
40 Fleisch
133 Fleischer
93 fleißig wie eine Biene
32 Fliege
17 fliegen
20 fliehen
20 fließen
20 flink
109 Flinte
95 Flitterwochen
72 fluchen
20 Flucht
63 flüchtiger Blick
65 ~
33 Flügel
50 ~
114 ~
83 flüssig
140 Flüssigkeit
137 Flüssigunze
73 flüstern
9 Flug
78 Flugblatt
9 Flughafen
12 Flugkapitän
9 Fluglinie
9 Flugsteig
9 Flugzeug
64 Flur
1 Fluß
153 Flußufer
3 Flut
34 Föhre
119 Förderer
58 förmlich
148 Folge
18 folgen
68 folgern
68 Folgerung
102 Folie
74 fordern
123 Form
124 ~
163 ~
58 formell
76 Formular
150 Forscher
124 Forschung
2 Forst
50 Fort
31 Fortbestand
154 fortgeschritten
18 Fortschritt
27 fortschrittlich
22 fortsetzen
23 fortwährend
115 Foto
115 Fotoapparat
68 fotografieren

46 Fotomodell
91 Fräulein
71 Frage
74 Frage aufwerfen
83 Frageanhängsel
71 fragen
121 Fragespiel
76 Fragezeichen
101 Französisch
91 Frau
92 ~
91 Frau *(Anrede)*
91 Frauen
56 frech
58 ~
97 frei
93 frei wie ein Vogel
127 frei *(Tag, Woche)*
78 frei erfundene Erzählung
127 freie Stelle
97 Freiheit
99 ~
112 Freispruch auf Bewährung
146 freistehend
24 Freitag
111 freiwillig
109 Freiwilliger
114 Freizeit
97 fremd
97 Fremde(r)
83 Fremdsprache
81 Frequenz
116 ~
40 fressen
57 Freude
55 Freude haben an
57 Freude machen
57 freudig
92 Freund(in)
55 freundlich
58 ~
92 freundlich gesinnt
58 Freundlichkeit
95 Freundschaft
92 freundschaftlich
62 Frieden
104 ~
103 Friedhof
62 friedlich
4 frierend
27 frisch
46 Friseur
46 Friseuse
57 fröhlich
54 froh
55 ~
57 ~
33 Frosch
4 Frost
4 frostig
33 Frucht
127 fruchtbar
43 Fruchtsaft
43 Fruchttorte
22 früh
96 Frühaufsteher
26 früher
25 Frühling
40 Frühstück
32 Fuchs
52 fühlen
18 führen
20 ~
31 ~
99 Führer
10 Führerschein
153 füllen, (sich)
76 Füller
164 für den Fall, daß
66 für etwas sein
28 für immer
160 für jemanden tun
30 für jetzt
61 fürchten
56 fürchterlich
105 Fürst
82 Fürwort
40 füttern
7 Fundamt
116 Funkamateur
141 Funke
125 Funktion
125 funktionieren
128 ~
59 Furcht
55 furchtbar
153 ~
13 Fuß
35 ~
137 ~
118 Fußball
119 ~
118 Fußball(spiel)
119 Fußballrowdy
48 Fußboden
64 ~
10 Fußgänger
36 Fußknöchel

• • • • • • • • • • • • •

160 Gabe
41 Gabel
37 gähnen
127 Gärtner(in)
6 Gästehaus
137 Gallone
10 Gang
42 ~
97 ~
33 Gans
153 ganz
155 ~
37 ganz gut
37 ganz wohl
127 Ganztags-
48 Garage
75 Garantie
75 garantieren
50 Garderobe
49 Gardine
33 Garnele
138 Garnitur
55 garstig
48 Garten
129 Gartenarbeit
138 Gas
11 Gasse
6 Gast
7 Gastfamilie
7 Gastfreundschaft
7 Gastgeber
7 Gastgeberin
6 Gasthaus
48 Gastwirt
92 Gatte
92 Gattin
80 Gebärde
48 Gebäude
159 geben
103 Gebet
2 Gebiet
96 ~
98 ~
31 geboren
125 Gebrauch
128 Gebühr
98 gebürtig
31 Geburt
27 Geburtstag
69 Gedächtnis
68 Gedanke
80 Gedankenaustausch
76 Gedankenstrich
149 gedeihen
77 Gedicht
96 Gedränge
76 Gedrucktes
62 geduldig
156 geeignet
163 gefährlich
110 Gefängnis
113 ~
163 Gefahr
52 Gefallen
55 ~
64 Gefallen tun
55 Gefallen finden an
160 gefangen
110 Gefangener
5 gefrieren
143 Gefrierschrank
4 gefroren
52 Gefühl
53 ~
53 gefühlsbetont
53 Gefühlsregung
14 gegen
15 ~
28 ~
2 Gegend
98 ~
154 gegenseitig
102 Gegenstand
138 ~
140 ~
83 Gegenteil
162 ~
164 gegenteilig
162 gegenüber
63 gegenüberstehen
27 gegenwärtig
22 Gegenwart
153 ~
95 Gegner
127 Gehalt
128 Gehalt empfangen
128 Gehaltserhöhung
55 geheim
108 Geheimagent
55 Geheimnis
63 ~
63 geheimnisvoll
61 gehemmt
16 gehen
17 ~
128 ~
95 gehen mit
36 Gehirn
2 Gehölz
158 gehören
75 gehorchen
11 Gehsteig
116 Geige
108 Geisel
66 Geist
103 ~
69 Geistes-
68 Geistesgegenwart
69 geistig
70 geistig gesund
103 geistlich
58 geizig
60 Gelächter
17 gelangen
57 gelangweilt
4 gelb
130 Geld
128 Geld verdienen
45 Geldbörse
130 Geldinstitut
130 Geldschein
153 Geldstrafe
43 Gelee
15 gelegen sein
22 Gelegenheit
162 ~
23 gelegentlich
30 ~
69 Gelehrsamkeit
102 Gelehrter
69 Gelehrtheit
20 geleiten
75 geloben
36 gelockt
122 Gemälde
123 ~
74 gemäß
157 gemäßigt
58 gemein
97 Gemeinde
154 gemeinsam
160 ~
61 ~
97 Gemeinschaft
40 Gemüse
53 Gemütszustand
73 genannt
152 genau
156 ~
158 ~
165 ~
109 General
93 Generation
40 genesen
40 Genesung
7ß Genie
91 Gentleman
123 genügen
152 genug
154 ~
85 Genus des Verbs
146 geöffnet
2 Geographie
140 Gepäck
9 Gepäckträger
153 ~
47 gepflegt
47 geputzt
136 Gerade
136 gerade
152 ~
142 Gerät
43 geräucherter Hering
148 Geräusch verursachen
64 geräuschvoll
158 gerecht
111 Gerechtigkeit
158 ~
40 Gericht
110 Gericht(shof)
52 gern haben
52 gern tun
60 gerne wissen mögen
64 Geruch
80 Gerücht
155 gesamt
101 Gesamtschule
125 Geschäft
132 ~
134 geschäftlich
134 Geschäftsabschluß
134 Geschäftsfrau
126 Geschäftsführer
134 Geschäftsmann
161 geschehen
67 gescheit
159 Geschenk
160 ~
110 ~
153 ~
77 Geschichte
101 ~
23 geschichtlich
23 geschichtlich (bedeutend)
67 Geschicklichkeit
67 geschickt
70 geschickt in
70 Geschicktheit
92 geschieden
49 Geschirrschrank
41 Geschirr spülen
31 Geschlecht
146 geschlossen
64 Geschmack
65 geschmackvoll
109 Geschoß
150 geschützt
18 Geschwindigkeit
11 Geschwindigkeitsbegrenzung
111 Geschworene
95 Gesellschaft
96 ~
97 ~
125 ~
98 gesellschaftliche Stellung
97 Gesellschaftsklasse
12 Gesellschaftsraum
109 Gesetz
110 ~
110 Gesetzesvorlage
111 Gesetzgebung
35 Gesicht
155 gespannt
103 Gespenst
73 Gespräch
83 Gesprächsthema
35 Gestalt
123 ~
80 Geste
24 gestern
24 gestern abend
24 gestern nacht
32 gestreift
37 gesund
39 ~
69 gesunder Menschenverstand
37 Gesundheit
37 Gesundheitszustand
41 Getränk
129 Getreidefeld
146 getrennt
60 Getue
111 gewähren
60 Gewalt
148 ~
153 gewaltig
60 gewalttätig
60 Gewalttätigkeit

36 Gewebe
109 Gewehr
109 Gewehrkugel
127 Gewerkschaft
136 Gewicht
52 gewillt sein
133 Gewinn
118 gewinnen
128 ~
119 Gewinner
165 gewiß
56 Gewissen
5 Gewitter
69 gewitzt
99 gewöhnlich
155 ~
158 ~
156 gewöhnt sein an
109 Gewohnheit
43 Gewürz
2 Geysir
148 gezwungen sein
58 gierig
3 gießen
19 ~
39 Gift
110 ~
39 giftig
153 gigantisch
1 Gipfel
12 ~
116 Gitarre
5 glänzend
42 gläsernes Gefäß
42 Glas
139 ~
155 glatt
68 Glaube
103 ~
52 glauben
67 ~
68 ~
103 glauben an
162 gleich
164 ~
28 ~
55 ~
164 gleichen
154 gleichfalls
136 Gleichgewicht
62 gleichgültig gegenüber
8 Gleis
19 gleiten
2 Gletscher
36 Glied
149 ~
36 Gliedmaßen
142 Globus
140 Glocke
57 Glück
162 ~
165 ~
55 glücklich
163 glücklicherweise
57 Glücksgefühl
58 Gnade
91 gnädige Frau
91 gnädiges Fräulein
138 Gold
2 Golf
120 ~
100 Gott
103 Gottesdienst
100 Gottheit
130 graben
138 Grad
3 Grad *(Temperatur)*
99 Graf (engl.)
98 Grafschaft
156 ~
137 Gramm
83 Grammatik
34 Grapefruit
33 Gras
2 Grasland
132 gratis
73 gratulieren
4 grau
59 grausam
60 Grausamkeit
160 greifen
27 Greisenalter
12 Grenze
15 ~
15 Grenzland
140 Griff
160 ~
64 ~
44 Grill
44 Grillparty
60 grinsen
60 Grinsen
38 Grippe
184 Größe
150 ~
154 größer
107 ~
54 groß
151 ~
137 groß *(Personen)*
54 großartig
56 ~
107 ~
153 ~
76 Großbuchstabe
92 Großeltern
134 Großhandel
91 Großmutter
96 Großstadt
91 Großvater
56 großzügig
58 Großzügigkeit
4 grün
48 Grünanlage
148 gründen
155 gründlich
94 grüßen
107 ~
13 Grund
71 ~
145 ~
148 Grundlage
165 grundlegend
101 Grundschule
96 Gruppe
97 ~
116 Gruppe *(Musik)*
117 Gruselstück
158 gültig
162 günstige Gelegenheit
46 Gürtel
141 Gummi
54 gut
153 ~
96 gut auskommen mit
67 gut in
54 gutaussehend
56 ~
133 gute Gelegenheit
133 gutes Geschäft
60 gutgelaunt
101 Gymnasium *(GB)*
102 ~

35 Haar
35 Haare
46 Haarschnitt
159 haben
43 Hackfleisch
136 Hälfte
94 Händedruck
134 Händler
11 Hängebrücke
12 hängen
113 ~
55 häßlich
22 häufig
99 Häuptling
11 Hafen
9 Hafen(stadt)
11 Hafenanlagen
43 Haferbrei
51 Hahn
51 Haken
136 halb
102 Halbjahr
16 halbwegs
50 Halle
88 Hallo
89 ~
35 Hals
47 Halskette
17 Halt
26 ~
26 halten
159 ~
68 halten für
51 Halterung
53 Haltung
42 Hamburger
43 Hammelfleisch
35 Hand
101 Handarbeit
132 Handel
134 ~
64 ~
133 handeln
145 ~
133 handeln mit
134 ~
117 handelnde Person
36 Handgelenk
128 handhaben
132 Handlungsreisender
77 Handschrift
47 Handschuh
46 Handtasche
49 Handtuch
125 Handwerker
149 harmlos
116 Harmonie
155 hart
40 hartgekochtes Ei
32 Hase
54 Haß
52 hassen
18 Hast
156 hatte
141 Haufen
151 Haupt-
154 ~
42 Hauptgericht
40 Hauptmahlzeit
128 Hauptquartier
151 hauptsächlich
154 ~
96 Hauptstadt
8 Hauptverkehrsstraße
11 ~
8 Hauptverkehrszeit
82 Hauptwort
48 Haus
127 Hausarbeit
102 Hausaufgabe
100 Hausaufgaben
64 Hausaufgaben machen
92 Hausfrau
93 Haushalt
133 ~
99 Hausmädchen
49 Hausmeister
48 Hauswirt
48 Hauswirtin
101 Hauswirtschaft
35 Haut
129 Hecke
105 Heer
60 heftig
40 heilen
103 heilig
103 Heilige(r)
40 Heilmittel
34 Heilpflanze
48 Heim
121 Heimtier
92 heiraten
3 heiß
4 heiter
57 ~
143 Heizgerät
143 Heizkörper
49 Heizung
59 Held
117 ~
117 Heldin
147 helfen
4 hell
5 ~
35 ~
4 Helligkeit
46 Helm
45 Hemd
29 ~
33 Henne
147 herausfinden
118 herausfordern
118 Herausforderung
79 Herausgeber
144 herausnehmen
69 herausragend
71 herausschreien
18 herbringen
25 Herbst
143 Herd
32 Herde
19 hereinschauen
110 herkömmlich
40 Heroin
97 Herr
91 Herr *(Anrede)*
50 Herrenhaus
32 herrenlos
106 Herrschaft
105 Herrschaftsgebiet
106 herrschen
104 herrschen über
104 Herrscher
122 herstellen
124 ~
128 Hersteller
13 herum
20 herumführen
75 herumnörgeln
13 herunter
73 hervorheben
74 ~
35 Herz
96 herzlich
99 Herzog
99 Herzogin
129 Heu
23 heute
24 heute abend
24 heute morgen
24 heute nacht
29 heutzutage
13 hier
13 hierfür
147 Hilfe
150 ~
72 Hilfe leisten
56 hilfreich
130 Hilfsarbeiter
56 hilfsbereit
85 Hilfsverb
3 Himmel
15 hinauf
14 hinaus
15 Hindernis
104 Hindu
14 hindurch
30 ~
14 hinein
143 hineinlegen
113 hinrichten
14 hinten
13 hinter
14 ~
123 Hintergrund
14 hinüber
15 hinunter
74 Hinweis
64 Hinweis(schild)
32 Hirsch
23 historisch
3 Hitze
113 Hobby
137 hoch
132 hoch *(Preis)*
17 hochheben
2 Hochland
99 Hochschule
102 ~
95 Hochzeit
95 Hochzeitsreise
95 Hochzeitstag
151 höchst
11 Höchstgeschwindigkeit
32 Höcker
56 höflich
74 höflich ersuchen
58 Höflichkeit
50 Höhe
138 ~
154 höherstehend
2 Höhle
100 Hölle
139 hölzern
64 hören
75 hören auf
48 Hof
50 ~
55 ~
52 hoffen
53 hoffentlich
52 Hoffnung
53 hoffnungslos
18 holen
159 ~
123 Holographie
139 Holz
43 Honig

128 Honorar
2 Horizont
2 horizontal
45 Hose(n)
6 Hotel
6 Hotelzimmer
11 Hovercraft
12 Hubschrauber
54 hübsch
1 Hügel
2 hügelig
32 Hühnchen
118 hüpfen
120 ~
112 Hüter
49 Hütte
33 Hummer
113 Humor
115 humorvoll
32 Hund
42 Hunger
42 Hungern
42 hungern
40 hungrig
5 Hurrikan
38 husten
38 Husten
45 Hut
156 ~

• • • • • • • • • • • • •

86 ich
162 ich bin an der Reihe
147 ich kann nichts dafür
52 ich möchte lieber
66 Idee
164 identisch
164 Identität
33 Igel
86 ihm
86 ihn
86 ihnen
86 Ihr
86 ihr
106 Ihre Königliche Hoheit
86 ihres
111 illegal
123 illustrieren
27 im Alter von
27 im Augenblick
6 im Ausland
30 im Begriff sein
109 im Dienst
138 im Durchschnitt
119 im Freien
19 im Gänsemarsch
155 im ganzen
157 ~
164 im Gegenteil
119 im Haus
84 im Komparativ stehend
84 im Positiv stehend
84 im Superlativ stehend
30 im voraus
42 Imbiß
42 Imbißstube
44 ~
125 imitieren
28 immer
28 immer noch
28 immer noch nicht
30 immer wenn
85 Imperativ
105 Imperium
134 Import
134 importieren
13 in
14 ~
46 in (Mode) sein
90 in Anbetracht dessen, daß
61 in Angst versetzen
160 in der Falle
98 in der Innenstadt
157 in der Lage sein
13 in der Nähe
15 ~
98 in der Öffentlichkeit
110 in der Regel
163 in der Tat
162 in diesem Fall
61 in Gefahr
14 in hinein
149 in Kontakt sein
29 in kurzem
37 in Ordnung
45 in Ordnung bringen
127 in Pension gehen
15 in Reichweite
13 in Richtung
156 in Schwierigkeiten
61 in Sicht
7 in Übersee
64 in Verbindung mit
62 in Verlegenheit
59 in Verlegenheit bringen
138 indirekt
85 indirekte Rede
85 indirektes Objekt
93 Individuum
125 Industrie
125 Industrie-
125 industriell
85 Infinitiv
89 infolge
148 ~
79 Information
73 informieren (über)
122 Ingenieur
138 Inhalt
78 Inhalt(sverzeichnis)
90 inklusive
16 Innen-
119 ~
16 innen
98 Innenstadt
16 inner
14 innerhalb
14 innerhalb von
63 ins Auge blicken
6 ins Ausland
32 Insekt
1 Insel
82 inserieren
129 Installateur
111 instand halten
142 Instrument
117 Inszenierung
67 intelligent
70 Intelligenz
53 interessant
52 Interesse
52 interessieren
52 interessiert (an)
59 ~
52 interessiert sein
97 international
85 Interrogativ
6 Interview
6 interviewen
83 Intonation
85 intransitives Verb
108 Invasion
30 inzwischen
87 irgendein
86 irgend etwas
86 irgendwelche
87 irgendwie
87 irgendwo
57 irreführen
158 Irrtum

• • • • • • • • • • • • •

89 Ja
45 Jacke
20 jagen
150 Jäger
25 jährlich
50 Jagdhütte
24 Jahr
25 Jahreszeit
24 Jahrhundert
117 Jahrmarkt
50 Jalousie
24 Januar
28 je
162 je nachdem
141 Jeansstoff
86 jede(r,-e,-es)
165 jedenfalls
87 jeder
152 ~
88 jedoch
89 ~
28 jemals
87 jemand
88 jene
88 jener
88 jenes
14 jenseits
27 jetzt
29 ~
62 ~
126 Job
120 Jockey
120 joggen
43 Joghurt
81 Journalist(in)
104 Jude
121 Judo
27 jünger
27 jüngste(r/e)
27 Jugend
7 Jugendherberge
31 jugendlich
93 Jugendlicher
24 Juli
27 jung
91 Junge
93 ~
95 Junggeselle
24 Juni
111 Jury
141 Juwel
47 Juwelen

• • • • • • • • • • • • •

142 Kabel
11 Kabine
33 Käfer
143 Käfig
5 Kälte
45 kämmen
108 kämpfen
104 kämpfen mit/gegen
41 Käse
41 Kaffee
105 Kaiser
105 Kaiserin
105 Kaiserreich
11 Kajüte
34 Kaktus
32 Kalb
43 Kalbfleisch
25 Kalender
4 kalt
96 ~
93 kalt wie ein Frosch
32 Kamel
115 Kamera
50 Kamin
45 Kamm
107 Kampagne
104 Kampf
105 ~
108 ~
117 Kampfrichter
2 Kanal
81 ~
107 Kandidat
32 Kaninchen
162 kann
164 kann *(Möglichkeit)*
6 Kanne
105 Kanone
109 ~
16 Kante
44 Kantine
11 Kanu
106 Kanzler
138 Kapazität
103 Kapelle
69 kapieren
9 Kapitän
77 Kapitel
143 Kappe
12 Kapsel
156 kaputt
63 ~
61 ~
38 kaputtschlagen
44 Karamel
123 Karikatur
34 Karotte
127 Karriere
76 Karte
118 Karten(spiel)
7 Kartenbüro
34 Kartoffel
121 Karussell
7 Kasse
135 ~
117 Kasse *(Theater/Kino)*
44 Kasserolle
114 Kassettenrekorder
135 Kassierer(in)
34 Kastanie
153 Kasten
78 Katalog
103 Kathedrale
104 Katholik
32 Katze
42 kauen
133 Kauf
132 kaufen
133 ~
132 Kaufhaus
152 kaum
154 ~
34 Kauribaum
33 Kea *(Papageienart)*
35 Kehle
86 kein
86 keine
152 keiner von beiden
136 keiner,-e,-es
41 Keks
50 Keller
42 Kellner
42 Kellnerin
66 kennen
5 kennenlernen
95 ~
66 Kenntnisse
2 Kennzeichen
163 ~
163 kennzeichnend
138 Kennziffer
93 Kerl
34 Kern
142 Kerze
44 Kessel
142 Kette
8 Kfz-Werkstatt
119 kicken
34 Kiefer
137 Kilogramm
137 Kilometer
91 Kind
93 ~
91 Kinder
10 Kinderwagen
27 Kindheit
93 kindisch
93 kindlich
36 Kinn
80 Kino
82 ~
43 Kipper
101 Kirche
103 Kirchhof
34 Kirsche
51 Kissen
140 Kiste
143 ~
33 Kiwi
57 kläglich
75 Klage
72 klagen über
76 Klammer
64 Klang
95 Klaps
3 klar
4 ~
63 ~
162 ~
100 Klasse
100 Klassenzimmer
116 Klassik
78 klassisch
116 klassische Musik
80 Klatsch
114 Klavier
126 Klavierspieler(in)
142 Klebeband
140 kleben
142 klebrig
142 Klebstoff
44 Kleid
44 Kleider
51 Kleiderschrank
44 Kleidung
46 ~
137 klein

151 ~
115 ~
10 Kleinbus
42 kleine Gaststätte
154 kleiner
51 kleiner Teppich
138 kleines Stück
130 Kleingeld
17 klettern auf
17 klettern gehen
4 Klima
51 klimatisiert
65 klingen
2 Klippe
51 Klo(sett)
65 klopfen
104 Kloster
96 Klub
67 klug
70 Klugheit
42 Kneipe
35 Knie
19 knien
36 Knochen
36 Knöchel
45 Knopf
140 ~
149 knoten
149 Knoten
32 knurren
42 Koch
6 ~
41 kochen
44 Kochrezept
78 Kode
42 Köchin
104 König
104 Königin
106 königlich
105 Königreich
157 können
164 ~
164 könnte
162 könnte vielleicht
35 Körper
36 körperlich
119 körperliche Bewegung
65 köstlich
140 Koffer
34 Kohl
139 Kohle
34 Kohlkopf
99 Kolleg
92 Kollege
105 Kolonie
105 kolonisieren
105 Kolonisierung
76 Komma
16 kommen
17 ~
16 kommen aus
73 Kommentar
73 kommentieren
106 Komitee
80 Kommunikation
117 Komödie
84 Komparativ
70 kompetent
73 Kompliment
108 Komplott
116 komponieren
116 Komponist
116 Komposition
75 Kompromiß
85 Konditional
85 konditional
73 Konferenz
41 Konfitüre
108 Konflikt
106 Kongreß
119 Konkurrent(in)
157 konnte
107 konservativ
107 Konservativer
85 Konsonant
49 Konstruktion
65 Kontakt
149 Kontakt haben zu
149 Kontakt verlieren
143 Kontaktlinse
83 Kontext
1 Kontinent
2 kontinental
130 Konto
145 Kontrolle
145 kontrollieren
50 Kontur(en)
114 Konzert
117 Konzerthalle
35 Kopf
156 ~
34 Kopfsalat
38 Kopfschmerzen
122 Kopie
122 kopieren
140 Korb
34 Korn
156 korrekt
102 Korrektur
81 korrespondieren
100 korrigieren
2 Kosmos
64 kosten
130 ~
107 ~
128 Kosten
130 ~
131 ~
45 Kostüm
46 ~
29 ~
46 kostümieren, (sich)
33 Krabbe
19 krabbeln
65 Krach(en)
65 krachen
65 krachend stürzen
139 Kraft
79 kräftig
10 Kraftfahrer
157 kraftvoll
141 Kraftwerk
47 Kragen
37 krank
38 Krankenhaus
40 Krankenpflege
38 Krankenschwester
40 Krankenwagen
37 Krankheit
39 ~
34 Kraut
45 Krawatte
100 Kreide
136 Kreis
71 kreischen
11 Kreisverkehr
136 Kreuz
121 Kreuzworträtsel
19 kriechen
104 Krieg
109 Kriegsmarine
112 kriminell
110 ~
110 Krimineller
68 Kritik
56 ~
69 ~
69 Kritiker
56 ~
69 kritisch
68 kritisieren
106 krönen (zu)
106 Krone
41 Kuchen
49 Küche
4 kühl
96 ~
140 Kühlschrank
143 ~
123 Künstler
27 kürzlich
29 ~
128 Kürzung
92 küssen
72 ~
1 Küste
103 ~
1 Küste(nbereich)
109 Kugel
55 ~
142 ~
76 Kugelschreiber
32 Kuh
129 kultivieren
97 Kultur
97 kulturell
58 Kummer
132 Kunde
8 Kundendienst
132 Kundin
122 Kunst
101 Kunsterziehung
123 Kunstgalerie
141 Kupfer
100 Kurs
101 Kurs für Autoreparatur
77 Kursivdruck
8 Kurve
22 kurz
137 ~
45 kurze Hose(n)
22 kurze Pause
22 kurze Zeit
77 Kurzschrift
92 Kuss
10 Kutsche
76 Kuvert

• • • • • • • • • • • • •

124 Labor
124 Laboratorium
60 Lachen
58 lachen (über)
132 Laden
135 Ladenkasse
134 Ladung
99 Lady
58 Lächeln
58 lächeln
70 lächerlich
138 Länge
2 Längengrad
55 Längenmaß
15 längs
64 Lärm
64 lärmend
60 lästig
51 Läufer
64 läuten
12 Lage
15 ~
161 ~
7 Lager
6 ~
134 ~
44 Lager *(Bier)*
7 lagern
160 ~
41 Laib *(Brot)*
32 Lamm
140 Lampe
1 Land
156 ~
96 ~
9 landen
99 Landfahrer
1 Landkarte
2 Landschaft
98 ~
99 Landstreicher
12 Landung
11 Landungsbrücke
127 Landwirt
129 Landwirtschaft
129 landwirtschaftlich
136 lang
46 langärmlig
22 lange
46 lange Damenhose
46 lange Hose
46 langes Kleid
18 langsam
70 langsam von Begriff
20 langsamer fahren
63 langweilen
60 langweilig
109 lassen
134 Last
8 Lastwagen
101 Latein
118 Lauf
127 Laufbahn
17 laufen
118 ~
17 laufen gehen
52 Laune
60 ~
64 laut
74 ~
73 lauter reden
116 Lautsprecher
116 Lautstärke
31 Leben
31 leben
47 ~
149 ~
31 lebend
31 lebendig
149 ~
97 Lebensart
133 Lebenshaltungskosten
134 Lebensmittelgeschäft
133 Lebensmittelhändler
127 Lebensunterhalt
128 Lebensunterhalt verdienen
97 Lebensweise
165 lebenswichtig
36 Leber
32 Lebewesen
37 lebhaft
139 Leder
92 ledig
153 leer
153 leeren
111 legal
18 legen
31 legen *(Eier)*
103 Legende
21 lehnen, (sich)
78 Lehrbuch
129 Lehre
100 lehren
100 Lehrer
100 Lehrerin
101 Lehrerzimmer
100 Lehrgang
129 Lehrling
129 Lehrzeit
155 leicht
156 ~
157 ~
4 leicht neblig
4 leichter Nebel
157 leichtgewichtig
38 leiden an
53 Leidenschaft
131 leihen
142 Leim
142 Leine
141 Leinen
141 Leinwand
64 leise
149 Leistung
50 Leiter
99 ~
126 ~
100 Lektion
77 Lektüre
102 ~
10 Lenkrad
33 Lerche
67 lernen
77 Lesen
76 lesen
76 Leser(in)
26 letzt(er/e/es)
112 letzter Wille
75 leugnen
91 Leute
156 ~
93 ~
107 liberal
107 Liberaler
4 Licht
52 Liebe (zu)
52 lieben
55 ~
58 Liebenswürdigkeit
54 lieber als
95 Liebling
54 Lieblings-
144 Lied
79 liefern
160 ~
159 liefern an
20 Lieferung
160 ~
10 Lieferwagen
12 liegen
15 ~
153 ~
48 Lift
78 Limerick
40 lindern
78 Lineal
136 Linie
13 link-
13 links
143 Linse
36 Lippe
76 Liste
78 ~

137 Liter
78 Literatur
31 live
149 ~
109 Lizenz
8 LKW
73 Lob
73 loben
1 Loch
150 Loch im Reifen
155 locker
107 ~
36 lockig
41 Löffel
127 Löhne
66 lösen
68 Lösung
128 Lösung finden
32 Löwe
32 Löwin
69 Logik
127 Lohn
128 Lohn empfangen
158 lohnend
10 Lokomotive
23 Los
155 lose
107 ~
144 loswerden
15 Lücke
57 Lüge
153 ~
57 lügen
157 ~
3 Luft
80 Luftpost
36 Lunge
57 lustig
113 ~
133 luxuriös
133 Luxus

• • • • • • • • • • • • •

145 machen
158 Macht
91 Mädchen
91 Männer
31 männlich
24 März
35 Magen
103 Magie
103 magisch
40 Mahlzeit
24 Mai
34 Mais
61 Majestät
47 Make-up
135 mal
122 malen
123 Maler
93 Mami
89 man
128 Management
126 Manager
154 manch
28 manchmal
53 Mangel
46 Manie
53 Manieren
91 Mann
92 ~
9 Mannschaft
118 ~
118 Mannschafts-kapitän
45 Mantel
46 ~
1 Mappe
120 Marathon
43 Margarine
109 Marine
121 Marionette
102 Marke
117 Markt
132 ~
132 Marktplatz
134 Marktstand
41 Marmelade
6 ~
19 Marsch
19 marschieren
157 Marsmensch
140 Maschine
142 Maschinen
57 Maske
46 (Masken)Kostüm
57 maskieren
138 Maß
138 Maße
141 Masse
81 Massenmedien
141 Mast
117 Match
138 Material
101 Mathematik
51 Matratze
9 Matrose
4 matt
51 Matte
48 Mauer
33 Maus
154 Maximum
124 Mechaniker
122 mechanisch
119 Medaille
81 Medien
38 Medizin
124 ~
38 Medizin-
1 Meer
1 Meeresufer
43 Mehl
151 mehr
151 mehr als
151 mehrere
154 ~
137 mehrfach
107 Mehrheit
131 Mehrwertsteuer
84 Mehrzahl
137 Meile
86 mein
91 mein Herr
67 meinen
79 ~
86 meines
55 ~
67 Meinung
79 ~
68 ~
107 Meinungsum-frage
151 meist-
119 Meister
129 Meister *(Hand-werk)*
118 Meisterschaft
123 Meisterwerk
80 melden
116 Melodie
96 Menge
150 ~
153 ~
93 Mensch
98 Menschheit
91 menschlich
67 merken
2 Merkmal
117 Messe
136 messen
41 Messer
140 ~
138 Metal
137 Meter
122 Methode
133 Metzger
86 mich
131 Miete
131 mieten
134 ~
116 Mikrophon
41 Milch
135 Milchmann
157 mild
58 Mildtätigkeit
109 Militär
137 Milliliter
137 Millimeter
107 Minderheit
154 minderwertig
154 mindestens
55 Mine
154 Minimum
104 Minister
138 minus
24 Minute
86 mir
41 mischen
44 Mischung
149 Mißerfolg
103 Missionar
74 Mißtrauen
157 mißtrauisch
69 mißverstehen
14 mit
9 mit *(Verkehrs-mittel)*
76 mit der Maschine schreiben
122 mit Hilfe
51 mit Klimaanlage
20 mit knapper Not davonkommen
154 mit Mühe
73 mit Namen
164 ~
126 Mitarbeiter(in)
58 Mitgefühl
158 ~
92 Mitglied
97 Mitgliederschaft
97 Mitgliederzahl
55 Mitleid
58 ~
158 ~
8 mitnehmen *(Auto)*
23 Mittag
40 Mittagessen
13 Mitte
25 ~
73 mitteilen
79 Mitteilung
40 Mittel
122 ~
25 Mittel-
122 mittels
97 Mittelschicht
23 Mitternacht
30 mittlerweile
24 Mittwoch
49 Mobiliar
85 Modalverb
46 Mode
46 Mode(torheit)
46 Modell
124 ~
26 modern
27 ~
46 modisch
49 Möbel
51 möblieren
49 möbliert
52 mögen
54 ~
162 möglich
162 möglicherweise
164 Möglichkeit
160 Möglichkeiten
34 Möhre
103 Mönch
112 Mörder(in)
110 ~
55 mogeln
43 Molkerei
22 Moment
29 momentan
105 Monarch
105 Monarchie
24 Monat
25 monatlich
1 Mond
157 Monster
24 Montag
124 montieren
110 Mord
23 Morgen
24 morgen
102 Morgenandacht
104 Mormone
104 Moschee
104 Moslem
7 Motel
120 Moto-cross
140 Motor
8 Motorrad
10 ~
120 Motorrennen
36 müde
59 Mühe
125 ~
128 mühelos
157 Mühsal
144 Müll
129 Müller
80 mündlich
83 ~
130 Münze
145 müssen
148 ~
128 müßig
46 Mütze
98 multinational
137 multiplizieren
35 Mund
73 murmeln
33 Muschelschale
122 Museum
116 Musical
101 Musik
114 ~
116 Musiker
126 ~
114 Musikinstrument
114 Musikkassette
36 Muskel
165 muß
114 Muße
124 Muster
125 ~
163 ~
61 Mut
59 mutig
93 mutig wie ein Löwe
91 Mutter
83 Muttersprache
93 Mutti

• • • • • • • • • • • • •

122 na und?
13 nach
28 ~
74 ~
24 nach *(bei Zeit-angaben)*
89 nach alledem
16 nach innen
48 nach oben
148 nach sich ziehen
7 nach Übersee
48 nach unten
125 nachahmen
96 Nachbar(in)
98 Nachbarschaft
68 Nachdenken
68 nachdenken über
107 Nachfolger
124 nachforschen
71 Nachforschung
75 Nachfrage
28 nachher
23 Nachmittag
25 nachmittags
94 Nachname
79 Nachricht(en)
74 nachschlagen
72 nachsehen
86 Nachsilben
23 Nacht
117 Nachtclub
165 Nachteil
42 Nachtisch
96 Nachtschwärmer
107 Nachwahl
46 nackt
15 nächste(r,s)
58 Nächstenliebe
123 nähen
19 Näherkommen
143 Nähmaschine
140 Nähnadel
42 nähren
90 nämlich
142 Nagel
15 nahe
40 Nahrung
82 Name
92 ~
94 ~
44 Napf
39 Narbe
67 Narr
35 Nase
3 naß
96 Nation
97 national
98 Nationalität
31 natürlich
156 ~
162 ~
1 Natur
31 Naturgeschichte
122 Naturwissen-schaft
3 Nebel
15 neben
163 nebenbei be-merkt
13 nebeneinander
82 Nebensatz
4 neblig
60 necken
93 Neffe
85 negativ

36 Neger
18 nehmen
41 ~
45 ~
159 ~
62 Neid
62 neidisch sein auf
163 neigen zu
163 Neigung
89 Nein
70 nennen
36 Nerv
39 Nervenzusammenbruch
59 nervös
32 Nest
47 nett
54 ~
55 ~
120 Netz
142 ~
27 neu
26 ~
26 neueste
62 neugierig
25 Neujahr
27 neulich
23 ~
29 ~
136 nicht
70 nicht beachten
145 nicht dürfen
152 nicht einmal
37 nicht gut in Form
53 nicht haben
136 nicht im geringsten
154 ~
157 nicht in der Lage
54 nicht mögen
165 nicht notwendig
165 nicht notwendigerweise
147 nicht umhin können
63 nicht vorrätig
148 nicht wirkungsvoll
84 nicht zählbar
93 Nichte
87 nichts
89 nichts als
37 Nickerchen
28 nie
19 niederknien
109 Niederlage
76 niederschreiben
77 Niederschrift
137 niedrig
132 niedrig *(Preis)*
28 niemals
87 niemand
39 niesen
44 nippen an
87 nirgends
50 Niveau
28 noch (nicht)
154 noch dazu
162 noch ein(e/es)
28 noch einmal
1 nördlich
107 nominieren
103 Nonne
1 Nord-
1 Norden
67 normal
155 ~
158 ~
155 normalerweise
57 Not
102 Note
164 ~
116 Note *(Musik)*
164 Notfall
64 Notiz
76 ~
76 Notizblock
76 Notizheft
56 notwendig
163 ~
53 Notwendigkeit
165 ~
24 November
44 nüchtern
128 nützen
157 nützlich
138 nuklear
136 Null
84 Numerus
89 nun
89 nur
152 ~
34 Nuß
125 Nutzen
129 Nutzpflanze

• • • • • • • • • • • • •

88 ob
150 Obdach
48 oben
12 obenauf
42 Ober
107 Oberbürgermeister
13 Oberfläche
14 oberhalb
106 Oberhaus
97 Oberschicht
112 Oberster Gerichtshof
2 Observatorium
33 Obst
134 Obst-/Gemüsehändler
88 obwohl
156 ~
32 Ochse
152 oder
97 öffentlich
61 ~
97 öffentliche Einrichtung
68 öffentliche Meinung
106 öffentlicher Dienst
97 Öffentlichkeit
146 öffnen
15 Öffnung
135 Öffnungszeiten
130 ökonomisch
41 Öl
139 ~
141 Ölleitung
97 örtlich
98 ~
1 östlich
143 Ofen
56 offen
146 ~
56 offen (gesagt)
65 offenbar
50 offener Kamin
65 offensichtlich
109 offiziell
105 Offizier
28 oft
14 ohne
46 ohne Kopfbedeckung
99 ohne Rang
35 Ohr
37 OK
24 Oktober
118 Olympische Spiele
43 Omelette
8 Omnibus
92 Onkel
116 Oper
117 ~
40 Operation
40 operieren
117 Opernhaus
40 Opfer
103 Opfer(gabe)
103 opfern
108 Opposition
108 Oppositionspartei
4 orange
33 Orange
43 Orangenmarmelade
6 ~
116 Orchester
45 ordentlich
47 ~
58 ordinär
158 ~
78 Ordner
145 Organisation
31 organisch
145 organisieren
5 Orkan
12 Ort
1 Ost-
1 Osten
25 Ostern
138 oval
102 Overheadprojektor
1 Ozean

• • • • • • • • • • • • •

45 Paar
136 ~
160 packen
143 Packung
140 Päckchen
95 Pärchen
79 Paket
50 Palast
150 Panne
26 Panne haben
109 Panzer
33 Papagei
93 Papi
76 Papier
115 Papierbild
78 Papierstreifen
103 Papst
103 Paradies
65 Parfüm
48 Park
8 parken
8 Parkhaus
8 Parkplatz
106 Parlament
104 Partei
60 Partei ergreifen für
85 Partizip Perfekt
85 Partizip Präsens
92 Partner
113 Party
109 Paß
83 Passage
50 ~
6 Passagier
45 passen
160 ~
62 passend
156 ~
161 passieren
163 ~
85 Passiv
85 passiv
43 Pastete
40 Patient
7 Pauschalreise
2 Pause
102 ~
22 pausieren
62 peinlich
32 Pelz
130 Pence
130 Pennies
130 Penny
6 Pension
7 ~
64 ~
128 ~
128 Pensionierung
136 per
19 per Anhalter fahren
156 perfekt
141 Perle
91 persönlich
158 ~
93 Persönlichkeit
84 Person
91 ~
127 Personal
158 ~
34 Petersilie
8 Pfad
150 Pfadfinder
150 Pfadfinderin
141 Pfahl
43 Pfeffer
43 Pfefferkuchen
43 Pfefferminze
42 Pfeife
60 pfeifen
60 Pfeifen
32 Pferd
129 Pferdestall
60 Pfiff
69 pfiffig
25 Pfingsten
34 Pfirsich
33 Pflanze
127 pflanzen
34 Pflaume
55 Pflicht
144 pflücken
160 ~
129 Pflug
48 Pforte
2 Pfütze
130 Pfund
137 ~
68 Phantasie
56 phantastisch
69 Philosoph
69 Philosophie
115 Photograph
115 Photographie
83 Phrase
101 Physik
114 Pianist
40 Picknick
103 Pilger
39 Pille
12 Pilot
45 Pinsel
49 Pionier
141 Pipeline
109 Pistole
112 plädieren
143 Plakat
66 Plan
69 ~
66 planen
125 ~
2 Planet
129 Plantage
139 Plastik
142 Platte
114 Plattenspieler
47 plattiert
8 Platz
12 ~
15 ~
119 ~
73 Plauderei
73 plaudern
22 plötzlich
43 Plumpudding
84 Plural
138 Plus
79 Poet
117 Pokal
118 Pokalendspiel
2 Pol
142 polieren
112 Politesse
104 Politik
107 ~
104 Politiker(in)
104 politisch
107 politische Linie
142 Politur
110 Polizei
110 Polizeibeamter
110 Polizeiwache
111 Polizist
110 Polizist(in)
51 Polster
103 Poltergeist
43 Pommes frites
32 Pony
116 Pop(musik)
53 populär
9 Portier
153 ~
42 Portion
123 Portrait
123 Porzellan
15 Position
98 ~
85 Positiv
84 ~
79 Post
81 ~
81 Post-
79 Postamt
79 Postbote
127 Posten
140 ~
143 Poster
79 Postgebühr
76 Postkarte
81 Postkasten
81 postlagernd
81 Postleitzahl
56 prächtig
86 präpositional
104 Präsident
158 präzise
61 prahlen
2 Prairie
122 praktisch

103 Preis
131 ~
156 ~
134 Preisnachlaß
132 preiswert
104 Premier(minister)
80 Presse
146 pressen
103 Priester
54 prima
105 Prinz
105 Prinzessin
110 Prinzip
91 privat
61 ~
101 Privatschule (mit Internat) *(GB)*
136 pro
145 probieren
59 Problem
136 ~
122 Produkt
117 Produktion
124 ~
124 Produktionsmenge
122 produzieren
101 Professor
117 Profi
133 Profit
128 profitieren
138 programmieren
136 Programmierer
69 Projekt
117 Projektionsfläche
117 projizieren
65 prominent
77 Prospekt
78 ~
108 Protest
104 Protestant
104 protestieren
98 Provinz
136 Prozent
122 Prozeß
100 Prüfung
39 Psychiater
124 Psychologie
42 Pub
115 Publikum
79 publizieren
42 Pudding
141 Puder
78 pünkteln
23 pünktlich
45 Pullover
36 Puls(schlag)
49 Pult
141 Pulver
142 Pumpe
142 pumpen
78 Punkt
119 ~
140 ~
136 Punkt *(Geometrie)*
120 (Punkte) erzielen
78 punktieren
118 Punktzahl
121 Puppe
104 Puritaner
4 purpurrot
33 Puter
45 putzen
63 Puzzle

136 Quadrat
136 quadratisch
104 Quäker
103 Qualifikation
161 Qualität
2 Quelle
26 ~
14 quer über
132 Quittung
79 ~
121 Quiz

54 Rache
138 Rad
20 radfahren
10 Radfahrer(in)
126 ~
78 Radiergummi
80 Radio
81 Radiogerät
114 ~
63 Rätsel
121 ~
112 Räuber
142 Rahmen
12 Rakete
109 ~
50 Rampe
129 Ranch
16 Rand
98 Rang
27 ranghöher
50 Rasen
18 rasen
45 Rasierapparat
45 rasieren, (sich)
96 Rasse
55 ~
98 Rassen-
153 Rast
72 Rat
72 Rat geben
106 Rat(sversammlung)
135 Rate
107 Rathaus
72 Ratschläge
113 Raub
113 Raubüberfall
139 Rauch
42 rauchen
58 Raufbold
155 rauh
1 Raum
12 ~
49 ~
96 ~
138 Rauminhalt
12 Raumschiff
39 Rauschgift
74 reagieren
148 ~
74 Reaktion
148 ~
163 realistisch
163 Realität
108 Rebell
108 Rebellion
136 Rechenmaschine
124 recherchieren
137 Rechnen
138 rechnen mit
132 Rechnung
131 Rechnung begleichen
55 Recht
55 recht
55 recht haben
111 Recht und Ordnung
13 recht-
74 rechtfertigen
111 rechtlich
13 rechts
110 Rechtsanwalt
112 ~
77 Rechtschreibung
22 rechtzeitig
61 ~
118 Redakteur
71 Rede
71 Rede (über)
71 Rede halten
71 reden
83 Redensart
83 Redewendung
73 Redner
108 Reform
108 Reform durchführen
108 reformieren
109 Regel
23 regelmäßig
155 ~
85 regelmäßiges Verb
3 Regen
4 Regen-
4 Regenbogen
46 Regenmantel
3 Regenschauer
45 Regenschirm
106 regieren
104 Regierung
106 Regierungszeit
98 Region
98 regional
115 Regisseur
78 Register
78 registrieren
3 regnen
4 regnerisch
158 regulieren
21 reiben
130 reich
133 ~
160 reichen
152 reichlich
133 Reichtum
15 Reichweite
27 reif
27 reif *(Obst)*
8 Reifen
150 Reifenpanne
136 Reihe
78 Reim
45 rein
34 Reis
6 Reise
68 Reise machen
148 Reise unternehmen
6 Reise(n)
7 Reisebüro
10 Reisebus
6 Reiseführer
6 reisen
109 Reisepaß
130 Reisescheck
19 Reiseziel
18 reißen
149 ~
46 Reißverschluß
118 reiten
120 Reiter
120 Reitsportfest
59 reizbar
54 reizend
54 reizvoll
80 Reklame
157 relativ
103 religiös
103 religiöse Überzeugung
103 religiöse Verehrung
100 Religion
101 Religionslehre
120 Rennbahn
118 rennen
118 Rennen
55 ~
128 Rente
64 ~
131 ~
123 Reparatur
123 Reparaturarbeiten
123 reparieren
81 Reporter
106 Repräsentantenhaus
105 Republik
105 republikanisch
117 Requisiten
150 Reservat
150 Reserve
6 reservieren
96 reserviert
7 Reservierung
49 Residenz
61 Respekt
61 respektieren
153 Rest
42 Restaurant
118 Resultat
147 retten
150 ~
108 Revolution
108 revolutionär
109 Revolver
40 Rezept
79 ~
6 Rezeption
116 Rhythmus
120 richten auf
110 Richter
111 richterlicher Beamter
55 richtig
156 ~
158 ~
1 Richtung
64 riechen (nach)
153 riesenhaft
153 riesig
32 Rind
129 Rinderfarm
43 Rindfleisch
138 Ring
163 Risiko
59 riskieren
17 Ritt
99 Ritter
119 Rivale
119 Rivalin
32 Robbe
142 Roboter
45 Rock
29 ~
139 Röhre
43 rösten
44 ~
42 roh
59 ~
139 Rohr
138 Rohstoff
140 Rohstoffe
117 Rolle
39 Rollstuhl
50 Rolltreppe
78 Roman
4 rosa(rot)
33 Rose
34 Rosine
4 rot
32 Rotwild
11 Route
119 Rowdy
143 Rucksack
120 rudern
35 Rücken
39 Rückenschmerzen
9 Rückfahrkarte
25 rückgängig machen
13 Rückseite
68 Rücksicht
16 rückwärts
99 Ruf
73 Rufen
119 Rugby
62 Ruhe
65 ~
153 ~
35 Ruhepause
59 ruhig
62 ~
29 ~
64 ~
61 Ruhm
69 ~
123 Ruine
123 ruinieren
136 rund
81 Rundfunkstation
6 Rundreise
19 rutschen

50 Saal
112 Sache
138 ~
159 Sachen
143 Säge
143 sägen
114 Sänger(in)
142 säubern
91 Säugling
123 Säule
7 Safari
133 Safe
41 Saft
103 Sage
70 sagen
41 Sahne
41 Salat
58 salopp
41 Salz
144 sammeln
144 Sammlung
24 Samstag
139 Sand
41 Sandwich
58 sanft
103 Sankt
2 Satellit
79 satt haben
120 Sattel
82 Satz
83 ~
138 ~
85 Satzaussage
85 Satzgegenstand
83 Satzteil
45 sauber
45 saubermachen

43 Sauce
64 sauer
141 Sauerstoff
140 Schachtel
147 schaden
147 Schaden
149 ~
46 schäbig
44 schälen
143 schärfen
67 schätzen
68 Schätzung
32 Schaf
31 schaffen
145 ~
10 Schaffner
46 Schal
33 Schale
44 ~
64 Schall
114 Schallplatte
62 Scham
62 Schande
140 scharf
65 scharf (gewürzt)
4 Schatten
4 Schattenbild
95 Schatz
133 ~
110 ~
63 schauen
3 Schauer
121 Schaukel
98 Schauplatz
65 Schauspiel
114 ~
117 ~
117 Schauspiel-
115 Schauspieler
115 Schauspielerin
130 Scheck
141 Scheibe
95 Scheidung
149 ~
4 scheinen
161 ~
163 ~
146 scheitern
149 Scheitern
143 Schere
113 Scherz
113 scherzen
47 scheuern
97 Schicht
129 ~
47 schick
79 schicken
20 schicken nach
23 Schicksal
18 schieben
119 Schiedsrichter
105 schießen
105 schießen auf
109 Schießpulver
9 Schiff
79 Schild
43 Schinken
45 Schirm
108 Schlacht
36 schläfrig
120 Schläger
35 Schlaf
37 ~
46 Schlafanzug
35 schlafen
71 ~
35 schlafend
49 Schlafzimmer
39 Schlag
59 ~
119 ~
65 schlagen
113 ~
118 ~
149 ~
116 Schlager
78 Schlagzeile
141 Schlamm
141 schlammig
16 Schlange
16 Schlange stehen
36 schlank
37 ~
37 Schlankheitskur machen
67 schlau
70 Schlauheit
37 schlecht
55 ~
55 schlechter
60 schlechtgelaunt
19 schlendern
83 schleppend
129 Schlepper
68 schließen
146 ~
28 schließlich
30 ~
23 ~
62 ~
120 Schlittschuh
120 schlittschuhlaufen
15 Schlitz
48 Schloß
140 ~
42 schlucken
140 Schlüssel
143 Schlüsselloch
26 Schluß
132 Schlußverkauf
65 schmackhaft
115 schmal
64 schmecken (nach)
73 schmeicheln
5 schmelzen
37 Schmerz(en)
38 schmerzen
39 ~
38 schmerzhaft
33 Schmetterling
44 schmoren
47 Schmuck
45 Schmutz
47 ~
45 schmutzig
47 ~
47 schmutzige Wäsche
160 schnappen
117 Schnappschuß
3 Schnee
38 schneiden
41 ~
47 Schneider
3 schneien
18 schnell
20 ~
38 Schnitt(wunde)
123 Schnitzarbeit
158 Schnitzer
139 Schnur
36 Schnurrbart
59 Schock
59 schockieren
3 schön
54 ~
57 ~
153 ~
41 Schokolade
28 schon
131 schonen
50 Schornstein
142 Schottenmuster
46 Schottenrock
142 Schottenstoff
49 Schrank
15 Schranke
140 Schraube
143 Schraubkappe
61 Schrecken
55 schrecklich
56 ~
153 ~
71 Schrei
73 ~
78 Schreibblock
75 schreiben
77 Schreiben
126 Schreibkraft
76 Schreibmaschine
49 Schreibtisch
78 Schreibwaren
71 schreien
71 schreien (um)
129 Schreiner
77 Schrift
77 schriftlich
77 Schriftsteller
16 Schritt
17 Schritt machen
23 schrittweise
47 schrubben
154 schrumpfen
143 Schubfach
18 Schubs
61 schüchtern
100 Schüler
156 ~
7 Schüleraustausch
100 Schülerin
44 Schüssel
19 schütteln
21 Schütteln
19 schütten
150 schützen
147 schützen vor
45 Schuh
100 Schularbeiten
75 Schuld
112 ~
133 ~
75 Schuld geben für
130 schulden
133 Schulden
110 schuldig
99 Schule
35 Schulter
102 Schulversammlung
102 Schulzeugnis
49 Schuppen
109 Schuß
147 Schutz
150 ~
150 Schutz gewähren
46 Schutzhelm
157 schwach
156 Schwachstelle
158 Schwäche
158 schwächen
94 Schwägerin
94 Schwager
33 Schwalbe
47 Schwamm
31 schwanger
33 Schwanz
4 schwarz
36 Schwarzer
41 schwarzer Tee
96 schwarzes Schaf
32 Schwein
43 Schweinefleisch
36 Schweiß
29 ~
39 schwer
155 ~
156 ~
130 Schwerarbeiter
70 schwerfällig
91 Schwester
94 Schwiegermutter
94 Schwiegervater
156 schwierig
59 Schwierigkeit
156 ~
157 ~
72 Schwierigkeiten bereiten
118 Schwimmbecken
19 schwimmen
118 ~
71 ~
17 schwimmen gehen
120 Schwimmer
96 Schwindel
55 schwindeln
36 schwitzen
75 schwören
78 Science Fiction
1 See *(f)*
1 See *(m)*
2 See *(Schottland)*
7 Seebad
32 Seehund
103 Seele
9 Seemann
7 Seereise
9 segeln
120 ~
17 segeln gehen
141 Segeltuch
63 sehen
6 Sehenswürdigkeit
63 Sehkraft
151 sehr
37 sehr gut
52 sehr mögen
133 sehr wertvoll
109 Sehrohr
64 Sehvermögen
53 sei brav
137 seicht
141 Seide
139 Seife
29 ~
142 Seil
31 sein
29 ~
161 ~
64 seine Pflicht tun
149 sein Bestes geben
64 ~
106 Seine Königliche Hoheit
128 seinen Lebensunterhalt verdienen
86 seines
29 seit *(Zeitpunkt)*
29 seit *(Zeitraum)*
30 seit der Zeit
29 seit(dem)
30 seitdem
76 Seite
13 Seite(n)
50 Seitenflügel
8 Seitenstraße
126 Sekretär(in)
141 Sektion
24 Sekunde
152 selbst
132 Selbstbedienung
54 Selbstbeherrschung
61 selbstbewußt
113 Selbstmord
28 selten
30 ~
156 seltsam
157 ~
102 Semester
106 Senat
106 Senator
79 senden
81 ~
80 Sendung
81 ~
43 Senf
63 Sensation
63 sensibel
158 ~
24 September
138 Serie
160 Service
41 servieren
44 Serviette
49 Sessel
51 ~
18 setzen
118 setzen auf *(Geld)*
39 seufzen
39 Seufzer
31 Sex
114 Show
86 sich
21 sich abreiben lassen
164 sich ändern
66 sich anders besinnen
92 sich anfreunden (mit)
126 sich anschließen
62 sich aufregen
19 sich ausbreiten
125 sich ausdenken
71 sich ausruhen
42 sich bedienen
18 sich beeilen
20 ~
115 sich befassen mit
145 ~
17 sich begeben
138 sich belaufen auf
59 sich bemühen
53 sich benehmen
145 ~
125 sich bereit machen
37 sich besser fühlen
16 sich bewegen
119 sich Bewegung verschaffen
126 sich bewerben um
67 sich bewußt sein
74 sich beziehen auf
122 sich bilden
21 sich bücken
148 sich einmischen
66 sich entschließen

75 sich entschuldigen
37 sich erbrechen
163 sich ereignen
105 sich ergeben
109 ~
19 sich erheben
66 sich erinnern
69 sich erinnern (an)
38 sich erkälten
64 ~
74 sich erkundigen
42 sich etwas nehmen
125 sich fertigmachen
59 sich fragen
55 sich freuen (über)
67 sich freuen auf
52 sich fühlen
53 sich gefallen lassen
157 sich gewöhnen an
12 sich hinlegen
68 sich interessieren für
38 sich kümmern um
68 ~
131 sich leisten (können)
107 ~
19 sich nähern
49 sich niederlassen
103 sich qualifizieren
78 sich reimen
95 sich schneiden lassen
38 sich schneiden
12 sich setzen
59 sich sorgen
160 sich teilen
5 sich treffen
19 sich trennen
66 sich überlegen
20 sich umdrehen
71 sich unterhalten
164 sich unterscheiden
146 sich verbessern
149 sich verbeugen
149 sich vereinen
149 sich vereinigen
71 sich vergewissern
19 sich verirren
132 sich verkaufen lassen
57 sich verkleiden
57 sich verlassen auf
19 sich verlaufen
95 sich verlieben
95 sich verloben
41 sich vermischen
73 sich verständigen
147 sich verstecken
67 sich vorstellen
68 ~
72 sich weigern
108 sich widersetzen
59 sich wundern
21 sich zerstreuen
95 sich zum Ausgehen verabreden
61 sich zusammenreißen
74 sicher
147 ~
150 ~
162 ~
147 Sicherheit
150 ~
162 sicherlich
165 ~
165 sicherstellen
63 Sicht
65 sichtbar
86 sie
41 sieden
49 Siedler
98 Siedlung
109 Sieg
78 Siegel
79 Signal
80 signalisieren
84 Silbe
138 Silber
123 Silhouette
114 singen
84 Singular
9 sinken
12 ~
17 ~
79 Sinn
52 Sinn für Humor
80 Sinnbild
64 Sinne
157 sinnlos
158 ~
93 Sippe
99 Sir *(Anrede)*
109 Sitte
29 ~
161 Situation
51 Sitzbank
49 Sitz(platz)
12 sitzen
120 Skateboard
120 Ski
120 Ski fahren
17 Ski fahren gehen
77 Skizze
123 ~
123 skizzieren
99 Sklave
99 Sklaverei
82 Slang
98 Slum
42 Snackbar
88 so
89 ~
162 so . . . wie
88 so daß
89 ~
162 so ein
57 so tun als ob
122 so was
28 sobald
45 Socke
51 Sofa
22 sofort
27 ~
28 ~
62 ~
152 sogar
90 sogenannt
91 Sohn
2 Solar-
162 solch ein
162 solch(e)
105 Soldat
140 solid
145 sollen
163 ~
145 sollte
162 ~
164 ~
25 Sommer
157 sonderbar
114 Song
24 Sonnabend
1 Sonne
2 Sonnen-
23 Sonnenaufgang
4 Sonnenschein
23 Sonnenuntergang
1 sonnig
24 Sonntag
152 sonst
152 sonst noch etwas
58 Sorge
147 ~
38 sorgen für
147 Sorgfalt
161 Sorte
164 sortieren
43 Soße
160 Souvenir
159 soweit
154 sowie
87 sowieso
89 ~
152 sowohl . . . als auch
96 sozial
106 Sozialarbeiter(in)
107 Sozialist
107 sozialistisch
124 Soziologie
22 spät
26 später
28 ~
30 ~
15 Spalte
149 spalten
22 Spanne
59 spannend
62 ~
63 Spannung
130 sparen
131 ~
133 sparsam
113 Spaß
115 ~
113 Spaß machen
140 Spaten
17 spazierengehen
17 Spaziergang
43 Speck
10 Spedition
160 speichern
40 Speise
41 Speiseeis
42 Speisekarte
42 Speiselokal
42 Speisenfolge
34 Speisepilz
49 Speiseschrank
48 Speisezimmer
131 spenden
82 Spezialbeitrag
122 Spezialist
156 speziell
157 spezifisch
49 Spiegel
40 Spiegelei
113 Spiel
117 ~
113 Spielen
113 spielen
117 ~
71 ~
114 ~
114 spielen *(Musik)*
119 spielen *(um Geld)*
119 Spieler(in)
119 Spielfeld
121 Spielplatz
118 Spielzeug
34 Spinat
33 Spinne
108 Spion
108 spionieren
44 Spirituosen
1 Spitze
12 ~
16 ~
94 Spitzname
119 Sponsor
101 Sport
117 ~
117 Sportler
117 Sportlerin
82 Sprache
21 Spray
21 Spraydose
71 sprechen
70 ~
71 sprechen über
73 Sprecher
82 Sprecher *(Radio/TV)*
83 Sprichwort
118 springen
120 ~
21 sprühen
36 spucken
52 spüren
150 Spur
96 Staat
105 Staatenbund
96 Staats-
97 Staatsbürger
98 Staatsbürgerschaft
104 Staatspräsident
127 Stab
33 Stachel
34 Stachelbeere
119 Stadion
115 ~
164 Stadium
115 ~
96 Stadt
8 Stadtbus
50 stadteigenes Wohnhaus
6 Stadtrundfahrt
98 Stadtviertel
30 ständig
158 Stärke
158 stärken
139 Stahl
93 Stamm
16 stammen aus
134 Stand
110 Standard
141 Stange
115 Star
39 stark
79 ~
155 ~
156 ~
93 stark wie ein Pferd
3 stark regnen
65 starren
61 starrköpfig
12 Start *(Flugzeug)*
9 starten
26 ~
150 statt zu
160 statt dessen
161 stattfinden
123 Statue
45 Staub
47 staubig
143 Staubsauger
40 Steak
39 stechen
140 ~
113 Steckenpferd
140 Stecknadel
12 stehen
163 stehen für
110 stehlen
155 steif
19 steigen
85 Steigerung
1 steil
2 steiler Abhang
34 Stein
139 ~
141 Steinbruch
12 Stelle
15 ~
83 ~
126 ~
18 stellen
126 Stellung
127 ~
76 Stempel
76 stempeln
34 Stengel
77 Steno
126 Stenotypistin
31 sterben
110 ~
1 Stern
131 Steuer
20 steuern
9 Steward
9 Stewardess
47 Stiefel
34 Stiel
44 Stieltopf
76 Stift
123 Stil
64 still
65 Stille
19 Stillstand
26 ~
123 Stilrichtung
82 Stimme
104 Stimme abgeben für
85 stimmhaft
85 stimmlos
107 Stimmrecht
52 Stimmung
53 ~
60 ~
62 stimulieren
102 Stipendium
139 Stock
48 Stockwerk
64 ~
39 stöhnen
59 stören
61 ~
148 ~
26 Störung
19 stolpern
62 Stolz
59 stolz
25 stoppen
18 Stoß
18 stoßen
8 Stoßzeit
113 Strafe
155 straff
110 Strafgebühr
4 strahlend
5 ~

1 Strand (flach)
8 Straße
8 Straßenbahn
8 Straßenecke
11 Straßenkreuzung
11 Straßenübergang
141 Strauß
11 Strecke
157 strecken
19 streichen
140 Streichholz
153 ~
32 Streifen
142 ~
127 Streik
129 streiken
59 Streit
60 ~
104 ~
105 ~
59 streiten
71 ~
108 ~
58 streng
79 ~
63 Streß
21 streuen
32 streunend
76 Strichpunkt
123 stricken
1 Stömung
1 Strom
139 ~
142 Struktur
45 Strumpf
45 Strumpfhose
100 Student(in)
126 ~
50 Studierzimmer
124 Studium
123 Stück
138 ~
141 ~
25 stündlich
108 stürmen auf
164 Stufe
164 stufen
49 Stuhl
39 stumm
4 stumpf
143 ~
24 Stunde
11 Stundenplan
100 ~
61 stur
3 Sturm
5 Sturmwind
47 stutzen
137 subtrahieren
147 Suche
20 suchen
147 ~
150 ~
1 Süd-
1 Süden
1 südlich
64 süß
29 ~
41 Süßigkeiten
136 Summe
137 ~
84 Superlativ
132 Supermarkt
40 Suppe
29 ~
120 Surfbrett
120 surfen
80 Symbol
80 symbolisch
158 Sympathie
83 Synonym
142 System
142 systematisch
1 Szene
114 ~

• • • • • • • • • • • •

42 Tabak
143 Tablett
40 Tablette
75 tadeln
25 täglich
114 Tänzer(in)
36 tätig
82 Tätigkeitswort
95 tätscheln
57 täuschen
100 Tafel
142 ~
23 Tag
24 ~
25 Tagebuch
5 Tageslicht
80 Tageszeitungen
36 Taille
116 Takt
70 Takt(gefühl)
107 Taktik
70 taktlos
58 taktvoll
70 ~
1 Tal
70 Talent
70 talentiert
8 Tankstelle
11 ~
92 Tante
114 Tanz
55 Tanzabend
114 Tanzen
114 tanzen
17 tanzen gehen
59 tapfer
61 ~
140 Tasche
45 Tasche *(Kleidung)*
128 Taschengeld
136 Taschenrechner
45 Taschentuch
25 Taschenuhr
42 Tasse
64 Taste
54 Tat
161 Tatsache
90 tatsächlich
23 ~
61 ~
161 ~
163 ~
39 taub
33 Taube
39 Taubheit
120 tauchen
130 tauschen
133 ~
8 Taxi
10 ~
118 Team
124 Technik
124 Techniker
122 technisch
101 technische Fachhochschule
101 Technisches Zeichnen
124 Technologie
124 technologisch
41 Tee
44 Teekessel
93 Teenager
2 Teich
138 Teil
99 Teil der Universität
137 teilen
160 ~
96 teilnahmslos
115 teilnehmen (an)
83 Teilsatz
127 Teilzeit-
80 Telefon
81 Telefonhörer
80 telefonieren
81 Telefonnummer
81 Telefonzelle
80 Telegramm
41 Teller
104 Tempel
3 Temperatur
18 Tempo
163 Tendenz
120 Tennis
120 Tennisschläger
49 Teppich
51 ~
5 Termin
50 Terrasse
2 Territorium
61 Terror
108 Terrorismus
108 Terrorist(in)
100 Test
132 teuer
82 Text
141 Textilien
83 Textzusammenhang
114 Theater
114 Theaterstück
82 Thema
83 ~
124 theoretisch
68 Theorie
143 Thermometer
117 Thriller
106 Thron
137 tief
137 Tiefe
31 Tier
32 ~
32 Tiergarten
32 Tiger
139 Tinte
76 tippen
49 Tisch
18 Tisch decken
77 Titel
43 Toast
43 toasten
5 toben
91 Tochter
31 Tod
31 töten
49 Toilette
51 ~
58 tolerant
58 Toleranz
54 toll
56 ~
153 ~
34 Tomate
64 Ton
114 Tonband
114 Tonbandgerät
137 Tonne
41 Topf
48 Tor
119 ~
120 Tore schießen
119 Torhüter
43 Torte
119 Torwart
107 Tory
31 tot
6 Tour
7 Tourismus
6 Tourist(in)
126 ~
110 Tradition
110 traditionell
36 Träne
149 ~
35 träumen
20 tragbar
18 tragen
44 ~
117 tragisch
117 Tragödie
118 Trainer
69 trainieren
119 Training
129 Traktor
8 Tram
99 Tramp
19 trampen
44 tranchieren
85 transitives Verb
10 Transport
10 Transportfirma
20 transportieren
80 Tratsch
34 Traube
35 Traum
55 traurig
5 Treffen
5 treffen
118 ~
150 treffen auf
119 Treffer
19 treiben
146 trennen, (sich)
19 trennen
149 ~
149 Trennung
48 Treppe
50 ~
50 Treppenhaus
133 Tresor
110 ~
17 treten
119 ~
56 treu
57 Treue
55 Trick
102 Trimester
41 trinken
71 ~
42 Trinkgeld
44 Trinkgeld geben
42 Trinkglas
3 trocken
3 trocknen
40 trösten
62 ~
116 Trommel
116 Trompete
139 Tropfen
62 Trost
88 trotz
89 ~
89 trotz alledem
89 trotzdem
109 Truppe(n)
33 Truthahn
140 Tube
67 tüchtig
148 ~
48 Tür
140 Türklinke
140 Türschloß
140 Tüte
145 tun
11 Tunnel
142 Turbine
48 Turm
120 Turnhalle
102 ~
142 Tweed
163 typisch
56 Tyrann

• • • • • • • • • • • •

9 U-Bahn
109 U-Boot
37 übel
37 Übelkeit verspüren
146 üben
14 über
16 ~
151 ~
158 ~
13 überall
16 ~
87 ~
65 Überblick
57 überdrüssig
72 Übereinkommen
72 Übereinstimmung
19 Überfahrt
108 Überfall
108 überfallen
155 Überfluß
155 überfüllt
109 übergeben
88 überhaupt
136 überhaupt nicht
20 überholen
11 Überlandstraße
159 überlassen
31 überleben
31 Überleben
154 überlegen
68 Überlegung
57 überlisten
24 übermorgen
6 Übernachtung mit Frühstück
38 überprüfen
147 ~
150 Überprüfung
18 überqueren
60 überraschen
63 überraschend
60 Überraschung
74 überreden
160 überreichen
12 Überschall-
76 Überschrift
3 Überschwemmung
7 Übersee-
7 überseeisch
82 übersetzen
83 Übersetzung
65 Übersicht
69 überspringen
127 Überstunden
118 übertreffen
73 übertreiben
157 überwältigend
155 überzählig
74 überzeugen
74 Überzeugung
46 Überzieher
131 übrig sein

152 übrigens
100 Übung
146 ~
1 Ufer
24 Uhr
25 ~
25 Uhr *(bei Zeitangaben)*
129 Uhrmacher
33 Uhu
13 um
157 ~
13 um . . . herum
90 um . . . willen
100 um Gottes willen
90 um zu
157 ~
113 umbringen
20 umdrehen
21 ~
65 Umfrage
83 umgangssprachlich
144 umgeben
98 Umgebung
11 Umgehungsstraße
13 umher
2 umkreisen
2 Umlaufbahn
123 Umriß
44 umrühren
83 Umschreibung
132 umsonst
164 Umstände
82 Umstandswort
108 Umsturz
122 umtauschen
8 Umweg
98 Umwelt
47 Umweltverschmutzung
16 umziehen
46 umziehen, (sich)
57 unabhängig von
105 Unabhängigkeit
150 Unachtsamkeit
56 unangenehm
158 Unannehmlichkeit
58 unanständig
57 unaufrichtig
59 unbarmherzig
165 unbedeutend
54 unbeliebt
158 unbequem
127 unbesetzt
88 und
65 undurchsichtig
57 unehrlich
54 uneigennützig
23 unentrinnbar
56 unerläßlich
153 unermeßlich
62 unerwartet
157 unfähig
70 unfähig zu
158 unfair
8 Unfall
11 ~
96 unfreundlich
60 Unfug treiben
70 ungebildet
63 Ungeduld
62 ungeduldig
30 ungefähr
151 ~
154 ungenügend
158 ungerecht
111 Ungerechtigkeit
111 ungesetzlich
156 ungewöhnlich
157 ~
56 ungezogen
58 ungezwungen
68 unglaublich
57 unglücklich
165 ~
58 unhöflich
46 Uniform
105 Union
99 Universität
2 Universum
70 Unkenntnis
128 Unkosten
22 unmittelbar
162 unmöglich
59 unnachgiebig
47 Unordnung
54 unparteiisch
148 unrationell
55 unrecht haben
155 unregelmäßig
85 unregelmäßiges Verb
55 unrichtig
86 uns
133 unschätzbar
65 unschmackhaft
112 unschuldig
86 unser
86 unseres
61 unsicher
79 Unsinn
128 untätig
15 unten
48 ~
14 unter
16 ~
151 ~
88 unter der Bedingung, daß
71 unterbrechen
48 unterbringen
11 Unterführung
48 Untergeschoß
14 unterhalb
115 unterhalten
57 unterhaltsam
71 Unterhaltung
115 ~
106 Unterhaus
48 unterkommen
49 Unterkunft
69 unterlassen
154 unterlegen
125 Unternehmen
100 unterrichten
102 ~
100 Unterichtsstunde
102 Unterrichtsvorbereitung
46 Unterrock
111 untersagen
164 unterscheiden
97 Unterschicht
162 Unterschied
150 Unterschlupf
76 unterschreiben
76 Unterschrift
74 unterstreichen
72 unterstützen
72 Unterstützung
38 untersuchen
38 Untersuchung
44 Untertasse
46 Unterwäsche
102 Unterweisung
76 unterzeichnen
23 unvermeidlich
22 unverzüglich
155 unvollständig
147 unvorsichtig
3 Unwetter
165 unwichtig
154 unzählig
137 Unze
57 unzuverlässig
26 Ur-
141 Uran
127 Urlaub
129 ~
6 Urlauber
145 Ursache
26 ursprünglich
26 Ursprung
68 Urteil
90 usw

• • • • • • • • • • • • •

117 Varietétheater
143 Vase
91 Vater
93 Vati
5 Verabredung
6 ~
111 verabschieden *(Gesetz)*
5 veränderlich
122 verändern
63 veraltet
145 veranlassen
123 veranschaulichen
112 verantwortlich
112 Verantwortung
85 Verb
86 Verb-Adverb-Verbindung
83 verbal
40 Verband
57 verbergen
147 ~
149 Verbesserung
146 verbessern
111 verbieten
40 verbinden
146 ~
149 ~
65 Verbindung
146 ~
73 Verbindung aufnehmen mit
50 Verbindungsgang
131 verbrauchen
134 Verbraucher
110 Verbrechen
110 Verbrecher
139 verbrennen
22 verbringen
74 Verdacht
157 verdächtig
74 verdächtigen
147 verderben
128 verdienen
159 ~
127 verdienen *(Geld)*
21 verdrehen
61 verehren
103 ~
97 Verein
149 vereinen
157 vereinfachen
146 vereinigt
97 Vereinigung
105 ~
123 Verfahren
78 Verfasser
110 Verfassung
111 verfassungsmäßig
118 verfehlen
18 verfolgen
20 ~
154 verfügbar
161 Verfügung
22 Vergangenheit
72 vergeben
158 vergebens
158 vergeblich
22 vergehen
110 Vergehen
112 ~
66 vergessen
69 vergeßlich
123 vergeuden
144 vergießen
162 vergleichen mit
55 Vergnügen
47 vergoldet
117 vergrößern
82 Verhältniswort
113 verhängen
110 verhaften
53 Verhalten
54 ~
134 verhandeln
134 Verhandlung
92 verheiratet mit
147 verhindern
74 verhören
42 verhungern
42 Verhungern
61 verjagen
132 Verkäufer(in)
132 Verkauf
132 verkaufen
132 Verkaufsregal
131 verkauft
8 Verkehr
151 ~
112 Verkehrsaufseher
10 Verkehrsmittel
8 Verkehrsunfall
149 verknoten
73 verkünden
15 verkürzen
79 Verlag
52 Verlangen
53 ~
74 verlangen
17 verlassen
20 ~
127 ~
79 Verleger
39 verletzen
146 ~
39 Verletzung
95 verliebt sein in
61 ~
105 verlieren
107 ~
119 Verlierer
92 verlobt mit
56 ~
95 Verlobte
95 Verlobter
95 Verlobung
133 Verlust
18 vermeiden
131 vermieten
41 vermischen
52 vermissen
81 Vermittlung
133 Vermögen
67 vermuten
68 Vermutung
40 vernachlässigen
85 verneinend
85 Verneinung
123 vernichten
156 vernünftig
158 ~
66 Vernunft
79 veröffentlichen
79 Veröffentlichung
113 verprügeln
154 verringern
154 Verringerung
67 verrückt
70 ~
70 Verrücktheit
78 Vers
26 versagen
111 ~
146 ~
149 Versagen
5 Versammlung
106 ~
25 verschieben
26 ~
162 verschieden von
162 verschiedenartig
60 verschiedener Meinung sein
37 verschlafen
47 verschmutzen
47 Verschmutzung
123 verschwenden
57 Verschwiegenheit
16 verschwinden
108 Verschwörung
39 versehrt
9 versenken
73 versichern
131 ~
131 Versicherung
78 versiegeln
83 Version
160 versorgen mit
160 Versorgung
72 versprechen
72 Versprechen
58 Verständnis
69 Verständnis(test)
36 Verstand
66 ~
147 verstecken
67 verstehen
69 ~
112 verstoßen gegen
21 verstreuen
148 Versuch
64 versuchen
145 ~
148 ~
105 verteidigen
112 ~
108 Verteidigung
112 ~
19 verteilen
161 ~
134 Vertrag
55 vertrauen
56 Vertrauen
57 ~
157 vertraut mit
107 Vertreter(in)
128 Vertretung
47 verunreinigen
145 verursachen
110 verurteilen
106 Verwaltung
93 verwandt
92 Verwandte(r)
158 verwechseln

72 verweigern
74 Verweis
123 verwenden
158 Verwendung
148 verwickeln in
145 verwirklichen
148 Verwirklichung
39 verwunden
60 Verwunderung
78 Verzeichnis
72 Verzeihung
25 verzögern
26 verzögert
25 Verzögerung
53 verzweifelt
53 Verzweiflung
108 Veto
108 Veto einlegen gegen
93 Vetter
16 via
81 Video
81 Videorecorder
32 Vieh
129 Viehrost
151 viel
152 ~
154 ~
151 viele
137 vielfach
164 Vielfalt
162 vielleicht
32 vierfüßiges Tier
136 Viertel
25 vierzehn Tage
50 Villa
116 Violine
111 Visa
64 Vision
111 Visum
56 vital
106 Vizepräsident
96 Völker
155 völlig
105 völlig besiegen
31 Vogel
85 Vokal
96 Volk
93 Volk(s)-
153 voll
59 voll Scham
35 Vollbart
153 vollbesetzt
53 voller Hoffnung
120 Volleyball
153 vollgestopft
156 vollkommen
153 vollständig
155 ~
138 Volumen
163 vom Glück begünstigt
63 vom Sehen kennen
164 ~
26 vom Stapel lassen
13 von
159 ~
163 von Bedeutung sein
157 von Nutzen
30 von Zeit zu Zeit
14 vor
28 ~
29 ~
24 vor *(bei Zeitangaben)*
157 vor allem
26 vor allen Dingen
23 vor einigen Tagen
29 vor kurzem
161 vor sich gehen
19 vorangehen
26 vorausgehend
89 vorausgesetzt, daß
15 vorbei
16 ~
19 vorbeischauen
125 vorbereiten
125 Vorbereitung
13 Vorderseite
94 Vorfahr(en)
164 Vorfall
54 Vorgang
57 vorgeben
24 vorgestern
49 Vorhang
30 vorher
26 vorhergehend
23 Vorhersage
30 vorläufig
124 Vorlage
76 vorlesen
73 Vorlesung
102 ~
54 Vorliebe
25 vormittags
112 Vormund
126 ~
92 Vorname
94 ~
98 Vororte
134 vorrätig
132 vorrätig haben
134 Vorrat
160 ~
99 Vorrecht
142 Vorrichtung
20 Vorrücken
72 Vorschlag
74 ~
72 vorschlagen
74 ~
148 ~
110 Vorschrift
147 vorsichtig
86 Vorsilbe
42 Vorspeise
96 Vorstadt
92 vorstellen
94 Vorstellen
66 Vorstellung
114 ~
123 ~
6 Vorstellungsgespräch
68 Vorstellungskraft
57 vortäuschen
163 Vorteil
73 Vortrag
16 vorübergehen
19 Vorübergehen
127 vorübergehend
54 Vorurteil
7 Vorverkaufsstelle
13 vorwärts
52 vorziehen
54 vorzuziehen
58 vulgär
3 Vulkan

• • • • • • • • • • • • •

143 Waage
2 waagerecht
35 wach
110 Wache
112 Wachmeister
27 wachsen
154 Wachsen
124 Wachsfiguren (kabinett)
154 Wachstum
104 wählen
81 wählen *(Telefon)*
104 wählen (zu)
27 während
30 ~
89 ~
133 Währung
164 wäre
5 Wärme
110 Wärter
47 Wäsche
142 Wäscheleine
47 Wäscherei
105 Waffe
10 Wagen
61 wagen
10 Wagen *(Eisenbahn)*
10 Waggon
104 Wahl
159 ~
107 Wahlkreis
70 Wahnsinn
161 wahr
161 Wahrheit
162 wahrscheinlich
164 ~
164 Wahrscheinlichkeit
2 Wald
48 Wand
100 Wandtafel
123 Wandteppich
36 Wange
28 wann
87 ~
30 wann immer
89 ~
134 Waren
134 Warenrechnung
3 warm
96 ~
72 warnen
72 Warnung
12 Wartehalle
12 warten
81 ~
10 Wartesaal
16 Warteschlange
87 warum?
87 was?
89 was (auch immer)
163 Was ist los?
152 was noch
51 Waschbecken
45 waschen, (sich)
139 Wasser
150 wasserdicht
51 Wasserhahn
1 Wasserlauf
34 Wassermelone
49 WC
51 ~
122 Wechsel
130 Wechselgeld
130 wechseln
24 Wecker
8 Weg
14 weg
13 weg von
18 wegbringen
88 wegen
89 ~
17 wegfahren
16 weggehen
17 ~
18 wegnehmen
160 wegräumen
37 weh
38 weh tun
3 wehen
31 weiblich
155 weich
129 Weide
75 Weigerung
2 Weiher
25 Weihnachten
88 weil
89 ~
156 ~
22 Weile
41 Wein
59 weinen
60 ~
67 weise
70 Weisheit
4 weiß
151 weit
153 ~
15 weit entfernt
16 weit weg
15 weiter
16 weiter *(räumlich)*
101 weiterführende Schule *(GB)*
101 weiterführende Schule *(USA)*
154 weiterhin
22 weitermachen
23 ~
34 Weizen
89 welch(er,e,es)
87 welcher
2 Welle
1 Welt
1 Weltall
1 Weltraum
105 Weltreich
2 weltweit
19 wenden
151 wenig
151 wenige
151 weniger
151 weniger als
154 wenigstens
88 wenn
88 wenn nicht
87 wer?
156 ~
89 wer auch immer
82 werben
82 Werbespruch
80 Werbung
82 Werbung *(Radio/TV)*
29 werden
147 ~
161 ~
161 werden (lassen)
131 ~
18 werfen
123 Werk
101 Werken
124 Werkstatt
24 Werktag
139 Werkzeug
142 ~
130 wert
130 Wert
133 wertlos
132 wertvoll
133 ~
165 wesentlich
87 wessen?
1 West-
1 Westen
115 Western
1 westlich
118 Wettbewerb
118 wetten
3 Wetter
4 Wetterbericht
4 Wettervorhersage
117 Wettkampf
118 ~
118 Wettlauf
153 Wettspiel
44 Whisky
163 wichtig
163 Wichtigkeit
154 wichtigst-
148 Widerhall
148 widerhallen
95 Widersacher
108 Widerstand
108 widerstehen
89 wie
55 ~
156 ~
162 ~
72 Wie bitte?
155 wie gewöhnlich
55 wie schade
62 ~
28 wieder
40 wieder gesund werden
125 wiederaufbereiten
67 wiedererkennen
71 wiederholen
146 ~
22 wiederholt
148 Wiederholung
136 wiegen
129 Wiese
31 wild
54 Willen
94 willkommen heißen
3 Wind
32 Windhund
3 windig
129 Windmühle
21 winken
25 Winter
153 winzig
86 wir
5 Wirbelsturm
165 wird bestimmt
162 wird vielleicht
90 wirklich
122 ~
161 ~
161 Wirklichkeit
163 ~
148 wirksam
148 Wirksamkeit
145 Wirkung
148 wirkungsvoll
134 Wirtschaft
133 wirtschaftlich
130 Wirtschafts-
134 Wirtschaftswissenschaft
47 wischen
66 Wissen
66 wissen

59 wissen wollen
122 Wissenschaft
122 Wissenschaftler (in)
124 wissenschaftlich
95 Witwe
95 Witwer
113 Witz
87 wo?
156 ~
89 wo immer
24 Woche
24 Wochenende
24 Wochentag
80 Wochenzeitung
25 wöchentlich
82 Wörterbuch
2 Woge
89 wohingegen
39 Wohlergehen
39 Wohlfahrt
65 Wohlgeschmack
130 wohlhabend
133 ~
134 Wohltätigkeitsbazar
52 Wohlwollen
50 Wohnanlage
48 Wohnblock
47 wohnen
7 Wohnmobil
50 Wohnschlafzimmer
49 Wohnsitz
48 Wohnung
7 Wohnwagen
49 Wohnzimmer
32 Wolf
3 Wolke
50 Wolkenkratzer
4 wolkenlos
139 Wolle
52 wollen
139 ~
46 wollene Strickjacke
82 Wort
83 Wortschatz
12 Wrack
52 wünschen
121 Würfel
41 Würstchen
2 Wüste
5 wüten
60 wütend
60 wütend werden
37 wund
39 Wunde
60 Wunder
63 ~
54 wunderbar
56 ~
52 Wunsch
69 ~
120 Wurfpfeilspiel
33 Wurm
41 Wurst
34 Wurzel
60 Wut

• • • • • • • • • • • • •

137 Yard

• • • • • • • • • • • • •

90 z.B.
158 zäh
84 zählbar
136 zählen
58 zärtlich
135 Zahl
131 zahlreich
133 Zahlung(en)
35 Zahn
38 Zahnarzt
45 Zahnbürste
39 Zahnpasta
38 Zahnschmerzen
58 zart
103 Zauberei
117 Zauberkünstler
50 Zaun
32 Zebra
11 Zebrastreifen
96 ~
36 Zehe
79 Zeichen
102 ~
122 zeichnen
123 Zeichnung
147 zeigen
150 ~
150 zeigen auf
22 Zeit
128 Zeit finden
22 Zeitabschnitt
23 Zeitalter
22 Zeitraum
80 Zeitschrift
81 ~
80 Zeitung
77 Zeitungsartikel
81 Zeitungshändler
115 Zeitvertreib
6 Zelt
6 Zelten
7 Zeltplatz
102 zensieren
136 zentral
128 Zentrale
49 Zentralheizung
13 Zentrum
96 ~
103 Zeremonie
149 zerreißen
18 zerren
18 Zerren
143 zersägen
149 zerschlagen
44 zerschneiden
123 zerstören
123 Zerstörung
125 ~
113 Zerstörungswut
149 zertrümmern
138 Zeug
112 Zeuge
112 Zeuge sein von
100 Zeugnis
138 zickzack
32 Ziege
141 Ziegel
18 ziehen
18 Ziehen
66 Ziel
69 ~
120 Ziel(scheibe)
120 zielen auf
150 ~
158 ziellos
29 ziemlich
152 ~
29 ziemlich bald
135 Ziffer
42 Zigarette
42 Zigarre
99 Zigeuner
6 Zimmer
49 ~
48 Zimmerdecke
129 Zimmermann
141 Zinn
74 Zitat
742 zitieren
34 Zitrone
97 Zivilisation
22 zögern
131 Zoll
29 ~
9 Zollabfertigung
9 Zollbeamter
131 zollfrei
98 Zone
32 Zoo
32 Zoologischer Garten
60 Zorn
13 zu
152 ~
64 zu einer Einigung kommen
26 zu Ende sein
22 zu früh
17 zu Fuß gehen
48 zu Hause
62 ~
161 zu Ihrer Verfügung
120 zu Pferd
67 zu schätzen wissen
41 zu sich nehmen
31 zu spät
131 zu verkaufen
131 zu vermieten
80 zu verstehen geben
41 zubereiten
41 Zucker
127 züchten
26 zuerst
28 ~
62 ~
66 zufällig
164 ~
150 zufällig finden
162 Zufall
164 ~
7 Zuflucht
55 zufrieden
57 Zufriedenheit
62 ~
55 zufriedenstellen
56 zufriedenstellend
8 Zug
19 Zugang
48 Zuhause
64 zuhören
115 Zuhörer
26 zukünftig
22 Zukunft
53 zulassen
109 ~
111 ~
153 zuletzt
90 zuliebe
90 zum Beispiel
57 zum Narren halten
113 zum Spaß
146 zumachen
29 zumindest
62 ~
154 Zunahme
36 Zunge
121 Zungenbrecher
147 zunichte machen
17 zur Jagd gehen
79 zur Post geben
49 zur Ruhe kommen
74 zur Sprache bringen
154 zur Verfügung
13 zurück
159 zurückbekommen
159 zurückbringen
160 zurückgeben
17 zurückkehren
17 zurücklassen
159 zurücklegen
80 zurückrufen
47 zurückschneiden
160 zurückstellen
153 zusätzlich
154 zusätzlich zu
155 ~
15 zusammen
128 zusammenarbeiten
39 Zusammenbruch
78 zusammenfassen
78 Zusammenfassung
146 zusammenfügen
144 zusammenkommen
47 zusammenlegen
124 zusammensetzen
11 Zusammenstoß
11 zusammenstoßen
136 zusammenzählen
111 Zusatz (Verfassung)
44 Zusatzstoff
82 Zuschauer
115 ~
74 zusichern
146 zusperren
161 Zustand
147 zustande bringen
20 Zustellung
72 zustimmen
75 ~
72 Zustimmung
44 Zutat(en)
19 Zutritt
56 zuverlässig
57 Zuverlässigkeit
30 zuvor
128 Zuwendung *(Geld)*
18 zuwerfen
58 zwanglos
66 Zweck
158 ~
157 zwecklos
71 Zweifel
74 zweifelhaft
74 zweifellos
165 ~
71 zweifeln
34 Zweig
126 Zweigstelle
135 zweimal
65 zwicken
34 Zwiebel
93 Zwilling
145 zwingen
14 zwischen
22 Zwischenraum

My own notes